Contesting Inequality and Worker Mobilisation

Contesting Inequality and Worker Mobilisation: Australia 1851–1880 provides a new perspective on how and why workers organise, and what shapes that organisation.

The author's 2018 *Origins of Worker Mobilisation* examined the beginning of worker organisation, arguing inequality at work and regulatory subordination of labour, drove worker resistance, initially by informal organisation that slowly transitioned to formal organisation. This new volume analyses worker mobilisation in the period 1851–1880, drawing data from a unique relational database recording every instance of organisation. It assesses not only the types of organisation formed, but also the issues and objectives upon which mobilisation was founded. It examines the relationship between formal and informal organisation, including their respective influences in reshaping working conditions and the life-circumstances of working communities. It relates the examination of worker mobilisation to both historical and contemporary contexts and examines mobilisation by different categories of labour. The book identifies important effects of mobilisation on economic inequality, hours of work (including the eight-hour day and the beginnings of the weekend) and the development of democracy.

It will be of interest to researchers, academics, and students in the fields of social mobilisation, social and economic history, industrial relations, labour regulation, labour history and employment relations.

Michael Quinlan is Emeritus Professor of Industrial Relations, University of NSW and adjunct professor School of History and Humanities, University of Tasmania.

Routledge Studies in Employment and Work Relations in Context

Edited by Tony Elger and Peter Fairbrother

The aim of the *Employment and Work Relations in Context Series* is to address questions relating to the evolving patterns and politics of work, employment, management and industrial relations. There is a concern to trace out the ways in which wider policy-making, especially by national governments and transnational corporations, impinges upon specific workplaces, occupations, labour markets, localities and regions. This invites attention to developments at an international level, marking out patterns of globalization, state policy and practices in the context of globalization and the impact of these processes on labour. A particular feature of the series is the consideration of forms of worker and citizen organization and mobilization. The studies address major analytical and policy issues through case study and comparative research.

Contesting Inequality and Worker Mobilisation
Australia 1851–1880
Michael Quinlan

Previous titles to appear in Routledge Studies in Employment and Work Relations in Context include:

Work, Locality and the Rhythms of Capital
The Labour Process Reconsidered
Jamie Gough

Trade Unions in Renewal
A Comparative Study
Edited by Peter Fairbrother and Charlotte Yates

Reshaping the North American Automobile Industry
Restructuring, Corporatism and Union Democracy in Mexico
John P. Tuman

For more information about this series, please visit: www.routledge.com

Contesting Inequality and Worker Mobilisation

Australia 1851–1880

Michael Quinlan

Routledge
Taylor & Francis Group

NEW YORK AND LONDON

First published 2021
by Routledge
605 Third Avenue, New York, NY 10017

and by Routledge
2 Park Square, Milton Park, Abingdon, Oxon OX14 4RN

First issued in paperback 2022

Routledge is an imprint of the Taylor & Francis Group, an informa business

© 2021 Taylor & Francis

Publisher's Note
The publisher has gone to great lengths to ensure the quality of this
reprint but points out that some imperfections in the original copies
may be apparent.

British Library Cataloguing-in-Publication Data
A catalogue record for this book is available from the British Library

Library of Congress Cataloging-in-Publication Data
Names: Quinlan, Michael, 1951– author.
Title: Contesting inequality and worker mobilisation : Australia
    1851–1880 / Michael Quinlan.
Description: New York : Routledge, 2020. | Series: Routledge
    studies in employment and work relations in context | Includes
    bibliographical references and index.
Identifiers: LCCN 2020017658 | ISBN 9780367861780
    (hardback) | ISBN 9781003018971 (ebook)
Subjects: LCSH: Labor unions—Australia—History—
    19th century. | Labor unions—Australia—History—
    18th century. | Equality—Australia—History—19th century.
Classification: LCC HD6892 .Q5596 2020 | DDC
    331.880994/09034—dc23
LC record available at https://lccn.loc.gov/2020017658

ISBN: 978-0-367-53725-8 (pbk)
ISBN: 978-0-367-86178-0 (hbk)
ISBN: 978-1-003-01897-1 (ebk)

DOI: 10.4324/9781003018971

Typeset in Sabon
by Apex CoVantage, LLC

You have not spoken of the duty of Governments to procure pleasures for their subjects. Sufficient attention has never been paid to this subject.
Maria Therese Rodet Geoffrin, French Enlightenment figure's deathbed statement (1777) cited by London newspaper advocating the weekly half-holiday movement and reproduced by *Adelaide Times* 16 December 1854. http://nla.gov.au/nla.news-article207020283

Sons of labor through the land, Men of hard and horny hand, 'Gainst each proud oppressor stand, And ye shall be free. . . . Ye for honest ample pay, Eight hours' working every day, Eight for sleep and eight for play, Or your minds to free.
'To The Workmen of The Land' (excerpts) by William Stitt Jenkins, Geelong bricklayer and universal short hours advocate in *The Leader* 16 January 1864. http://nla.gov.au/nla.news-article197291452

The effects of the drought of 1865 will be felt for many a long year to come . . . What if the ensuing. . . . years should be similar to this? The consequence must be that hundreds and thousands of sheep and cattle will perish. Farmers must leave their lands and seek other occupations, the necessaries of life raised in the colonies must rise to famine prices, a large proportion of the labouring population will be thrown out of employment, and starvation, distress, and disease will become prevalent over the broad face of the Australia's.
Avoca Mail 28 October 1865. http://nla.gov.au/nla.news-article190702367. These prescient observations about Australia as a hard-land of recurrent droughts are a reminder that human interactions with climate have shaped history— we ignore it at our peril.

Contents

Tables and Figures

Tables

Figures

Abbreviations

ACL	Anti-Chinese League
AMA	Amalgamated Miners Association
ANU	Australian National University Noel Butlin Archives
ASCJ	Amalgamated Society of Carpenters and Joiners
ASE	Amalgamated Society of Engineers, Machinists, Millwrights, Smiths and Pattern Makers
ASN	Australian Steam Navigation Company
CRO	Crowther Collection State Library of Tasmania
CSD	Colonial Secretary's Office Despatches
ECA	Early Closing Association
HHA	Half-holiday Association
ITUC	Intercolonial Trades Union Congress
LC	Lower Court records TAHO/State Library of Tasmania
ML	Mitchell Library, State Library of NSW
MLA	Member of Legislative Assembly
MSS	Manuscript
MUA	Melbourne University Archives
NSCA	Non-Strike Collective Action
NSHLL	National Short Hours Labour League
NSW	New South Wales
NT	Northern Territory
SA	South Australia
TAFE	Technical and Further Education
TAHO	Tasmanian Archives and Heritage Office
THLI	Trades Hall and Literary Institute
THC	Trades Hall Council
TLC	Trades and Labour Council
VDL	Van Diemen's Land (Tasmania)
VOBS	Victorian Operative Bricklayers Society
VTHC	Victorian Trades Hall Council
WA	Western Australia
WMA	Working Mens Association
WMDA	Working Mens Defence Association

Acknowledgements

Like *The Origins of Worker Mobilisation: Australia 1788–1850*, this book forms part of a project on how and why workers come together which began in 1982. I acknowledge assistance and encouragement from Malcolm Rimmer, Greg Patmore, Richard Croucher, Eric Tucker, Doug Hay, Paul Craven, Hamish Maxwell-Stewart, Barrie Dyster, Terry Irving, Rowan Cahill, Bradon Ellem, Mary Turner, Margaret Gardner, Peter Akers, Liang Li, Tom Dunning, Michael Roe, Ian Pearce, Vicki Pearce, Trudy Cowley, Wayne Lewchuk, Sarah Gregson, Tony Sheldon, Claire Williams, Collette Smith-Strong, Christine Smith, Robyn Hollander, Danielle Thyer, Mark Dunn and Kim Pearce. Malcolm alerted me that unilateral regulation suited dealing with fractured capital. Mark Gregory shared his important collection of Australian working-class songs and poems. Andrea Tompkins created several critical charts. I owe a huge debt to Laura Bennett who suggested I make political economy a key analytical component, pointed to the pivotal redistributive effects of shorter working hours and informed my understanding of capital's use of categories of workers like immigrants and women to undermine labour market controls erected by organised labour.

Digitalisation of union minute-books, court, newspapers and other records were instrumental in facilitating this research. I especially acknowledge the importance of the National Library's Trove collection, the Noel Butlin Archives ANU, the Tasmanian State Library/TAHO and Mitchell Library. Their digitalisation of records and making them publicly available online are exemplars of how libraries/archives can facilitate researchers (regardless of means) in a democratic society. Visiting libraries and archives remain essential. I am grateful to the assistance the Mitchell Library (with a vast collection of extending beyond NSW), the Victorian State Library, the University of Melbourne Archives and the Auchmuty Library archives University of Newcastle. Libraries/archives limiting digital access to state-residents or charging for access do not serve Australia-wide research or the principle of free access to public documents that should mark a democracy.

Finally, I thank David Varley, Mary de Plato and the Routledge team. David's support for *Origins* was pivotal to the current book. Those involved in producing this book were a joy to work with. When considering the subtitle for this book I was tempted to add 'after the Gold Rush' not because the discovery of globally significant gold deposits in 1851–1852 was a turning point in Australian history (it wasn't), but to draw connections between the past and present which is the essential contribution of history to humanity. In September 1970 Neil Young released the album 'After the Gold Rush' referring to the 1849 California Gold Rush. The album was emblematic of the flowering of popular/rock/blues music unleashed by the great post-war shift to income equality in the West then at its height. This book examines organised labour's challenge to inequality 1851–1880, important steps towards building a more equal and democratic society now dangerously in retreat.

Introduction

This book is about how and why workers come together. Drawing primarily on Australian data for 1851–1880 it places this in a wider context. It continues examinations begun in *The Origins of Worker Mobilisation*; including the shifting relationship between informal and formal organisation, between different categories of labour, and between industrial and political organisation. It charts how workers sought to challenge inequality at work and its wider social consequences. This included not only craft methods but other strategies like the output-restricting Vend used by Newcastle coalminers and widespread efforts to restrict working hours. As evident prior to 1850, industrial struggles readily transferred into the political sphere. The eight-hour-day campaign secured gains industrially reinforced by large community demonstrations and demands to legislate. The same mix is evident in parallel campaigns to shorten hours, like early closing. Other measures aimed at general labour market exclusion, notably campaigns to restrict European immigration and the Chinese.

It is important to understand the rationale for these practices and lessons that can be drawn from them. This book doesn't ignore the plight of vulnerable groups, and their resistance, but locates it within a broader struggle against subordination and inequality at work. Simply labelling some union practices as craft-exclusionist, racist or sexist and ignoring strategic efforts by capital to break down labour market controls detracts from the prospects of building more genuinely inclusive societies where the underlying drivers of inequality are addressed. Though now deemed unfashionable by individualised discourse which interprets inequality as a series of human rights, reducing socio-economic inequality at local and global levels requires implementing controls on work/labour markets and business organisation. Under neoliberalism, labour markets are still regulated but in ways that perpetuate and extend inequality. Neoliberalism wasn't about deregulation but shifting government policies and regulation in ways that wrought more profoundly unequal outcomes for working communities and societies.

The book uses the same methods/approach as its predecessor, drawing on a database recording every instance of worker organisation—no matter how small or ephemeral—and all types of collective action as well as political mobilisations. Organisation and collective action overlap but are not equivalent terms. Informal organisation (where there is no institutional body, even a committee) entailed workers acting collectively making a demand, restricting output, striking or group-absconding. Most involved only a single action—generally short-lived—though some involved multiple actions over a period of time. On the other hand, formal organisations (unions) generally undertook multiple actions (including some unavailable to informal organisations) though short-lived unions did little more than try to form. This book deems collective action as any refusal to work/temporary absence, absconding, sabotage, demand, litigation, go-slow and the like by two or more workers. Strikes are important. However, viewing collective action predominantly through the lens of strikes as much labour historiography has, results in a distorted picture. In 1851–1880, as for 1788–1850, strikes represented a minority of collective action and were often preceded by, coincident with or followed other forms of collective action.

Data collection involved trawling colonial newspapers, courts records, government records, diaries, business and union records. Multiple sources had both quantitative and qualitative benefits. Newspaper reports of . court cases and court records each contain information not found in the other. Reporters attending trials made observations not found in court bench-books. In total 5,059 instances of worker organisation (industrial and political) were identified, representing probably about 70% of those for which evidence survives. This estimate is based on assumptions similar to *The Origins of Worker Mobilisation* tweaked a little. The *Origins* 60–70% estimate was based on around 800 instances of group-absconding in Tasmania compiled by Hamish Maxwell-Stewart (most not in my database), the known 'hit-rate' in Tasmanian Court records projected to other colonies' court records only partially examined as well as logbooks and other records I knew existed but was unable to examine. This estimate proved conservative. Subsequent research (mainly for a project on convict worker resistance with Hamish) has yielded over 1,000 instances of worker organisation additional to the 6,426 reported in *Origins* for 1788–1850.

The database affords opportunities for further analysis as well as a template for comparable research in other countries. Digital mapping techniques could be used to identify/track networks of activists while the capture-recapture method enables estimating worker organisation and activity where records are missing or lost. The book uses a big-data approach along with qualitative methods that add depth/meaning and retain the subjective experiences of workers and their organisations. An advantage of combined methods is mitigating selection-bias risks in qualitative material used. The big-data/qualitative approach is particularly suited to a systematic evaluation of worker mobilisation.

Examining all organisations has strengths for understanding how and why mobilisation occurred, including the often complex transition of informal to formal organisation and building more robust unions.[1] The logic of wider organisational strategies also becomes evident. Craft unions were keen to maximise the spread of eight-hours to other workers, deploying considerable resources to employer counter-attacks, conducting large anniversary demonstrations and pressing for eight-hour laws. This reflected a strategic understanding of how to hold onto gains.[2] The significance of particular statements also becomes more apparent. At an 1856 eight-hour meeting a Sydney carpenter (Marlow) argued reducing hours would eliminate unemployment for 200 carpenters and in so doing strengthen their capacity to bargain over wages.[3] This observation highlighted that the campaign wasn't just about leisure and health but redistributing available work and enhancing bargaining power. It also helps explain why unions sometimes offered reduced wages for shorter hours because in the long term they could more than retrieve this loss. It was a strategy recognised and pursued elsewhere but Australian unions were especially adept in this regard. For obvious reasons Marlow's points were not going to be articulated publicly too often. Other 'understandings' might not find their way into union records because they were so well understood there would seem no need to record them. The underlying rationale for the eight-hour campaign and methods used become evident once the struggle is examined as a whole. This book also reveals other hitherto neglected hour-related campaigns, especially the early-closing and half-holiday movements as well as interconnections between them. Important contemporary lessons can be drawn from hour struggles in terms of means of regulating labour markets to mitigate inequality.

The first chapter examines relevant theories/literature, sources and methods used, and the political economy of the colonies which shaped worker organisation. Chapter 2 overviews patterns of organisation, Chapters 3–10 examine organisation in specific industries, Chapter 11 deals with peak and political organisation, while Chapter 12 draws key findings together and sets them in a wider context. For reasons of brevity some issues examined by *The Origins of Worker Mobilisation*, including use of the courts against individual workers and elements of working-class culture/identity, are not repeated in this book.

Some Conventions and Terms Used

Following Tilly, this book adopts a broad definition of organisation (how a group structures to pursue its interests), mobilisation (acquiring collective control of resources to take action) and collective action (joint action pursuing a common interest).[4] In examining organisation and action, a distinction is drawn between informal and formal organisation including their inter-relationship—something often missing from earlier research. The book uses a broad definition of collective action, and compares the use of different forms of action, especially strikes and non-strike collective action (NSCA). To minimise repetition/confusion a number of conventions are followed. Rather than using the full union title (often subject to change) they have been abbreviated. For example, the Sydney Shipwrights Provident Society is referred to simply as the Sydney Shipwrights. Where several unions competed for the same members and this convention might cause confusion, the bodies are distinguished, notably the Amalgamated Society of Carpenters and Joiners and rival Progressive Society of Carpenters and Joiners.

Aside from general chapters, the book's primary framework is based around industries, using contemporary definitions. Apart from making the findings more comparable with later periods this was done for other reasons. First, it helps make sense of an otherwise complex array of occupational-specific organisation as well as highlighting the extent of organisation in economic sectors neglected by past labour histories. Second, this framework is more compatible with the political economy themes underpinning the analysis. Organisation becomes more explicable when industry-specific economic, political and labour market characteristics are recognised within the wider experience of particular countries. An industry approach involved trade-offs and discretionary decisions. Some occupational unions operated across a range of industries. Occupational data breakdowns help offset this limitation as do qualitative discussion (for example boilermakers working in mines). For reasons of logic, railway workers were included in transport although the vast majority were government employees. Whatever organising principle is used, compromises are inevitable. I believe the industry focus is more appropriate than others for examining how and why workers come together, and the consequences of that mobilisation.

Finally, in addition to tables the book describes the spread of organisation in particular industries and occupations by listing their locations and formation dates/first known report. In some instances, especially retailing in larger towns, multiple bodies organised in the same year. Listings may seem lengthy but actually concisely summarise the geographic spread of organisation often neglected in labour historiography. It enables discussion to focus on illustrative examples while also identifying areas for future research. The book is self-standing but some data from earlier periods is included in charts and tables to contextualise trends and emphasise that unions and political organisation after 1850 built on earlier developments. Post-1881 data in charts is incomplete but indicative. Membership/involvement figures are mostly presented in decade-long blocks which are more reliable than annual figures and a more indicative of long-term trends.

Notes

1. Cooperatives were excluded. They are being researched by Greg Patmore and Nikki Balnave.
2. *Evening Journal* 3 April 1879.
3. *Empire* 26 September 1856.
4. Tilly, C. (1977) From Mobilisation to Revolution, *Centre for Research on Social Organization Working Paper 156*, University of Michigan, Ann Arbor, 11–12.

1   The Collective Impulse, Mobilisation and Political Economy

Introduction: The Collective Impulse and Mobilisation

The collective impulse and worker mobilisation have been examined by an array of historical literatures including studies of unions and political parties, customary/informal resistance, the history of work regulation and of female, unfree/semi-free labour. Reviewing this literature, *The Origins of Worker Mobilisation* made several points relevant to this book.[1] First, while the industrial revolution was transformative, worker organisation long predated it and included groups overlooked in pioneering union histories by the Webb's, John R. Commons and others. Research by Rudé, Thompson, Rediker and Linebaugh indicated worker organisation should be viewed broadly, including informal combinations/ social networks.[2] *The Origins of Worker Mobilisation* identified substantial informal collective action transitioning into formal organisation, more rapidly in some industries than others. Second, the state was pivotal to the development of capitalism, regulating categories of labour (free, indentured workers, convicts and slaves). Courts played a critical role subordinating labour notwithstanding ongoing struggles over terms and conditions of employment. This struggle predominantly involved individuals and small groups. Laws specifically targeting combinations were used against unions but overall unionists were at less risk of being prosecuted than those taking collective action informally.

Reframing worker mobilisation has implications for fields including industrial relations, labour law, economic and labour history.[3] There are good reasons for industrial relations scholars to re-examine the history of labour law, strike waves and employer organisation, something John Kelly's book *Rethinking Industrial Relations: Mobilization, Collectivism and Long Waves* initiated 20 years ago.[4] Drawing on extensive literatures including Shorter and Tilly's *Strikes in France*, Kelly's portrayal of industrial relations emphasised confrontation and resistance to injustice at work as the propelling force underpinning mobilisation manifested in long waves.[5] Kelly's approach was criticised by Fairbrother as mechanistic and too reliant on a leadership approach to worker organisation.

Croucher and Wood pointed to historically contingent (and therefore not comparable) features of particular mobilisations.[6] This book argues resistance to inequality at work underpins worker organisation. It charts waves of mobilisation but one which incorporates 'resistance from below,' collaborative networks and multiple organisational forms without gainsaying the pivotal role of unions. Inequality is preferred over injustice because it is broader, more elemental and some aspects more measurable.[7]

Organisation Objectives, Methods and Recruitment/Coverage

A longstanding focus for analysing worker organisation has been examining different models of organisation and recruitment/coverage. As union density plummeted from the 1980s, unions sought recruitment methods to arrest this (like young and ethnic organisers and borrowing techniques used in the more union-hostile US) but largely failed to address labour market flooding, business/labour practices and regulatory changes or give sufficient attention to mobilising issues.[8] Recruitment methods and mobilisation are often used interchangeably but the former is tactical while the latter is strategic, based on organisation and long-term, issue-based campaigning. This book makes some observations about recruitment but focuses on mobilisation.

The Webb's pioneering examination of union development identified two pivotal organisational types. First, new model craft unions originating in the early 1850s typified by the Amalgamated Society of Engineers (ASE), marked by bureaucratic governance, high membership fees, extensive friendly benefits, tight craft entry controls, unilateral regulation, insular outlook and eschewing strikes and politics. Second, the new unionism or mass mobilisation of semi- and unskilled workers typified by the London Dockers (1889) with low membership fees, no friendly benefits and embracing both strikes and politics. While a valuable heuristic device, Archer observed many unions didn't entirely conform to the criteria with 'new unions' of miners and dockworkers operating accident funds—friendly benefits.[9] This book reinforces Archer's point, identifying craft unions that embraced politics and unskilled/semi-skilled unions practicing unilateral regulation. This is not simply nuance. In Australia the shift to mass organisation began in the 1850s and accelerated after 1870 not 1880. These points apply equally to peak and political organisation. Attempts at wider organisation long predated 1850, like the Grand National Consolidated Trades Union in the UK (1834). The period 1851–1880 witnessed experiments with more broadly based organisation. In the US the National Labor Union (1866–1873) sought to bring local unions and other bodies like eight-hour leagues together. The Knights of Labor (1869–1886), a more radical body enrolling blacks and women, initially advocated cooperative production. Similar attempts can be identified in the UK, Australia and elsewhere which clearly involved borrowing ideas although there were also country-specific trajectories of development, reflecting differences in societies, their history and political economies like the aggressiveness of capital and violent repression of unions in the US.

Notwithstanding extensive research in the 120 years since the Webb's wrote, there have been remarkably few attempts to systematically re-examine objectives/mobilising issues and methods in historical context, including the relationship between informal and formal organisation or the implications of earlier studies' failure to consider organisation amongst clerks, teachers and other workers. Historians are hardly alone in building scholarship silos. The last decade has witnessed numerous publications dealing with informal collective action, especially amongst immigrants or workers in the 'Global South,' worker-community alliances, as well as the perils of the gig economy/precarious work and supply chains. Much of this research is ahistorical, ignoring similar phenomena in earlier periods and consequently proffering impoverished understandings of what is occurring.[10]

One subject attracting attention since the 1980s is sources of union power. Visser identified three central sources of union power, namely organisational, institutional and economic, while also recognising union structure (the degree of cooperation and ideological splits) would influence this.[11] Drawing on subsequent work by Silver (see later in the chapter), Lehndorff et al. identified four sources of union power: structural power (bargaining power in the labour market and labour process), organisational power (numerical strength and the capacity to mobilise members), institutional power (bargains struck as a result of structural and organisational power as well as regulated minimum labour standards) and societal power (building collaborate networks within civil society to represent workers in the political sphere as well as political representation).[12] These categorisations are attractive but rather mechanistic, leaving little scope for significant differences in worker agency. Their application is also challenging when dealing with a diffuse array of organisational forms, overlapping networks and historically contingent aspects of particular eras or countries. Nonetheless, it is possible to relate sources of union power with earlier typologies of union methods like unilateral regulation, bargaining and legal enactment as well as align this with significant shifts. Historically, skilled male workers were able exercise power via their critical location in the labour process, especially when products were always changing or market demand was small. This rapidly eroded where mass production was viable, enabling changes to the labour process through mechanisation and introducing unskilled/semi-skilled workers. Chapters 7 and 8 examine these struggles, reinforcing Bennett's point that while the construction of skill is gendered, simplistic critiques of labour market barriers erected by unions paying no attention to employer strategies detract from wider understandings of how and why working communities organise to protect themselves.[13] To make mobilisation more comprehendible to sociologists, political-scientists and others interested in power, this book applies these frames of reference on power in chapter conclusions, highlighting their strengths and weaknesses.

Studies have examined worker mobilisation comparatively, though largely focused on the post-1880 era, partly due to data gaps but more generally because 1880–1930 is deemed pivotal at least for the 'old' rich countries. Beverly Silver's *Forces of Labor: Workers' Movements and Globalisation since 1870* examined peaks in labour unrest in over 20 countries in selected industries (textiles, automobiles and education). Importantly the examination is not confined to formal organisation or strikes (including demonstrations, bans, riots and other actions). Silver used a database constructed by the World Labour Research Group covering the period 1870–1996 with over 90,000 references to labour unrest from two newspapers with global coverage (*The Times* and the *New York Times*).[14] To explain unrest-peaks, changing bargaining power and national accommodations, Silver points to structural factors like shifts in capital mobility, product markets and production processes like extensive subcontracting in Japanese manufacturing later exported to other countries. Her examination of globalisation over a long time-frame is welcome in an age where narrow research dominates. Silver doesn't entirely reject Thompson's argument about the cultural component whereby taking collective action builds class identity but doesn't deem it important.[15]

This book is more sympathetic to Thompson's approach, arguing that notwithstanding structural factors there are contingent aspects to worker mobilisation in particular countries, regions and epochs. Research pointing to the historically contingent nature of worker mobilisation includes Shorter and Tilly's study of French strikes from 1830 which highlighted large numbers of strikes occurring outside unions—an observation reinforced by this book.[16] In a later book, *The Contentious French*, Tilly emphasised the need to analyse worker dissent over longer time-frames (from the 17th century). In conjunction with shifts in wages and hours, Tilly identified several influential factors notably particular features of the French-state, the greater significance of agricultural capitalists (compared to Britain) and regional differences (including access to food).[17] The research of Tilly and others (outlined later) demonstrate that amidst substantial global commonalities in capitalism and worker responses to it there are contingent elements, both historically and in the configuration of conflict within particular societies. This point is relevant to understanding what has and will occur amongst industrialising countries in Asia.

Also relevant is the notion of American Exceptionalism contending early Puritan settler ideas, the American Revolution and frontier/

settlement patterns spawned a unique ideology in the US combining liberty, individualism, egalitarianism, laissez-fare economics, democracy and republicanism. This had implications for class relations including the size/nature of union organisation and the failure to develop a mass working-class political party. Rejecting crude variants and responding to postmodernist critics, political scientist Seymour Lipset argued American Exceptionalism should be viewed from the perspective of comparative social analysis—a spectrum of traits and their relative strengths. The US shared traits with Anglophone societies like Canada, Britain, Australia and New Zealand, but there were also differences. Canada appeared more elitist, law-abiding and statist than the US but more anti-statist, violent and egalitarian compared to Britain.[18] These observations are relevant although Lipset focuses on the post-1880 period and says little about Australia—ironic given American social reformers' (like Henry Demarest Lloyd and John R. Commons) interest in Australia as a social-welfare reform pioneer in 1880–1920.[19]

Comparing 'settler' capitalism in Australia and the US hasn't been ignored.[20] Robin Archer's *Why there is no Labor Party in the United States* makes Australia the key comparator, using both quantitative and qualitative data.[21] Archer's findings resonate with this book, reinforcing some key points but also raising questions about others. Archer demolishes several US exceptionalism arguments, notably that greater prosperity and earlier enfranchisement compared to Europe inhibited a Labor Party. Per capita GDP and real wages were higher in Australia than the US for much of the 19th century and roughly equal in the early 20th century. Australia secured universal male suffrage around the same time (mid-19th century) and Archer cannot discern other compelling differences between the countries' political apparatuses like voting methods or paying representatives. The capacity of workers to attend polls/vote is not examined and this book identifies this as important (Chapter 11). Archer finds other comparison points ambiguous. This includes the urban-rural divide where the proportion of small-holders differed, but large land-holders and regional capital (like mining companies) provided a base for small-holder/labour alliances in both—even if it wasn't realised. Archer points to the importance of shearers/rouseabouts unions in mobilising a rural vote. As this book shows, to this could be added shop-workers, carriers/carters, tradesmen, general and construction labourers, railway workers and miners, although at least some like metalliferous miners, retail-workers and carriers also organised in the US prior to 1880. Archer finds another common explanation, namely race/immigration is not as compelling as expected. The labour movement of both countries demonstrated a strong antipathy to Chinese and black labour. The Chinese constituted a higher proportion of the Australian population but still relatively small. Archer finds anti-Chinese sentiment actually bolstered political mobilisation, a finding this book supports. While Australia's population included proportionately more immigrants, far fewer came from southern and eastern Europe. The timing of this wave and growing ethnic divisions might be a difference. Perhaps more compelling, the sheer number of immigrants weakened union organisation and bargaining power in the US at a critical point, whereas Australia's remoteness meant passage assistance was essential for most working-class migrants and efforts to restrict immigration became a political mobilisation point for labour far earlier than the US, as this book will show.

Archer found one persuasive difference was that the shift to new unionism/mass unionism was more belated in the US. In the early 1890s over 60% of unionists belonged to new unions in NSW and with the TLC actively organising others. This compared to 15–20% in the US where the American Federation of Labor (AFL) didn't following the TLC path, preferring to build unions more closely resembling the Webb's new model unions. Archer echoes Markey's pioneering research indicating Australia led the UK too in forming stable unions of seamen and wharf-labourers/dockers. While Australian workers (many British emigrants) drew heavily on British organisational forms and ideas, they were able to implement some more rapidly.[22] The Melbourne Trades Hall Council (founded in 1856) predates its UK equivalents by several years and a more rapid trajectory is also evident for the eight-hour day and extended franchise. This book reinforces the more rapid rise of mass unionism in Australia, arguing unions of semi-skilled/unskilled workers outnumbered craft union membership probably by around 1875 and certainly by 1880.

In both the US and Australia, organising semi-skilled/unskilled workers encountered employer resistance aided by governments though most virulently in the US. This difference was magnified by US craft unions' failure to provide logistical/financial and political support whereas Australian unions and peak bodies (headed by craft union officials) did, exemplified by the 1878 seamen's strike. Craft unions involved themselves in politics in both countries. If craft exclusivism typified by the 'aristocracy of labour' thesis has an evidentiary base it was in the US, encouraging divisions/competitive movements like the Knights of Labor and later the Congress of Industrial Organisations. Even so, the Knights of Labor demonstrate the danger of viewing this purely as American Exceptionalism or a reaction to craft-exclusivity. Formed by dissidents from the collapsed Philadelphia Garment Cutters Union in 1869 (turnover of Australian clothing trades unions was common for the same reasons), and drawing on religious zeal, the Knights of Labor grew slowly during the 1870s before peaking during the industrial upheavals of the 1880s. Branches were formed in other countries including the UK, Ireland, Belgium, Italy, South Africa, New Zealand and Australia. The Knights faced hostility from governments and established unions and faded—typical of many bodies. Nonetheless, Parfitt argues they represented a globally important worker organisation whose policy agenda shaped progressivism in New Zealand

and Australia.[23] The Knights need to be seen as part of a broader spectrum of organisational experimentation. The aristocracy of labour, coined by revolutionary anarchist Mikhail Bukanin in 1872 to debunk organised workers as the most radical, was popularised by labour and social historians from the late 1970s to explain working-class divisions, US-style business unionism and conservative voting patterns by craft workers in the 19th century.[24] Notwithstanding criticism of its analytical value, the aristocracy of labour thesis influenced scholarship for over two decades.[25] While acknowledging divisions and tensions within organised labour this book finds Australian evidence doesn't support the thesis.

Politics and the Role of the State

Thompson, Linebaugh, Hay and others initiated new understandings of the state, capitalism and worker resistance pertinent to understanding later developments.[26] Linebaugh's *The London Hanged* demonstrated interconnections between rapacious capitalism, labour process changes in particular trades and an array of punitive property, trade and anti-combination laws and capital offences in the 18th century.[27] Convict transportation was part of this regime. After the American Revolution transportation shifted primarily to Australia, reaching historically unprecedented levels, simultaneously controlling dissent in Britain/Ireland and providing labour to build capitalist colonies enriching the empire. *The Origins of Worker Mobilisation* showed law, courts and police undertook critical roles, subordinating convict and later free labour in the colonies as well as safeguarding the colonial elite's property.

Criticising Polanyi's notion of a great transformation between the 18th and 19th century when pre-capitalism (enclosures, poor laws) gave way to a self-regulating economy. Stanziani argued regulation wasn't abandoned per se but reconfigured to support social and economic inequalities, later redressed in part by interventions in the 20th century.[28] *The Origins of Worker Mobilisation* disputed such time-confined periodisation, arguing the state facilitated capitalism from the 14th century even if this intensified from the 18th century. Efforts to subordinate workers and their communities encountered increasing resistance which mitigated aspects and exacted political (increased franchise/representation) and industrial concessions (like union recognition and work safety laws). Unions and their political allies also took steps to ensure protective laws were implemented/enforced—something less discussed by historians.[29] This book traces this shift in Australia, highlighting its importance for later developments. Returning to Archer's examination of American Exceptionalism, one factor driving working-class politicisation identified in this book was the centrality of the colonial state in economic affairs, including infrastructure like railways and land policies (generally favouring large landholders) and financing immigration.[30] Another facilitating factor was the greater success of the shorter hours' movement increasing time to politically engage and vote.

The Political Economy of the Colonies

By 1850 Australia was an integral part of global capitalism. Nonetheless, significant gold discoveries in NSW and Victoria in 1851–1852 accelerated growth, with substantial inflows of people and capital.[31] The 1850s also witnessed increased production and export of coal, lead, tin and copper. Gold exports were globally significant. Victorian gold production alone approached three million ounces in 1856, employing a workforce of over 140,000 in 1859 (declining to 80,000 by 1865).[32] In the mid-1840s South Australian mines became globally significant copper suppliers and exports grew substantially in succeeding decades. The value of copper and lead exports grew over fivefold from £94,831 in 1854 to £542,393 in 1863, increasing further after 1863.[33] Like gold, this attracted population to the colony, increased manufactured imports as well as encouraging local engineering/manufacturing. Like the rural/ farming sector, mining was volatile. Between 1861–1863 and 1868–1870, mining's share of gross domestic product fell from 15.1 to 10.6% while rural industry's share rose from 8 to 11.3%. During the same period manufacturing and construction's share rose from 12.9 to 17.3%.[34] Mining fuelled other activities. Copper and other ores were smelted, most for export. However, ironworks were established near Mittagong (NSW) in the 1840s, followed in the 1870s by Beaconsfield (Tasmania), Ballarat (Victoria) and on the Fleurieu Peninsula (South Australia), along with several small blast furnaces at Maldon/Castlemaine and Hindmarsh. Major ports became hubs for engineering/manufacturing activities. In Newcastle boilermakers, toolmakers, moulders and others were employed building and maintaining equipment for Hunter Valley collieries; in family-owned engineering firms manufacturing coal wagons and boilers as well as ship repair; and in government railways and the harbour and rivers department.[35]

Wool production and export (mainly to British textile mills) expanded substantially, as did agricultural and rural food production with increasing exports of wheat and the beginnings of a substantial meat export industry facilitated by refrigeration in the 1870s.[36] Regional towns were integral to the expansion of rural production.[37] While smaller landholdings grew (especially in dairying and some agricultural activities) along with small retailers, manufacturers and mining companies, the colonies were still dominated by large capital and a more economically engaged state sector than the UK or the US.[38] Large landholders exerted considerable, if slowly diminishing political influence. Unlike Argentina they were unable to entrench property rights, stunt democracy and inhibit economic growth.[39] Growing population, urban settlements and primary production contributed to an expansion of local manufacturing and boosted private, commercial and civil construction. Overall, exports fell as a proportion of GDP while the colonies' isolation/remoteness encouraged some entrepreneurial innovation in business development.[40]

The prolonged construction boom (bridges, railway culverts and public buildings) is still evident in almost every sizeable town throughout eastern-Australia. Metal/engineering, food processing, clothing/footwear, transport equipment and household items dominated local manufacturing, concentrated in major centres. Average enterprise size remained modest but grew with a shift away from small craft-based workshops (less so in country towns) and emergence of larger manufacturing companies like the Colonial Sugar Refining Company (1855). Employer organisation was dominated by craft-masters associations but from the 1870s industry-based associations representing large employers were formed in key sectors like the Northern Coal Sales Association and the Steamship Owners Association (1878), followed by others in the 1880s. There was little collective bargaining between unions and masters' and industry associations, with many unions opting for unilateral regulation or agreements underpinned by community pressure in the case of retail-workers.[41]

By global standards the colonies were comparatively urbanised by 1850 and this intensified in 1851–1880. By 1881, 30% or more of the population of NSW, Victoria, South Australia and Western Australia lived in the colonial capital. Sydney and Melbourne, with populations over 200,000, were globally significant cities for the period, comparable to Baltimore and Chicago.[42] Lipset and Lakin argue urbanisation encouraged class identification and Australia provides evidence of this.[43] Working-class districts marked by overcrowding and poverty existed before 1850 but had grown substantially by the 1870s, especially in Sydney and Melbourne. Environmental problems from industry discharges and public health problems (sickness and the threat/reality of epidemics) led to government inquiries and the establishment of bodies like Sydney City and Suburban Sewage and Health Board (1875).[44]

There were also important changes to transport. Railways—moving people and bulk goods rapidly over long distances—began in NSW, Victoria and South Australia in the early 1850s, followed by Queensland (mid-1860s), Tasmania (early 1870s) and Western Australia (early 1880s). Private initiatives rapidly gave way to government ownership/control becoming a major component of colonial budgets and borrowing. Like roads, railways radiated from major ports (two initially separate networks in NSW and three in Queensland) connecting to rural and mining centres. Total railway mileage in South Australia and the three eastern mainland colonies grew from a few hundred miles in 1860 to 953 (1,533 km) in 1870, 3,347 (5,386 km) in 1880 and 8,416 (13,544 km) in 1890.[45] From the early 1850s, shallow-draft paddlewheel steamers were important for moving people and bulk goods, especially on the only major inland river system—the Murray-Darling covering a basin of over one million square kilometres of flat and poorly-watered land stretching across Queensland, NSW, Victoria and South Australia.[46] Tiny by global standards, this (with related Macquarie and Murrumbidgee rivers) facilitated pastoral expansion, enabling wool to be moved from remote areas yet to be reached by railways. Wilcannia on the Darling River almost 1,000 kilometres west of Sydney became the country's third largest inland port. The 1878–1881 logbook of an unidentified paddle-wheeler provides vivid testimony to active trade in goods and people, moving wool bales from towns like Wilcannia, Wagga, Hay, Wellington, Yanko, Port Murrumbidgee and small riverside jetties near sheep-stations.[47]

The state played a critical role in economic development, building infrastructure like ports, railways (maintaining engines and rolling stock), roads and bridges, funding education and providing assisted-passage to immigrants. Borrowing by colonial governments represented an important capital inflow, augmenting the private sector.[48] Enfranchisement also empowered rural communities to secure access to water, enhancing growth.[49] The contribution of the state to Australia's distinctive development should not be underestimated.

Overall, the economy became more diversified and complex, though still vulnerable to external economic shifts affecting export demand and capital inflows along with local factors, notably droughts like one in the mid-1860s that severely impacted rural production and employment. Climate shaped economic activity, favouring pastoralism over agriculture, but it was an accommodation rife with shortcomings.[50] Australia continued its trajectory to becoming one of the richest societies on the planet.[51] Exceptional growth in per capita GDP prior to 1890 was not simply a product of Australia's resource endowment but its combination with labour participation and productivity.[52] Aided by mechanisation, pastoral activities became more capital intensive with abrupt shifts in employment levels during droughts/business downturns. Construction experienced similar volatility. Employment growth/stability was greater in manufacturing in part due to protective tariffs. Import duties weren't new to the colonies but Victoria led the post-goldrush extension, ultimately setting policy parameters for post-federation Australia.[53] Australia's road to prosperity built on pre-1851 foundations facilitated by a diversifying economic base (including mineral and rural/agricultural exports and local manufacturing), urbanisation and the comparatively early shift to democratic institutions in which, as this book demonstrates, organised labour played a pivotal role.

Changing Labour Markets

By 1850 the non-indigenous population reached 405,400 mainly through convict transportation and migration. While natural growth increased, heavy dependence on migration continued, the vast majority of emigrants receiving passage assistance apart from the period immediately after gold was discovered when population jumped to 648,900 by 1852 and almost tripled in the decade to 1860 (1,145,600). The 1860s were marked by weaker economic conditions and total population grew more slowly to 1,647,700 in 1870 before reaching 2,231,500 in 1880. Economic conditions already described created a labour market that experienced periodic labour shortages but was also marked by rapid shifts in demand and periodic bouts of unemployment especially in the major urban centres. The latter has often been glossed over by historians but (see Chapter 11) severe if mostly short-lived joblessness sparked significant social unrest.

Episodic labour shortages like that in the early 1850s exacerbated problems of labour control. Government workers finding their wages eroded by inflation could only complain, while others like seamen deserted in droves. Levels of maritime insubordination which had fallen during the 1840s depression rebounded. In November 1852 William Parfitt, master of the *Formosa*, lamented his experience and called for 'a more healthy system in the administering of the laws relating to shipping, in the place of the rotten and unjust one at present in practice.'[54] Arriving in Victoria the Williamstown Water Police Court dealt with several 'troublesome' ringleaders but sailing onto Sydney, Parfitt's control of his crew unravelled. A litany of complaints about prolonged and ineffective legal processes then followed, Parfitt arguing he was now short-handed for the ongoing voyage. Parfitt's complaint wasn't isolated and colonies rapidly introduced more stringent maritime labour laws, also retaining legally dubious practices ostensibly removed from earlier punitive laws, notably police arresting suspected deserters without warrant in Sydney and Tasmania.[55] Amidst hysteria, seamen were arrested on suspicion, reminiscent of the treatment of convicts. Captain Escott gave his crew a half-holiday but 18-year-old John Dawson was arrested while travelling to visit friends in Ashfield, tried before the Sydney Police Court and released with a warning even after Escott corroborated his claims.[56] This wasn't an isolated incident. Nor was it confined to the gold rush years—the same fate befalling two seamen granted a half-holiday from the *Red Gauntlet*.[57]

Importing Labour

The colonies relied heavily on immigration, overwhelmingly passage-assisted British/Irish while non-British Europeans commonly arrived under employer-sponsored indenture. Convict transportation to Tasmania ended in 1853 with small numbers transported to Western Australia until 1868. The gold rushes encouraged greater diversity amongst arrivals, still mainly from Europe but also the US and over 38,000 Chinese by 1861—Chinese constituted 9% of the Victorian population in 1857.[58] Responding to remoteness and high travel costs, colonial parliaments expended substantial budget funds on passage assistance. While population/defence considerations played a part, the key driver was capital whose representatives dominated parliament resisting immigration cutbacks even during downturns—as they still do today with misguided backing from the Australian Council of Trade Unions. There was no subtlety. During one debate in 1874 the *Ballarat Courier* observed:

> Of course, petitions in favour of assisted-immigration will be sent in in response to Mr Highett's invitation. Employers of labor are interested in obtaining it as cheaply as possible, and there is no surer method of bringing down wages than free immigration.[59]

Employers in manufacturing, mining and agriculture repeatedly pushed for more immigrants. Given their dominance within legislatures, there was limited need for overt pressure but their influence is manifest in budgetary debates as well as petitions mostly from rural/agricultural bodies.[60] Largely escaping systematic analysis by historians, employers imported workers from Europe, Asia and the Pacific under indenture. The advantages of 'coolie' labour in terms of their alleged servility and cheapness had been lauded since the 1830s, with small groups of Indian, Chinese and Pacific Islanders imported mainly by pastoralists. The ending of convict transportation to NSW (1840) sharpened the push along with periodic employer efforts to reintroduce transportation, the latter overlooked by historians seemingly because it failed. In March 1852 the *People's Advocate* argued employers inured to cheap convict labour were unhappy with reduced revenue of paying European labourers and sought alternatives in India and China, aided by Chinese 'crimps' (contract labour providers). Several days earlier WC Wentworth prosecuted Chinese servants who complained about their food, ill-treatment and having no shoes. Wentworth appeared before the court later that year, admitting he hadn't paid one Chinese servant and paid several others in kind.[61] These cases typified employer treatment of non-Europeans they imported.

The largest non-European group were 62,000 Pacific islanders used in Queensland agriculture, especially sugar plantations from the 1860s. While subjected to extensive historical research, the role/practices of employers have been neglected. Employers agitated for the importation, driven by one objective cheap and servile labour.[62] Speakers at an East Moreton Farmers Association meeting in February 1868 compared the cheapness and availability of indentured German workers (14s 6d per week and 7s 6d for their wives) to Pacific Islanders (9s per week or £18 for a three-year agreement). This was well below 4s per day (24s per week) paid to resident 'white' Europeans—still a low wage by colonial standards.[63] One speaker complained resident Europeans were 'so difficult to control.'[64] Euphemistic variants of these arguments continue with regard to harvest and other work today, like locals won't work hard enough or do these jobs—meaning not under wages offered. Queensland's Pacific Islanders' regime differed only by degree from slavery, highlighted when the schooner *Daphne* was intercepted in 1869 with 100 islanders crammed in a hold licensed to carry 50 and with agreements signed by 'interested parties' rather than those contracted.[65] Islanders were often blackbirded (kidnapped), engaged under exploitative contracts (even then frequently flouted) and mistreated, leading to levels of morbidity/mortality that eventually sparked British government intervention. Regulatory protections improved but belatedly. There were numerous smaller importations of Asia-Pacific workers under similarly exploitative conditions in agriculture, fishing and pearling, some only coming to light incidentally. In January 1878 the *Cooktown Herald* reported 37 De La Warr Island natives engaged in fishing on the schooner *Kingston* had mutinied, probably accounting for its abrupt disappearance.[66]

The Regulatory Apparatus for Subordinating Labour

Subordinating Labour and Wage Recoveries

Table 1.1 summarises laws affecting work enacted in 1850–1885. Lopsided master and servant and maritime labour laws continued as the main regulator of work arrangements. Dissenting workers were regularly gaoled in the 1850s though this slowly declined. As earlier, colonies amended laws to address changing labour market conditions. Apart from seamen, colonial labour laws were largely free from UK oversight. Amidst widespread desertion and dissent by seamen in the early 1850s, Imperial authorities urged the colonies to introduce more punitive laws.[67] Some changes echoed the convict era by enabling twice-convicted seamen to be treated as convicted felons. In January 1852 the Sydney Bench warned several *Osprey* seamen gaoled twice for refusing work that a recent legislative change meant they could be sent to the Cockatoo Island penal establishment or the Newcastle breakwater. Treating deserters as vagrants—the *Vagrancy Act* enabled up to two years' imprisonment—was also considered.[68] Seamen lodging complaints of ill-treatment seldom received a fair hearing except in the most egregious cases and they could only claim wages at the end of their voyage. Whalers paid under the lays system (sharing the voyage catch of oil, bone and ambergris) were in a worse situation if few whales were caught or the vessel wrecked. Indeed, poor returns became common as the industry declined due to falling whale numbers and growing use of petroleum oil.[69]

Absconding/dissent amongst land-workers in the early 1850s occasioned revised master and servant laws interlinked with new assisted-emigrant laws to prevent emigrants brought out at considerable state or

Table 1.1 Work and Labour Market Related Laws Enacted in the Australian Colonies 1850–1885

	New South Wales*	Queensland	South Australia	Tasmania	Victoria	Western Australia
1850	Master & servants Steam navigation				Master & servant Seamen	
1851	Apprentices					
1852	Assisted-immigration, Foreign seamen, Master & servants		Master & servant Seamen	Master & servants Mercantile marine	Master & servant Seamen	
1853	Seamen/water police				Seamen	
1854	Assisted-immigration, Coal Mines, Master & servants		Civil service	Master & servants Immigrants	Foreign seamen	
1855	Immigration, Seamen lodging				Master & servants Assist immigration.	
1856			Aliens	Master & servants		
1857	Master & servants		Chinese, Immigration		Chinese	Port Safety
1858	Immigration loan		Convict prevention			
1859				Foreign seamen Seamen	Chinese	
1860	Seamen		Civil service			
1861	Chinese, Immigration loan	Master & servants		Aliens		Explosives
1862	Coal Fields	Coolie Act		Public works	Chinese Civil service	
1863			Aliens, Master & servants		Chinese, aliens Immigration	

(Continued)

Table 1.1 (Continued)

	New South Wales*	Queensland	South Australia	Tasmania	Victoria	Western Australia
1864	Seamen		Aliens, Industrial Societies, Marine Board		Master & servant, apprentices, Immigration	
1865	Industrial societies, Seamen		Civil service, Convict prevention,	Marine Board, Public works	Chinese Seamen Aliens	
1866	Public Schools, Workhouse					
1867	Chinese			Public works, Immigration, Marine Board		
1868		Polynesian Labourers		Public works (2)		Master & servants
1869					Aborigines	
1870		Wages		Foreign seamen	Railway pay (2) Wages (contractors)	
1871	Navigation					Aboriginal Pearl, Distressed seamen
1872						
1873	Navigation		Immigration			Aboriginal Pearl, Apprentices
1874				Immigration, Marine Board, Marine Officers	Factory/workshops Mines regulation	Imported labour registry, Aboriginal Offenders
1875						Pearl Fishery, Seamen

Year						
1876	Agreements validation, Coal Mines		Trade Unions, Marine Board			
1877			Master & servants	Marine Officers		Mines regulation
1878			Conspiracy, Marine Board, Master & servants			
1879	Islander engagements, Navigation		Marine Board, NT immigration,			Convict discipline
1880	Public instruction	Pacific Island Labourers		Marine Board		
1881	Chinese, Trade Union, Navigation		Marine Board	Marine Board, Mines Regulation	Mines regulation	Superannuation, Mines regulation
1882	Employers liability	Pacific Island Labourers, Assist. immigration	NT Indian migration	App, Marine Board. Master & servant		Master & servant
1883	Seamen		Mines regulation			Mines regulation
1884	Butchers Sunday closing, Civil service	Pacific Islanders, Wages, Assist. immigration	Employers liability	Machinery inspect, Marine Board, Master & servant, Mines Regulation, Women & Child employment	Mine Acc. Fund, Trades Union	
1885	Pacific Island Labourers	Pacific Island Labourers	Civil Service	Immigration (2), Marine Board	Explosives, Factories & shops, Companies, Wages	Explosives, Superannuation

* Covered areas which became Victoria until it separated in 1852 and Queensland which separated in 1859.

private expense leaving their employer or the colony.[70] Viewed by the labour movement as an attempt to depress wages, the mismatch was especially intense in Tasmania which was already losing workers, especially ex-convicts, to more attractive (jobs and wages-wise) mainland colonies and after 1853 no longer had transportation. Debating a new Master and Servant Bill in 1854, landholder Robert Kermode bemoaned clauses dealing with servants' ill-treatment and facilitating wage recoveries including additional penalties/compensation. More sympathetic members pointed to the collateral damage of imprisoning young females and imposing severe penalties on emigrants who broke their agreements.[71] Clauses imposing severe fines on those harbouring absconders or shipmasters aiding their escape smacked of convict regulations. The critics proved prescient. In October 1856 an assisted-emigrant couple named Ahern were arrested trying to depart the colony. Their imprisonment under the *Assisted Emigrants Act* 1854 created a public furore when it became known their departure was prompted by inability to find work.[72] The only immigrant group increasingly targeted for control and discouragement were the Chinese from the late 1850s (Table 1.1), a push that would intensify in the 1880s.

There were sporadic attempts to improve wage recovery provisions for rural workers like shepherds—who suffered from a mixture of sharp practice, insolvency or changes of rural holdings ownership—along with domestics and other vulnerable groups. Gains were slow, bills frequently rejected by landholder-dominated legislatures.[73] Wage theft was widespread, many workers having to resort to the courts to secure their entitlements.[74] For labourers working for contractors/subcontractors, including those engaged by local government or on construction projects like railways, slippery practices (via subcontracting chains and the truck-system) and insolvencies were common. Unpaid wages led to hundreds of protests, numerous court cases and, together with the truck-system, a stream of newspaper reports, letters and editorials.[75] Bills to remedy this were introduced into the Victorian and South Australian legislatures in the late 1850s amidst a tsunami of wage-defaults occasioning widespread distress.[76] Recovering pay was particularly difficult for self-employed workers not covered by master and servant laws. A Victorian bill covered both wage-earners and self-employed subcontractors thereby crossing a legal-artefactual divide that still advantages exploitive strategies by capital (like franchising and Uber-type arrangements).[77] In South Australia the Public Works Commissioner received multiple petitions from workmen complaining of wage-defaults and the truck-system.[78] The government promised to legislate but, as in Victoria, didn't.[79]

Other proposed remedies included requiring contractors to pay weekly in cash or to lodge security payments with the administering government authority. The latter was raised with the South Australian Central Road Board—beset by numerous contractor defaults—in 1860 but rejected. One board member cynically acknowledged contractors were 'men of straw.'[80] Bound by competitive tendering to engage the cheapest contractor, in 1870 the Board took out an advertisement telling workers their only resort lay with contractors.[81] The situation was similar in other colonies. An NSW MLA (Hoskins) recited a case where men paid by a government road-contractor near Grafton travelled to Sydney but had to return when their payment-cheques bounced.[82] Payment scheduling by some government authorities rendered regular payment by contractors more difficult than it should have been.[83] Notwithstanding repeated complaints/protests reaching colonial parliaments, legislative intervention took over a decade. In 1870 NSW and Victoria enacted contractor wage recovery laws. It was an important step. However, as one Victorian Legislative Council member (Kitto) noted, the law didn't help 90% of the working classes whose wage recoveries still depended on the none-too-tender mercies of the *Master and Servant Act*.[84]

Queensland introduced laws regulating 'coolie' and pacific island labour in 1862, 1868 and 1880 (Table 1.1). Like master and servant laws, their principal objective was facilitating the regime and advantaging capital notwithstanding evidence of widespread wage theft, misuse/ill-treatment and high morbidity/mortality. Numerous protests (Chapter 4) demonstrated widespread flouting of the few legal entitlements these workers had. In 1876–1877 Queensland parliament debated amending the *Polynesian Labourers Act* but was stymied by employer-dominated opposition, with ex-premier and Port Curtis landholder Arthur Palmer denying the scheme sought to drive down wages and ludicrously asserting there had only been one refusal to pay wages.[85]

Previously confined to opposing laws hostile to their interests from the 1850s, labour began promoting laws to protect/progress their interests. In November 1859 Victorian MLA Charles Don pushed for eight-hours to be made a condition in all government contracts.[86] This and legislative campaigns on safety and other matters are examined in later chapters.

The Courts, Judiciary and Prisons

As earlier, courts remained pivotal to subordinating labour. Even in convict-'endowed' Tasmania significant numbers of free workers were prosecuted, the Hobart Bench alone facing 16 unresolved master and servant cases on 29 June 1854.[87] The scale of litigation is essential to understanding collective action especially during the 1850s when large numbers were imprisoned for dissent, especially rural workers and seamen. The incarceration rate of seamen in ports like Melbourne and Brisbane required prison hulks—redolent of 18th-century England and the convict period.[88] In Tasmania convict insubordination and absconding was widespread. Many absconders tried to reach Victoria, some found secreted on vessels while braver souls aimed to Bass Strait in small boats like nine apprehended at Little Sandy Bay on 3 September 1852.[89] Some reached Victoria only to be apprehended, returned and tried.[90] Victorian authorities engaged men at the docks skilled at identifying convicts' distinctive appearance like tattoos and scarring from the lash. Absconders were also apprehended in Sydney.[91] Successful escapees, and there were many, simply vanished from the records. Rewards for capturing absconders encouraged VDL police constables (commonly ex-convicts) to be zealous—sometimes too zealous. In April 1852 three men dragged before the Hobart Bench were found to be free.[92] Groups of convicts seeking recreational absences like visiting pubs were also prosecuted mostly with unauthorised absence although those returning inebriated could be charged with being drunk and disorderly or creating a disturbance in their master's premises.[93] Though rarer, multi-workplace absences did occur like servants working for John Miller and Reverend W Reiley in March 1853.[94] As charges were laid by individual employers, court records probably understate multi-workplace absences and wider collaborations.

From the mid-1850s gaol remedies were progressively curtailed in colonial master and servant laws and courts were more likely to fine offenders, including those taking collective action. Imprisonment remained a default option where fines were unpaid. On occasion courts imposed heavy fines to ensure imprisonment. David Gibson's Ticket-of-Leave servants Samuel Smith and Hamilton Kelsey were fined £5 for being absent on 13 November 1860, and then committed to Launceston Gaol for a month with hard labour.[95] This penalty was probably at the employer's behest, with other workers convicted of disobedience around the same time escaping with small fines.[96] By the mid-1870s the same bench was imposing fines of several shillings for workers engaging in collective absence, helping to explain why employers were abandoning master and servant laws.[97]

Subordinating laws were accentuated by stilted benches composed of part-time magistrates especially in rural districts. The laws bestowed few rights on workers, mainly recovering unpaid wages, which did become proportionally more significant as employer prosecutions declined. Even here, courts often gave employers time to make restitution or discounted amounts for rations, losing sheep and the like. There was, as still pertains today, no gaol option for guilty employers except rare cases of prolonged refusal to pay. Courts didn't impose fines and, unlike workers, rarely condemned employers for their offences. In essence, courts afforded no deterrence to wage theft, with the burden on workers to secure their legal entitlements. On 1 April 1862 the Longford Bench gave James Freborough 14 days to pay two servants £6 15s 6d and £6 10s respectively plus court costs. Highlighting disparate treatment, servant James Smith tried immediately beforehand was fined 20 shillings for breaching the *Master and Servant Act* or in default 14 days' imprisonment.[98] As today, wage theft was treated as an administrative breach, not a criminal act.

Epitomising this, some benches didn't record employer's pleas as guilty or not guilty but rather as 'claim admitted' or 'claim disputed.' In July 1862, seven seamen sought unpaid wages from the *Union*'s master (Jacobs). The Hobart Bench awarded amounts from £6 8s 8d to £25 18s 8d (depending on offsets including goods provided) plus 12s 6d court costs in each case.[99] The amounts were substantial and court costs indicative of the expense of bringing proceedings and loss to workers if claims were rejected—as many were. Unpaid wages imposed considerable financial hardship on workers and their families, and even stress-related health effects exemplified by two Newcastle brothers whose mental instability was attributed to this cause.[100]

Sources and Methods

Sources

This book uses quantitative and qualitative methods, drawing on a range of sources. One source was union records. Few pre-1851 union records survive but thereafter material slowly increases, including account and minute-books, circulars, certificates, badges and addresses. Almost all 1851–1880 records were examined for information on union government, inter-linkages, objectives, methods, and activities, including collective action. Sydney Shipwrights took collective action around 70 times between 1866 and 1880, less than 15% being reported in newspapers. Importantly, surviving records refer to other unions/branches whose records have not survived. Nevertheless, records (often incomplete) survive for less than 10% of known unions, are biased towards craft unions (and some trades within this group) and pertain to NSW and Victoria apart from a handful from South Australia and Queensland.

Colonial newspapers provide the most extensive evidence of worker organisation, formal and informal, including many for which no other evidence survives. Newspapers were interrogated using two complementary methods. First, for a decade from the mid-1980s newspapers were manually searched, including advertisements/notices, news items, editorials, obituaries and court reports. Information was then organised chronologically according to occupation. Second, over the past decade the National Library's impressive Trove digital collection of newspapers was searched using many terms/phrases. This yielded more material but was dependent on search-terms developed from the manual search and still missed information uncovered in the original search. Digital searches are valuable, not exhaustive.

Magistrate court records were another important source, especially for informal collective action. All surviving Tasmanian magistrates' bench-books were examined along with some records for other colonies. Over 100 whaling and merchant vessel logbooks were also examined. The

Mitchell Library holds more than 100 logbooks and 250 ship journals. The Tasmanian Archives and Heritage Office (especially the Crowther collection) includes numerous logbooks, ship journals, crew lists/agreements and related material. Shipmasters were required to record seamen's dissent in the logbook for any subsequent court proceedings providing information on maritime working conditions and collective action unrecorded in other sources. Government records examined included public inquiries; laws, draft bills, legal advice; petitions/memorials, statistical reports, correspondence and register of friendly societies records. Searching these vast materials was necessarily selective. Finally, other sources consulted included contemporary diaries, biographies and books; theses, books (including a number of union histories) and journal articles. More exhaustive examination of government and court records, local histories, diaries/journals, company/business records, ship logbooks, regional libraries/archives, family histories and UK records would add further information.

Extensive examination of diverse sources took decades but was essential for the book's purpose identifying 5,059 instances of worker organisation in 1851–1880 (4,822 informal organisations, 1528 unions, 93 informal and 144 formal peak/political bodies). Confining examination to surviving union records would be misleading, missing over 1,000 unions whose records didn't survive, including whole categories like clerks, teachers, shop-assistants, public servants, road transport workers and shearers.

Methods

Understanding worker mobilisation requires examining different forms of organisation including seemingly ephemeral informal associations. Evidence of informal organisation commonly pertains to a single instance of collective action. Not all involved might be prosecuted. Ticket-of-Leave holders Samuel Gale and John Delaney were imprisoned for six months in March 1855 for being absent until 11 pm and 'decoying' Mr Benjamin's men to join them.[101] Similarly in August 1862 *Sapphire* whalers Martin Shean and William Price were charged with 'combining with others of the crew to disobey lawful commands.'[102] As actions could involve more workers than reported, database figures on worker involvement are conservative. While some collective action appears as a spontaneous protest, others involved planning and employers targeted those deemed ringleaders. In April 1854 the schooner *Proserpine*'s master charged three men who came aft to announce the crew refused to work.[103] Collective action often drew on shared understandings involving a larger group with surviving records only capturing fragments of the contestation. On occasion successive court actions provide evidence of prolonged contestation, especially amongst seamen. In September 1852 the Hobart Bench sentenced four *Martin Luther* crewmembers to 60 days' hard labour for refusing work over poor rations and forecastle conditions. When later returned on board they joined others in striking—seven being sentenced to three weeks' hard labour.[104] In early November 11 crewmembers were charged before the George Town Bench with combining to disobey lawful commands, along with other crew. Charges were withdrawn but relations deteriorated. Five crewmembers were variously charged with assaulting the Chief Officer and several constables on 21 November. Those assaulting the Chief Officer were sentenced to 12 weeks' hard labour.[105] Logbooks and court records afford evidence of prolonged rounds of informal collective action amongst seamen that likely occurred in other industries.

Central to recording and analysing material was a relational database with files for each organisation (formal, informal, industrial or peak/political), its objective, methods, affiliation/mergers and government, with separate sub-files for strikes, non-strike collective action (NSCA), petitions, deputations and court actions.[106] Coding and its conventions involve difficult decisions. Dates and numbers of workers involved can be imprecise. Some absconding workers were charged with absence and vice versa, types of action or reasons for it were sometimes difficult to determine and records occasionally fail to report occupation (colonial business directories helped). Overall, the number of ambiguous cases was small (around 2–8% depending on category). Occupational coding is consistent with the Historical International Standard Classification of Occupations but sometimes abbreviated where the incidence of collective action was very low. The database isn't simply quantitative including large amounts of qualitative material (over 10,000 words for larger organisations). This assisted combining 'big data' with qualitative analysis although the latter drew on additional material. I collected over 80% of the primary information and did almost all data entry, helping ensure consistency, adapt coding where necessary and dovetail the strengths/weaknesses of 'big data' and qualitative research. Reading original sources not only provided context but identified actions like incendiarism where reported instances of collective sabotage almost certainly understated instances involving collaboration. It also enhanced the database's capacity to cross-match names and organisations to reveal informal networks and organisational activist carryovers known at the time but rarely documented. Digital hubs enabling large historical databases to 'talk' to each other offer enormous potential to extend research in the future.

Notes

1. Quinlan, M. (2018) *The Origins of Worker Mobilisation: Australia 1788–1850*, Routledge, New York, 1–11.
2. Rudé, G. (1964) *The Crowd in History: A Study of Popular Disturbances in France and England 1730–1848*, John Wiley & Sons, New York; Thompson, E. (1968) *The Making of the English Working-class*, Penguin,

Harmondsworth; Thompson, E. (1991) *Customs in Common*, Merlin Press, London; Linebaugh, P. (1991) *The London Hanged: Crime and Civil Society in the Eighteenth Century*, Penguin, London; Linebaugh, P. and Rediker, M. (1990) The Many-Headed Hydra: Sailors, Slaves, and the Atlantic Working-class in the Eighteenth Century, *Journal of Historical Sociology*, 3(3): 225–52.

3. Tucker, E. (2017) On Writing Labour Law History: A Reconnaissance, *International Journal of Comparative Labour Law and Industrial Relations*, 33(1): 39–58.

4. Kelly, J. (1998) *Rethinking Industrial Relations: Mobilization, Collectivism and Long Waves*, Routledge, London.

5. Shorter, E. and Tilly, C. (1974) *Strikes in France 1830–1968*, Cambridge University Press, Cambridge.

6. Cited in Gall, G. and Holgate, J. (2018) Rethinking Industrial Relations: Appraisal, Application and Augmentation, *Economic and Industrial Democracy*, 39(4): 561–76; Croucher, R. and Wood, G. (2017) Union Renewal in Historical Perspective, *Work, Employment and Society*, 31(6): 1010–20.

7. Quinlan, M. and Bohle, P. (2014) Re-Invigorating Industrial Relations as a Field of Study: Changes at Work, Substantive Working Conditions and the Case of OHS, *New Zealand Journal of Employment Relations*, 38(3): 1–24.

8. Gall, G. (ed.) (2009) *Union Revitalisation Strategies in Advanced Economies*, Palgrave Macmillan, Basingstoke; Cooper, R. and Patmore, G. (2002) Union Organising and Labour History, *Labour History*, 83: 3–18; Heery, E. (2015) Unions and the Organisation Turn: Reflections after 20 Years of Organising Works, *Economic and Labour Relations Review*, 26(4): 545–60.

9. Archer, R. (2007) *Why Is There no Labor Party in the United States?* Princeton University Press, Princeton.

10. Eaton, A., Schurman, S. and Chen, M. (eds.) (2017) *Informal Workers and Collective Action: A Global Perspective*, Cornell University Press/ILR Press, Ithaca.

11. Visser J. (1995) Trade Unions from a Comparative Perspective, in Van Ruysseveldt J. Huiskamp, R. and van Hoof J. (eds.) *Comparative Industrial and Employment Relations*, Sage, London, 37–67.

12. Lehndorff, S., Dribbusch, H. and Schulten, T. (eds.) (2018) *Rough Waters: European Trade Unions in a Time of Crises*, European Trade Unions Institute, Brussels, 10–11.

13. Bennett, L. (1984) The Construction of Skill: Craft Unions, Women Workers and the Conciliation and Arbitration Court, *Law in Context*, 2: 118–32; Bennett, L. (1994) *Making Labour Law in Australia*, Law Book Company, Sydney.

14. Silver, B. (2003) *Forces of Labor: Workers' Movements and Globalisation since 1870*, Cambridge University Press, Cambridge, 187–94.

15. Thompson, *The Making of the English Working-class*; Thompson, *Customs in Common*.

16. Shorter and Tilly, *Strikes in France 1830–1968*.

17. Tilly, C. (1986) *The Contentious French*, Belknap Press of Harvard University Press, Cambridge, MA.

18. Lipset, S. (1996) *American Exceptionalism: A Double-Edged Sword*, WW Norton, New York, chapter 1.

19. See too Kirkby, D. (1991) *Alice Henry: The Power of Pen and Voice—the Life of an Australian-American Labor Reformer*, Cambridge University Press, Cambridge, 50.

20. Lloyd, C. (1998) Australian and American Settler Capitalism: The Importance of a Comparison and Its Curious Neglect, *Australian Economic History Review*, 38(3): 280–305.
21. Archer, *Why Is There no Labor Party in the United States?*
22. Markey, R. (1997) Colonial Forms of Labour Organisation in Nineteenth Century Australia, *Department of Economics University of Wollongong Working Paper*, No. 97–6, 8–10.
23. Parfitt, S. (2016) *Knights Across the Atlantic: The Knights of Labor in Britain and Ireland*, Liverpool University Press, Liverpool, 8–19. See also Churchward, L. (1953) The American Influence on the Australian Labour Movement, *Historical Studies*, 5: 258–77.
24. Pelling, H. (1954) The American Labour Movement: A British View, *Political Studies*, 2(3): 227–28; Pelling, H. (1956) *America and the British Left, from Bright to Bevan*, Adam and Charles Black, London; Gray, R. (2001 reprint) The Labour Aristocracy in the Victorian Class Structure, in Parkin, F. (ed.) *The Social Analysis of Class Structure*, Routledge, London, 19–38.
25. Moorhouse, H. (1981) The Significance of the Labour Aristocracy, *Social History*, 6(2): 229–33.
26. Hay, D., Linebaugh, P. and Thompson, E.P. (eds.) (1975) *Albion's Fatal Tree: Crime and Society in Eighteenth Century*, Pantheon Books, New York.
27. Linebaugh, *The London Hanged*.
28. Stanziani, A. (2018) Labor and Historical Periodization of Capitalism, *ISHA Newsletter*, 7(1): 1–6.
29. But prevalent in contemporary research, see Morantz, A. (2017) What Unions Do For Regulation, *Annual Review of Law and Social Science*, 13: 514–34.
30. Archer, *Why Is There no Labor Party in the United States?*
31. Reeves, K., Frost, L. and Fahey, C. (2010) Integrating the Historiography of the Nineteenth-Century Gold Rushes, *Australian Economic History Review*, 50(2): 111–28.
32. Sinclair, W. (1983) *The Process of Economic Development in Australia*, Longman Cheshire, Melbourne, 81.
33. *Wallaroo Times and Mining Journal* 6 September 1865.
34. Sinclair, *The Process of Economic Development in Australia*, 82.
35. Robinson, G. (1977) *A History of the Newcastle Branch of the Boilermakers Society 1877–1977*, Amalgamated Metal Workers and Shipwrights Union, Sydney, 3.
36. Greasley, D. and Oxley, L. (1997) Segmenting the Contours: Australian Economic Growth 1828–1913, *Australian Economic History Review*, 37(1): 39–53; Banerjee, R. and Shanahan, M. (2016) The Contribution of Wheat to Australian Agriculture from 1861 to 1939, *Australian Economic History Review*, 56(2): 125–50.
37. Frost, L. (1998) The Contribution of the Urban Sector to Australian Economic Development before 1914, *Australian Economic History Review*, 38(1): 42–73.
38. Ostapenko, D. (2014) 'Does Farming Pay in Victoria?' Profit Potential of the Farming Industry in Mid-Nineteenth Century Victoria, *Australian Economic History Review*, 54(1): 37–61.
39. McLean, I. (2013) *Why Australia Prospered: The Shifting Sources of Economic Growth*, Princeton University Press, Princeton.
40. Ville, S. (1998) Business Development in Colonial Australia, *Australian Economic History Review*, 38(1): 16–40; Jackson, R. (1998) The Colonial

Economies: An Introduction, *Australian Economic History Review*, 38(1): 1–15.

41. Markey, R. (2004) A Century of the Labour Movement in Australia, *Illawarra Unity—Journal of the Illawarra Branch of the Australian Society for the Study of Labour History*, 4(1): 42–63.
42. Sinclair, *The Process of Economic Development in Australia*, 108.
43. Lipset, S. and Lakin, J. (2004) *The Democratic Century*, University of Oklahoma Press, Norman, 379–89.
44. Recent archaeological work is adding to this *Darling Quarter (formerly Darling Walk), Darling Harbour, Sydney Report to Lend Lease Development*, Casey and Lowe, Leichhardt, December 2013.
45. Jackson, R. (1991) *Australian Economic Development in the Nineteenth Century*, ANU Press, Canberra, 87.
46. *Adelaide Times* 3 August 1854.
47. The log recorded numerous vessels passed during its travels. ML MSS8094 Logbook of unidentified paddle steamer July 1878 to August 1881.
48. Attard, B. (2007) New Estimates of Australian Public Borrowing and Capital Raised in London 1849–1914, *Australian Economic History Review*, 47(2): 155–77.
49. Harris, E. (2008) Colonialism and Long-Run Growth in Australia: An Examination of Institutional Change in Victoria's Water Sector During the Nineteenth Century, *Australian Economic History Review*, 48(3): 266–79.
50. Bassino, J-P. and van der Eng, P. (2010) Responses to Economic Systems to Environmental Change: Past Experiences, *Australian Economic History*, 50(1): 1–5.
51. Irwin, D. (2017) The Third Noel Butlin Lecture: Australian Exceptionalism Revisited, *Australian Economic History Review*, 47(3): 217–37.
52. Greasley, D. and Madsden, D. (2017) The Rise and Fall of Exceptional Australian Incomes since 1800, *Australian Economic History Review*, 57(3): 264–90.
53. Sinclair, *The Process of Economic Development in Australia*, 76–125; Lloyd, P. (2017) The First 100 years of Tariffs in Australia: The Colonies, *Australian Economic History Review*, 57(3): 316–44.
54. *Sydney Morning Herald* 9 November 1852.
55. Quinlan, M. (1997) Balancing Trade and Labour Control: Imperial/Colonial Tensions in Relation to the Regulation of Seamen in the Australian Colonies 1788–1865, *International Journal of Maritime History*, 9(1): 19–56.
56. *Empire* 2 December 1853.
57. *Empire* 28 September 1855.
58. Reeves, K. (2010) Sojourners or a New Diaspora? Economic Implications of the Movement of Chinese Miners to the South-West Pacific Goldfields, *Australian Economic History Review*, 50(2): 181.
59. *Ballarat Courier* 20 August 1874.
60. See for example *Argus* 16 September 1874.
61. *Peoples' Advocate* 27 March 1852; *Empire* 10 November 1852.
62. When ended by 'White Australia' in 1901 farms were paid a bounty to offset the higher cost of European labour. Griggs, P. (2011) *Global Industry, Local Innovation: The History of Cane Sugar Production in Australia, 1820–1995*, Peter Lang, Bern, Switzerland.
63. *Sydney Mail* 3 April 1869.
64. *Brisbane Courier* 3 February 1868.
65. Mortensen, R. (2000) Slaving in Australian Courts: Blackbirding cases, 1869–1871, *Journal of South Pacific Law*, 4: 7–37.

66. Reproduced in *Daily Northern Argus* 1 February 1878.
67. Quinlan, Balancing Trade and Labour Control, 26.
68. *Sydney Morning Herald* 26 January 1852; *Shipping Gazette* 31 January 1852.
69. *Mercury* 15 December 1870.
70. Quinlan, Balancing Trade and Labour Control; Quinlan, M. (2004) Australia 1788–1902: A 'Working Man's Paradise'? in Hay, D. and Craven, P. (eds.) *Masters, Servants, and Magistrates in Britain and the Empire, 1562–1955*, University of North Carolina Press, Chapel Hill, 219–50.
71. *Hobart Courier* 25 August 1854.
72. LC247-1-26 Hobart 14 October 1856.
73. *Queensland Times* 17 October 1867.
74. Multiple cases tried the same day were typical see *Age* 26 April 1856; *Sydney Morning Herald* 10 April 1858.
75. *Maryborough and Dunolly Advertiser* 5 November 1858; *Bendigo Advertiser* 16 May 1859, 9 September 1867; *Argus* 21 May 1859; *South Australian Advertiser* 2 December 1859; *Mercury* 19 July 1861; *Empire* 29 October 1863; *Dalby Herald* 23 February 1867.
76. *Age* 20 October, 29 November, 7 December 1859.
77. *Argus* 28 December 1859.
78. *South Australian Register* 10 May 1860.
79. *South Australian Register* 27 June 1860.
80. *South Australian Register* 17 August 1860.
81. *South Australian Advertiser* 21 February 1870.
82. *Sydney Morning Herald* 7 June 1862.
83. *Express and Telegraph* 18 April 1867.
84. *Argus* 9 November 1870.
85. *The Week* 15 July 1876; *Queensland Times* 24 May 1877.
86. *Age* 29 November 1859.
87. LC247-1-25 Hobart 29 June 1854.
88. *Brisbane Courier* 15 September 1863; *North Australian* 27 September 1864.
89. LC247-1-20 Hobart 24 September 1852.
90. LC247-1-20 Hobart 23 August 1852.
91. LC247-1-23 Hobart 6 December 1853.
92. LC247-1-20 Hobart 19 April 1852.
93. See LC362-1-8 Longford 16 May 1853.
94. LC362-1-8 Longford 10 March 1853.
95. LC83-1-12 Campbell Town 15 November 1860.
96. LC83-1-12 Campbell Town 29 November, 18 December 1860.
97. See LC83-1-14 Campbell Town 26 January 1876.
98. LC362-1-10 Longford 1 April 1862.
99. LC247-1-26 Hobart 3 July 1862.
100. *Melbourne Herald* 9 March 1877.
101. LC362-1-9 Longford 12 March 1855.
102. LC247-1-26 Hobart 23 August 1862.
103. LC156-1-4 George Town 5 April 1854.
104. LC247-1-21 Hobart 9 September 1852; *Empire* 4 October 1852.
105. LC156-1-3 George Town 6, 23 & 26 November 1852.
106. Quinlan, M. and Gardner, M. (1994) Researching Industrial Relations History: The Development of a Database on Australian Trade Unions 1825–1900, *Labour History*, 66: 90–113; Quinlan, M. and Gardner, M. (1995) Strikes, Worker Protest and Union Growth in Canada and Australia 1801–1900, *Labour/Le Travail*, 36: 175–208.

2 Overview of Organisation, Methods and Patterns of Struggle

Introduction

Large gold discoveries near Bathurst, Ballarat and Bendigo had complicated effects on worker organisation. There was a spike of informal dissent as some workers deserted for the goldfields or demanded higher wages, including public sector workers whose salaries were eroded by inflation. Simultaneously, losses of workers to the goldfields or regional construction activities disrupted existing craft unions like the Melbourne Stonemasons Mutual Benefit Society.[1] Disruption was short-lived, just another round of organisational volatility that had been occurring for decades. Rising population and wealth accelerated demand for food and other goods, housing, civil construction and brought workers, many with union experience, to the colonies. This assisted union growth in numbers, membership and geographical spread particularly in NSW and Victoria. There were some positive flow-on effects to South Australia and what became Queensland, but not Western Australia and Tasmania, the latter losing labour and economic activity to the mainland. Tasmanian courts like George Town were kept busy trying to prevent convicts absconding to Victoria by secreting themselves on vessels like two men and Mary Smith found on board the barque *Favourite*, and John Reid and John Sadler on the schooner *Tamar* in 1852.[2]

In industries with longstanding customs of workplace organisation like coalmining and printing organisation at this level often preceded unions. Early unions were largely confined to colonial capitals. This pattern continued after 1851 but organisation slowly spread to other towns like Newcastle, Maitland, Launceston, Geelong and Moonta, sometimes as branches but many formed independently. Even amongst affiliated bodies local independence and inter-branch friction occurred over issues like accepting member clearances. On the other hand, inter-union solidarity/support was common during strikes and grew in strength. Although by no means immune to lapses, minutes and press reports of small and localised unions attest to democratic processes, including regular, well-attended meetings (commonly fortnightly, some craft unions fining non-attendees), six-month or annual office-holder elections, careful consideration of issues and vigorous debate. This chapter overviews worker organisation, many key observations amplified by industry chapters.

Overall Patterns of Organisation

Worker organisation prior 1850 was predominantly informal (6,524 instances) but a transition was underway with 150 unions formed between 1826 and 1850. For 1851–1880 there is evidence of 1,528 unions and 3,294 instances of informal organisation. Figure 2.1 demonstrates the transition to unions although informal organisation continues (post-1881 data is incomplete). Organisation numbers cross-over in 1858, relapse briefly in 1861–1863 and diverge strongly thereafter, notwithstanding some year-on-year volatility. Union numbers grew from 341 in 1851–1860 to 528 in 1861–1870 and 892 in 1871–1880 while informal organisation numbers declined from 1,550 to 917 and 836 in the corresponding decades. Declining organisation in the early 1860s reflected the impact of economic depression and government indebtedness (Figure 2.1).

Organisation remained male-dominated, with 4,675 instances of male organisation, 19 female-only bodies and 113 involving both genders (mostly teachers and shop-assistants). Only perhaps two female unions

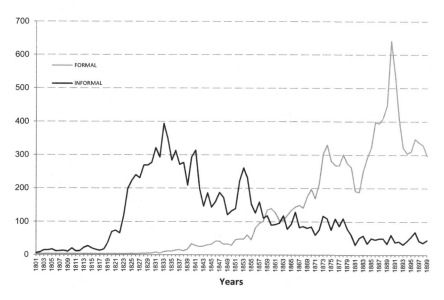

Figure 2.1 Instances of Informal and Formal Worker Organisation: Australia 1801–1900

are known before 1850 but female union involvement, though modest, far outstripped informal organisation especially after 1870. Figure 2.2 also shows the geographic spread of unionism after 1870 as miners, shop-assistants and transport workers organised.

The pre-1851 cycle of union formation/collapse/renewal continued. Economic downturns precipitated waves of collapse but median union duration increased and gaps between collapse and renewal narrowed. Median union duration increased from 162.5 days in 1841–1850 to 303.5 days by 1861–1870 falling back temporarily to 242 days in 1871–1880 due to a spate of union formation. Median duration of informal organisation remained unchanged at four days. Union consolidation occurred faster in some occupations, industries and regions. Median duration for 1851–1880 was highest in printing (4,322 days) followed by the metal trades (925 days), mining (746 days), miscellaneous manufacturing (739 days) clothing/footwear (368 days), transport equipment (353 days), food (324 days), building materials (313 days) and building (157 days). Shorter duration bodies included retailing (84 days) and services (71 days). Business cycle sensitivity and regional projects like railway building helps explain shorter duration of building unions notwithstanding long-lived bodies of carpenters, stonemasons and bricklayers in major towns. The longer duration of mining unions is notable, influenced by well-organised Hunter Valley coalminers and Victorian highland gold-miners notwithstanding numerous short-lived unions elsewhere. Intense

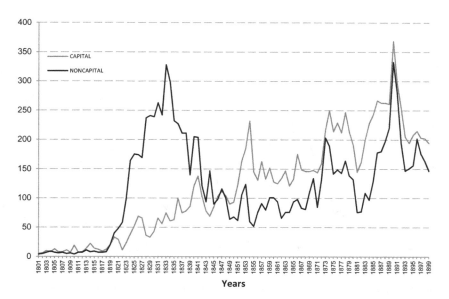

Figure 2.2 Organisation by Capital and Non-Capital Location

competition in baking, butchering and retailing was conducive to turn-over, though larger establishments were beginning to assist. Enduring organisation was challenging for rural workers, manufacturing affected by mechanisation like clothing and footwear, government, road and rail transport and the service sector where many women were employed.

Table 2.1 summarises indicators of worker mobilisation in specific colonies.[3] Informal organisation gives way to unions most rapidly in Victoria and NSW followed by South Australia, Tasmania and Western Australia. Notwithstanding promising beginnings in the 1830s, unionisation in Tasmania stalled amidst ongoing use of convicts, economic stagnation and losing workers to the mainland. Convicts, like other unfree labour, inhibited union formation but once freed, readily joined unions, a number taking leadership roles. The shift to unions is also evident with regard to membership/involvement, duration, strikes and non-strike collective action (NSCA) although less conspicuous for strikes, most still informal even in Victoria.

Intercolonial comparisons provide insights into factors affecting union growth. Table 2.2 indicates 1871–1880 union numbers broadly align with intercolonial population differences, although South Australia outperforms while Queensland and Tasmania lag. Greater urban concentration measured by the relative importance of colonial capitals of South Australia, Victoria and NSW (Adelaide, Melbourne and Sydney) helps explain this difference. Victoria and NSW account for 71.5% of total population but 82.4% of union membership. However, other factors operated with Sydney only accounting 43.8% of total worker involvement, reflecting the strength of coalmining unions and reinforcing an argument that union membership also reflected differences in colonial economies—with protectionist Victoria having more manufacturing compared to free-trade coal exporting NSW. There is evidence protectionism advantaged Victorian unionism where numbers/membership in areas prone to import competition (metal, clothing/footwear, coach/shipbuilding and printing/publishing) exceeded NSW (96 to 58 unions and 9,755 to 8,128 members or 54.5/44.5%) for 1871–1880, more than proportional to the population difference (53.1/46.9%) although figures are too close to be definitive.

The transition to unions was complex and not simply a mechanistic response to demographic and socio-economic changes. Like 1826–1850 informal collaborative networks were critical to building unions and political bodies. Simply charting organisational history omits these transmission-belts of ideas and continuity. Charting these networks in detail would be a major undertaking. For this book's purpose some illustrative examples are sufficient. Many immigrants arrived with prior union experience. Compositor Charles Ross, formerly a Dublin Typographical Association Secretary, migrated to Melbourne, joined the *Age* Chapel and Melbourne Typographical Society.[4] Arriving in 1855, James

Table 2.1 Summary of Worker Organisation by Colony 1831–1880

	1831–1840	1841–1850	1851–1860	1861–1870	1871–1880	Total 1851–1880*
New South Wales						
Informal organisations	1915	420	497	215	153	860
Unions	32	46	82	141	284	445
Informal involvement	7017	2915	2847	2226	1648	6721
Union membership	353	749	5369	13681	51569	70619
Union median members	35	30	32	60	106.5	
Union median duration	639	615	227	369	271	
Union strikes	17	10	10	18	80	108
Non-union strikes	215	119	315	149	71	543
Union NSCA	9	10	51	79	357	487
Non-union NSCA	1849	314	212	66	63	341
Queensland						
Informal organisations	18	20	27	152	128	306
Unions			5	51	81	127
Informal involvement	115	88	228	1327	859	2414
Union membership				1182	3427	4609
Union median members				35	45.5	
Union median duration			1471	40	159	
Union strikes				6	16	22
Non-union strikes		10	19	112	72	103
Union NSCA			2	32	59	93
Non-union NSCA	22	11	14	50	49	113
South Australia						
Informal organisations	13	77	121	154	238	512
Unions	3	11	35	59	141	220
Informal involvement	33	536	876	1853	4181	6910
Union membership	114	473	878	3657	17981	22516
Union median members	114	55	60	35	60	
Union median duration	2615	174	116	139	54	
Union strikes	1	4	2	4	23	29
Non-union strikes	4	46	65	93	155	313
Union NSCA		5	33	102	171	306
Non-union NSCA	8	37	54	65	92	211
Tasmania						
Informal organisations	874	907	589	103	94	785
Unions	12	20	21	10	39	67
Informal involvement	3608	3703	2319	465	1218	4002

	1831–1840	1841–1850	1851–1860	1861–1870	1871–1880	Total 1851–1880*
Union membership	77	273	706	57	1037	1800
Union median members	38.5	8	22	28.5	79	
Union median duration	116	11.5	55	86.5	49	
Union strikes	1	3	6		9	15
Non-union strikes	511	597	371	60	49	480
Union NSCA	3	10	12	6	19	37
Non-union NSCA	534	401	264	43	46	353
Victoria						
Informal organisations	27	157	299	282	210	659
Unions	6	37	198	264	339	790
Informal involvement	88	1139	6243	5053	2331	13627
Union membership	30	418	12150	15842	60554	88546
Union median members	30	30	50	77	130	
Union median duration	77.5	40	500	516	368	
Union strikes	4	17	45	18	82	145
Non-union strikes	10	65	156	157	112	425
Union NSCA	1	16	97	136	292	525
Non-union NSCA	19	96	143	112	90	345
Western Australia						
Informal organisations	20	11	17	11	3	41
Unions	1	1		3	8	10
Informal involvement	69	5	68	14	465	547
Union membership				1188	1590	2778
Union median members				117.5	106	
Union median duration	1	17		2342	33.5	
Union strikes						
Non-union strikes	9	5	16	18	4	28
Union NSCA				1	7	8
Non-union NSCA	13	3	3	8	5	16

* To avoid double-counting, organisations surviving more than one decade only counted once. ⁺Adjusted by multiplying number of zero-reporting organisations/years by median membership for each colony in that decade.

Beddows helped found the Victorian Boilermakers Society before going to Sydney, helping to form the union there with others like James Sinclair McGowen (later leader of the NSW Labor Party). Beddows moved onto Newcastle, helped form a Boilermakers Society branch in 1877 and remained a union stalwart until his death (1902).[5]

Table 2.2 Union Organisation 1871–1880 and Population (1881) by Colony

State	Unions 1871–1880	Union membership 1871–1880	Population 1881 (proportion of total)	Colonial capital population 1881 (proportion of total)	Capital total involvement % of total
New South Wales	284 (31.8%)	51,569 (37.9%)	751,468 (33.6%)	224,939 (33.6%)	43.8%
Queensland	81 (9.1%)	3427 (2.5%)	213,525 (9.5%)	30,955 (14.5%)	26%
South Australia	141 (15.8%)	7,981 (5.8%)	279,865 (12.5%)	103,942 (33.3%)	60%
Tasmania	39 (4.3%)	1,037 (0.8%)	115,705 (5.2%)	33,000 (28.5%)	27.6%
Victoria	339 (38%)	60,554 (44.5%)	849,438 (37.9%)	282,847 (33.3%)	70.8%
Western Australia	8 (0.9%)	1,590 (1.2%)	29,708 (1.3%)	8,500 (28.6%)	77.5%
Total	892	136,158	2,239,709		

Collaborating groups revived organisations that collapsed—sometimes repeatedly. In January 1865 members of a re-established plasterers' society requested funds loaned to the Melbourne Trades Hall by the predecessor body (1856–1861), providing a receipt proving their connection.[6] Seven months later Melbourne United Labourers Friendly Society (1863–1886) members made a similar request, again demonstrating their connection to an earlier body (1856–1861) whose records they held.[7] In 1871 the Sydney Typographical Society asked its Melbourne counterpart for information on four members of an earlier Melbourne Typographical Society prosecuted for collective action at the *Argus* in 1857. A year later the Melbourne Society asked for records of the earlier society held by Messrs Robinson and Fielding.[8] Printers' chapels collaborated prior to and after the formation of typographical unions. The 1854 conspiracy prosecution of 17 members of the Sydney *Empire*'s companionship afforded insights into customary pay and work practices and their transmission via printers moving between different workplaces and colonies.[9] Another illustration of collaborative networks is found in the minutebook of the Vale of Clywdd Lodge/Western District Coalminers Association (1878–1881) which contains minutes of the first meeting reviving the association in Hartley in 1886. The Melbourne Stonemasons Union (established 1856) kept the minute-book of an earlier body and minutebooks of stonemason lodges that collapsed in both NSW and Victoria were recycled by later lodges. Union records also point to collaborative networks amongst unions whose records haven't survived.

There is evidence of continuity/collaboration amongst other unions including seamen, teachers and early-closing/half-holiday associations. WA Cawthorne, founding secretary of the Adelaide Preceptors Association in 1851, performed this role when it was revived in 1857. Melbourne ECA (1866–1882) Secretary TJ Jackman told its 1872 annual dinner he had been involved in the early-closing movement since 1853.[10] Similarly, G Ford and W Bennett, amongst others, took leading roles in the Maryborough Half-Holiday Association established in 1869 and revived it two years later. Bennett was active in another body established in 1874. Several half-holiday advocates in Goulburn in 1877 like HB Watts had been involved in earlier campaigns.[11] At least as important were those bringing organisation to new locations whose names are unrecorded epitomised by 'the few Sydney agitators' who engineered an eight-hour day campaign in Armidale (NSW) in 1878.[12]

Individuals should be viewed as part of networks not in isolation. This is well-evidenced by the Melbourne eight-hour movement, subject to retrospective mythmaking. William Taylor's activist account (1884) tried to dispel myths, pointing to New Zealand (1847) and Sydney (1855) precedents prior to Melbourne. Acknowledging stonemason James Galloway's contribution (including his May 1856 address to Kilmore mechanics), Taylor noted Galloway (who died in 1860) never claimed to be the movement's originator unlike James Stephens whose claims he thought baseless. Emphasising the group aspect, Taylor wrote that after the stonemason's initial breakthrough they were rapidly joined by bricklayers, carpenters, joiners, plasterers and slaters.[13] Together with interviews (presumably), Taylor's account used union records and his interpretation matches my own reading of surviving evidence.

There were important geographic aspects to networking/collaboration and mobilisation. In major towns housing-costs and transport caused workers to congregate in specific areas. As in the past, individual trades/occupations used specific hotels for recreation, information exchange and union formation/meetings.[14] Some hotels like the *Swan with Two Necks* in Sydney and *Bristol Tavern* in Adelaide were hubs for union gatherings and broader alliances including union peak bodies. Hotels were eventually displaced by dedicated union meeting places, the Melbourne Trades Hall being a global pioneer.

Mobilising Numbers and the Shift to Mass Unionism

Unionisation translated into greater numbers of workers joining together collectively. In 30 years to 1850 the database records 26,412 workers organising informally compared to only 2496 in unions adjusted to 27546 and 6492 respectively if zero reports are attributed median membership/involvement. Corresponding numbers are 12,581 informal/19,103 formal in 1851–1860, 10,938 informal/35,607 formal in 1861–1870 and 10,702 informal/136,158 formal in 1871–1880. Median involvement in informal organisation slowly rose from three in 1831–1860 to four in 1861–1870 and six in 1871–1880 while median union membership increased from 30 in 1841–1850 to 49 in 1851–1860, 51 in 1861–1870 and 100 in 1871–1880. Adjusted involvement/membership numbers are 13,217 informal/31,059 formal in 1851–1860, 11,702 informal/59,373 formal in 1861–1870 and 12,430 informal/230,358 formal in 1871–1880. Given fragmented reporting, annual membership needs to be treated cautiously. Taking years where reporting is highest gives total union membership of 3,652 (or 4,792 adjusted by adding median to zero counts) in 1859, 6,275 (9,437 adjusted) in 1870, 20,902 (31,202 adjusted) in 1874 and 17,585 (33,713 adjusted) in 1879. This doesn't correspond to those for informal organisation, which had conspicuous peaks in 1853, 1857 and 1872 (all over 2,200) with smaller peaks in 1870 (1,382 or 1,472 adjusted) and in 1874 (1,429 or 1,669 adjusted). These figures require caution but are consistent with qualitative evidence in later chapters. Overall, workers organising informally stagnates while union membership grows substantially, supplanting the former in the 1850s. Numbers are based on reported membership/involvement for every organisation each year so decade figures double-count individuals belonging to unions over one year. It also masks considerable year-on-year membership volatility but captures growth over time and unionisation's importance for worker mobilisation.

Worker mobilisation was male-dominated. Female involvement grew mainly through teachers and retail-worker associations recruiting male and female members (over 60 bodies in 1871–1880) although a handful of female-only bodies like tailoresses emerged in the 1870s. In 1851–1860 unions recruiting both genders grew in absolute numbers from 2,631 to 12,133 (raw numbers) between 1851–1860 and 1871–1880 but fell as a proportion of total union membership from 8.3% to 4.5%. Female-only union membership grew from zero to 1,815 or 0.7% of total membership in the same period. Urbanisation, changes to industry-mix and unionisation also affected the geographic spread of worker involvement. In 1801–1850 colonial capitals accounted for only 36.22% of total worker involvement but by 1851–1880 this had risen to 56.7%. Table 2.3 provides an industry breakdown of worker organisation and demonstrates the wider spread of organisation than is typical for discussions of this period, especially with regard to transport, retailing and government.

Chapter 1 identified debate over dating the transition to mass unionism which the database contributes to although some caveats should be acknowledged. There are no government/official membership-statistics and membership could only be deduced from surviving union records and newspaper reports using meeting attendances when other information isn't available. Decade-grouping helped provide a sufficient pool of data notwithstanding obvious double-counting of individuals. Non-craft union membership was generally more volatile although 20% or more annual membership turnover was common for craft unions. Table 2.4 divides membership data into trade/craft unions and two others, manual workers—the focus for the Webb's, Markey and Archer—and another group of service/white-collar workers generally overlooked for this period. It uses raw numbers to avoid distortions from small cell-sizes in some occupations and because the point of comparison is identifying

Table 2.3 Instances of Worker Organisation and Involvement by Industry 1831–1880

Industry	1831–1840	1841–1850	1851–1860	1861–1870	1871–1880	Total 1851–1880
Building/construction						
Organisations	32	44	174	192	174	465+
Raw involvement	217	648	10206	8861	16387	35454
Adjusted involvement*	268	1348	12555	16757	34287	63599
Building materials						
Organisations	34	32	30	23	35	82+
Raw involvement	166	455	37	653	2772	3462
Adjusted involvement*	200	511	227	14753	20672	35652
Clothing, boots etc.						
Organisations	36	35	36	21	47	95+
Raw involvement	278	472	176	750	3457	4383
Adjusted involvement*	308	535	196	1200	7057	8453
Commercial services						
Organisations	126	44	63	18	22	102+
Raw involvement	257	1108	386	76	424	886
Adjusted involvement	261	1130	394	118	1448	1960
Food manufacture						
Organisations	29	29	35	24	59	108+
Raw involvement	106	214	779	896	833	2508
Adjusted involvement*	121	254	807	1656	3615	6078
General						
Organisations			2	34	25	50+
Raw involvement			600	3042	3865	7507
Adjusted involvement*			900	5422	7665	13987
Government/community						
Organisations	1443	511	154	108	120	365+
Raw involvement	6161	2305	1767	1853	5489	9101
Adjusted involvement*	6257	2428	2044	3397	10139	15580
Maritime/whaling						
Organisations	264	471	985	614	491	2086+
Raw involvement	1332	2396	6413	3348	13085	22846
Adjusted involvement*	1562	2692	6763	3524	13460	23747
Metal manufacture						
Organisations	4	8	21	31	67	97+
Raw involvement		52	636	5809	9774	16219
Adjusted involvement		54	972	9009	15724	25705

(Continued)

Table 2.3 (Continued)

Industry	1831–1840	1841–1850	1851–1860	1861–1870	1871–1880	Total 1851–1880
Mining						
Organisations	109	41	75	79	140	271+
Raw involvement	645	671	6963	12071	47156	66202
Adjusted involvement*	673	721	8263	17831	72482	98576
Misc. manufacturing						
Organisations	6	7	10	5	17	28+
Raw involvement	14	10	10	0	370	380
Adjusted involvement*	16	10	24		1140	1164
Printing & publishing						
Organisations	11	12	25	37	57	87+
Raw involvement	79	190	1196	1164	4501	6861
Adjusted involvement*	93	318	1716	2267	5731	9714
Retailing						
Organisations	13	20	58	102	212	352+
Raw involvement	21	421	1591	3590	12010	17191
Adjusted involvement*	25	1441	3191	8640	23395	35226
Road/rail transport						
Organisations		9	18	55	101	166+
Raw involvement		2	210	2552	18112	20874
Adjusted involvement*		27	990	5464	24992	31446
Rural & farming						
Organisations	751	393	168	74	82	323+
Raw involvement	2039	1221	541	432	2310	3283
Adjusted involvement*	2127	1339	565	577	2531	3673
Transport equipment						
Organisations	8	14	14	21	53	82+
Raw involvement	47	30	33	1100	3607	4740
Adjusted involvement*	75	62	429	2140	9991	12560
Unknown						
Organisations	53	37	30	18	15	61+
Raw involvement	142	104	140	348	2708	3196
Adjusted involvement*	150	104	173	387	4553	5113
Total						
Organisations	2921	1707	1891	1445	1728	4822+
Raw involvement	11504	9651	31684	46545	146860	
Adjusted involvement*	12136	12974	40161	93334	259490	

* Adjusted by multiplying number of zero-reporting organisations/years by median membership for each industry in that decade. +For totals, organisation spanning multiple decades only counted once.

differences in trade and non-trade union membership composition. More conservative figures bias towards craft bodies (commonly reporting membership more frequently), providing a more robust test.

Table 2.4 indicates craft union membership outstripped non-craft unions (subgroup 1) prior to 1860 although a narrowing trend is

Table 2.4 Trade and Non-Trade Union Membership Australia Decade Totals 1831–1880

Industry	1831–1840	1841–1850	1851–1860	1861–1870	1871–1880
Craft/Trade Unions					
Building Trades	206	441	7659	5502	13304
Build material & furniture	304	464	56	490	2408
Metal Trades		52	636	5809	9774
Boots, apparel	334	478	185	870	4833
Printing trades	79	197	1196	1164	4501
Food trades	38	172	707	596	1088
Transport equip.	47	30	33	1100	3607
Misc. Skilled	14	10	10		370
Total	1022	1844	10482	15531	39885
Non-Trade Unions—Subgroup 1					
Engine-drivers				774	1526
Quarrymen			39	163	368
Miners		343	3688	10156	41538
Seamen		74	690		3362
Labourers			397	1045	2081
Dock labour		61	120	120	8135
Road transport	49	2	214	584	3408
Rail workers				1544	12843
Shearers			34	170	2108
Total	49	478	5182	14556	75369
Non-Trade Unions—Subgroup 2					
Retail-workers	24	424	1587	2776	5113
Domestics/ waiters/cooks				20	91
Postal workers					470
Clerks		24	456	600	1704
Teachers			705	567	2972
Misc. unskilled			154	504	314
Total	24	448	2902	4467	10664
Grand Total	1095	2770	18566	34554	125918

apparent. Narrowing accelerates after 1860 almost reaching parity in 1861–1870 before non-craft union membership becomes almost twice as large in 1871–1880. Subgroup 2 of teachers, clerks and retail-workers also grew strongly after 1850 and if added by 1871–1880, two-thirds of union members weren't tradesmen. While reiterating a note of caution, the shift coincides with the formation of stable unions in subgroups 1 and 2 from the early 1870s—not in all locations. Australian unions were expanding well beyond the skilled trades, evident even in the 1850s but gaining traction over time. While craft unions dominated union peak councils and political bodies, they no longer dominated union membership. Their officials knew this and generally viewed it positively (Chapter 11). The need to acknowledge more diverse union organisation prior to 1881 and the unionate status of subgroup 2 is reinforced by later chapters. Australian colonies may have led the transition to mass unionism but the UK, the US and other countries' experience require re-examination in this regard.

Objectives, Methods and Patterns of Collective Action

Table 2.5 summarises organisation objectives/issues and methods. With regard to totals and percentages, organisations—especially unions—pursued multiple objectives and deployed multiple methods. Several trends are clear and connected to unionisation. Regarding objectives wages, hours, health and safety (OHS), jobs/employment, friendly benefits, trade control, unionism and legislation became more important over time. A similar trend (at lower levels) applies to hostility to European and non-European (especially after 1870) immigration and subcontracting along with support for mutual-improvement, conciliation/arbitration, pensions, licensing and gender exclusion. Hours represented the single most important objective (43.6% of organisations) followed by OHS (41.1%), unionism (36.7%), wages (37.5%), trade control (18.7%), job security (16.1%) and friendly benefits (13.2%). The significance of OHS arises from its connection to campaigns against long-hours, friendly benefits (like accident/sickness funds), legislative/licensing campaigns (like mine safety and certifying engine-drivers) and other claims like unseaworthy ships and poor rations. Unions enabled workers to pursue issues difficult to resolve at workplace level (like hours) and engage in politics (legislation, opposition to immigration and conciliation/arbitration). The legislative sphere was unavoidable for teachers and public servants because governments determined pay, pension, discipline, credentials and other conditions.

Unionisation also influenced methods. Methods typically associated with informal organisation like group-absconding, go-slows, insolence/abuse and misconduct declined over time. There is no clear trend for threats, assault, sabotage and riots because these were uncommon, also

Table 2.5 Worker Organisation Objectives/Issues and Methods: Australia 1831–1880*

	1831–1840	1841–1850	1851–1860	1861–1870	1871–1880
Issues/Objectives					
Wages/ remuneration	128 (4.4%)	260 (15.2%)	473 (25%)	475 (32.9%)	648 (37.5%)
Working conditions	2443 (83.6%	1053 (61.7%)	938 (49.6%)	572 (39.6%)	481 (27.8%)
Hours of work	341 (11.7%)	371 (21.7%)	524 (27.7%)	499 (34.5%)	753 (43.6%)
Health & safety	264 (9%)	260 (15.2%)	427 (22.6%)	455 (31.5%)	711 (41.1%)
Management behaviour	218 (7.5%)	215 (12.6%)	159 (8.4%)	143 (9.9%)	125 (7.2%)
Jobs/employment	64 (2.2%)	85 (5%)	278 (14.7%)	258 (17.9%)	278 (16.1%)
Friendly benefits	30 (1%)	56 (3.3%)	136 (7.2%)	177 (12.2%)	228 (13.2%)
Apprentice/trade control	22 (0.8%)	60 (3.5%)	210 (11.1%)	242 (16.7%)	323 (18.7%)
Legislation		1	52 (2.7%)	90 (6.2%)	160 (9.3%)
Licensing			3 (0.2%)	2 (0.1%)	9 (0.5%)
Subcontracting	3 (0.1%)	8 (0.5%)	37 (2%)	34 (2.4%)	49 (2.8%)
Unionism	10 (0.3%)	16 (0.9%)	258 (13.6%)	388 (26.9%)	634 (36.7%)
Anti-Europe immigration	4 (0.1%)	4 (0.2%)	10 (0.5%)	20 (1.4%)	38 (2.2%)
Racial/anti-Chinese		1	7 (0.4%)	18 (1.2%)	55 (3.2%)
Gender exclusion				3 (0.2%)	8 (0.5%)
Self-improvement	1	1	26 (1.4%)	32 (2.2%)	34 (2%)
Conciliation/ arbitration			3 (0.2%)	10 (0.7%)	29 (1.7%)
Pensions		3 (0.2%)	1	8 (0.6%)	13 (0.8%)
Unknown	54 (1.8%)	88 (5.2%)	2 (0.1%)	2 (0.1%)	2 (0.1%)
Methods					
Strike	713 (24.4%)	838 (49.1%)	976 (51.6%)	648 (44.8%)	621 (35.9%)
Group-absconding	1820 (62.3%)	505 (29.6%)	405 (21.4%)	139 (9.6%)	114 (6.6%)
Made demands	40 (1.4%)	78 (4.6%)	280 (14.8%)	371 (25.7%)	650 (37.6%)
Court action	65 (2.2%)	93 (5.4%)	108 (5.7%)	67 (4.6%)	67 (3.9%)
Petition	19 (0.7%)	47 (2.3%)	93 (4.9%)	105 (7.3%)	139 (8%)
Deputation	3 (0.1%)	8 (0.5%)	40 (2.1%)	85 (5.9%)	144 (8.3%)
Go-slow	274 (9.4%)	113 (6.6%)	32 (1.7%)	11 (0.8%)	7 (0.4%)
Misconduct	143 (4.9%)	140 (8.2%)	72 (3.8%)	24 (1.7%)	13 (0.8%)
Larceny/stealing food	36 (1.2%)	12 (0.7%)	20 (1.1%)	17 (1.2%)	15 (0.9%)
Insolence/abuse	118 (4%)	80 (4.7%)	10 (0.5%)	7 (0.5%)	7 (0.4%)
Threats	29 (1%)	21 (1.2%)	18 (1%)	16 (1.1%)	12 (0.7%)
Assault	44 (1.5%)	38 (2.2%)	57 (3%)	67 (4.6%)	50 (2.9%)

(Continued)

Table 2.5 (Continued)

	1831–1840	1841–1850	1851–1860	1861–1870	1871–1880
Sabotage	24 (0.8%)	16 (0.9%)	5 (0.3%)	13 (0.9%)	13 (0.8%)
Riot	3 (0.1%)	7 (0.4%)	16 (0.8%)	13 (0.9%)	9 (0.5%)
Bans	9 (0.3%)	21 (1.2%)	10 (0.5%)	11 (0.8%)	21 (1.2%)
Mutual insurance	31 (1.1%)	55 (3.2%)	139 (7.4%)	185 (12.8%)	225 (13%)
Craft/skill control	22 (0.8%)	54 (3.2%)	202 (10.7%)	238 (16.5%)	307 (17.8%)
Unilateral regulation	9 (0.3%)	21 (1.2%)	117 (6.2%)	143 (9.9%)	190 (11%)
House-of-call	14 (0.5%)	18 (1.1%)	19 (1%)	15 (1%)	15 (0.9%)
Closed shop	1	1	3 (0.2%)	4 (0.3%)	5 (0.3%)
Strike-fund	5 (0.2%)	9 (0.5%)	58 (3.1%)	59 (4.1%)	61 (3.5%)
Picketing			8 (0.4%)	14 (1%)	24 (1.4%)
Education	1	1	18 (1%)	29 (2%)	32 (1.9%)
Public Demonstration	19 (0.7%)	41 (2.4%)	153 (8.1%)	225 (15.6%)	363 (21%)
Political/legal enactment	15 (0.5%)	33 (1.9%)	78 (4.1%)	129 (8.9%)	209 (12.1%)
Agreement	1	2 (0.1%)	27 (1.4%)	66 (4.6%)	133 (7.7%)
Collective bargaining	4 (0.1%)	8 (0.5%)	19 (1%)	26 (1.8%)	57 (3.3%)
Conciliation/ arbitration			2 (0.1%)	9 (0.6%)	24 (1.4%)
Workshop organisation		1	49 (2.6%)	47 (3.3%)	41 (2.4%)
Cooperation		2	2 (0.1%)	5 (0.3%)	8 (0.6%)	17 (1%)
Inter-union solidarity	1	2 (0.1%)	106 (5.6%)	178 (12.3%)	317 (18.3%)
Unknown	27 (0.9%)	25 (1.5%)	12 (0.6%)	21 (1.5%)	24 (1.4%)
Total Organisations	2921	1707	1891	1445	1728

* Expressed as numbers and proportion of organisations for each period.

occurring during bitter/protracted disputes involving unions. Unionisation was associated with increased petitioning and deputations less available to informally organised workers but also methods almost entirely dependent on formal organisation like mutual insurance, craft control, unilateral regulation, public demonstrations, legal enactment, strike funds, picketing, agreements, collective bargaining, conciliation/arbitration, education and cooperation. The rise of inter-union solidarity reflects growing webs of interlinked unions extending well beyond formal affiliation to peak bodies. The importance of particular functions for sustaining organisations like craft controls, mutual insurance and unilateral regulation (the latter two extending beyond craft unions), together with public demonstrations and legal enactment, is evident. Some old methods like the House-of-Call for controlling recruitment stagnated while others like mutual-improvement/education remained subsidiary to other methods.

Unilateral regulation and agreements secured through moral suasion/public pressure were suited to dealing with fractured capital. This, together with limits to organisation, explains the slow growth of collective bargaining and small but growing support for conciliation/arbitration. As unions became larger, more formal arrangements for workshop organisation emerged where they didn't already exist. The effect of unionisation on strikes and its relationship to other forms of collective action is more complicated than commonly portrayed in labour historiography. In the decade to 1880 only 36.7% of unions struck in part because organisation had spread to workers where striking was difficult or not favoured.

Several methods warrant elaboration because they enhance understanding of worker mobilisation and industry-specific developments examined later.

Mutual Insurance and Financial Governance

Mutual insurance was important for many unions, not simply craft unions. Life expectancy was short by modern standards, accidental death more common, there was no welfare state, and health-related insurance covering accidents, illness and funerals made sense. Citing UK mortality data in 1872 the *Queenslander* noted average life expectancy of clerks and shopmen was 33 years, teachers 34 years, engineers 36 years, printers 38 years, tailors 41 years, painters 42 years, stonemasons 47 years, carpenters 49 years, blacksmiths 51 years, shipwrights, hatters and ropemakers 54 years and coopers 55 years.[15] Some unions sought registration as friendly societies to secure funds, place rules on a firmer footing and on occasion to fund a union hall.[16] Following generalised models, union governance became more elaborate over time, especially rules/procedures on expenditure authorisation, account-reporting and signing cheques (multiple signatures), with dedicated roles of treasurer, trustees to overview expenditure and auditors to periodically check accounts.[17]

While generally adequate, there were instances of officials defalcating followed by difficult and costly attempts to recover funds. In September 1861 Victorian Stonemason ex-treasurer James Cassells agreed to repay £27 10s 4d by instalments. He did and was sufficiently redeemed to join the Central Committee.[18] The Waterloo and Sydney Stonemasons lodges both experienced incidents in early 1871 and rules were changed regarding trustees signing off funeral funds. The society prosecuted its Sydney treasurer John Campbell for £20 8s 9d. Engaging solicitors, Campbell argued as a member he was a 'partner' in an unregistered organisation and therefore as entitled to the money as anyone else. The court dismissed the case which had cost the society £3 18s 5d in legal fees.[19] In December 1872 the Sydney Progressive Carpenters investigated discrepancies involving their 'late treasurer.'[20] In December 1878 the Sydney Painters pursued its ex-treasurer (Edwards) for £15 5s 1d: the case not resolved until May 1880 when Edwards agreed to pay 2s 6d per week in order to rejoin the union.[21] In August 1879 the Western Districts coalminers Vale of Clywdd Lodge refused to issue a clearance to ex-treasurer Richard Owen after he left with money, notifying the lodge where he was now employed.[22] Fraud cases were sufficiently concerning for societies to register as a Friendly Society and pursue a *Trade Union Act*.

Unilateral Regulation

Like mutual insurance, unilateral regulation was a longstanding method whereby wages, hours, working conditions and labour market controls were specified in union rules binding members and presented to employers. Members were required to warn, and if ignored withdraw from, employers flouting rules including employing non-unionists. Unilateral regulation originated as early journeymen's society mimicked trade-regulation by medieval guilds. Indeed, some trade restriction rules were similar like setting apprentice/tradesmen ratios for each workplace. Unilateral regulation didn't preclude strikes, with gains later being incorporated into union rules as the Melbourne Stonemasons did following its 1874 Saturday half-holiday success.[23] Although the Webb's saw unilateral regulation as characteristic of new model craft unions, Rimmer and Sheldon demonstrated colonial non-craft unions (labourers, carters and shearers) used it in the 1880s because it suited fractured capital.[24] This book reinforces this argument, demonstrating shearers, carters, builders' labourers and wharf-labourers deployed unilateral regulation prior to 1880 (see later chapters).

Strike Funds and Picketing

Early colonial unions used strike funds, special levies and picketing but these practices became more common after 1850 and not simply for large strikes. It was common for pickets to be paid an additional rate to normal strike pay.[25]

Petitions and Deputations

Deputations were increasingly favoured over petitions, enabling union officials to directly deal with ministers supported/introduced by sympathetic political representatives and with implicit recognition of the organisation's importance. Deputations demanded respectful behaviour but petition rules required supplicating language that irked unions' democratic sentiments. In 1878 a Sydney TLC deputation to the Colonial

Secretary objected to the Speaker of the House of Assembly rejecting petitions for failing to include the concluding 'prayer.'[26]

Demonstrations and Community Engagement

Public demonstration methods included mass meetings, marches/torchlight processions, consumer-boycotts, excursions/celebrations, advertisements/public notices, concerts/soirees, theatrical productions and donations. Many unions regularly donated to hospitals and orphanages/benevolent-funds. Hospital donations helped secure treatment for members, especially those in hazardous industries. It also popularised campaigns—noted when the Echuca ECA donated to the local hospital.[27] While raising their community standing, it wasn't simply instrumental but arose from wider social engagement and reciprocity. Reflecting this, eight-hour committees regularly donated funds to hospitals, relief-funds, charities and Mechanics Institutes.[28] Public demonstrations were an increasingly important means of affirming organisational identity and reinforcing a campaign/victory. Eight-hour and early-closing demonstrations commonly dovetailed this with well-attended family activities like picnics, entertainments and sports. Individual unions also held annual dinners or picnics attended by hundreds or thousands in the case of the Hunter Valley Coalminers.[29] Demonstrations became larger and more multi-faceted. In 1874, eight-hour celebrations in Melbourne included a comedy and a poetic address on eight-hours by Miss Carey at the Lyceum Theatre. Four years later, Governor Bowen and family attended a committee-sponsored Theatre Royal performance of the 'The Hypocrite and the Honeymoon' to aid Melbourne Hospital.[30] Sister bodies in Williamstown and Echuca ran school-essay and speech competitions.[31]

Patterns of Collective Action

Figure 2.3 records strikes and non-strike collective action (NSCA) by year. Strike waves are evident in 1826, 1840, 1853, 1874 and 1890. This only partially corresponds with NSCA peaks in 1833, 1854, 1874 and 1890. Differentiating informal and union-based strikes only slightly alters the pattern, with 1853 strikes being predominantly informal. For NSCA, apart from 1833 (overwhelmingly informal), peaks are more evident for formal organisation but these are small (including the 1856 eight-hour struggle) apart from 1874, 1878 and the 1890 spike. There were also geographic shifts. Before 1851 most collective action occurred outside colonial capitals. However, in 1851–1880, 2,311 strikes (67.7% of the total) occurred in colonial capitals. The shift is less marked for NSCA (1,659 or 58.5% of all NSCA) and narrows considerably in 1871–1880 with 600 regional NSCA (47.9% of the total) compared to 653

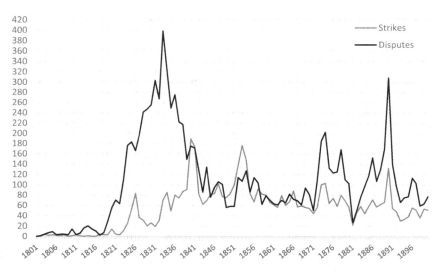

Figure 2.3 Number of Strikes and Non-Strike Collective Actions by Year Australia 1801–1900

in colonial capitals. This reflects growing regional unionisation amongst miners, shop-assistants and others.

Table 2.6 summarises strikes and NSCA by decade 1831–1880, including numbers of workers and establishments involved. Before 1851 most strikes and NSCA occurred outside of a union. While this pattern continued there is a clear trend towards unionised strikes which were significantly larger in numbers involved and median duration (median informal strike duration was unchanged). This highlighted the capacity of unions to sustain strikes, also evident in the growth of working days lost. By the decade to 1880 unionised strikers outnumbered informal strikers by three to one. For NSCA the transition was two decades earlier (Table 2.6). Median number of workers per strike grew for both unionised and informally organised workers but more rapidly for the former. The same trend is apparent for NSCA. Unions' ability to mount multi-establishment strikes is also clear, including the first colony-wide and intercolonial strikes. Nonetheless, most strikes remained workplace-based. Picking off or dealing with recalcitrant employers was preferable to expensive multi-establishment strikes. The two most conspicuous spikes in working days lost were 1874–1875 (97,825 days) and 1878–1879 (117,095 days), both reflecting key mobilisation struggles described elsewhere.

Unionisation profoundly influenced NSCA. Overall, NCSA outnumber strikes, involved more workers, were of longer duration and were more likely to entail multi-establishment, town/region and colony-wide

Table 2.6 Number and Size of Collective Action: Australia 1831–1880

	1831–1840	1841–1850	1851–1860	1861–1870	1871–1880	Total 1851–1880
			Strikes			
Formal						
Number	23	34	63	46	210	319
Total involvement	232	1043	1509	4238	16563	22310
Median involvement	30	12	45	80	61.5	
Adjusted involvement*	742	1271	3579	6318	24681	34578
Total duration days	387	470	978	1010	5166	7154
Median duration	6	3	7	8.5	8	
Working days lost+	11610	5640	44010	080800	317709	442519
Number of establishments						
One	3 (13%)	17 (50%)	33 (52.4%)	25 (54.3%)	000133 (63.3%)	199
Multiple	5 (21.7%)	5 (14.7%)	14 (22.2%)	13 (26.3%)	29 (13.8%)	56
Town/regional	14 (60.1)	12 (35.3%)	15 (23.8%)	7 (15.2%)	47 (22.4%)	69
Colony-wide				1 (2.2%)		1
Intercolonial					1 (0.5%)	1
Unknown	1 (4.3%)		1 (1.6%)			2
Informal						
Number	749	842	942	579	471	1992
Total involvement	2754	4541	7486	6588	5615	19689
Median involvement	3	3	4	4	5	
Adjusted involvement*	2955	4790	7802	6872	6130	20804
Total duration days	1866	12365	4499	39316	3362	47177

(Continued)

Table 2.6 (Continued)

	1831–1840	1841–1850	1851–1860	1861–1870	1871–1880	Total 1851–1880
Median duration	1	1	1	1	1	
Working days lost⁺	5598	37107	17996	157264	16810	190270
Number of establishments						
One	736 (98.3%)	819 (97.3%)	905 (96.1%)	552 (95.3%)	428 (90.9%)	1885
Multiple	8 (1.1%)	10 (1.2%)	27 (2.9%)	17 (2.9%)	20 (4.2%)	64
Town/regional	4 (0.5%)	10 (1.2%)	9 (1%)	10 (1.7%)	23 (4.9%)	42
Colony-wide						
Intercolonial						
Unknown	1 (0.5%)	3 (0.4%)	1 (0.1%)			4
Strike Total	772	876	1005	625	681	2311
Non-strike collective action (nsca)						
Formal						
Number	13	41	196	356	905	1457
Total involvement	57	763	4041	10799	36262	51102
Median involvement	11	30	30	40	45	
Adjusted involvement*	156	1753	8421	22439	68527	99387
Total duration days	268	565	4980	6948	23323	35251
Median duration	8	5	8	7	6	
Working days involved+	2948	16950	149400	277920	1049535	1476855
Number of establishments						
One	3 (23.1%)	10 (24.4%)	52 (26.5%)	76 (21.3%)	302 (33.4%)	430
Multiple	5 (38.5%)	3 (7.3%)	12 (6.1%)	17 (4.8%)	71 (7.8%)	100

Town/regional	5 (38.5%)	28 (68.3%)	120 (61.2%)	245 (68.8%)	487 (53.8%)	852
Colony-wide			12 (6.1%)	18 (5.1%)	45 (5%)	75
Intercolonial						
Informal						
Number	2445	866	690	339	348	1377
Total involvement	8089	3406	2988	3843	4214	11045
Median involvement	2	3	3	4	5	
Adjusted involvement*	8219	3649	3324	4243	4979	12546
Total duration days	74413	41822	10369	4084	3883	18336
Median duration	8	4	3	3	3	
Working days involved+						
Number of establishments						
One	2428 (99.3%)	830 (95.8%)	618 (89.6%)	289 (85.3%)	235 (67.5%)	1142
Multiple	12 (0.5%)	23 (2.7%)	41 (5.9%)	13 (3.8%)	25 (7.2%)	79
Town/regional	5 (0.2%)	11 (1.3%)	23 (3.3%)	27 (8%)	66 (19%)	116
Colony-wide		2 (0.2%)	8 (1.2%)	10 (2.9%)	22 (6.3%)	32
Intercolonial						
Nsca total	2458	907	886	695	1253	2834
All Action Total	3230	1760	1891	1320	1934	5145

* Adding median involvement multiplied by number of zero counts +Total duration multiplied by median involvement.

action. Nonetheless, informal multi-establishment action became more common in 1871–1880 and differences in median duration of informal and formal NSCA are less pronounced than strikes. Unlike strikes, total days involved in NSCA don't equate to working days lost (some like absconding did while others interrupted/reduced work) which helps explain the longer median duration of informal NSCA. Table 2.6 reinforces the importance of considering both formal and informal organisation, and strikes and NSCA, in examining worker mobilisation.

Table 2.7 summarises collective action by issues, revealing significant trends and differences. Unionised workers were more likely to strike over wages followed by hours while wages and working conditions were most important for informally organised workers. For NSCA hours and OHS assume greater significance for unionised workers, reinforcing their importance for worker mobilisation. Hours account for roughly 20% of strikes and NSCA by informally organised workers but wages, working conditions and health and safety were more frequent issues. Beyond these broad observations there were inter-industry differences. In the metal and maritime industries hours were more important for strikes than wages. Numbers were roughly comparable in building materials, government, rural and transport equipment while wages were more dominant in printing, mining, road transport, building and clothing/footwear. For NSCA, hours were the dominant issue for retail and food trade (butchers, bakers) workers. Hours were of equal importance with wages for building, metal and transport equipment workers. Wages were more important for printers, miners, government, road transport, clothing/footwear and rural workers and the combination of wages, jobs and OHS for maritime workers.

The database gives collective action outcomes, although this should be treated cautiously and dovetailed with later qualitative analysis. Aside from record gaps and complexities determining outcomes, there are reporting biases. Informal collective action was often reported when workers were prosecuted and there are reasons (press hostility and employer sensibilities) to believe some successful actions were not reported. Acknowledging these caveats Table 2.8 indicates unionised workers were more likely to win both strikes and NSCA than their informally organised counterparts, further evidence of unionisation's significance.

The Courts and Collective Action

Both before 1851 and in 1851–1880 around 90% of court actions involved workers prosecuted for collective action. Worker-initiated actions accounted for 10% of collective court cases, 200 for unpaid wages (6.2% of all court actions), 94 for OHS (2.9%) and 30 (0.9%) for other employer offences. Maritime and rural workers dominated those prosecuted for collective action accounting for 76.8% and 8.9%

Table 2.7 Strikes and Non-strike Collective Action by Issue* in Australia 1831–1880

	1831–1840	1841–1850	1851–1860	1861–1870	1871–1880	Total 1851–1880
Strikes						
Formal						
Wages	22 (95.7%)	25 (73.5%)	37 (58.7%)	29 (63%)	119 (56.7%)	185
Hours		7 (20.6%)	23 (36.5%)	11 (23.9%)	65 (31%)	99
Working conditions			4 (6.3%)	7 (15.2%)	8 (3.8%)	19
Jobs/ employment	1 (4.3%)	5 (14.7%)	1 (1.6%)	2 (4.3%)	12 (5.7%)	15
Unionism	2 (8.7%)	2 (5.9%)	7 (11.1%)	6 (13%)	49 (23.3%)	62
Management behaviour				2 (4.3%)	18 (8.6%)	20
Work methods	1 (4.3%)	2 (5.9%)	2 (3.2%)	3 (6.5%)	23 (11%)	28
Subcontracting		1 (2.9%)	5 (7.9%)	4 (8.7%)	5 (2.4%)	14
Health & safety		1 (2.9%)	1 (1.6%)	1 (2.2%)	9 (4.3%)	11
Unknown		1 (2.9%)	2 (3.2%)		1 (0.5%)	3
Informal						
Wages	34 (4.5%)	80 (9.5%)	114 (12.1%)	102 (17.6%)	138 (29.3%)	354
Hours	327 (43.7%)	329 (39.1%)	291 (20.3%)	119 (20.6%)	99 (21%)	509
Working conditions	377 (50.3%)	449 (53.3%)	450 (47.8%)	317 (54.7%)	169 (35.9%)	936
Jobs/ employment	16 (2.1%)	25 (3%)	73 (7.7%)	46 (7.9%)	32 (6.8%)	151
Unionism		1 (0.1%)	1 (0.1%)		6 (1.3%)	7
Management behaviour	126 (16.8%)	118 (14%)	113 (12%)	100 (17.3%)	56 (11.9%)	269
Work methods	11 (1.5%)	17 (20.2%)	24 (2.5%)	14 (2.4%)	12 (2.5%)	50
Subcontracting			4 (0.4%)		4 (0.8%)	8
Health & safety	158 (21.1%)	134 (15.9%)	179 (19%)	103 (17.8%)	104 (22.1%)	386
Unknown	7 (0.9%)	5 (0.6%)	5 (0.5%)	5 (0.9%)	2 (0.4%)	12
Non-strike collective action (NSCA)						
Formal						
Wages	9 (69.2%)	20 (48.8%)	61 (31.1%)	84 (23.6%)	265 (29.3%)	410
Hours	1 (7.7%)	17 (41.5%)	124 (63.3%)	263 (73.9%)	529 (58.5%)	916
Working conditions	5 (38.5%)	1 (2.4%)	16 (8.2%)	15 (4.2%)	69 (7.6%)	100
Jobs/ employment	5 (38.5%)	3 (7.3%)	11 (5.6%)	14 (3.9%)	78 (8.6%)	103
Unionism		1 (2.4%)	7 (3.6%)	9 (2.5%)	73 (8.1%)	89
Management behaviour		1 (2.4%)	8 (4.1%)	4 (1.1%)	38 (4.2%)	50
Work methods	1 (7.7%)	2 (4.9%)	8 (4.1%)	7 (2%)	76 (8.4%)	91
Subcontracting		2 (4.9%)	8 (4.1%)	4 (1.1%)	9 (1%)	21

(Continued)

Table 2.7 (Continued)

	1831–1840	1841–1850	1851–1860	1861–1870	1871–1880	Total 1851–1880
Health & safety		10 (24.4%)	57 (29.1%)	185 (52%)	408 (45.1%)	650
Legislation				5 (1.4%)	11 (1.2%)	16
Pensions					5 (0.6%)	5
Grievance procedures				1 (0.3%)	4 (0.4%)	5
Unknown				1 (0.3%)	1 (0.1%)	2
Informal						
Wages	76 (3.1%)	130 (15%)	191 (27.7%)	125 (35.1%)	136 (39.1%)	452
Hours	40 (1.6%)	26 (3%)	41 (5.9%)	26 (6.7%)	76 (21.8%)	143
Working conditions	2286 (93.5%)	659 (76.1%)	474 (68.7%)	184 (47.2%)	129 (37.1%)	787
Jobs/ employment	15 (0.6%)	16 (1.8%)	91 (13.2%)	55 (14.1%)	34 (9.8%)	180
Unionism		1 (0.1%)		2 (0.5%)	1 (0.3%)	3
Management behaviour	130 (5.3%)	135 (15.6%)	49 (7.1%)	35 (9%)	29 (8.3%)	113
Work methods	12 (0.5%)	10 (1.2%)	3 (0.4%)	2 (0.5%)	4 (1.1%)	9
Subcontracting	1		14 (2%)	21 (5.4%)	10 (2.9%)	45
Health & safety	104 (4.3%)	79 (9.1%)	62 (9%)	45 (11.6%)	88 (25.3%)	195
Legislation	1	1 (0.1%)	1 (0.1%)	6 (1.5%)	3 (0.9%)	10
Pensions				2 (0.5%)	3 (0.9%)	5
Unknown	38 (1.6%)	63 (7.3%)	6 (0.9%)	3 (0.8%)	1 (0.3%)	10

* Percentages exceed 100% due to multiple issues in same strike/dispute.

respectively of all court proceedings. Shipmasters could directly punish those involved in dissent at sea, confining them in irons or placing them on subsistence rations. In July 1858 two strike ringleaders on the Emigrant Ship *Africa* were confined in chains and fed bread and water for 23 days after assaulting the captain and another officer. The Williamstown Bench only imposed one additional day's imprisonment on them but such accommodations were rare.[32] Naval sailors were still flogged for mutinous conduct although a public furore erupted in Sydney when five sailors from the steam sloop *Pioneer* were lashed before being marched to prison in 1862.[33] Amongst land-based workers convict or free, conviction was an almost a foregone conclusion unless employers withdrew charges or failed to appear before the court.[34]

Traditionally labour historians focused on courts being used to suppress unions via conspiracy/combinations laws. This has resulted in a distorted picture. Workers prosecuted for taking collective action were predominantly informally organised and charged with refusing work or absence under master and servant and maritime laws. Confirming

Table 2.8 Outcomes of Collective Action in Australia 1831–1880

	1831–1840	1841–1850	1851–1860	1861–1870	1871–1880	Total 1851–1880
Strikes						
Formal						
Won	7 (30.4%)	9 (26.5%)	16 (25.4%)	9 (18.8%)	54 (25.5%)	79
Draw		1 (2.9%)		2 (4.2%)	4 (1.9%)	6
Lost	4 (17.4%)	11 (32.4%)	9 (14.3%)	9 (18.8%)	38 (17.9%)	56
Unknown	12 (52.2%)	13 (38.2%)	38 (60.3%)	28 (58.3%)	116 (54.7%)	182
Total	23	34	63	48	212	323
Informal						
Won	34 (4.8%)	66 (8.5%)	84 (9.5%)	38 (7%)	52 (10.7%)	174
Draw	14 (2%)	22 (2.8%)	34 (3.9%)	22 (4.1%)	7 (1.4%)	63
Lost	651 (91.6%)	680 (87.1%)	725 (82.3%)	453 (83.7%)	310 (63.9%)	1488
Unknown	12 (1.7%)	13 (1.7%)	38 (4.3%)	28 (5.2%)	116 (23.9%)	270
Total	711	781	881	541	485	
Non-strike collective action (NSCA)						
Formal						
Won	1 (7.7%)	20 (48.8%)	72 (36.7%)	153 (42.9%)	329 (36.3%)	554
Draw			1 (0.5%)	4 (1.1%)	20 (2.2%)	25
Lost	6 (46.2%)	6 (14.6%)	20 (10.2%)	37 (10.4%)	98 (10.8%)	155
Unknown	6 (46.2%)	15 (36.6%)	103 (52.6%)	163 (45.7%)	460 (50.7%)	726
Total	13	41	196	357	907	
Informal						
Won	46 (2%)	89 (10.4%)	147 (21.5%)	60 (18.3%)	101 (28.9%)	308
Draw	30 (1.3%)	21 (2.4%)	16 (2.3%)	4 (1.2%)	5 (1.5%)	25
Lost	1278 (54.4%)	471 (54.8%)	363 (53%)	163 (49.7%)	125 (35.8%)	651
Unknown	994 (42.3%)	278 (32.4%)	159 (23.2%)	101 (30.8%)	118 (33.8%)	378
Total	2348	859	685	328	349	

pre-1851 experience in 1851–1880 unionised workers were far less likely to come before the courts—87 cases involving 148 unionists compared to 3,161 cases involving 13,145 informally organised workers. When weighted according to the number of organisations and membership/ involvement, the disparity is accentuated and the gap grows over time. These observations are reinforced when outcomes (more fully reported than NSCA/strike outcomes) are considered. Most unionised workers prosecuted for collective action (including picketing, assault, unauthorised absence or unlawful combination) were convicted but proportionally fewer than informally organised workers. Gaol sentences imposed on convicted unionists were lower too, a gap that widens over time (temporarily reversed during the 1890s struggles).

Table 2.9 Court Action and Workers Involved in Collective Action: Australia 1831–1880

	1831–1840	1841–1850	1851–1860	1861–1870	1871–1880	*Total 1851–1880*
			Formal			
Number of court actions	9	22	21	18	48	87
As percentage of organisations	16.7%	19.1%	6.2%	3.4%	5.4%	
Workers involved	12	20	40	33	75	148
Percentage of membership (raw)	2.1%	1%	0.2%	0.1%	0.1%	
Won	2 (22.2%)	7 (31.8%)	3 (14.3%)	7 (38.9%)	9 (18.8%)	19
Draw					2 (4.2%)	2
Lost	7 (77.8%)	13 (59.1%)	15 (71.4%)	8 (44.4%)	29 (60.4%)	52
Unknown		2 (9.1%)	3 (14.3%)	3 (16.7%)	8 (16.7%)	14
Total	9	22	21	18	48	87
Median gaol term (days)	60	40	28	22	17.5	
Average gaol term	25.7	8.8	34	2.4	20.7	
Total gaol terms	231	194	713	44	994	1751
			Informal			
Number of court actions	2533	2098	1687	859	615	3161
As percentage of organisations	88.3%	131.8%	108.8%	93.7%	73.5%	
Workers involved	4860	4526	6831	3607	2707	13145

	44.5%	64.7%	54.3%	40%	25.3%	
Percentage of total worker involvement						
Won	94 (3.7%)	189 (9%)	230 (13.6%)	85 (9.9%)	101 (16.4%)	416
Draw	15 (0.6%)	22 (1%)	65 (3.9%)	23 (2.7%)	4 (0.7%)	92
Lost	2250 (88.8%)	1680 (80.1%)	1254 (74.3%)	651 (75.8%)	469 (76.3%)	2374
Unknown	174 (6.9%)	207 (9.9%)	138 (8.2%)	100 (11.6%)	41 (6.7%)	
Total	2,533	2098	1687	859	615	3161
Median gaol term (days)	30	30	30	30	30	
Average gaol term	53	52.1	35.3	24.4	20.1	
Total gaol terms	134238	109321	59567	21042	12389	92998

Courts were used against unions but overall unionisation was protective—a finding that warrants investigation in other countries. Factors influencing the protection effect included unions' greater financial resources and employers' considering the consequences of court proceedings for future relations, including advantaging rival employers. When shipbuilder John Cuthbert threatened legal proceedings during a wages/union membership strike, Sydney Shipwrights resolved to indemnify the legal costs of anyone prosecuted. One member (JG Connor) apologised to Cuthbert but another (W Ford) was indemnified.[35] Employer threats were more common than actual resort to the courts. The argument is not that court cases were ineffective. In early 1854, 17 compositors at Henry Parkes *Empire* newspaper were convicted of conspiracy in the Supreme Court for leaving without notice when their wage demands were rejected. Ringleader Henry John Bone received six weeks in Parramatta Gaol, the others gaoled for terms ranging from one day to four weeks. Judge Dowling was annoyed operative classes' meetings protested their prosecution and bemoaned the workmen's costly imposition on a capitalist like Parkes. These observations became bitterly ironic four years later when Parkes' mismanagement led to the dismissal of 37 printers owed 15 months' wages.[36] At no risk of being brought before the Supreme Court let alone gaoled for his costly imposition on workmen and their families, Parkes continued his stellar political career.[37] A year earlier (1857) four Melbourne *Argus* printers adjudged strike ringleaders were gaoled for 30 days for breaching their contract under the *Master and Servants Act*. Another accused, Thomas Hurst, successfully challenged his imprisonment.[38] Like the Hunter Valley coalminers and others, printers disputed their coverage under the law. Aside from challenging their coverage, unions mobilised against these lopsided laws.[39] Prosecution of unionists was rare and didn't stop unionisation that reduced the overall risk of being prosecuted for collective action—an effect probably known to workers but unlikely to be publicised by employers or newspapers. There were campaigns to curb anti-worker labour laws that continued long after 1880 but unionisation itself was reshaping the regulatory regime.

Mobilisation Issues/Points

Building on the preceding quantitative assessment, the following section examines some mobilising issues, particularly working hours as the most encompassing point of mobilisation. The discussion also provides context for detailed examination by later chapters.

Hours of Work

The most pivotal mobilisation issue in 1851–1880 (still relevant) was working hours. The eight-hour and early-closing/half-holiday campaigns each mobilised tens of thousands of workers. Their impact stretched far beyond those directly involved. A half-holiday agreement signed in just one Melbourne working-class suburb (Richmond) in 1878 covered nearly 2,000 retail-workers and bootmakers and this figure can be multiplied at least four times to capture family and other community members thereby affected.[40] This observation applies equally to eight-hours, early-closing and struggles against excessive hours by butchers, bakers, clothing outworkers and others.

Best-known, the eight-hour-day campaign began in the building trades before spreading to other industries and working communities generally. The eight-hour idea originated in England where socialist factory owner Robert Owen advocated an eight-hour day from 1817 coining the slogan 'eight hour's work, eight hour's recreation, eight hour's rest.' This slogan is on a commemorative monument surmounted by a triple 8 symbol close to the Melbourne Trades Hall Council. Owen's ambitions gained traction more rapidly in the colonies than Britain (where workers were still demanding a nine-hour day in the 1870s), firstly by Otago (New Zealand) carpenters in 1847. In Port Adelaide a Building Trades Committee formed to agitate for eight hours without reduced pay in August 1854.[41] In 1855 Sydney stonemasons initiated the first sustained campaign after an earlier push for a 4 pm Saturday finish-time (with cabinetmakers and carpenters) in 1853.[42] Melbourne stonemason soon followed in 1856, rapidly encompassing other building trades. Immediately following their success, in April 1856 Melbourne stonemasons planned a large demonstration and established a defence fund and Trades Hall Council to cement the gain.[43] These prescient plans were a model for other locations. In 1859 labourers, ten trades and over 7,000 people attended the 3rd anniversary Melbourne demonstration.[44] By 1858 the movement reached Brisbane and regional towns like Castlemaine, Ballarat, Warrnambool, Bendigo, Williamstown and Beechworth. There were further attempts/gains (like Launceston and Sale) in the 1860s and early 1870s (Adelaide, Port Adelaide, Sydney) involving wider groups of workers like coachbuilders and the iron-trades. The campaign included intense struggles against pockets of resistance/employer pushback like prolonged strikes at William's Batman's Swamp railway carriage works (1863–1864) and at Tunbridge's Ballarat in 1869.[45]

Consistent with its centrality, the Sydney Progressive Carpenters made eight-hours a condition for Bathurst and Orange unions becoming branches. Sydney Carpenters also supported (financially and through boycotts) hour struggles by building labourers, harness-makers, ironworkers, mill-sawyers, wharf-labourers and bakers. Bakers received help because they were committed to the eight-hour principle (their actual hours were far longer) unlike bootmakers who also requested help.[46] Eight-hours were an initiating point for organisation. In Adelaide (1873) and Sydney (1874) iron-trades committees formed to coordinate eight-hour campaigns involving unionised and non-union workers. Some groups campaigned before unionising like Sydney sawmill workers who struck for eight-hours in late 1873, requesting craft union help.[47] Craft societies mobilised resources to assist other unions' struggle like Melbourne gas stokers, bakers (both 1873), tanners and brickmakers (both 1874). Eight-hours prompted renewed unionisation amongst Melbourne brickmakers in 1873. Notwithstanding gains especially in Hawthorne, by October 1874 it confronted ten-hour pushback, particularly from one Brunswick master. The Victorian Operative Bricklayers Society (VOBS) provided assistance, pressuring non-compliant master brickmakers and sympathetically receiving brickmaker deputations (but rejecting suggestions non-unionism was their responsibility).[48]

Combined union bodies mobilised against breaches, the Sydney Trades and Labour Council informing affiliates of an Adelaide strike over reintroducing the ten-hours system in March 1879.[49] To extend and entrench the system, unions repeatedly agitated for legislation mandating the eight-hour day—a number of bills being introduced by sympathetic politicians.[50] In 1869 the *Adelaide Evening Journal* noted a numerously signed petition to the Victorian Legislative Assembly, with similar moves underway in the US (Massachusetts).[51] This highlights the political engagement of colonial unions, their wider agenda and historical lessons to be drawn from running simultaneous industrial, community and political campaigns around mobilising issues.

Community recognition of the movement's importance was immediate, including a competition for the best short hours essay adjudicated by Melbourne University professors. The winning entry penned in May 1856 by AT Best referred to the hot/enervating and changeable climate, social progress and improved family life. Compare the latter to the disingenuous corporate mantra of promoting work/life balance while simultaneously extending hours, precarious work and 24-hour technological surveillance of workers today. Best argued eight-hours was the most practical means of securing shorter hours and refuted contentions it would cause pauperism by noting Britain's overworked population hadn't avoided pauperism—another prescient observation for this neoliberal age. Critically, Best concluded the movement's success depended on unity of action amongst all trades.[52] Others argued the movement wasn't just about recreation but increasing employment, improving health, reinforcing mutual insurance, demonstrating unionism's value and enabling workers to pursue social and political activities as engaged citizens. Sydney Stonemasons encapsulated this in a July 1857 circular issued to the workmen of Sydney and surrounds.[53] It was subsequently published as a public notice in Brisbane, an introductory letter extolling what unionism could achieve, stating they were not:

> absorbed by that selfish wealth-craving spirit which reads such a satire on our country. They are seeking after intelligence, taste, and

moral worth, those virtues which alone can adorn humanity. And from their union they derive strength, warmth, and earnestness, and can command a force of thought which can never be attained by isolated individuals.[54]

These sentiments were echoed repeatedly. Addressing an 1861 Brisbane eight-hour meeting a speaker stated the Sydney School of Arts had enrolled 300 extra members since eight-hours was secured.[55]

The anniversary of securing eight-hours became a marker for public demonstration and celebrations (marches, fetes, picnics, sporting events and gala balls) in every sizeable town, affirming the movement and its wide community support. Size mattered. In 1870 the Sydney United Labourers fined nine members for failing to attend the demonstration.[56] The Sydney Shipwrights fined members found working on demonstration day.[57] Most unions relied on moral suasion. Eight-hour demonstrations were symbolic and aspirational, involving miners and seamen working longer hours. Individual unions hired bands/musicians to play before their contingent. By the late 1850s Victorian Stonemasons had their own band with others like the Melbourne Bricklayers and Gas Stokers following suit over succeeding decades.[58] Considerable planning, funds and logistical support went into celebrations. Bigger demonstrations like Melbourne eventually involved months of planning, detailed financing, balloting to determine the march-order of societies, and awards for the best banner.[59] Union representatives were trustees on the Friendly Society Gardens. Notwithstanding instances of friction eight-hour demonstrations were displays of unity.[60] The eight-hour system was widespread in major towns of all colonies (except Perth) by the late 1870s, extending beyond tradesmen to quarrymen, labourers and others. In November 1877 early-closing advocate David Rodger claimed 19 of 20 Williamstown workingmen worked eight-hour days.[61] Such claims require caution—workers on docks, in boot and clothing factories, butchers and bakers worked far longer hours. Nonetheless, available evidence indicates shorter hours were secured by a significant part of the male manual workforce (reinforced for some women by the Victorian *Factories Act* of 1873), setting the base for further expansion. The eight-hour campaign raised social discourse on working hours, reinforcing other hour-related campaigns—as Rodger's letter indicates.

Eight-hour gains in Australia need to be viewed as part of a wider mobilisation on hours encompassing almost all workers. Trade societies saw the link. Collingwood stonemasons supported bakers and butchers for whom even ten hours would have been an improvement.[62] The eight-hour movement increasingly aligned with the early-closing movement that began in 1840, involving thousands of retail-workers copying UK struggles. Retail-workers associations lacked structural power and used moral suasion to secure retailer agreement to close shops in particular towns at set hours. From 1853 onwards a parallel campaign, initiated by NSW civil servants, sought a weekly half-day break—the half-holiday movement. The movement spread throughout the colonies facilitated by informal networks, generally sympathetic newspapers and immigrants involved in British struggles. In December 1857 the *Age* stated:

> It is gratifying to observe the progress the Saturday half-holiday movement is making throughout a number of trades in town . . . the whole of the ironmongers are now unanimous and close, without a single exception at the appointed hour on Saturday. Many more of the trades ought to follow the example, but it requires the employees to initiate the movement.[63]

Early-closing and half-holidays both attracted civic and religious leaders, including church sermons.[64] The half-holiday movement ultimately involved the widest array of workers—shop-assistants/warehouse workers, hairdressers, government officers, mechanics and labourers and private sector clerks—even figuring in job advertisements.[65] For some manual workers, like glass and china trade workers, half-holidays not eight-hours initiated organisation.[66] There was a reinforcing interchange between various hour campaigns. Shop-assistants referred to eight-hour gains to bolster early-closing claims while mechanics with eight-hours pushed for a Saturday half-holiday.[67] Ballarat factory operative 'Ginger Pop' urged his employer (Lewis) to translate his support for early-closing into giving employees a half-holiday.[68] A January 1856 *Empire* editorial compared eight-hours to prior early-closing struggles, acknowledging these tough-minded men would bring a hard edge to the hours struggle. The *Empire* noted piecework had weakened the British ten-hour law push.[69] This became a key reason for colonial unions' greater hostility to piecework than their British counterparts.

Half-holidays were a longstanding practice for celebratory or sporting events taken up with vigour in the colonies for Christmas/new year, royal birthdays, governor visits, Regatta Day (Hobart), visiting cricketing teams, annual race-meetings and specialised events like ship launchings.[70] However, the movement sought a regular weekly business/office closure at around noon/1 pm for recreational purposes. In the UK, Saturday half-holiday campaigns began in the 1840s with a Leeds agreement followed by Edinburgh, Manchester, Glasgow, Liverpool, Nottingham and other towns by the early 1850s.[71] The movement spread to Australia, Canada and the US (where by 1871 it was labelled a major institution).[72] In 1854 most colonies introduced midday Saturday closing for government offices before expanding into local government and the private sector (even some Northern Territory workers).[73] Like eight-hours and early-closing, half-holidays were advocated on moral/self-improvement, leisure/recreation, increased musical/artistic/theatrical activities, religious-observance and health/hygiene grounds. Connections were made with building sports like cricket as well boosting voluntary militias.[74] In Portland the formation of a militia drove the movement while the *Age* reported Saturday half-holidays had regularised weekly rifle-shooting competitions.[75] Social volunteering benefits were reinforced by philanthropic actions of half-holiday associations (HHAs), including supporting fire brigades, local hospitals and benevolent societies.[76] In 1857 the *North Australian* pointed to productivity and economic benefits:

> Saturday ought throughout the colony to be kept as a half-holiday. All work should be suspended at noon . . . the wages of the week having been paid on the previous evening. This would afford the labourer and the shopmen some time for relaxation, and he would return with redoubled vigour to his work on Monday. The merchant would not suffer . . . as there would be precisely the same amount of money in the hands of purchasers. . . . It is a well-known fact that many mechanics habitually neglect to work on Monday. . . . A half-holiday on Saturday would induce nearly all this class cheerfully to resume work on Monday. . . . Indeed, it may be doubted if the gross production of the colony would be at all effected by it.[77]

As in Europe, in cities like Adelaide and mining towns like Moonta it was argued the half-holiday enabled clerks and others to escape unsanitary conditions.[78] Reverend JG Wright told a Moonta meeting that sanitary reform, early-closing and half-holidays were conducive to temperance.[79] The value of fresh-air was advocated for shop-assistants, clerks and others even in small towns.[80]

In South Australia half-holidays were secured by some manual workers prior to eight-hours. Foundry and building workers, coachmakers and wheelwrights in Gawler secured a Saturday half-holiday in September 1861.[81] The agreement survived some time and, as elsewhere, bodies like mechanics/literary institutes and volunteer rifle/defence brigades benefited.[82] In Adelaide and Port Adelaide building tradesmen gained a Saturday half-holiday during an eight-hour push in the mid-1860s. Mine-mechanics, labourers and building tradesmen in Moonta, Wallaroo and Kadina followed suit with claims.[83] During the latter, agitation speakers at a *Cornucopia Hotel* (Wallaroo) meeting stated Port Adelaide Shipwrights had eight-hours and a Saturday half-holiday.[84] Tradesmen's campaigns moved onto other towns like Mount Gambier.[85] Amidst a colony-wide push for eight-hours in 1873, Adelaide harness and saddle-makers sought eight-hours incorporating a Saturday half-holiday but, facing employer resistance, pragmatically opted for the latter as did Moonta mine-mechanics.[86] In other colonies individual mine-owners had already granted this. An *Australian Town and Country Journal* correspondent reported the Britannia tin mine Copes Creek was well-liked by workmen for regular hours, regular pay and a Saturday half-holiday and miners at the Lord Nelson tin mine Scrubby Creek could organise their hours to do the same.[87]

Wider colonial movements occurred during 1873, Goulburn master saddlers agreeing to a Saturday half-holiday and an Echuca saddler (Ferguson) agreeing to a 2 pm Saturday knock-off amidst a half-holiday push by retail-workers in both towns.[88] The more businesses closing, the less likely country-customers would come to town to shop. In some towns the movement closed virtually every business. The January 1873 Wednesday half-holiday agreement signed in Grafton covered retail-workers, bakers, butchers, carpenters, tanners, confectioners, tailors, cordial-makers, tinsmiths, painters, bank and solicitor's clerks. In February it was extended to bootmakers, jewellers and dressmakers amongst others.[89]

Largely ignored by historians, efforts to coordinate various hours campaigns began in the late 1850s and progressively strengthened. The Ballarat Eight Hours and General Short Hours Association formed in 1859 combined eight-hours and early-closing as core objectives. Its November anniversary soirees/demonstrations celebrated both. Collaboration extended to individual unions. The Ballarat Carpenters and Joiners supported the ECA while he ECA joined Ballarat's annual eight-hour celebrations.[90] In 1862 bricklayer William Stitt Jenkins told the *Geelong Advertiser* shorter hours included the 'glorious boon' of a universal Saturday half-holiday in return for diligent work when 'at it.'[91] Collaboration worked both ways. In 1869 the Brisbane Building Trades Committee organising eight-hour anniversary celebrations asked the ECA to cooperate.[92] In working-class suburbs like Collingwood and Richmond, towns like Grafton and elsewhere, half-holidays incorporated bootmakers, clothing workers, bakers and others subject to excessive hours.[93] Like eight-hours the movement involved a virtuous circle whereby it was in proponents' interests to extend the 'boon' widely to neighbouring towns and beyond. The Sandhurst ECA repeatedly sought early-closing amongst the city's bootmakers and organised a petition from plumbers and gasfitters urging the minister to shift the day for installing water-services from Wednesday.[94]

There were challenges. One tension point was widespread payment of building and other workers on Saturday thereby encouraging shopping later that day. In 1873 a HHA secured agreement by over 60 Maitland and Morpeth employers to pay their workers on Friday. Well beyond informal accommodations that were the norm, it still proved inadequate.[95] Another friction point was competing claims for early-closing and half-holidays. This only splintered a handful of campaigns.[96] A third tension arose from ECAs/HHAs not affiliating to trades and labour councils signifying allegiance to the wider labour movement.[97] Some bodies feared this would alienate influential middle- and upper-class supporters. In 1874 'workingman' criticised Echuca's Mayor for backing early-closing/half-holidays but not laws mandating eight-hours. The Mayor made some amends organising a park and a half-holiday for the town's annual eight-hour celebration.[98] Notwithstanding tensions, links strengthened over time. In 1868 the Melbourne ECA met with unions at the Trades Hall to increase cooperation.[99] It renewed efforts in 1874, sending deputations to individual societies, with building unions promising support. The Melbourne Grocers Assistants also received support, telling the VOBS that 12 hours 'was quite long enough.'[100] Parallel trends are evident in other colonies. Sydney Painters initially told the ECA to join the TLC but within three months (October 1874) joined a TLC ban on shops open after 7 pm.[101] Alliances had reciprocal benefits. In April 1875 Melbourne associated building trades and labourers pressed the Builders and Contractors Association for weekly payment, arguing it was part of their pledge to assist the ECA.[102] Combining eight-hours with a half-holiday initially caused disagreements amongst trades, eventually resolved by coordinated campaigns like that of Sydney building unions in 1874.[103] In South Australia it was claimed problems had been reconciled by building and engineering workers commencing a half-hour earlier at 7.30 am to secure the half-holiday.[104] In 1874 Melbourne stonemasons secured a Saturday half-holiday, a supporting wife stating it would mitigate intemperance and was already the practice in London.[105] Efforts to broaden the campaign to the entire building trade proved difficult but were revived two years later.[106]

Half-holidays or shortened hours appealed to others like carriers, gardeners, labourers, brickmakers, and factory workers.[107] In 1873 a Richmond tailoress wrote to the *Age* about horrendous factory conditions.[108] Shortening hours was a key objective of the Melbourne Tailoresses Mutual Protection Society established a year later.[109] The New Zealand *Employment of Women and Others Act* (1873 and 1874) imposed an eight-hour daytime limit on women in factories.[110] Victoria followed suit. This sparked petitions from Ballarat and Melbourne female factory operatives requesting dispensation because it reduced their piecework earnings—some signatories later recanted.[111] Newspapers regularly published letters requesting help, like Maria, a single seamstress outworker in Norwood working from 8 am to 7 pm in 1867.[112] For domestic servants too, even a Sunday off would have been an improvement. In 1863 one mistress indicated her benefice extended to conceding servants several half-holidays a year for the 'general peace of the family.'[113] Outworkers and domestics remained outside the orbit of organisation. Rare exceptions like a domestic servants union in Dundee, Scotland calling for every second Sunday off in 1872 were widely publicised.[114] Others like carters, book-keepers and mercantile clerks wrote letters lamenting long-hours and pleading for a half-holiday.[115]

Municipal labourers repeatedly petitioned for Saturday half-holidays from the mid-1860s and slowly made ground with periodic reverses over the ensuing decade.[116] Again there is evidence of inter-changeable claims. Hobart City Council labourers petitioned for eight-hours but were granted a Saturday half-holiday (along with carpenters). Alderman Joseph Risby stated he didn't support eight-hours but endorsed Saturday half-holidays with Friday payment having recently granted it to his sawmill workmen.[117] As with eight-hours and early-closing there were wider half-holiday campaigns episodically. In 1875 Hobart City Council labourers' request coincided with claims/gains involving coachmakers, agricultural implement makers, commercial and law-firm clerks, retail-workers, government officers and auction-house employees in the city. Its applicability to rural workers was also canvassed after the Shoobridge hops-growing estate Bushy Park granted a half-holiday—still operating three years later.[118]

The half-holiday movement had wide social and political dimensions. An 1866 the *Maitland Mercury* stated it represented an important counterpoint to the march of industrial civilisation whereby access to cheaper goods entailed longer hours, drudgery and the rise of sweating eloquently described in Tom Hood's 1843 seamstress poem, 'Song of the Shirt.'[119] Arguments extended to nation-building, the better life owed to citizens and meeting immigrant aspirations. In Hobart reviewing 16 years of unsuccessful struggle, an exasperated 'Looker-on' told a critic:

> Surely people do not leave England and cross the seas but to better their condition . . . I am afraid the writer does not drink in the spirit of the age. Certainly it is not by thus looking behind that this infant State is to grow up to a vigorous nation.[120]

Half-holidays entered politics, most commonly in calls for it to be granted to government workers but also during elections and more generally.[121] During the 1874 NSW election, campaign-notices for Clarence urged voters to support Madgwick not Bawden who opposed eight-hours and weekly half-holidays.[122] At a North Adelaide electoral meeting in March 1878 the Minister for Education pledged to support a Saturday half-holiday for letter-carriers like that secured in Melbourne.[123] Most importantly, as moral suasion repeatedly failed, the movement became increasingly politicised and aligned with the labour movement, culminating in 1885 when Victoria pioneered laws mandating trading hours thereby limiting working hours, a precedent adopted throughout Australia and beyond over the next two decades.[124]

In sum, the eight-hour movement was one of four pillars of hours-mobilisation after 1850, the most significant pillar but misconstrued if viewed in isolation. The inter-linkages and wider ramifications were recognised from the outset. In October 1856 the *Argus* labelled the shorter hours' push a step to civilisation, as new ideas and discoveries gave the labouring class an opportunity to liberate themselves. It lauded predominantly self-employed goldminers' decision not work on Sunday and urged carriers (again largely self-employed) to follow suit.[125] There were complex interactions between campaigns in terms of periodisation, who was involved and collaboration. While independently organised, there were growing alignments. In late 1870 assistant drapers in Adelaide pursued a Saturday half-holiday with coachmakers following suit in April/ May 1871 while journeymen butchers, too, secured shorter hours.[126] The half-holiday push in Launceston sparked renewed calls for shorter hours by others like bakers.[127] As with eight-hours, advocates recognised that encompassing as many workers (including self-employed) and employers as possible into agreements enhanced their longevity.[128] The movement also overlapped with celebratory holidays. Hobart butchers and bakers couldn't secure shorter hours but did manage a half-holiday to play cricket in February 1878.[129] Finally, there is extensive evidence of networking within and between towns. Launceston and Hobart, Sydney and Newcastle, Brisbane and Ipswich, and Adelaide and Port Adelaide were exemplars in this regard. In 1877 Launceston and Hobart acted in unison to secure a Wednesday half-holiday, the day itself chosen after considering experiences elsewhere (like Melbourne) and how to enroll all trades.[130]

Howsoever secured, shorter hours had profound social consequences. As in Britain, alarmist claims it would increase alcoholism/vandalism were countered with more persuasive connections between long-hours and drinking—something reaffirmed by contemporary research.[131] Shorter hours gave time for more family and social activities, intellectual, recreation, cultural and religious pursuits as well as time to read newspapers and engage in political discourse. Observing two Saturday afternoons, a Muswellbrook correspondent wrote they caused no inconvenience and 'the young people betake themselves to cricket and to similar games, while the older ones pass the hours in reading and the like.'[132] The liberation from endless drudgery extending to the entire community was evident even in remote towns like Tumut where its 1874 inauguration celebrations were described:

> At 1 o'clock p.m. all the principal places of business were closed, and the event was celebrated by the strains of Parker's brass band, the performers being driven round in Caspersonn's Express and playing a selection of lively airs. In the afternoon a large number of ladies and gentlemen congregated on the race-course and amused themselves with a variety of out-door exercises, until the shades of evening closed over the scene and warned them to wend their way homewards. All who were present seemed to be fully animated by a holiday spirit, and for the time to have cast aside the worry and cares of everyday business life.[133]

Half-holiday associations sponsored public lectures, penny-readings, dramas/theatricals, balls and soirees as well as recreational excursions.[134] Greater time increased working-class opportunities for self-improvement and, as in Britain, public and parliamentary debates over opening-times of museums, libraries and botanical gardens.[135] Half-holidays increased recreational activities like dancing, fishing and picnics along with public recreational areas/parks and holiday-spots like Manly.[136] Some organisations initiated/facilitated recreational grounds as the Grafton HHA did in 1874.[137] Bodies became involved in managing gardens/grounds used to celebrate eight-hour day or half-holidays, the Melbourne Trades Hall and Newcastle HHA being two examples.[138] More generally, growing demand for recreational space encouraged public reserves/gardens to a degree unmatched in the UK or the US—an important heritage of worker-initiated/state-facilitated public space.[139] Half-holiday associations—like the Prahran United Tradesmen in 1865—and their sporting offshoots/beneficiaries campaigned via deputations to local and colonial governments.[140] In port-towns steamers and ferries offered day trips and coaching schedules between towns were revised.[141] In colonial capitals railway timetables were re-scheduled with special low-fare trains for family outings, though sometimes disrupting mail/goods deliveries to outlying towns.[142]

Half-holidays gave scope for working people to attend and participate in sports, with mechanics, apprentices and other workers joining and helping to form athletics, football (various codes) and cricket teams, including mechanic and early-closing specific clubs, across the colonies from Melbourne to Perth.[143] Newspapers repeatedly identified the connection. In 1867 the *Maitland Mercury* reported Newcastle's first half-holiday would be celebrated by a cricket match between drapers and grocers (repeated in subsequent years). In 1869 the *Maryborough Chronicle* stated the newly secured half-holiday led to cricket matches and formation of a new club with similar observations about Muswellbrook in 1873.[144] Associations like Echuca and Newcastle fielded their own teams.[145] It wasn't just cricket. The Grafton rowing club labelled the half-holiday a great assistance. In 1878 an Illawarra District 'Victoria rules' football club was labelled an auxiliary of the HHA and the Echuca HHA also formed a team.[146] By 1878 Melbourne boasted at least four suburban HHA football teams—St Kilda, Brighton, North Fitzroy and South Yarra.[147] Athletic events were common during half-holiday excursions and HHAs also organised specific events like regattas/rowing matches.[148] The half-holiday/organised sport connection was recognised across the length and breadth of the colonies. In 1868 Queanbeyan and Goulburn cricketers both lamented they needed a Saturday half-holiday for the game to prosper.[149] Newspapers acknowledged half-holidays enabled thousands to attend events like the Victorian Racing Club's November race meeting. But not the Melbourne Cup held on Tuesday with requests by public works officers for a half-holiday being refused in 1866.[150] Half-holidays were increasingly proclaimed for eight-hour anniversary celebrations.[151]

Acknowledging the profound changes, in 1880 the *Illawarra Mercury* observed:

> Although we live in a fast age, people, nevertheless, appear to be learning more than ever that 'all work and no play makes Jack a dull boy,' and in order to provide means of healthful relaxation for people generally, public recreation grounds and weekly half-holidays are becoming far more common than heretofore in all civilized communities.[152]

The Saturday half-holiday movement in the UK, North America and Australasia heralded the beginning of the weekend and facilitated the emergence of popular sports (baseball, cricket, rugby and soccer). In Australia it was a step towards a society where sport secured a culturally iconic status. Shorter hours democratised sport and other recreational activities, cultural exhibits and flower shows being increasingly aligned with half-holidays.[153] But it was more profound than this. The weekend represented sanctioned time for socialising and relaxation of immense value, rightly seen as civilising capitalism. Those advocating its demise/irrelevance today represent a return to barbarism. Time is essential for engaged citizens and a democratic society—anyone viewing the lengthening working hours in recent decades (for those 'lucky' enough to have full-time jobs), the 24/7 work-world created by the digital economy and streams of commuters glued to their smart-phones should ponder this. More generally, shorter hours increased time available for families (even if not always used) and increased scope for consumption of goods and services (like excursions), in so doing enhancing economic as well as social wellbeing and health.

Wages, Cheap Labour/Jobs and De-unionisation

Economic inequality is fundamental to capitalism and workers' attempts to improve wages and associated remuneration were a central mobilising issue (Table 2.5 and 2.7). While important in aggregate effects and demonstrating the value of unions, it didn't involve as much inter-union collaboration as hours. Nonetheless, benefits of extending common-rule wages were recognised. Victorian Bricklayers financially supported the recently established the Agricultural Implement and Machine Makers campaign for increased uniform wages in August–October 1874.[154] There were also coordinated responses to employer attempts to undermine wages, especially those seeking to eliminate unions altogether epitomised by the 1878 seamen's strike (Chapter 3).

Health and Safety

Health was another major mobilising issue but took diverse forms. Health was integral to hours' campaigns, especially early-closing/half-holidays for retail-workers and anti-long hour campaigns by butchers, bakers and tailors/tailoresses. Another health issue was the provision of accident, illness and funeral benefits by manual unions to assist members and families meet morbidity/mortality risks. Providing friendly benefits extended well beyond craft unions. Finally, OHS was an important issue for groups like miners and seamen facing especially hazardous working conditions.

Conclusion

Prior to 1851 tens of thousands of workers took collective action, overwhelmingly informally, although unionisation began in 1826 and was well underway by the 1840s. Unionisation accelerated after 1850. Informal organisation didn't disappear but numbers stagnated while formal organisation grew, sometimes fitfully, sometimes rapidly. Even during the economically blighted 1860s there were three times as many unionists as informally organised workers. The gap widened considerably in the 1870s. Importantly, this growth involved a wide array of occupations—the shift to mass unionism was well underway with most unionists being non-craftsmen by around 1875. Labour market conditions, the economic mix and high-urbanisation in the colonies help explain this. However, absence of comparable detailed research for other countries caution against exaggerating differences. This chapter demonstrated the array of methods used by workers and distortions arising from a preoccupation with strikes. Sources of union power at this time also require re-evaluation. Structural power was significant for tradesmen but so too was societal power manifested in wider community campaigns and, as Chapter 11 will reinforce, growing pressure for political 'voice.' There is some evidence of organisational power and (less so) institutional power which later chapters will elaborate.

Unions pursued multiple objectives addressing inequality at work but hours were especially significant in mobilisation. While the colonies pioneered eight-hours campaigning they drew on British ideas in particular, aided by inter-union communication and a steady flow of industrially experienced immigrants. In 1880 *Fraser's Magazine* observed that the 1859 London builders' strike/lockout involving 10,000–16,000 workers (and another 40,000 indirectly), costing over £50,000 in strike pay alone and widely viewed as a defeat, nonetheless resulted in 100,000 ceasing work at noon on Saturday for more pay than they would have received for working an additional four hours. The magazine concluded the strike had cost but a fraction of the gain it secured for workers (at least £562,500 in wages), a gain only such action could have secured.[155]

To this could be added the social/health benefits and potential job gains well-articulated by Sydney carpenter and eight-hour campaigner (Marlow) in 1856. The tangible benefits of hour campaigns to wider communities and the logic of even apparently sacrificial collective action warrant recognition.

Notes

1. P94-19 Melbourne Stonemasons Mutual Benefit Society minutes.
2. LC156-1-3 George Town 25 February 1852, 29 October 1852.
3. Excluding 18 instances of organisation in the Northern Territory then administered by South Australia, mostly seamen, labourers and miners.
4. *Age* 12 October 1872.
5. Robinson, *A History of the Newcastle Branch of the Boilermakers Society 1877–1977*, 2.
6. ML MSS308 THLI minutes 20, 27 January, 24 February, 16 March 1865, 18 May 1866.
7. ML MSS308 THLI minutes 11, 18 August, 1, 15 September 1865.
8. MUA Melbourne Typographical Society minutes 4 February 1871, 13 July 1872.
9. *Sydney Morning Herald* 11, 15 February 1854.
10. *Argus* 6 September 1872.
11. *Goulburn Herald and Chronicle* 14 February 1877.
12. *Sydney Mail* 9 November 1878.
13. ML331.811T Taylor, W. (1884) *A Brief Account of the Origin of the Eight Hours of Labour*, Victorian Operative Stonemasons Society, Melbourne.
14. Quinlan, *The Origins of Worker Mobilisation.*
15. *Queenslander* 5 October 1872.
16. T46-3 NSW Stonemasons Society Central Committee minutes (hereafter NSW Stonemasons Central Committee) 15 September 1857; T46-1-1 NSW Stonemasons Society Sydney minutes 26 July 1858.
17. Z291-17-1 NSW Bricklayers Society Sydney minutes 19 September 1871.
18. E117-2-2 Victorian Operative Stonemasons Society Central Committee minutes (hereafter Victorian Stonemasons Central Committee) 12 September, 21 November 1861, 13 March, 11 September 1862.
19. T46-4 NSW Stonemasons Central Committee minutes 20 January, 3 February 1871.
20. A2795 Sydney Progressive Carpenters and Joiners Society (hereafter Sydney Progressive Carpenters) minutes 30 December 1872.
21. MUA Sydney Painters Trade Society minutes 16 December 1878, 24 February 1879, 9 February, 19 May 1880.
22. E165-33-1A Western District Coalminers Mutual Protection Association minutes (hereafter Western Districts Coalminers) 6 September 1879.
23. *Age* 10 September 1874.
24. Rimmer, M. and Sheldon, P. (1989) 'Union Control' Against Management Power: Labourers' Unions in New South Wales before the Maritime Strike, *Australian Historical Studies*, 23(92): 274–92.
25. E117-2-1 Victorian Stonemasons Central Committee minutes 28 May 1857; E117-58 Victorian Stonemasons Riddles Creek minutes 3 November 1859.
26. *Evening News* 30 March 1878.
27. *Riverine Herald* 29 June 1878.
28. *South Australian Chronicle* 21 September 1877; *Williamstown Chronicle* 12 April 1879.

29. E165-28 Hunter Valley Coalminers Association (hereafter Hunter Valley Coalminers) minutes 12 January 1876.
30. *Leader* 25 April 1874.
31. *Riverine Herald* 25 March 1875.
32. *Age* 19 August 1858.
33. *Age* 21 June 1862.
34. LC247-1-21 Hobart 6 January 1852.
35. ML MLK00049 Sydney Shipwrights Society (hereafter Sydney Shipwrights) minutes 1, 11 May, 22 June 1871.
36. *Sydney Morning Herald* 11, 15 February 1854, 23 April 1858.
37. *Illawarra Mercury* 12 September 1859.
38. *Argus* 10, 12 January, 2 April 1857.
39. At a trial of stonemason refusing to act as strike-breakers it was claimed the law no longer applied to printers. *Geelong Advertiser* 19 January 1859.
40. *Bendigo Advertiser* 4 March 1878.
41. *South Australian Register* 16 August 1854.
42. *Peoples Advocate* 7 May 1853.
43. *Argus* 1 May 1856.
44. *Argus* 23 April 1859.
45. *Age* 12 November 1863, 5 May 1864; *Star* 4, 7 August 1869.
46. A2795 Sydney Progressive Carpenters minutes 11 September 1871, 26 February, 25 March, 6 May 1872, 13 January, 2 June, 17 November 1873, 24 January, 23 February, 5, 19 October, 16 November, 28 December 1874, 8 February, 1 November 1875.
47. *Argus* 3 November 1873; T46-1-3 NSW Stonemasons Sydney minutes 19 November, 3, 12 December 1873.
48. T8-2A-3 VOBS Melbourne minutes 5, 12 October, 24, 30 November, 1, 14 December 1874.
49. E235-2 Sydney United Plasterers minutes 31 March 1879.
50. T8-2A-3 VOBS Melbourne minutes 7 August 1871.
51. *Evening Journal* 17 December 1869.
52. ML MSS308 Box 7 Best, A.T. (1857) *Essay on the Eight Hours Question Which Obtained the Prize Given by the Ex-Mayor JT Smith Esq under the Adjudication of the Professors of the University of Melbourne*, G Salter, Melbourne, 5–11.
53. ML61SLNSW Operative Stonemasons Institution, To the Operative Stonemasons of Sydney and Vicinity, Haymarket, 15 July 1857.
54. *Moreton Bay Courier* 7 November 1857.
55. *Moreton Bay Courier* 13 April 1861.
56. ML MSS208 Box 02 Item 7 Sydney United Labourers Protection Society fine book 1 October 1870.
57. ML MLK00049 Sydney Shipwrights minutes 16 September, 20 October 1875.
58. E117-2-2 Victorian Stonemasons Central Committee minutes 10 June 1859.
59. ML MSS308 Box 6 Eight Hour Anniversary Committee minutes 8 April 1874.
60. A2795 Sydney Progressive Carpenters minutes 7 July, 18 August 1879.
61. *Williamstown Chronicle* 10 November 1877.
62. E117-39 Victorian Stonemasons Collingwood minutes 17 April 1860.
63. *Age* 16 December 1857.
64. *Telegraph, St Kilda, Prahran and South Yarra Guardian* 25 May 1867.
65. *South Australian Register* 14 April 1873.
66. *Argus* 16 November 1872.
67. *Maitland Mercury* 10 September 1874.
68. *Ballarat Star* 28 October 1869.
69. *Empire* 16 January 1856.
70. *South Australian Register* 7 January 1873; *Mercury* 9 June 1875.

71. *South Australian Register* 13 December 1853.
72. *Sydney Morning Herald* 12 August 1871; *Sacramento Daily Union* 8 June 1883.
73. *South Australian Weekly Chronicle* 17 March 1866; *South Australian Register* 26 April 1869.
74. *South Australian Weekly Chronicle* 21 July 1866; *Mercury* 12 August 1878.
75. *Age* 24 December 1861.
76. *Portland Guardian* 28 May 1866; *Riverine Herald* 5 November 1873.
77. *North Australian* 27 January 1857.
78. *Adelaide Times* 15 December 1853; *South Australian Register* 21 December 1853.
79. *Evening Journal* 20 May 1878.
80. *Border Watch* 14 November 1866.
81. *South Australian Advertiser* 5 September 1861.
82. *South Australian Advertiser* 10 April 1862.
83. *South Australian Advertiser* 18, 19 August 1864; *Wallaroo Times* 21, 28 June, 8 July 1865.
84. *Wallaroo Times* 9 September 1865.
85. *Border Watch* 28 July, 25 August 1866.
86. *South Australian Advertiser* 9 July 1873; *Yorke's Peninsula Advertiser* 22 July 1873.
87. *Australian Town and Country Journal* 16 November 1872; *Armidale Express* 11 January 1873.
88. *Goulburn Herald* 18 October 1873; *Riverine Herald* 1 November 1873.
89. *Clarence and Richmond Examiner* 21 January, 11 February, 20 May 1873.
90. *Star* 21 November, 3 December 1861, 22 April, 21 November 1863.
91. *Geelong Advertiser* 4 February 1862.
92. *Queenslander* 27 February 1869.
93. *Mercury and Weekly Courier* 13 July 1878.
94. *Bendigo Advertiser* 4 September 1878.
95. *Maitland Mercury* 18 October, 20 November 1873.
96. *Mercury* 14 September 1878.
97. A2795 Sydney Progressive Carpenters minutes 27 July 1874.
98. *Riverine Herald* 21 January, 18 April, 2 May 1874.
99. *Argus* 13, 17 March 1868; *Age* 18 March 1868.
100. T8-2A-3 VOBS, Melbourne minutes 9, 16, 23 March, 11, 25 May, 1, 22 June 1874; *Age* 16 July 1874.
101. MUA Sydney Painters minutes 27 July, 9 October 1874.
102. *Age* 3 June 1875.
103. T46-1-3 NSW Stonemasons Sydney minutes 14, 28 January, 2 February 1874.
104. *Age* 23 August 1873.
105. *Age* 18, 20 June, 10 September 1874.
106. *Argus* 16, 18 July 1874.
107. *Age* 16 March 1878.
108. *Age* 23 May 1873.
109. *Argus* 20 July 1874.
110. Graham, J. (1987) Child Employment in New Zealand, *New Zealand Journal of History*, 21: 62–78.
111. *Age* 18 January 1874.
112. *Express and Telegraph* 7 March 1867.
113. *Argus* 19 January 1863.
114. *Argus* 29 June 1872; *Tasmanian* 6 July 1872.
115. *Argus* 17 February 1865; *Age* 14 June 1873.
116. *South Australian Advertiser* 22 August 1876.

117. *Mercury* 13 October 1874.
118. *Mercury* 26 June 1877; *Tasmanian Tribune* 3, 21, 22 October, 16, 18, 26 November 1874.
119. *Maitland Mercury* 1 December 1866.
120. *Colonial Times* 22 September 1855; *Mercury* 11 July 1871.
121. *Express and Telegraph* 29 November 1867.
122. *Clarence and Richmond Examiner* 22 December 1874.
123. *South Australian Register* 20 March 1878.
124. Quinlan, M. and Goodwin, M. (2005) Combating the Tyranny of Flexibility: The Struggle to Regulate Shop Closing Hours in Victoria 1880–1900, *Social History*, 30(3): 342–65.
125. *Argus* 30 October 1856.
126. *Advertiser* 22 May 1871.
127. *Weekly Examiner* 2 September 1876.
128. *Mercury* 13 September 1877.
129. *Mercury* 5 February 1878.
130. *Mercury* 1 October 1877; *Launceston Examiner* 11 October 1877.
131. *Sydney Morning Herald* 25 November 1868; Virtanen, M. et al. (2015) Long Working Hours and Alcohol Use: Systematic Review and Meta-Analysis of Published Studies and Unpublished Individual Participant Data, *British Medical Journal*, doi: 10.1136/bmj.g7772.
132. *Maitland Mercury* 16 June 1874.
133. *Gundagai Times* 21, 28 February 1874.
134. *Clarence and Richmond Examiner* 11 February 1873.
135. *Age* 23, 27 October, 5 November 1874.
136. For fishing see *Hamilton Spectator* 9 July 1878.
137. *Clarence and Richmond Examiner* 10 February 1874.
138. *Newcastle Chronicle* 20 December 1873.
139. *Inquirer* 25 August 1875; *Western Australian Times* 7 November 1876; *Eastern Districts Chronicle* 17 December 1880.
140. *Argus* 24 March 1865.
141. *Illawarra Mercury* 7 December 1880.
142. *Brisbane Courier* 25 July, 22 September 1877.
143. In country towns sporting games like cricket were played on Wednesday or Thursday half-holidays although inconsistent half-holidays presented problems. *Geelong Advertiser* 4 February 1864; *Evening News* 5 August 1870; *Border Watch* 15 December 1880.
144. *Maitland Mercury* 10 January 1867, 23 December 1873; *Maryborough Chronicle* 25 February 1869.
145. The Newcastle club donated £2 2s to the widowed-mother of young player fatally struck by a cricket ball in Sydney. *Newcastle Morning Herald* 10 September 1878.
146. *Clarence and Richmond Examiner* 21 January, 18 February 1873; *Illawarra Mercury* 12 April 1878; *Riverine Herald* 13 May 1879.
147. *Telegraph, St Kilda, Prahran and South Yarra Guardian* 6 July 1878.
148. *Newcastle Chronicle* 13 June 1871.
149. *Queanbeyan Age* 30 May 1868; *Goulburn Herald* 9 December 1868.
150. *Bendigo Advertiser* 2 November 1866.
151. *The Mercury* 11 November 1871; *Launceston Examiner* 3 February 1872.
152. *Illawarra Mercury* 2 March 1880.
153. *Kiama Independent* 19 March 1880.
154. T8-2A-3 VOBS Melbourne minutes 14 September, 12 October 1874.
155. Cited in *Geelong Advertiser* 3 March 1880.

3 Transport and Maritime Activities

Introduction

This chapter deals with land transport and maritime activities separately, beginning with the latter. As the colonies expanded, more ports became hubs of maritime activity, including Newcastle, Geelong, Adelaide and Brisbane. As in *The Origins of Worker Mobilisation*, maritime transport and whaling are examined together given overlapping regulation, issues and patterns of collective action. Whaling, in terminal decline accelerated by Yankee whaleship destruction by confederate raiders during the Civil War and the shift to petroleum, was increasingly concentrated in Hobart (ex-convicts an important source of crews) and declining catches and returns aggravated labour relations. In the merchant marine shipboard protests and employer resort to the courts remained endemic although court records only captured fragments of the struggle. Table 3.1 summarises patterns of maritime worker organisation. Shipboard protests, long common with 102 in 1841 alone, experienced a significant increase in 1851–1860 only partly coincident with the gold rushes (309 instances in 1853–1854 with another spike of 127 in 1857). Dominant issues were working conditions, hours, OHS, jobs/employment and wages, with workers overwhelmingly losing actions. Strikes significantly outweigh (in numbers and involvement) non-strike forms of collective action (NSCA) like group-absconding. Seamen's strikes exceed industry totals because some, like boatmen, were employed by government or on inland ferries. Collective action was largely confined to a single establishment/ship but unionisation's influence is evident after 1870, in growing multi-establishment/port and two colonial/intercolonial actions. Unionisation, especially amongst seamen and wharf-labourers, also affected membership/involvement, methods (petitions, deputations, marches and mass meetings) and issues like unionism (see Table 3.1 breakdowns). Nonetheless, informal organisation remained important because international-trade seamen and whalers remained unorganised, as were coasting seamen and wharf-labourers in small ports.

Table 3.1 Worker Organisation in the Maritime Industry 1831–1880

Industry	1831–1840	1841–1850	1851–1860	1861–1870	1871–1880	Total 1851–1880
Entire industry						
Organisations	264	471	985	614	491	2086⁺
Raw involvement	1332	2396	6413	3348	13085	22846
Est. involvement*	1562	2692	6763	3524	13460	23747
Strikes						
Won	20	44	59	26	41	126
Drawn	8	12	26	11	2	39
Lost	128	283	541	396	270	1207
Unknown	25	45	47	27	38	112
Total	181	384	673	460	351	1484
Est. total involvement*	1007	1880	4779	2540	4350	11669
Number of establishments						
One	179	378	661	457	327	1445
Multi	2	1	11	1	8	20
Regional/town	1	3	2	1	13	16
Intercolonial					1	1
Non-strike Collective Action						
Won	20	28	86	30	39	155
Drawn	3	5	14	10	4	28
Lost	39	56	232	112	91	400
Unknown	33	41	81	84	42	189
Total	95	130	413	236	176	825
Est. total ivolvement*	392	628	1759	826	4581	7166
Number of establishments						
One	94	127	409	189	171	769
Multi	1	3	7	3	9	19
Regional/Town				2	13	15
Colonial					1	1
Unknown						
Issues in collective action (strikes/ NSCA)						
Wages	17/36	29/31	53/86	29/31	55/56	137/173

Industry	1831–1840	1841–1850	1851–1860	1861–1870	1871–1880	Total 1851–1880
Hours	29/1	93/5	146/10	90/6	84/12	320/28
Working conditions	124/46	258/82	375/312	286/140	145/98	806/550
Health & safety	52/13	79/21	156/42	92/29	94/46	342/117
Management behaviour	42/12	62/23	99/32	91/27	52/18	242/77
Jobs/employment	12/8	22/6	68/74	41/44	30/29	139/147
Work methods	8/3	11/1	18/1	11	11/3	40/4
Unionism		1/		/1	11/7	11/8
Subcontracting					1/1	1/1
Legislation					/1	/1
Unknown	5/17	2/19	5/5	4/3	1/1	10/9
Total strikes/ NSCA	276	514	1086	696	527	2309
Breakdown of organisation and actions of two largest occupational subgroups						
Seamen and whalers						
Organisation numbers	285	504	1023	629	472	2118+
Est. involvement*	1714	2800	6844	3628	6614	17078
Strikes	188	395	690	467	336	1493
NSCA	108	152	433	205	185	823
Absconding	61	89	325	115	82	522
Petitions	2	11	4	2	16	22
Deputations					9	9
Mass meetings			1		19	20
Marches					8	8
Letters/public notices		1	2	2	9	13
Bans	2		1	4	7	12
Court Actions						
Won	33	94	173	67	80	320
Lost	234	497	935	588	423	1946
Drawn	8	13	45	15	3	63
Wharf-labourers						
Organisation numbers	8	6	6	7	22	35+
Est. involvement*	20	70	134	360	8855	9349
Strikes	6	5	4	2	16	22
NSCA	1			2	13	15
Absconding	1					

(*Continued*)

Table 3.1 (Continued)

Industry	1831–1840	1841–1850	1851–1860	1861–1870	1871–1880	Total 1851–1880
Petitions		1	1	1	2	4
Deputations					2	2
Mass meetings					6	6
Marches					4	4
Letters/public notices				2	3	5
Bans						
Court Actions						
Won			1 (100%)		3 (45.9%)	4
Lost	5 (100%)	4 (100%)			4 (54.1%)	4

* Adjusted by multiplying number of zero-reporting organisations/years by industry and occupation median membership for each decade. ⁺For totals, organisation spanning multiple decades only counted once.

Merchant Seamen, Whalers and Pearlers

Shipboard Protests

Desertion and insubordination spiked in 1852–1854, affecting most colonial ports, not just Sydney and Melbourne. Some deserting seamen headed for the goldfields but most exploited better job prospects. Desertion required organisation and planning given preventative measures including vigilant ship's officers, water police and constables; seamen's distinctive appearance/gait; the need for shore-passes; lucrative apprehension-rewards and courts and governments keen to minimise shipping disruptions. Seamen needed clothes and funds to avoid rapid apprehension as befell *Primula* deserters caught begging at New Town near Hobart.[1] Desertion was facilitated by elaborate crimping networks of watermen, publicans and hostel/brothel owners operating in sizeable ports.

Surviving evidence significantly understates the scale of dissent. Largely complete records for one port, Hobart, indicates newspapers reported under half the cases going before courts. For other ports court records are fragmentary or entirely lost so only newspaper reports survive, cautioning against interpreting too much from spikes in litigation. Further, courts only dealt with deserters who were apprehended. The *Neptune* lost three crewmembers to desertion on 23 February 1852, four more on 1 March, another two on 20 March and six more over the next ten weeks—none had been recaptured by 26 June.[2] Even seamen apprehended after their ship departed faced brighter prospects. Crewmembers of British vessels *Jane Catherine* and *Columbus* both escaped punishment before the Hobart Bench in September 1852 because their complainant's had left and couldn't press charges.[3] Some deserters from the *Tasman* also escaped detection, the master being charged for costs of issuing warrants in February 1853 when the ship was about to leave.[4] Evidence suggests numerous desertions succeeded. An August 1854 Hobart Bench return listed 48 warrants issued between October 1853 and July 1854 where seamen remained at large when ships left port.[5] On 31 December 1856, 31 cases of absent seamen and six of absent whalers remained undecided, six months later 26 seamen and three whalers, and in the six months to 31 December 1859 warrant fees for 38 unapprehended seamen and seven whalers were paid to the Crown.[6] Escape was more difficult where shipowners or their agents were domiciled in the port and seamen could be prosecuted after a vessel left. Several whaleship *Sussex* deserters (ex-convicts) were sentenced to two months hard labour plus 12s 6d court costs by the shipowner's agent.[7]

Other seamen struck with a view to remaining in the colonies, several *Aboukir* crewmembers telling the Hobart Bench they were 'dissatisfied with the ship.'[8] In August 1852 the *Tasmanian Colonist* complained the colony got no benefit from gold discoveries, just greater dissent amongst seamen with 50 currently in Hobart's House of Correction.[9] Seamen ashore without passes risked arrest by vigilant constables and could be imprisoned until their ship was ready to sail. Nonetheless, shipmasters found it politic to punish sparingly, like the *Blenheim*'s master who withdrew charges against deserters George Davison and John Wilson after losing eight other crewmembers to prison for misconduct, desertion and refusing work in the previous fortnight.[10] Some shipmasters offered substantial rewards. Moored in Sydney in May 1853, the Danish ship *Calloe*'s master offered £50 for six deserters and the German ship *Java*'s master £20 for three seamen.[11] Recently appointed police inspector McCook rapidly arrested and tried them under the *Foreign Seamen's Act* with six being imprisoned for eight weeks.[12] However, complications arose two days later. Legal counsel secured the release of two seamen who refused to join the Dutch ship *Nehalenia* arguing the *Foreign Seamen's Act* only applied in ports with a consul of the country where the ship was registered and there was no Dutch consul. There was also no Danish consul so the remaining two *Calloe* runaways were sent on board not imprisoned (one *Java* seamen remained at large). Inspector McCook still received £50.[13] Incentivising police to apprehend deserters emphasised the nexus between state and capital. Unlike convicts, deserting seamen were not already under sentence so the state's formal interest in their apprehension was not so direct. Those engaging or harbouring deserters faced serious penalties like the owner of the barge *Thistle* and master of *Maria* both fined £30.[14]

One desperate shipmaster in Melbourne urged crew wishing to desert to do so immediately, not when the vessel was about to sail.[15] Others offered more pay. William Parfitt (*Formosa*) offered his crew Singapore £10 more per month which was initially accepted 'but in the evening I received a letter signed by twenty-one seamen and firemen, stating that unless I cancelled my old articles and agreed to bring them back from Singapore on the terms I offered, they would "stand their chance."'[16] Informal wage-bargaining was probably more common than incidental references to it in letters, newspapers and court proceedings, like the *James Brown* master's agreement to pay his crew six shillings a day while the vessel was in Port (Melbourne).[17] Melbourne didn't experience the numerous crewless-ships left stranded in San Francisco in 1849 but seafaring wasn't well-paid. Some crews demanded a discharge and their wages so they could rehire at higher colonial rates. The brig *Panama*'s 'coloured crew' did this in Sydney in June 1854.[18] Court proceedings invariably record cases where efforts failed but wage disparities prompted tacit bargaining before and after the goldrushes. In 1876 the *Crested Wave*'s master discharged several crewmembers who agreed to forfeit two months' pay.[19] Maritime laws deemed collective wage demands illegal but there was an undercurrent of allowance-claims or on-shore spending money, epitomised by the *Dunrobin Castle* crew's strike in Hobart (June 1863). Conflict festered with some refusing to rejoin the ship, highlighting how regulation drove discharge/desertion options.[20]

Shipboard dissent expended large state resources. Notwithstanding rapidly dispensing 'summary justice,' even cases involving a single ship could be costly. Twelve *Caroline* crewmembers struck in Sydney (November 1853). Replacements were engaged for the voyage to discharge emigrants in Brisbane where the 12 continued their refusal, seven absconding on a raft they built.[21] Failed strikes were followed by mass absconding—or vice versa—emphasising the need to examine all collective action. In August 1855 the *Admiral Boxer*'s crew deserted in Port Adelaide, most quickly apprehended and gaoled for a month. Returned on board under guard didn't prevent a strike, 18 receiving three months' hard labour with several pledging to never serve again on the vessel.[22] Seamen found ways to protest even under escort back to their ship by rioting, damaging property or other more subtle devices. In September 1863 the *Hannah More*'s crew 'walked through the streets of the town at a snail-like pace, for the evident purpose of keeping their guards in the rain as long as possible; they also sung many sea songs on the way, and attracted a large crowd of persons to see them.'[23]

Dissent was driven by multiple factors including higher colonial living standards. In 1875 the *Geffrarde*'s Chinese and coloured seamen told Port Adelaide magistrates they had no complaint against the master but wanted to stay in the colony.[24] Whaleship *Julia* crew complained of harsh discipline but it was also alleged they wanted a discharge to go to the goldfields.[25] Rations (poor quality or insufficient) and harsh treatment caused strikes and desertion. The *Catherine Middleton*'s crew complained of being 'half-starved' during the voyage to the colonies—two months' gaol.[26] When the ship sailed, five crewmembers still in gaol (losing clothes and wages) petitioned for release and permission to work or join another vessel.[27] When US whaleship *Nautilus* crew tried to lodge a complaint over rations in March 1861 the Chief Officer placed them in irons and laid refusing work charges. The whaler's counsel secured their release after revealing these facts but three days later four were sentenced to 28 days' imprisonment for refusing work on Sunday.[28] Seamen also broached cargo for food, alcohol or as acts of revenge. In May 1876 the barque *Strathearn*'s crew were charged with larceny after breaking into a cask of ale worth £9 in Rockhampton. The incident followed a breakdown in shipboard relations, including physical confrontations and sabotage (damaging ship property), one crewmember stating their treatment was 'unfit for a dog.'[29]

Seamen's preference for collective action was influenced by knowledge lodging a complaint before a court generally resulted in it being trivialised and summarily dismissed. Assaults on seamen were common, often went unpunished and punishments were typically a fine—not imprisonment meted out to insubordinate seamen. In April 1859 the *Harrowby*'s master (William Storie) was fined £5 for maliciously assaulting William Dallinger the Hobart Bench, dismissing claims by another seamen William Davis 'as too trifling to merit notice.' Alarmed fellow crewmembers were sent on board under police escort.[30] Even in egregious cases officers were seldom gaoled, a rare exception being the *Bayswater*'s second mate who received five weeks' gaol in Rockhampton in 1866 for 11 counts of assaulting crew. Even here 17 crewmembers who struck over ill-treatment received one month's gaol, their fear and suffering not deemed sufficient mitigation.[31] Ill-treatment complaints were more common amongst non-European crews. In January 1861, 14 crewmembers of the *Norna* complained of being flogged, having stones hung around their necks, one crewmember murdered by officers and another dying of illness. The Sydney Water Police Court dismissed their claims and gaoled them for insubordination. Lawyer William Palmer Moffatt offered to represent them for a discharge and wages. Moffatt secured an agreement with the shipmaster (Crawford), no doubt keen to avoid public airing of evidence at a trial, but took half their wages (£60–70) as his fee and deducted another exorbitant £43 for lodging costs. The men were left homeless and destitute. Aided by a more humane lawyer (W James) they unsuccessfully petitioned the Supreme Court for restitution. James alleged Water Police Magistrate North suppressed evidence of appalling treatment, 'siding with the strong, oppressing the weak' and forcing the poor men 'to leave the colony, ill-used on their passage hither, robbed of their wages . . . and obliged to face tempestuous seas, and, to them, ungenial weather, in a state near to nudity.'[32] Racist imperial attitudes resonated in this incident—by no means atypical. Nevertheless, at its core were the social relations of production where labour is subordinated to the interests of capital. European seamen, too, suffered at the hands of rapacious lawyers, a stacked legal regime and powerful interests. The difference was one of degree, not kind.

Successful ill-treatment complaints by seamen, irrespective of their origin, were rare and often the result of unusual circumstances. The ship *Douglas*'s master Augustus Grossan was fined £415 for not providing crew with lime juice or sufficient or wholesome rations (weevil-ridden flour) and cramming them into a forecastle with insufficient bunks, poorly caulked (leaking) and ventilated.[33] What really drove Grossan's prosecution and conviction, however, was that he had breached passenger safety and immigration regulations, carrying 306 Chinese passengers from Hong Kong, including 83 sneaked aboard after official vetting was completed (fined £5 for each overloaded passenger). The aggrieved seamen were entitled to share (£60) of the fine but hadn't received it seven months later—their suffering wasn't pivotal.[34]

Other OHS issues sparking dissent included rotten/leaking or shorthanded vessels. In September 1861 the whaleship *Catherine*'s crew refused to put to sea, arguing the vessel lacked sufficient qualified seamen.[35] In May 1860, eight crew of the whaling brig *Victoria* crew were imprisoned for 12 weeks after alleging the vessel had almost sunk on three occasions. Their claims were rejected by shipbuilder Alexander McGregor whose inspection did however identify issues with rigging and stays. Two weeks later further seamen were gaoled for refusing to join the vessel.[36] Unseaworthiness claims were more common on merchant vessels. Another danger was drunk or incompetent officers. In September five seamen from the whaling brig *Highlander* complained the captain had been drunk and running around on deck with a loaded pistol after ordering them to raise anchor in Macquarie Harbour. The bench refused to allow witnesses on the grounds these crewmembers would 'bolt' if given a chance. The Hobart *Mercury* observed the captain was unable to answer basic questions and 'the men examined the Captain with great legal acumen and certainly placed him in very perplexing position.'[37] It still did them no good. Adjudged instigator James Murphy receiving one month's imprisonment.[38] In February 1860 the *Maid of Erin*'s crew were gaoled for a month and fined £1 for striking in Port Davey. They complained their captain was drunk and had battened down hatches almost suffocating them.[39]

Seamen could lodge ship-safety complaints but as with ill-treatment these seldom succeeded. In 1873 the *Anglesey*'s crew petitioned for an inspection. Her master rebuffed the Commissioner for Customs, claiming pumping was exceptional and threatening legal action if the ship was detained.[40] An unfortunate passenger later recounted the ship was only kept afloat during its voyage to Britain by continuous pumping, bypassing Cape Town (to avoid inspection), offloading 3,000 bales of wool and repairing leaks at St Helena.[41] In September 1877 the *Wild Rose*'s crew refused to leave Port Adelaide. The master conceded the vessel's poor recent history but the magistrate told them at least a quarter of the crew should lodge a formal protest just prior to its scheduled departure. Striking again, they were imprisoned for a month and mulcted two days' pay.[42] Importantly, incidents of this kind were occurring globally, involving ships of all nations. In August 1856 the Hawaiian ship *General Blanco*'s crew, unconvinced by repairs approved by the Collector of Customs and Port Adelaide Assistant Harbour Master, indicated they would prefer gaol to going 'to sea in a leaky vessel' (three months' hard labour).[43] The *Alfred*'s crew in Sydney took a similar view, refusing to proceed to sea repeatedly, culminating in three months' hard labour.[44]

All-too-common reports of ships foundering or simply disappearing lent weight to protests generally involving entire crews. Port authorities were cognisant of safety but more concerned about impeding shipping.[45] Regularly found in logbooks were instances acknowledging the vessel was labouring and shipping water especially during heavy weather, requiring pumping every two or four hours and sometimes continuously. Typical was the Hobart-Shanghai-Sydney voyage of English trading brig *Betah* (November 1853 to September 1854) while the brigantine *Sea Gull* was barely kept afloat between Hobart to San Francisco and there abandoned. Less fortunate was the schooner *Picard* taking water on 9 October 1867. Seven days later the sternpost fractured and with seven feet of water in the hold the master acquiesced to the crew's 'urgent solicitations to leave the ship,' taking to a boat which made it to Montague Island.[46] Captain and mate were subsequently prosecuted by the owners with 'casting away' the vessel—explaining why officers only reluctantly abandoned vessels.[47] Logs attest to voyages where vessel or crew survived. There were 'near misses' that likely explain many disappearances and observed vessel foundering during gales/storms. Long-simmering angst over 'coffin ships' finally erupted in the early 1870s. Campaigning by House of Commons member Samuel Plimsoll and seamen's unions flowed onto the colonies aided by colonial unions. However, like other social protection movements by working people there were no sudden shifts in safety practices. Seafaring was replete with other hazards, including falls (from the rigging or into holds), being hit by objects (like rigging, whale flukes or whaling equipment), fire (especially coal-export ships), boiler explosions and drowning. Whaleship logs in particular record a grim toll, especially those lost overboard where the frigid water and heavy clothing made survival unlikely irrespective of swimming ability.[48]

Hours of work/breaks, designated duties and work methods also sparked disputes. Consistent with their greater vulnerability, collective action over work methods, leaking ships or crewing-levels seems rarer amongst non-European crews. In July 1868, 12 'Lascars' on the Steamer *Bombay* refused to clean the bottom of the ship, arguing this wasn't part of their duty (four weeks' gaol).[49] In January 1877 the mail-steamer *City of Sydney*'s Chinese crew struck work after the boatswain was dis-rated.[50] Most hours-related disputes concerned seamen taking unauthorised absences but masters ordering prolonged hours, work before breakfast/during meals or Sunday work in port also sparked strikes.[51] Conviction usually followed though clever pleading sometimes succeeded. The steamer *European*'s crew resisted requests to square the yards during supper but escaped punishment, arguing they hadn't refused work, the magistrate finding insufficient evidence to convict them.[52] Strikes at sea over hours/workloads were uncommon, although activities like trying-out whale-oil involved long-hours, occasioning disputes notwithstanding the incentive of whalers' pay (lays') being linked to whale product value. After working until 11 pm the previous evening trying-out and stowing oil, the barque *Litherland*'s crew ignored repeated calls to duty at daybreak the next day. A deputation told the captain he 'gave them too much work to do.' Robert Duson was confined and the others ordered back to work, with deputation leader William Chambers joining Duson a day later after a heated exchanged with the master.[53]

Court appearances usually exacerbated shipboard relations but some resolved them. David Walker, master of an American vessel in Hobart, persuaded his crew to resume work and promptly withdrew charges against them.[54] Importantly, ship logs identify numerous instances of shipboard action never reaching court, including absconders, groups granted a discharge after striking or dissidents punished directly by the shipmaster.[55] On 23 September 1861 the schooner *Lady Leigh*'s crew struck and demanded their wages/discharge which was granted, log entries indicating the schooner was leaking badly probably prompting their action.[56] Safety concerns also sparked desertions from the whaling brig *Prince of Denmark* in January 1852, the voyage abandoned 20 days later due to the 'state of the ship' (built 1789).[57] In October 1861 the 184 ton whaleship *Australasian Packet*'s crew struck in Recherche Bay, one crewmember (J Timmins) being confined on bread and water. Relations didn't improve, a cutting-line used to cut blubber sabotaged four months later.[58] On 16 September 1871 the whaling barque *Othello*'s crew refused to man the windlass unless granted time ashore during reprovisioning. John Brown and Frank Bain were placed in irons and the others locked in the forecastle on bread and water til they relented the following day.[59] During an earlier voyage (1868) four whalers stole a boat and deserted. Discovered digging potatoes, they could not be forceably returned. The *Othello*'s master could only write a protest letter to the Chatham Island magistrate.[60] In December 1875 the *Velocity*'s crew complained of inadequate rations and clothing. Edward Medlen told the master ship's biscuit 'was not fit for a pig' while Henry Molloy was cautioned for stating he had no clothing 'but defied me to alter it.' The log had recorded sickness amongst crewmembers as well as regular pumping.[61]

Shipmasters could directly punish recalcitrant crewmembers when at sea or remotely from a court/watch-house. The *Aladdin*'s master did this to groups of deserters as an 'example to other men on board.'[62] Many shipmasters tolerated small instances of misconduct. Trading brig *Betah*'s master recorded seven crewmembers were allowed ashore for a bath but three didn't return until 7 am the following morning.[63] Logbooks suggest collective desertion, absences and (less so) work refusals were routine even on shorter voyages. Undertaking trading voyages around the east-coast of Australia and New Zealand (December 1861 and October 1862), the schooner *Jane Lockhart* experienced two group desertions and a collective absence in Sydney. None led to court proceedings, simply hiring replacement seamen.[64] Others probably didn't even record minor infractions they chose to ignore.

Informal action by merchant seamen and whalers was endemic—well beyond the litany of court cases. Patterns of collective action described were global, matching Cooper-Busch's extensive examination of American whaleship logbooks and also evident in US whaleship logs ending up in colonial ports like Hobart.[65] During the August 1851 to April 1854 voyage of the New Bedford whaler *Menkar*, seven whalers absconded in a boat off the Peruvian coast on 13 January 1852 (apprehended and punished). On reaching Hawaii 'some of the crew refused duty and were put in irons.' Six dissidents were discharged on the 30th and three replacements shipped.[66] This and another voyage log (9 August 1854 to 31 January 1856) documented whaling hazards, including sickness and losing a whaleboat crew when a crane broke, tossing them into the sea.

The growth of pearling from the 1860s witnessed collective action by culturally diverse crews over pay, safety and conditions on vessels sailing out of North Australian ports.[67] While few records survive, collective action was similar to other maritime workers, including 'sharp' practices like a group of seven Pacific Islanders hired as divers but denied payment.[68] Work was extremely dangerous (decompression sickness) and violent storms destroyed vessels, even entire fleets—one in 1899 killing 400.

Multi-ship Actions, Port Organisation and Unions

Shipboard actions drew on wider understandings, customs and labour market shifts. As in Europe and North America, informal networking occasionally transitioned into multi-vessel and port-wide actions. Colonial newspapers began reporting port-wide actions in the 1830s and evidence is also found in court records. Port organisation typically entailed wage demands but sometimes protested iniquities in maritime laws or their administration. In August 1857, 132 Hobart-based seamen petitioned for the dismissal of the port's shipping master (George Hawthorne), arguing his tyrannical behaviour 'will sooner or later cause a general strike.'[69] Eighteen months later a multi-ship strike occurred, three ringleaders receiving 30 days' gaol for insubordination. Another port-wide strike occurred in February 1860.[70] It was the same in other ports. In September 1861 the *Argus* reported Sydney seamen on intercolonial steamers 'are all demanding an increase of wages.' Six years later Newcastle seamen struck for increased wages.[71] Port Adelaide seamen too combined over wages in 1870.[72] Others demanding better wages included Brisbane dredge and tug men in 1864.[73] In 1877 and 1878 Port Phillip dredge-men protested losing job security after coming under control of the Melbourne Harbour Trust, and struck over wages in 1880.[74]

Port-wide action was a springboard to unions, especially amongst coasting seamen, but transitioning proved difficult. Sydney seamen operated a benefit society in 1839–1845 but a second effort didn't occur until July 1854 when 500 seamen striking against wage cuts (£9 to £7 per month) formed the Colonial Merchant Seamen's Society.[75] Focusing on mutual insurance, it lasted less than a year.[76] In July 1872 a strike over wages and oppressive behaviour by shipowners and government port officers prompted the formation of a Sydney union quickly followed by Newcastle.[77] In Brisbane a Seamen's Committee protested 'landsmen' discharging ships in 1862 soon lapsed as did the Brisbane Seamens Union and Benefit Association established in June 1873.[78] In December 1878 Rockhampton seamen organised to support the ASN Co. strike and in January 1879 a Queensland Seamens Union was established in Brisbane, initially as a branch of the NSW Union.[79] In Melbourne the United Seamens Society formed at Trades Hall in March 1866 was followed by an equally short-lived Committee of Seamen that made wage claims in October 1867—seamen accepting lower rates being assaulted.[80] In September 1872 a Seamens Union was established, which like Sydney proved permanent.[81] A Hobart Merchant, Coastal and River Seamen's Committee established in October 1872 amidst a wages strike didn't survive.[82] Hobart's seamen complained of job insecurity and wage cuts in 1879 but it was another decade before a union was formed.[83] Port Adelaide seamen made short-lived attempts to unionise and strike for increased wages in 1870 and 1872 but were successful five years later.[84] All the bodies just mentioned represented coasting and intercolonial seamen although overseas trade seamen did attempt organisation. Port Adelaide seamen sailing to Britain struck against a wage cut in April 1879 and for a wage increase nine months later.[85]

Health, Safety and Mutual Insurance

Like Britain, OHS was a mobilising point for colonial seamen. Engaged on fixed-term contracts (time-based for coasting seamen and voyage-based for intercolonial/international seamen), seafaring was extremely hazardous with a high incidence of injury (falls, drowning and hit by objects), disease/illness and premature infirmity/mortality. Colonial newspapers alone reported hundreds of fatalities.[86] Winter storms took a toll, especially amongst overloaded/unseaworthy vessels, as did tropical cyclones in the continents' northern waters. In July 1866 amidst a series of losses/disappearances, ASN Company seamen met to establish a widow and children's fund for those lost on the *Cawarra* but opposition from a captain fractured the venture.[87] Seamen's unions, like Brisbane, pursued mutual insurance and shipwreck funds to aid members and their families.[88] They also organised community appeals like a Sydney TLC-assisted public meeting following the loss of the *Yarra Yarra* in 1877.[89] Union formation in Sydney, Melbourne, Port Adelaide and Brisbane in the early 1870s coincided with Plimsoll's maritime safety campaign in Britain and like miners they pursued legal enactment to improve OHS. Reinforcing unseaworthiness protests from individual crews like the *Anglesey*, the Victorian Seamens Union petitioned government, demanding representation on Marine Boards (that investigated maritime incidents) in 1874 and pressed for more life-saving equipment on vessels in 1876.[90] The union also commended Plimsoll for his efforts.[91]

Wages, Jobs and Racism—The 1878 Seamen's Strike

In November 1878 the Australian Steam Navigation Company (ASN Co) began replacing all colonial crews with Chinese seamen at lower wages and conditions, sparking a strike in Queensland, NSW and Victoria. The company had increased Chinese crews prior to this, accommodating them in the old *Wonga Wonga* – points raised by Francis Dixon during a TLC-sponsored anti-Chinese immigration meeting in July 1878.[92] The meeting was part of a rising tide of anti-Chinese protests from the early 1870s involving wide sections of the community. A TLC-organised petition garnered 15,000 signatures by November. Fears were expressed the company's move, along with those in building and cabinetmaking, would encourage other employers to follow suit.[93] The ASN Company paid Chinese seamen £2.15 to £3 per month less than half European seamen, firemen and trimmer's rates (£6 to £8). Further, contracts bound Chinese seamen for three years compared to around three to six months for European seamen. Thousands of coalminers, coal-trimmers and wharf-labourers (from Melbourne to Rockhampton) took action supporting the strike. Numerous unions from other industries provided financial and logistical support.[94]

As at Clunes in 1873 (Chapter 5), from the outset the Chinese knew they were acting as union-busters and would face a hostile response, with 50 in Cooktown demanding a £5 advance before they would proceed to Sydney.[95] However, they weren't the only targets of hostility. In Sydney, wharf-labourers who scabbed were hooted by a crowd, which was itself attacked and many beaten by over 60 police, some mounted. Strike-breaking European deckhands on the largely Chinese-crewed *Gunga* were jeered and hooted, several being struck, by a dockyard-crowd in Newcastle. Similarly, several Brisbane wharf-labourers were charged for assaulting Peter Brennan and James Dwyer and labelling them 'black-legs.'[96] European seamen accepting lower wages had been attacked by union members prior to the strike, the Melbourne union defending nine involved in one assault in October 1878.[97] In early January 1879 the strike terminated with the company agreeing to substitute its Chinese crews with colonial seamen over two years. The strike was the first major intercolonial confrontation between capital and labour—earlier miners' strikes were building towards this—mobilising numerous workers, entailing strong organisational coordination and ramping up anti-Chinese immigration politics.

Most recent discourse on the strike is preoccupied with its racist overtones largely ignoring capital's strategy of introducing hyper-exploitable labour to undermine organised labour—still evident today. The Sydney Chamber of Commerce supported the company, condemned the Seamen's actions as illegal and congratulated ASN marine engineers for not supporting the strike.[98] Chamber members also resolved to exclude unionists from their workplaces.[99] It didn't proceed but indicated capital's asserted right to brook no union 'interference' when using cheaper labour characterised the titanic 1890s strikes. The NSW Political Reform Union used the strike to promote their anti-Chinese agenda, holding a public meeting in Hyde Park attended by 10,000 mainly working-class men—aided by the Saturday half-holiday.[100] With important exceptions like Griffith's, the role of bourgeois organisations building White Australia has been underplayed.[101]

The strike received widespread moral and financial community support, even in country towns like Morpeth where large quantities of wool, hay and other produce piled up, reinforcing the union's tactics.[102] Donations came from far and wide, from small bodies as well as ordinary citizens. Echuca Eight Hours Association subscriptions exceeded £21 by mid-December while the tiny Newcastle branch of the Boiler-makers Society donated £10, probably a quarter of its funds.[103] Craft unions provided substantial financial support. The Sydney Progressive Carpenters donated £50 and established a membership fund.[104] Coalminers' lodges also established subscriptions—a shilling per member per week from the AA Company's Borehole mine.[105] Audited accounts published by the NSW Seamens Union in mid-February 1879 listed hundreds of donations from unions, meetings and individuals totalling £3,303.10.15.[106] This was substantial but still well shy of the £30,000 the colonies donated to the London Dockers strike a decade later. This parallel should be recalled when evaluating the strike's racist element.

Both donations indicated the community solidarity unions were building and anti-immigration sentiments.

Another overlooked factor was that the ASN Company had 'form,' repeatedly challenging other unions prior to the incident. This included disputes with the Sydney Shipwrights—the most recent an attempted wage cut in July 1878. This helps explain why the shipwrights donated £100 and banned repairing ASN ships during the strike, as did Sydney Boilermakers—paying £40 compensation to members affected by the ban.[107] The ASN Company's use of cheaper Chinese crews following a well-trodden path globally—notable examples including employing sub-continent 'Lascar' crews in the British merchant marine—in what was already a low-paid, precarious and hazardous vocation.[108] Contemporary arguments unions should have embraced Chinese seamen and bargained up their wages ignore both the regulatory framework and laws of supply and demand. Nor is there evidence Chinese crews demanded the 'going rates' as immigrant workers had done elsewhere like indentured German stonemasons working on Victorian railway construction 20 years earlier (Chapter 6). Some Chinese crews did strike over excessive tasks, to retain their jobs or recover their wages/return passage after the strike.[109] Using Chinese workers as strike-breakers wasn't exceptional. Nor was it new for the ASN Co. In May 1877 Chinese were used to break a strike over wage cuts by Cooktown wharf-labourers discharging the ASN vessel *Leichhardt*.[110]

Importantly, it is worth recalling what happened subsequently. Over the next 50 years mobilisation by maritime labour—particularly in Europe, North America and Australasia—secured international codes, laws and collective bargaining that significantly improved employment conditions. This relied on nation-state registration of vessels. Over the past 60 years this regime has been progressively dismantled by shipping companies registering vessels in low/no-standard countries in Africa and the Caribbean (so-called flags of convenience), global crewing companies (temporary employment agencies) and crews deliberately drawn from poor countries with weak or non-existent unions and engaged under abysmal wages and conditions.[111] The issue here is not workforce diversity—seafaring has long been diverse—but capital strategies returning maritime working conditions to an earlier era.

Organisation Amongst Ship-Officers, Pilots, Marine Engineers and Stewards

Government employed marine pilots occasionally took collective action but didn't form unions until after 1880. In 1856 Tamar River pilots petitioned for increased wages. In June 1873 their Newcastle counterparts warned the Harbour Master port congestion was making it unsafe.[112] Informal organisation also predominated amongst cooks and stewards.

In 1876 the *Australia*'s stewards and stewardesses sought unsuccessfully to stop breakages being deducted from their wages.[113] In 1878 the
NSW Stewards and Cooks Mutual Association was established offering
friendly benefits.[114] Marine officers also attempted organisation, an association operating in Melbourne in 1873.[115] As with cooks and stewards,
more unions followed in the 1880s.

Like ship-officers and engine-drivers, safety regulation prompted
organisation and professionalisation amongst marine engineers, a historically pivotal link largely overlooked by contemporary scholarship
on professions. In October 1877 newspaper correspondence on safety/
competence and certification led to the formation of a Marine Engineers
Association in Port Adelaide.[116] Sydney marine engineers formed an association in 1873. ASN Company engineers refused to support the seamen's strike, despite pleas from the Iron Trades Eight Hours Committee,
only offering to mediate. Its stance earned no kudos and may explain
a second association formed in 1880 which sent delegates to form a
New Zealand branch and corresponded with bodies in other colonies.[117]
Marine engineer associations practiced unilateral regulation, the Sydney
body responding to wage cuts by banning members from Clarence and
Richmond River steamers and boycotting the steamer *Llewellyn* until
a full complement of engineers was aboard.[118] It also lobbied the shipping master on maritime regulations. Its Port Adelaide counterpart promoted mutual-improvement and technical knowledge through expert
lectures.[119] In December 1880 delegates from the Adelaide, Sydney and
Melbourne formed an intercolonial organisation with branches in Brisbane and other capitals added over the next decade.[120]

Organisation on the Docks/Wharves

Seamen were forming associations by the 17th century but dockworkers weren't far behind. To escape exploitation heightened by middle-
men (called undertakers), London coal-heavers formed a body offering
friendly benefits and a wage agreement in the early 18th century, only to
be crushed along with other unions.[121] Watermen had organised friendly
societies long before seamen (14th century) and colonial bodies were
operating by the 1840s. This said organisation amongst colonial dock
and associated workers was largely informal until the 1870s. In 1851
Hobart customs boatmen and weighers petitioned for a wage increase.[122]
In 1879 dockworkers at the inland port of Moama/Echuca secured
unpaid wages after striking and burning their employer in effigy.[123] In
1880 Fremantle boatmen protested the new *Passenger Act*.[124] Wharf-
labourers/lumpers and stevedore's labourers took port-wide action or
formed unions in Sydney (1872, 1873, 1878, 1879), Newcastle (1878),
Rockhampton (1865, 1878), Brisbane (1869, 1876, 1878), Cooktown
(1877, 1878), Port Adelaide (1858, 1865, 1872), Wallaroo (1865), Port

Pirie (1876), Port Augusta (1879), Hobart (1855), Melbourne (1857, 1872, 1874, 1876, 1878) and Williamstown (1861, 1870). Most unions rapidly collapsed but Sydney and Port Adelaide were notable exceptions. In Port Adelaide a short-lived attempt in 1865 was succeeded in 1872 by an enduring body, the Port Adelaide Working Mens Association.[125]

Wages and efforts to stabilise employment were important impetuses for unionisation, and some at least practiced unilateral regulation. In September 1873 the Sydney Labouring Mens Association asked the Sydney Shipwrights to acknowledge that, while moving vessel within docks was shipwrights' work, moving vessels from a wharf or anchorage to the slip/dock should be done by dockworkers, who earned tides-pay for this task.[126] This demarcation was accepted. The Port Adelaide Working Mens Association sought legal advice on the enforceability of its rules from William Henry Bundey who told them he saw no way rules governing work and sanctioning members who didn't comply with them could be legalised. Addressing the union's 1876 annual dinner, Bundey elaborated on rules deemed illegal actions including restricting an individual's right to labour and agreements amongst members as to when they would and wouldn't work. He listed other unlawful actions like those directed against third parties or secondary boycotts (shades of the iniquitous *Trade Practices Act* introduced in the 1970s), picketing and harassment and pointed to the penal provisions of the colony's *Master and Servant Act*. Bundey urged a colonial version of the UK *Trade Unions Act* 1871 to at least protect union funds.[127] Bundey's advice probably explains why the union's minute-book—a rare survivor for unskilled unions—only records trustees' financial dealings.[128] The association joined a multi-union deputation to the Attorney General in July 1876 which secured a *Trade Union Act*.[129]

The Port Adelaide body obtained an annual holiday to celebrate its anniversary and challenged the introduction of workers from Melbourne in 1872.[130] It had some success regulating wages but experienced ongoing challenges. In February 1879 labourers boycotted James Paterson after he engaged 'non-society' men. Paterson hired more non-unionists and the union, fearing a major confrontation, could do little although his actions were proscribed by its rules.[131] In December the Port Adelaide Bench fined lumper Frederick Miller 20 shillings for striking George Gifford. Gifford complained he was continually intimidated 'for not joining the others in raising the price of labour.'[132] Feverish bouts of work entailing long-hours coinciding with ship arrivals, interspersed with longer periods of unemployment, also caused tension. In May 1878 Association president Henry Tompkins was fined £5 for assaulting Edwin Dalby, master of the ketch *Portonian*, after telling Dalby 'you are making one man do three men's work.'[133] The Sydney Labouring Mens Association sought to regularise hours and work, campaigning for eight-hours. The resulting strike by 800 wharf-labourers in September 1875 proved a litmus test, encountering united resistance from merchants, lightermen and stevedores. Despite substantial craft union donations, they lost. Even offers to return under existing terms were rejected by merchants determined to destroy the union. Union activists were blacklisted, at least one (John Scott unemployed ten weeks) committing suicide, and the union collapsed.[134] Efforts were also made to destroy the Port Adelaide union via a non-union company in 1878 (shades of the Patrick's dispute 120 years later) but it survived.[135]

These incidents reflected difficulties organising an industry marked by irregular work and readily-replaceable labour. Mitigating the consequences of hazardous work was another mobilising point with the Port Adelaide, Port Pirie and other bodies establishing funeral and accident/illness funds.[136] Close interconnections between precarious work, exploitation and OHS were subsequently documented by royal commissions/investigations in the UK and Australia, culminating in permanency campaigns—succeeding in Australia in 1960s but undermined by the 1998 Patrick's dispute.[137] The 1878 seamen's strike sparked reorganisation by wharf-labourers in Sydney and Melbourne, and growing political alliances with seamen, including electing candidates sympathetic to developing the local maritime industry. In Newcastle seamen and wharf-labourers jointly supported the 1880 Hunter Valley coalminers strike (and arbitrated solution), and along with coal-trimmers actively engaged in elections.[138]

Coal-trimmers responsible for loading and handling coal in port, in bunkers and on ships (including dealing with spontaneous combustion) began organising in the 1850s. Sydney-based shipboard firemen and coal-trimmers formed a benevolent society (dissolved September 1859) that regulated wages. In November 1854, 11 steamship *London* firemen and trimmers were charged with conspiracy and another with assaulting the boatswain (all eventually acquitted on technical grounds) in a case highlighting wage and crewing disparities with colonial vessels.[139] Two weeks later the *Sydney Morning Herald* complained newly shipped hands at reduced wages had been forced to exit via the rear of the Shipping Office and a seamen shipping as a coal-trimmer on the *City of Sydney* had been assaulted 'by a man who had previously worked on board that vessel.'[140]

For port-based trimmers, interconnections between wages, contractors and jobs were critical. Following a failed attempt in 1872, in March 1874 Newcastle trimmers demanded 12 shillings wages from J Russell—granted a coal-trimming monopoly for the port. They protested Russell's steam crane contract with the Minister for Works and formed an association later that year.[141] In March 1876 the union opposed moves by the Railway Commissioner to put all trimming through a government contractor and in April became enmeshed in a dispute with Russell over work on the vessel *JL Hall*.[142] Between November 1877 and January 1878 large meetings and ministerial deputations protested the truck-system and Russell's coal-trimming monopoly, alleging Russell blacklisted any trimmer not spending 1s per day at Chapman's public house.[143] During 1878 there were further disputes over railway contractors doing coal-trimming especially after a poorly trimmed coal-train derailed near Quirindi.[144] Trimmers supported the seamen's strike, banning work on the ASN vessel *Wentworth*—Chinese crewmembers undertook coal-trimming—and other vessels like the *Gunga*.[145]

Building Maritime Unionism and Wider Alliances

After three decades of intermittent attempts, Sydney, Melbourne and Newcastle seamen and Port Adelaide wharf-labourers unionised in the early 1870s. By decade-end unionisation had spread to other ports and was also underway amongst coal-trimmers, marine engineers and officers. Seamen's unions rapidly affiliated to union peak bodies and forged intercolonial links. The 1878 seamen's strike reinforced solidarity amongst different categories of maritime workers and worker organisation more generally.

Land Transport Workers

Carriers/carters began organising in the 1840s, joined from the 1860s by cabdrivers, railway workers and, later, omnibus-drivers. Union membership more than quadrupled for all subgroups between 1861–1870 and 1871–1880 but in absolute terms railway workers now dominated (Table 3.2). Land transport workers were over four times more likely to take NSCA than strike. This disparity carries over to worker and establishment numbers involved. Known outcomes for strikes were poor. The number of multi-establishment/regional actions increased over time. There were 17 colony-wide NSCA (overwhelmingly rail-workers) but no colony-wide strikes. Both road and rail-workers unions used petitions and deputations. But road workers were more likely to publish letters/public notices and hold mass meetings—the latter mainly over remuneration including carters setting rates unilaterally and cabdriver protests against government-imposed fares. Overwhelmingly government employees, rail-workers were less likely to hold demonstrations let alone strike (Table 3.2). Unlike maritime workers, court actions were rare. Wages were the dominant issue for land transport workers (including pensions for rail-workers) followed by working conditions/work methods, jobs, hours and management behaviour.

Road Transport Workers

Informal Workplace Organisation

Workplace organisation was rare for road workers given the nature of their work. Carters/draymen employed on railway construction

Table 3.2 Worker Organisation in Land Transport 1831–1880

Industry	1831–1840	1841–1850	1851–1860	1861–1870	1871–1880	Total 1851–1880
Entire Industry						
Organisations		9	18	55	101	166*
Raw involvement		2	210	2552	18112	20874
Adjusted involvement*		27	990	5464	24992	31446
Strikes						
Won				1		1
Drawn						0
Lost	1			2	2	4
Unknown	3		1		12	13
Total	4		1	3	14	18
Est. total involvement*	?	?		60	1859	1919
Number of establishments						
One	1			1	4	5
Multi				1		1
Regional/town	3		1	1	10	12
Non-strike collective action						
Won	2		1		12	13
Drawn						
Lost	1			3	8	11
Unknown			5	14	34	53
Total	3		6	17	54	77
Number of establishments						
One	1		5		10	15
Multi			1	2	8	11
Regional/town	2		4	8	22	34
Colonial			1	2	14	17
Issues in collective action (Strikes/NSCA)						
Wages	4/3		/5	3/14	11/29	14/48
Hours				1/	/12	1/12
Working conditions	1			1/2	1/13	2/15
Health & safety					/4	/4

Industry	1831–1840	1841–1850	1851–1860	1861–1870	1871–1880	Total 1851–1880
Management behaviour				1/	/10	1/10
Jobs/employment				/4	2/10	2/14
Work methods					/2	/2
Unionism					/4	/4
Subcontracting						
Legislation		1	1/1	1/6	4/7	6/14
Pensions					/2	/2
Breakdown of organisation and actions of two largest occupational subgroups						
Road transport workers						
Organisation numbers	25	10	21	38	73	131+
Est. involvement*	53	22	929	1116	4695	6740
Strikes	1	5	1	2	13	16
NSCA	12	3	8	12	30	50
Absconding	12					
Petitions		3	6	7	12	25
Deputations				6	16	24
Mass meetings		1	8	15	29	52
Marches					3	3
Letters/public notices		1	3	7	4	14
Bans					2	2
Court actions						
Won						
Lost			3 (100%)	1 (100%)	2 (100%)	6
Railway workers						
Organisation numbers			1	18	24	37+
Est. involvement*				4074	20320	24394
Strikes				2	1	3
NSCA				5	15	20
Absconding						
Petitions				1	4	5
Deputations				4	6	10
Mass meetings				3	13	16
Marches					1	1
Letters/public notices				1	2	3
Bans					1	1
Court actions nil						

* Adjusted by multiplying number of zero-reporting organisations/years by industry median membership for each industry in that decade. +For totals, organisation spanning multiple decades only counted once.

projects sometimes joined action by navvies, as occurred at Sunbury Victoria in June/July 1861 resisting a contractor push for monthly not fortnightly pay.[146]

Multi-Workplace and Formal Organisation

Carters/carriers and cabdrivers organised sporadically during the 1840s. As population and road transport networks grew, organisation increased and spread beyond colonial capitals. Then—as now—many road workers were self-employed (including carters/carriers, cabdrivers, bread and milk-carters) although employee numbers grew especially in major towns. Self-employed workers dominated early organisations, some included both self-employed and employees, with predominantly employee bodies forming in the 1870s like the Hindmarsh Teamsters Union.[147] Self-employed carters tried to set rates or influence government regulation. Cabdriver's fares were set by government—a focus for agitation. Even where employees predominated, unions targeted regulation affecting jobs and working conditions like road laws and conditions.

In NSW there is evidence of organisation (first known date) by carriers/carters/draymen in Sydney (1852, 1854, 1859, 1864, 1866, 1870, 1871, 1873, 1874, 1875, 1876, 1878, 1880), Goulburn (1853, 1873, 1875), Singleton/Armidale (1866), Moama (1869), Kelso/Bathurst (1873), Mudgee (1873), Wallerawang (1873), Queanbeyan (1873), Tamworth (1873), Haydonton/Murrurundi (1875), Muswellbrook (1876), Newcastle (1878), Hay (1879, 1880), Balranald (1880), Deniliquin (1880) and Young (1880). For Queensland, organisations occurred in Brisbane (1864, 1872, 1880), Copperfield (1868, 1872), Maryborough (1868, 1872, 1876), Mount Perry (1872), Rockhampton (1878), Townsville (1880), Ipswich (1880) and Cooktown (1880). In South Australia organisations were formed in Port Adelaide (1851,1873), Adelaide (1851, 1865, 1866, 1868, 1878 and 1879), Port Wakefield (1852), Saltia (1861), Redruth (1868), Hindmarsh (1868, 1878), Clarendon (1868), Mount Gambier (1873), Kapunda (1876), Woodville (1877), Brighton and Glenelg (1878). In Tasmania, organisation occurred in Hobart (1851, 1854) and Launceston (1861). In Victoria, organisation occurred in Melbourne (1851, 1852, 1857, 1861, 1865, 1866, 1870, 1874, 1876, 1877, 1878), Geelong (1855, 1860, 1862), Ballarat (1861, 1877, 1879), Bendigo (1866, 1873), Hotham/North Melbourne (1870), Beechworth (1871), Linton (1873), Echuca (1873) and Gippsland (1878). A teamsters' association set rates at the Yam Creek gold-diggings in the Northern Territory in 1878—its first known union.[148] Cab, carriage and omnibus-drivers organised in Sydney (1871, 1872, 1873, 1874, 1875, 1878), Brisbane (1865, 1869, 1875, 1876 & 1879), Adelaide (1870, 1872, 1878), Hobart (1853, 1856, 1861, 1880), Launceston (1875), Melbourne (1858, 1859,

1866, 1867, 1868, 1869, 1873, 1879), Richmond, Hawthorn and Kew (1861), Sandhurst/Bendigo (1865) and Brunswick (1866).

In NSW, organisation of carters/carriers occurred in towns dotted along major road systems (then and now) south-west, west and north-west of Sydney and from Newcastle to New England, including the extending termini of railway lines from ports. A similar pattern is evident in Victoria with Geelong and Melbourne as road hubs, as was Port Adelaide/ Adelaide in South Australia and Brisbane, Maryborough and Rockhampton in Queensland. Organisation also occurred in ports servicing mining districts like Port Augusta and Townsville. Road networks were critical to the growing economy, notwithstanding railways and river/coastal shipping. Carriers/draymen serving country districts experienced long absences from family. Work was arduous and hazardous. In 1863 the *Singleton Times* described busy road to the Liverpool Plains (now New England Highway) and a fatality at Muswellbrook:

> The roads are tolerably sound, but in some places a succession of holes requiring attention, is a terrible strain upon the pole bullocks and shaft horses. . . . A carrier named Day, whose wife and family resided in Maitland, was returning from up-country with a dray load of hides; having arrived here shortly after dusk . . . he, it appears, commenced to unharness his horses . . . and . . . the dray by some means tilted up, and the tail fell on deceased between the neck and shoulders.[149]

Mutual Insurance

The Port Adelaide Licensed Carters Association and Sydney Licensed Drivers Mutual Benefit Association, amongst others, provided friendly benefits like funeral funds.[150] Combining mutual insurance with regulating cartage rates was central to the Great Northern Carriers Association's establishment.[151] Some cabdrivers' unions like the Hobart Cabmens Protective Union and Melbourne and Suburban Cabmens Protective Union (1879–1890) operated accident and funeral funds.[152] Few consolidated themselves sufficiently to sustain the activity but the objective was clear and manifested in more temporary measures. In April 1870 Melbourne carriers met to memorialise a colleague (Jewell) killed when gunpowder exploded on his dray and to assist his partner (Cruikshank) who was injured and lost his horses.[153]

Government, Business Costs and Working Conditions

Regulations affecting carters and draymen aroused antagonism. In March 1854 over 100 Sydney licensed-carters and draymen formed a committee and petitioned against a *Police Act* clause prohibiting draymen riding their drays even when holding the reins, claiming this adversely affected public safety. In October the committee organised further protests over 'obnoxious' licensing clauses in the *Carters and Draymen's Regulation Bill*.[154] In January 1855 Geelong licensed draymen also agitated against a ride-on ban and later (October) set cartage rates—suggesting ongoing informal organisation.[155] Double-standards in devising regulations drew ire. In January 1855 a *Sydney Morning Herald* letter complained the City Commissioners consulted the Sydney Chamber of Commerce over proposed changes in Hackney Carriage rates but extended no similar courtesy to draymen on cartage rates—considering employers' views but not workmen.[156] Precisely—and has this changed?

Licensing gaps also sparked protests. In October 1859 a Glebe 'licensed drayman' denounced a carters' meeting and petition against the *Carters Act* stating the movement involved multi-dray owners with special contracts to merchants who 'pay for no license whatever; they dare not ply for hire as licensed men do; if they could . . . two hundred odd poorer licensed men would stand no chance of a livelihood for themselves and families.'[157] In 1861 Launceston licensed draymen too protested merchants running unlicensed drays.[158] For licensed draymen regulating their practices warranted reciprocal market controls bestowing work and income benefits. Carters removing wood and stone from public lands felt burdened by high license fees or multiple-license requirements. In 1866 Bendigo wood carters and timber splitters (1866) demanded lower fees. Five years later Beechworth carters argued removing multiple licenses would 'commend itself to the whole of the labouring classes.'[159] Tensions between licensed and unlicensed carters/draymen, between self-employed operators, master-carriers and wage-earners emerged in other colonies, resulting in separate organisations. Local government bye-laws and decisions affecting work practices and jobs repeatedly sparked protests. In 1862 Geelong licensed-carters established a legal fighting fund to challenge a council bye-law.[160] In 1866 Sydney Licensed Draymen protested moves limiting access to the railway terminal, as did Brisbane draymen in 1880 when railway commissioners favoured the Railway Carrying Company.[161] In 1876 Sydney unlicensed van and draymen protested police harassment over government bye-laws that hindered carrying out tasks.[162] Self-employed carriers/carters also took action against others affecting their costs. In 1853 Goulburn District carriers banned carrying iron to protest high charges by blacksmiths.[163] In 1877 Ballarat wood carters demanded the Brown Coal Company halve the 'exorbitant' 6d per ton it charged for shunting wood along its half-mile siding, lobbying government when the company refused.[164]

Another work and remuneration-related impetus for organisation were efforts to rectify/improve roads, bridges and reserves to rest/park drays and feed animals.[165] In 1869 the Riverine Carriers Association petitioned for regulation preventing overzealous impounding of horses/bullocks, create road-side reserves sufficient to feed animals during dry-periods, and license carriers (annual fee of not more than £10) to protect the trade and fund these measures.[166] From the 1860s colonial governments introduced laws on vehicle weight and tyre width to protect/fund road maintenance. As still pertains, transport economics, vehicle dimensions and cartage rates were interconnected as these changes affected carter livelihoods. In July 1868 South Australian tyre-width legislation sparked protests by carters in Adelaide, Hindmarsh, Redruth/Kooringa and Clarendon, including petitions and parliamentary deputations. Speaking at Hindmarsh JW Burdon stated: 'Port-road carters had three-inch tires, and if they got one load a day they could earn 5s . . . but under the Act they would literally starve.'[167] M. Quinn (Redruth meeting) argued the Bill would cause 'great destitution and misery to the labouring classes' because few teamsters could afford to fit new wheels to drays.[168] Clarendon carters sought farmer support to oppose the law.[169] Adelaide carters tried to negotiate higher cartage rates with builders.[170] Wheel tax protests extended to other colonies. In 1880 timber trade bullock-drivers and carriers met in Ipswich, Laidley and Glamorgan Vale petitioning Queensland parliament against a wheel tax (based on width) by the Divisional Road Board.[171] Other regulatory charges sparked protests like an increased Council tariff on Adelaide sand-carters in 1879.[172]

Cab- and carriage-drivers too were licensed under local government bye-laws which on occasion sparked protests. In November 1858 Melbourne cabdrivers tried to change municipal bye-laws on cabstands with further protests on Hackney-Cab regulations in May 1859 and September 1868.[173] Regulatory concerns prompted formal organisation, though most like the Melbourne Cabmens Mutual Protection Society (1869) were short-lived. In 1873 the Victorian Cabmens Protective Union formed to oppose regulations reducing maximum passenger numbers from six to five and constables harassing cabdrivers, campaigning for two years without success. In 1876 Melbourne carriage-drivers struck over paying a £5 licence fee (cabdrivers only paid £3). The Mayor proved unresponsive.[174] Hobart cabdrivers protested bye-laws in 1853, 1856 and 1861 (included fares) and Launceston cab and carriage-drivers struck in 1875 when police banned them from leaving their vehicles to pick up steamer passengers.[175] Brisbane cabdrivers petitioned poor quality roads near the Union Hotel in 1869.[176] In October 1879 over 600 Sydney cabdrivers struck against bye-laws requiring passengers be provided with a card containing the cab's number, owner/driver's name and scale of charges.[177]

Omnibus-drivers also fell foul of council regulations. In December 1875 Brisbane omnibus and cabdrivers proposed amending bye-laws (including leaving vehicles), several accepted by Council, although there was another dispute in October 1876.[178] In May 1878, 32 Adelaide omnibus-drivers operating on the Kensington/Norwood route stopped running their buses to protest closure of their Grenfell St stand.

Two local councillors (Raphael and Richardson) took it on themselves to intimidate the drivers, demanding their names and numbers.[179] In December Melbourne Omnibus Company drivers protested aspersions on their character by legal counsel for the company when prosecuting a driver stealing fares.[180]

Cartage Rates, Cab-Fares and Wages

Rate-setting appealed to self-employed carters/carriers to proscribe rate-cutting competition and enhancing remuneration. In 1851 Melbourne water carriers increased their charges. The following year licensed-carters announced rates to offset increased hay, oats and bran costs, establishing the Licensed Carters Association of Victoria.[181] In July 1860 goldfields' carters meeting in Geelong bound themselves to adhere to new rates for each mining town including Ballarat, Creswick, Ararat and Back Creek.[182] The rates-schedule was printed in English and German. When John Daley breached the rate he was assaulted by an 'infuriated mob.'[183] William Kempmaer and Samuel Anniel were convicted and gaoled while Daley secured £10 plus damages to his wagon. The association distanced itself from the assault and sabotage, stating the men weren't members. Nonetheless, the incident coincided with 25 carters joining. The association offered Geelong merchants a discounted Ballarat rate in return for their support.[184] 'Fair play' gave the *Geelong Advertiser* a detailed account of carters' working costs and returns asked how 'could we blame the carters when their earnings had been cut down so low, for endeavouring, by forming a society, to obtain wages sufficient to keep their families free from debt?'[185] The *Argus* reinforced this, reporting that notwithstanding brisk business, teamsters were turning out their horses rather than accepting rates below those 'fixed by the Carters' Association.'[186] Eight months later an attempt to raise cartage rates in Ballarat failed.[187]

In February 1865 Adelaide carters established an association, amidst complaints rates driven down by builders were insufficient keep their families. One carter (Daniels) claimed they worked long-hours for below labouring-wages and hadn't come to strike but 'get fair wages for a good day's work.'[188] The association also tried to improve Glen Osmond mines' cartage rates, surviving over a year suggesting some success.[189] Like similar rate-setting bodies its monthly meetings were kept 'private.' Setting cartage rates became common by the 1870s.[190] Demonstrating the porous divide between self-employed and employees, an 1874 Hawthorn meeting resolved delegates representing Melbourne and suburbs should form 'a union to raise rates of cartage and wages.'[191] Milk and bread carters, as much retailers as transport workers, also organised to set prices, like a Melbourne dairymen's combination in 1866.[192]

The foregoing illustrates attempts at unilateral regulation binding members to adhere rates. There is evidence informal understandings existed elsewhere, warranting further research. On 10 August 1861 Melbourne coal-carters Richard Keenan and John Negelin were convicted of assaulting Spaniard Joseph Mendola for carting coal for Mr Lawrence for 1s 3d per ton rather than 1s 6d.[193] Formal action in one region spread to others, facilitated by transport workers' mobility. In mid-1873 Echuca wood carters set minimum rate of nine shillings per load—their Bendigo counterparts having already established an association—and those in Linton followed suit.[194] Six months earlier wood carters supplying mine furnaces at Copperfield Queensland sought pay increases to compensate for drought-associated difficulties.[195] Notwithstanding networking, available evidence suggests few agreements lasted any length of time, being hard to enforce even with formal organisation.

Where licensed-carters' rates were regulated, those deemed too low sparked protests, as in Tasmania in 1854.[196] Nonetheless, carters saw benefits in regulation. In 1864 Brisbane draymen and carters formed an association and successfully petitioned City Council for standardised charges under bye-law so they could be enforced.[197] In January 1873 Port Adelaide licensed-carters formed an association to fix cartage rates with a deputation proposing this to the Borough Council/Corporation.[198] In June 1874 they complained a corporation contractor (R Jones) was supplying ship ballast below association-rates. Further illustrating transport workers' unions deploying unilateral regulation Jones subsequently complained to the Corporation the association had fined him £5 for breaching their rates.[199] Addressing its 1876 anniversary dinner the Mayor said fears labouring men's combinations would have evil effects had proved unfounded, congratulating the association for securing common cartage rates which agents accepted.[200] Ironically, the body causing most problems was the Corporation. In April 1876 the association fined J. Manning for undertaking below-rate work, banning other members from working with him until the fine was paid. The Corporation threatened legal action unless the fine was refunded. The Corporation's chief overseer estimated it had spent £946 extra for cartage since the association's formation. The association tried to placate matters, indicating it probably wouldn't interfere in Corporation or District Council work over the ensuing year.[201] Aware of the risk of conspiracy charges against its officers, the association endorsed a joint union deputation to the Attorney General in July 1876, calling for a colonial *Trades Union Act*.[202] More successful than most, the association survived into the 1890s, forging links with other port unions, joining eight-hour marches, affiliating to the Maritime Labour Council and supporting the 1890 maritime strike.[203]

Regional carriers/carters' impetus to organise strengthened as mines, large landholders and other users tried to depress cartage rates. Salta mine carters prescribed rates in 1861 and there were strikes over unsatisfactory rates/wages (often indistinguishable) like that by Mount Perry ore carriers in 1872.[204] Sheep-station agents tried to play off carters against each other, as did steamship company agents. Country town residents viewed larger capital-based transport operations as taking income out and returning little. In 1861 the *Pastoral Times* argued Deniliquin would benefit from a local carriers association setting rates and attracting carriers and their families to the district.[205] Similarly, the *Armidale Telegraph* applauded a carriers association for the Singleton-Armidale road alleging goods were left at Singleton railway station for upwards of two months awaiting a '*fast* horse-team.'[206] The *Riverine Grazier* argued low rates didn't benefit wool-producers because it reduced teamster numbers to move loads quickly after shearing/harvest.[207] Shades of recent supply chain debates, ex-carrier George Loughnan complained steamer agents routinely forced carriers to sign forms incorrectly stating goods were in good condition thereby having breakages deducted from their rates.[208]

It made sense for district carrier associations to encourage organisation/collaboration with neighbouring districts to formalise rates across larger parts of road transport corridors. Some established cooperative companies to conduct business under association terms and secure funds to protect members.[209] Unlike master carrier associations these bodies were labelled unions and their actions were consistent with this label, the *Wide Bay News* (1874) stating the local body was:

> a trades union, the various members contributing to the expenses at a rate fixed by the amount of loading to carry. . . . The forwarding agent . . . has only to signify to the Secretary of the association that he has goods to be forwarded, and the latter will provide a carrier as soon as one is procurable, at the rates of carriage fixed by the association. The association will meet quarterly . . . the rates of carriage will be discussed and fixed, all the members pledging themselves to abide by the decision.[210]

Restricting worker organisation to wage-earners was and remains misleading (see Uber drivers) based on a legal construction of work to advantage capital. The wage relationship was never the only means of subordinating workers. In justifying regulation, Carriers' associations claimed they would provide faster and more reliable service, paralleling work-quality reassurances by craft unions. Strikes and strike funds were increasingly integral to organisation. In 1873 the Kelso association raised a £950 (projected £2,000) war-chest strike-fund for mutual protection. Mudgee and Wallerawang carriers followed and coordinated rates on roads linking the towns.[211] In June, Goulburn District carriers set minimum rates and a month later the *Southern Argus* lamented a strike had goods piling up at Goulburn railway station.[212] Queanbeyan carriers also organised against un-remunerative rates but failed.[213] In July 1880, Hay Carriers Association members rejected agent's rates, pledging to adhere to union rates, with financial support for those affected. The association applauded a Deniliquin carriers strike and another pending in Balranald.[214] In December, Young carriers formed the Southern Carriers Association setting minimum rates (including return load discounts) with similar meetings mooted for Grenfell, Murrumburrah, Cootamundra, Junee and Wagga. The *Cootamundra Herald* endorsed these moves, arguing 'the Monopoly Company' benefited a few but harmed carters and communities they served.[215]

More closely governed by regulation, cabdrivers tried to set rates or influence council bye-laws. In 1861 Richmond, Hawthorn and Kew cabdrivers set rates and working rules, followed by Brunswick cabdrivers in 1865. East Melbourne cabdrivers tried to double fares in 1866.[216] Outside Melbourne, Bendigo cabdrivers protested changes to Borough bye-laws lowering fares and altering stand locations in 1865.[217] Amidst public complaints of over-charging and anger at numerous small fines for bye-law infringements the Victorian Cabmens Protection Society formed in 1867, petitioning for fare increases and limited licence numbers because 800 cabmen were competing for jobs.[218] It was the same elsewhere. In January 1874 Sydney cabdrivers struck with pickets driving several cabs from the railway station after Metropolitan Transit Commissioners rejected their proposed fare-schedule. Three hundred drivers marched on Attorney General/Premier Henry Parkes, who told them to petition. A carriage and cab proprietors and drivers' union was rapidly established but didn't last. Drivers renewed fare protests in December 1875, detailing fuel and other costs justifying their claims.[219] In Adelaide the United Cabmens Association (1874–1885) fought disputes over fares/bye-laws in 1874, 1875, 1879 and 1880.[220] Similarly, Brisbane cabdrivers took action over fares in 1865, 1875 (twice), 1877 and 1879, including attempts to set fare-schedules.[221]

Omnibus-drivers in major towns also began organising over wages. The Sydney Omnibus Company's establishment (merging smaller operations) resulted in drivers petitioning for a 20% wage increase to offset longer hours in August 1872. Rebuffed, they pledged not to work below the specified amount (42s).[222] Like cabdrivers, unionisation followed British developments, notably the formation of the London Omnibus Mens Benefit Association.[223] The 15-hour days bemoaned in London paralleled Sydney complaints.

Hours of Work

While not pivotal, several road bodies supported the eight-hour movement. It was a stated objective, along with rate-fixing, for the Hotham Timber Carters' Association (established 1870).[224] In February 1877 Melbourne brewers' draymen secured a Saturday half-holiday with support from publicans and the Licensed Victuallers Association.[225] Others like Ballarat bread carters requested half-holidays.[226]

Inter-Union Relations and Politics

In 1865 Melbourne draymen, carters and warehousemen connected to the shipping industry protested new tariffs impacting on jobs—it was a short-lived.[227] As union organisation consolidated anti-tariff stances became incompatible with an increasingly protectionist labour movement and transport jobs linked to local manufacturers. By the 1870s they were forging links with other unions, Sydney draymen and van-drivers supporting the 1878 Seamen's strike, banning moving goods from ASN Company wharves.[228] In 1880 the Carriers joined other unions in supporting TLC Secretary Roylance's Legislative Assembly candidature.[229] Cab-drivers followed the same path, the Victorian Cabmens Protective Union (1873–1874) affiliating to the Trades Hall Council as did its successor, the Melbourne and Suburban Cabmens Protective Union (1879–1890).

Railway Workers

Unlike Britain and the US, railway construction and operation was undertaken by colonial governments, bringing stability at one level but also exposure to government finances. In 1866 a Victorian budget crisis impacted most on those not covered by the *Civil Service Act*, including railway workers. Those in railway sheds/workshops and stations in Williamstown, Sandhurst and Melbourne led protests (including deputations) over unpaid wages soon joined by Ballarat, Geelong and Castlemaine, with further protests in 1867.[230] From the early 1860s there were attempted unions, all but one involving government railways. Unions representing locomotive engine-drivers, firemen and later cleaners were formed in Victoria in 1861 followed by NSW in 1873, the South Australian Locomotive Enginemen, Firemen and Cleaners Association in 1875, and possibly a Queensland body in 1879.[231] Along with mutual-improvement (via regular lectures), mutual insurance was a key function, the Victorian Engine Drivers and Firemens Association making substantial donations to Melbourne Hospital.[232] Other issues were pursued, the NSW body securing paid holidays in 1874, but anti-unionism amongst railway authorities meant collective action was largely informal.[233] In September 1877 a Victorian deputation unsuccessfully protested mechanics driving engines in workshops and 11 months later junior running shed workers protested new promotion and salary-gradations affecting drivers, firemen and cleaners.[234]

Station staff, porters, gangers and others also organised—sometimes in conjunction with engine-drivers, establishing British-style railway benefit societies. In NSW the Great Southern and Western Railway Workmens Sick Society was established around 1864/65 (extant in 1880). By 1876 a Traffic Department Sick and Accident Society was operating with over 300 members.[235] In Victoria Melbourne and Hobson's Bay Railway

Company employees formed a benefit society in 1860 (lasting over a decade) advertising for a medical practitioner.[236] Government rail-workers also tried to form benefit societies from 1861 including platelayers on the Williamstown-Mount Alexander line who made donations to Ballarat Hospital from 1866 until the late 1870s.[237] Another attempt at general organisation, the Victorian Railways Mutual Benefit Society, garnered 230 members in 1866, 409 in 1867 and 1,059 by 1880, establishing branches (Ballarat) and operating well beyond 1890.[238] The society made substantial donations/payments to Melbourne Hospital (President WB Fife was made a Life Governor in 1872) and hospitals in Castlemaine, Kyneton, Wangaratta, Geelong and Ballarat giving members access to medical treatment. Platelayers and others between Footscray and Riddell's Creek did the same.[239] In South Australia a North-Line Benefit Society was established in 1861 and by May 1870 had dispensed £447 relief to 67 members for sickness, five for work injuries (one fatal), and ten for funeral benefits including member's wives.[240] In Queensland the Southern and Western Railway Servants Friendly Society established in Toowoomba in 1869 included engine-drivers.[241] Along with friendly benefits (dispensing £104 in six months to July 1880) the society supported Toowoomba Hospital so members and families received free treatment (the enginemen's department made extra donations) but Brisbane Hospital refused to match this.[242] The Queensland society's rules were models for the North and Western Tasmanian Railways Society established in Launceston in 1877 with another Hobart-based body operating by 1879.[243]

The focus on mutual insurance reflected the hazardous work. As elsewhere, railways were dangerous, serious incidents including derailments regularly reported and insurers charging higher rates for engine-drivers.[244] The South Australian Association's 1876 anniversary meeting recorded losing two 'valued members' at a Peaks Crossing incident in February. In February 1878 the Great Southern NSW engine-drivers association held a quadrille to assist widows and orphans of those killed in a recent incident.[245] Mutual insurance was equally important to other railworkers. When Phillip King died near Toowoomba in September 1873 he was decently interred (navvies dug his grave gratis), and his widow and children received £15 from the benefit society along with £30 from fellow-workers and residents. Less fortunate was John Reid, crushed in a November 1880 shunting incident, the *Ballarat Courier* noting he was not a benefit society member.[246] A female gatekeeper at Colac killed by train in 1877 probably lacked access to benefits.[247] The Victorian enginedrivers association also took up safety issues and represented members following incidents.[248]

Benefit societies stuck closely to mutual insurance given their reliance on railway authorities' largesse.[249] A special ball was run in a railway shed to boost the Victorian society's finances in February 1872. However, in 1877 the Minister for Railways rebuffed requests to remedy misapprehension over the relationship between society benefits and government entitlements.[250] Collective action on wages and jobs remained largely informal and was often dealt with disdainfully. In February 1867 the Victorian Commissioner for Railways told platelayers their difficulties and their children's want of education were 'inseparable from the nature of their employment.'[251] When Melbourne No. 4 goods shed casual workers struck over unpaid overtime and 'despotic management' in 1870 they were told to desist or be dismissed.[252] There were further disputes over wages and unpaid waiting-time/long-hours by Williamstown labourers (1873), Melbourne goods shed workers (twice in 1877) and nightwatchmen (1878).[253] Similar actions occurred elsewhere. In 1872, 217 South Australian platelayers and packers petitioned for increased wages and Port Adelaide porters protested draymen moving luggage and passengers from the station in 1878.[254]

Some disputes involved craftsmen in railway workshops or became aligned to broader movements as when railway workers joined wide-ranging protests over pay cuts, delegates from all three NSW railway-networks joining a deputation to the Minister for Works in February 1871.[255] Alliances were also forged with the wider union movement. In April 1873 mechanics, permanent-way and others on the Great Northern Railway petitioned for an eight-hour day, with sympathetic MLAs and TLC officials like Dixon taking up their cause.[256] Three years later Queensland railway workers secured an eight-hour day.[257] Railway workshops bringing together large numbers of tradesmen and labourers became a hub of worker organisation. Management behaviour and work-rules sparked disputes. In April 1875 Southern and Western Queensland railway workers accused the traffic manager of capricious behaviour/unfair dismissal and favouritism in promotion, calling for a review board like British railway companies.[258] Two years later Sydney railway employees refused to sign new work-rules issued by Superintendent Mason.[259] In April 1878 Redfern railway workshop coal-trimmers successfully petitioned for eight-hours while their Victorian counterparts complained at the lack of work.[260]

In 1879 Victorian rail-workers formed a union, the Victorian Railways Employees Association, which rapidly enrolled 4,000 members.[261] Setting a model for later colonial railway unions, it pursued claims on sickness and holiday-provisions, superannuation/pensions and less arbitrary promotion arrangements—pushing for legislatively mandated conditions comparable to the civil service.[262] While securing gains, this irked the Commissioner for Railways who ordered workers to sever their connections with the association. He also excluded Engine-driver and Firemens Association members from promotion. These anti-union measures were castigated by Victorian MLA, AT Clark, pointing to the hypocrisy of departmental heads joining clubs 'whilst the 6s per day men were tyrannised . . . and their association was to be dissolved.'[263]

Conclusion

Like earlier times, in 1851–1880 seamen's organisation was overwhelmingly informal. Nonetheless, port-wide organisation increased as did attempts at unions, creating durable seamen's unions by the early 1870s. Informal collective action amongst wharf-labourers/dockworkers also slowly gave way to unions in the 1870s though some succumbed to employer counter-attacks. By this time, coal-trimmers, marine officers and engineers were also unionising. Self-employed and employed carriers had formed unions since the 1840s and over the next three decades organisation by carters/draymen, cabdrivers and later omnibus-drivers proliferated, even if many were short-lived. The growing railway network saw instances of informal organisation alongside societies focusing on mutual insurance but with the beginnings of more industrially active organisation. Though lacking craft controls, seamen and wharf-labourers exercised some power given the pivotal role of maritime transport for geographically large, remote and trade-dependent colonies, augmented by their capacity to mobilise numbers and secure support from other workers in the export chain, notably miners, other unions/peak bodies and the wider community exemplified by the 1878 seamen's strike. Large ports were a hub for maritime worker recruitment/organisation and inter-union collaboration. With notable exceptions like railway workshops this was not the case for road and rail transport. Organisation remained weak and fragmented amongst road workers while rail-workers confronted the full might of the state as their employer.

Notes

1. LC247-1-27 19 September 1859.
2. *Sydney Morning Herald* 26 June 1852.
3. LC247-1-20 Hobart 27 September 1852.
4. LC247-1-23 Hobart 3 February 1853.
5. LC247-1-24 Hobart 25 August 1854.
6. LC247-1-28 Hobart 31 December 1856, 30 June 1857; LC247-1-26 Hobart 12 July 1862.
7. LC247-1-27 Hobart 22 November 1858.
8. LC247-1-21 Hobart 30 March 1852.
9. *Tasmanian Colonist* 5 August 1852.
10. LC247-1-20 & LC247-1-21 Hobart 15, 28, 29 November 1851.
11. *Sydney Morning Herald* 28 May 1853.
12. *Shipping Gazette* 4 June 1853.
13. *Shipping Gazette* 4 June 1853.
14. *Tasmanian Colonist* 26 April 1852.
15. *Cornwall Chronicle* 6 October 1852.
16. *Sydney Morning Herald* 9 November 1852.
17. *Argus* 22 March 1853.
18. *Sydney Morning Herald* 16 June 1854.
19. *Age* 30 October 1876.
20. LC247-1-27 Hobart 8 June 1863; *Mercury* 25 June 1863.

21. *Empire* 1 December 1853; *Moreton Bay Courier* 10 December 1853.
22. *Adelaide Times* 5 October 1855.
23. *Courier* 21 September 1863.
24. *South Australian Advertiser* 4 March 1875; *Express and Telegraph* 18 March 1875.
25. LC247-1-27 Hobart 30 April 1854; *Hobart Town Advertiser* 1 May 1860.
26. LC247-1-24 Hobart 2 October 1854.
27. TAHO CSO24/259/7027 Petition to Governor 2 December 1854.
28. LC247-1-27 Hobart 22, 25 March 1861; *Hobart Town Advertiser* 23 March 1861.
29. *Daily Northern Argus* 16 May 1876; *Rockhampton Bulletin* 20 May 1876.
30. LC247-1-26 Hobart 5 April 1859; LC247-1-27 Hobart 6 April 1859; *Hobart Town Courier* 6 April 1859.
31. *Brisbane Courier* 30 January 1866.
32. *Empire* 23 February 1861.
33. *Argus* 11, 29 August 1865.
34. *Argus* 2 March 1866.
35. LC247-1-27 Hobart 3 September 1861; *Mercury* 5 September 1861.
36. *Hobart Town Advertiser* 5 May 1860; LC247-1-26 Hobart 22 May 1860.
37. *Mercury* 16 September 1857.
38. LC247-1-27 Hobart 14 September 1857.
39. LC247-1-27 Hobart 29 February 1860; *Mercury* 1 March 1860.
40. *Argus* 10 March 1873.
41. *Argus* 1 November 1873.
42. *Express and Telegraph* 6 September 1877.
43. *Adelaide Times* 22 August 1856.
44. *Sydney Morning Herald* 30 July, 2, 21 August 1856.
45. Quinlan, M. (2012) The Low Rumble of Informal Dissent: Shipboard Protests Over Health and Safety in Australian Waters 1790–1900, *Labour History* 102: 131–55; Quinlan, M. (2013) Precarious and Hazardous Work: The Health and Safety of Merchant Seamen 1815–1935, *Social History*, 38(3): 281–307.
46. TAHO Crowther Collection *Betah* logbook (Log Box 2), CRO82/1/48 [provisional] *Sea Gull* logbook 27 December 1849, 13 April 1850; CRO82/1/37 *Picard* Logbook 9, 16 October 1867 (Log Box 12).
47. *Cornwall Chronicle* 14 December 1867.
48. See CRO27/1/12 Logbook *Litherland* 20 April 1851.
49. *Empire* 21 July 1868.
50. *Evening News* 11 January 1877.
51. ML A2596 Logbook *Louisa* 15 January 1854; ML A451 Logbook *Jane Lockhart* 5 September 1862.
52. *Sydney Morning Herald* 12 March 1857.
53. TAHO CRO27/1/12 Logbook *Litherland* 16, 17 May 1851.
54. LC247-1-21 Hobart 15 January 1852.
55. TAHO CRO27/1/90 Logbook *Terror* 8 February 1851; CRO27/1/84 Logbook *Julia* 8 June 1857.
56. TAHO CRO27/1/5 Logbook *Lady Leigh*.
57. TAHO CRO27/1/87 Logbook *Prince of Denmark* 27 January, 16 February 1852.
58. TAHO CRO27/1/93 Logbook *Australasian Packet* 19 October 1861, 16 February 1862.
59. TAHO CRO Logs Box 11 Logbook *Othello* 16, 17 September 1871.
60. TAHO CRO Logs Box 11 Logbook *Othello* 9 June 1868, 24 January 1869.

61. TAHO CRO Logs Box 11 Logbook *Velocity* 6, 9, 30 December 1875.
62. TAHO CRO Logs Box 1 Logbook *Aladdin* 15, 17 October 1880, 24 January, 4, 20 February 1881.
63. TAHO CRO Logs Box 2 Logbook *Betah* 8 February 1854.
64. The schooner later wrecked in 1868. ML A450 A451 Logbook *Jane Lockhart* 2 December 1861, 29–31 July, 11 October 1862.
65. Cooper-Busch, B. (1994) *Whaling Will Never Do for Me: The American Whaleman in the Nineteenth Century*, University Press of Kentucky, Lexington.
66. TAHO CRO27/1/71 Logbook *Menkah*.
67. *West Australian* 29 January 1873; *Inquirer* 20 May 1874; *Northern Times* 24 July 1875.
68. *Australian Town and Country Journal* 28 October 1876.
69. TAHO VDL CSD2/4/4096 Memorial *Tasmanian Daily News* 20, 28 August 1857.
70. LC247-1-26 Hobart 29 March 1859; *Argus* 3 March 1860.
71. *Argus* 27 September 1861; *Sydney Morning Herald* 4 November 1867.
72. *Sydney Morning Herald* 5 September 1870.
73. *Courier* 11 March 1864.
74. *Age* 4 July 1877, 1 March 1878, 21 January 1880.
75. *Sydney Morning Herald* 25 July 1854; *Cornwall Chronicle* 5 August 1854.
76. By then the Merchant Seamen's Provident Society, *Age* 25 June 1855.
77. *Evening News* 31 July, 2, 3 August 1872.
78. *Brisbane Courier* 12, 13, 18 November 1862, 26, 28 June 1873.
79. *Week* 7 December 1878; *Brisbane Courier* 8 March 1879.
80. *Argus* 27, 29 March 1866, 2, 3 October 1867.
81. *Argus* 17 September 1872.
82. *Mercury* 7, 9 October 1872.
83. *Mercury* 27 March 1879.
84. *Sydney Morning Herald* 5 September 1870; *Evening Journal* 24 September 1872; *Express and Telegraph* 27 April 1877.
85. *South Australian Register* 9 April 1879; *Argus* 15 January 1880.
86. Quinlan, Precarious and Hazardous Work, 281–307.
87. *Maitland Mercury* 24 July 1866.
88. *Brisbane Courier* 7, 9, 17 July 1873.
89. A2795 Sydney Progressive Carpenters minutes 30 July 1877.
90. *Argus* 10 March 1873, 25 June 1874, 1 November 1876.
91. *Argus* 25 March 1874.
92. *Sydney Morning Herald* 24 July 1878.
93. *Sydney Morning Herald* 19 November 1878.
94. *Sydney Morning Herald* 21 December 1878; E235-2 Sydney United Plasterers Society minutes 25 November, 2 December 1878; ML MSS2422 1(7) Sydney Boilermakers Society minutes 26 November, 10 December 1878.
95. *Sydney Morning Herald* 25 November 1878.
96. *Newcastle Morning Herald* 5 December 1878; *Brisbane Courier* 31 December 1878.
97. *The Argus* 24 October 1878.
98. *Sydney Mail* 30 November 1878.
99. *Sydney Morning Herald* 27 January 1879.
100. *Sydney Morning Herald* 30 December 1878.
101. Griffiths, P. (2006) *The Making of White Australia: Ruling Class Agendas, 1876–1888*, PhD Thesis, Australian National University.
102. *Evening News* 23 November 1878; *Armidale Express* 6 December 1878.

103. B5590 Newcastle Boilermakers minutes 4 December 1878; *Riverine Herald* 17 December 1878.
104. A2795 Sydney Progressive Carpenters minutes 2 December 1878.
105. *Armidale Express* 6 December 1878.
106. *Sydney Morning Herald* 11 February 1879.
107. ML MLK00049 Sydney Shipwrights minutes 12 December 1878; ML MSS2422 1(7) Sydney Boilermakers Society minutes 24 December 1878.
108. Quinlan, Precarious and Hazardous Work, 281–307.
109. *Brisbane Courier* 2, 11 December 1878, 5 March 1879.
110. *Maryborough Chronicle* 10 May 1877.
111. See Waters, D. and Bailey, N. (2013) *Lives in Peril: Profit or Safety in the Global Maritime Industry*, Palgrave Macmillan, Basingstoke.
112. TAHO VDL CSO24/188/6878 Memorial 12 March 1856; *Newcastle Chronicle* 28 June 1873.
113. *Glenn Innes Examiner* 6 September 1876.
114. *Sydney Morning Herald* 7 December 1878.
115. *Age* 5 September 1873.
116. *South Australian Register* 19, 20, 25 October 1877.
117. *Sydney Morning Herald* 21 July, 7 October 1873, 12 January 1874; *Newcastle Morning Herald* 29 November 1878.
118. T19-2 Sydney Marine Engineers Association minutes 1, 11 June, 9 August 1880.
119. *South Australian Register* 15 February 1878 and T19-2 Sydney Marine Engineers 3 September 1880.
120. T19-2 Sydney Marine Engineers minutes 2 November and 23 December 1880.
121. Linebaugh, *The London Hanged*, 306.
122. TAHO CSO24/280/6191 Memorial 28 June 1851.
123. *Geelong Advertiser* 10 June 1879.
124. *West Australian* 1 June 1880.
125. *South Australian Register* 15 September 1865; *Evening Journal* 19 August 1872.
126. ML MLK00049 Sydney Shipwrights minutes 18, 25 September, 2 October 1873.
127. ML61 SLNSW DSM/042/P10 Bundey, W.H. (1877) *Address to the Working Mens Association of Port Adelaide*, Webb, Verdon and Pritchard Adelaide, 3–7.
128. *South Australian Register* 21 August 1877.
129. *Evening Journal* 15 July 1876.
130. *Evening Journal* 23 September 1872.
131. *Newcastle Morning Herald* 4 March 1879.
132. *Express and Telegraph* 10 December 1879.
133. *South Australian Chronicle* 4 May 1878.
134. T46-1-3 NSW Stonemasons Sydney minutes 1 November 1875; ML MLK00049 Sydney Shipwrights minutes 4 November 1875; *Sydney Morning Herald* 30 September 1875; *Freeman's Journal* 4 December 1875.
135. *Melbourne Herald* 1 February 1878.
136. ANU E81 Port Adelaide Working Mens Association Funeral Benefits Records 1872–1940; *Express and Telegraph* 12 June 1876.
137. Quinlan, M. (2013) Precarious Employment, Ill-Health and Lessons from History: The Case of Casual (temporary) Dock Workers 1880–1945, *International Journal of Health Services*, 43(4): 721–44.
138. *Evening News* 15 January 1879; *Argus* 20 December 1878; *Newcastle Morning Herald* 4 June, 15 September 1880.

139. *Sydney Morning Herald* 30 November 1854, 12 February 1855.
140. *Sydney Morning Herald* 14 December 1854.
141. *Sydney Morning Herald* 9 March 1874.
142. *Newcastle Chronicle* 19 January 1875, 25 March, 5, 7, 20 April 1876.
143. *Newcastle Morning Herald* 13 November 1877.
144. *Australian Town and Country Journal* 1 June 1878.
145. *Evening News* 23 November 1878; *Newcastle Morning Herald* 5 December 1878.
146. *Age* 6 July 1860.
147. *South Australian Advertiser* 24 December 1878.
148. *Northern Territory Times* 12 October, 9 November 1878.
149. *Newcastle Chronicle* 1 April 1863.
150. *Sydney Morning Herald* 20 November 1878.
151. *Armidale Express* 10 January 1874.
152. *Mercury* 22 April 1880.
153. *Riverine Herald* 9 April 1870.
154. *Sydney Morning Herald* 28 October 1854.
155. *Geelong Advertiser* 10 January, 19, 22 October 1855.
156. *Sydney Morning Herald* 6 January 1855.
157. *Sydney Morning Herald* 8 October 1859.
158. *Cornwall Chronicle* 20 July 1861.
159. *Bendigo Advertiser* 8 December 1866; *Ovens and Murray Advertiser* 22 April 1871.
160. *Geelong Advertiser* 1 July 1862.
161. *Empire* 25 June 1866; *Telegraph* 14, 24 June 1880.
162. *Evening News* 8 February 1876.
163. *Goulburn Herald* 28 May 1853.
164. *Ballarat Courier* 20 November 1877.
165. *Maitland Mercury* 22 April 1875.
166. *Riverine Herald* 24 February 1869.
167. *Express and Telegraph* 13 July 1868.
168. *Express and Telegraph* 31 July 1868.
169. *South Australian Advertiser* 23 September 1868.
170. *South Australian Chronicle* 25 July 1868.
171. *Queensland Times* 29 July 1880.
172. *South Australian Advertiser* 15 July 1879.
173. *Argus* 19 November 1858, 4 May 1859, 18 September 1868.
174. *Telegraph* 4 January 1876.
175. *Hobart Guardian* 9 July 1853; *Mercury* 25 November 1856; *Hobart Town Advertiser* 8 January 1861; *Launceston Examiner* 26 October 1875.
176. *Brisbane Courier* 6 July 1869.
177. *Newcastle Morning Herald* 16 October 1879.
178. *Telegraph* 16 December 1875, 14 October 1876.
179. *Express and Telegraph* 2 May 1878.
180. *Argus* 16 December 1878.
181. *Melbourne Daily News* 12 April 1851; *Argus* 4 October 1852.
182. *Geelong Advertiser* 26, 27 July 1860.
183. *Geelong Advertiser* 15, 24 August, 6 December 1860.
184. *Geelong Advertiser* 3, 4 September 1860.
185. *Geelong Advertiser* 4 September 1860.
186. *Argus* 13 September 1860.
187. *Star* 2 May 1861.
188. *Adelaide Express* 22 February 1865.

189. *South Australian Advertiser* 26 May 1865.
190. *South Australian Advertiser* 4 January 1878; *Brisbane Courier* 21 September 1872, 23 June 1880; *Border Watch* 13 August 1873; *Age* 3 September 1874; *Armidale Express* 27 November 1874; *Freeman's Journal* 30 January 1875; *Maryborough Chronicle* 29 January 1876; *Daily Northern Argus* 15 January 1879.
191. *Age* 5 February 1874.
192. *Argus* 4 April, 1 May 1866.
193. *Argus* 12 August 1861.
194. *Bendigo Advertiser* 5, 31 May 1873; *Riverine Herald* 11 June 1873; *Ballarat Star* 1 October 1873.
195. *Rockhampton Bulletin* 9 November 1872.
196. *Launceston Examiner* 14 January 1854.
197. *Brisbane Courier* 5 July 1864.
198. *South Australian Register* 10 February 1873.
199. *Express and Telegraph* 29 June 1874; *Evening Journal* 11 August 1874.
200. *Evening Journal* 5 February 1876.
201. *Evening Journal* 18 April 1876; *South Australian Register* 1 May 1876.
202. *Evening Journal* 15 July 1876.
203. *Evening Journal* 4 February 1875.
204. *South Australian Register* 12 December 1861; *Brisbane Courier* 29 August 1872.
205. Reproduced in *Goulburn Herald* 12 June 1861.
206. Reproduced in *Maitland Mercury* 24 July 1866.
207. *Riverine Grazier* 24 April 1880.
208. *Riverine Grazier* 21 July 1880.
209. *Australian Town and Country Journal* 24 May, 12 July 1873.
210. *Armidale Express* 27 November 1874.
211. *Australian Town and Country Journal* 15 March 1873; *Armidale Express* 22 March 1873.
212. *Riverine Herald* 12 July 1873.
213. *Queanbeyan Age* 7, 21 August 1873.
214. *Hay Standard* 7 July 1880.
215. *Cootamundra Herald* 18 December 1880.
216. *Argus* 15 July 1861, 6 March 1865, 3 September 1866.
217. *Bendigo Advertiser* 24 June 1865.
218. *Argus* 5, 6 July 1867.
219. *Sydney Morning Herald* 6 March 1874, 31 December 1875.
220. *South Australian Advertiser* 7, 9, 24 July 1874, 10 October 1879, 16, 19 August 1880.
221. *Brisbane Courier* 11 March 1865, 7 September, 12 December 1875, 31 January 1877; *Telegraph* 11 April 1879.
222. *Evening News* 13 August 1872.
223. *Ballarat Star* 13 November 1872.
224. *Age* 28 January 1870.
225. *Argus* 25 November 1876, 13 February 1877.
226. *Ballarat Courier* 9 April 1879.
227. *Leader* 4 February 1865.
228. *Evening News* 23 November 1878.
229. *Riverine Grazier* 21 February 1880.
230. *Bendigo Advertiser* 12 April 1866; *Argus* 13 April 1866, 6 December 1867.
231. *Empire* 19 June 1874; *Evening Journal* 19 July 1875, 2 October 1876.
232. *Argus* 25 March 1865.

233. *Sydney Mail* 13 October 1877.
234. *Age* 25 September 1877, 24 August 1878.
235. *Evening News* 25 June 1877; *Australian Town and Country Journal* 1 May 1880.
236. *Argus* 25 September 1860.
237. *Argus* 7 June, 16 October 1861; *Ballarat Star* 4 January 1867, 1 March 1869.
238. *Australasian* 11 August 1866; *Kyneton Observer* 14 August 1866.
239. *Argus* 17 November 1869; *Mount Alexander Mail* 4 March 1871; *Ballarat Star* 2 August 1872; *Kyneton Guardian* 17 August 1872; *Ovens and Murray Advertiser* 30 August 1879; *Geelong Advertiser* 13 October 1881.
240. *Bunyip* 14 May 1870.
241. *Toowoomba Chronicle* 18 September 1869; *Darling Downs Gazette* 8 June 1872.
242. *Queensland Times* 23 December 1871; *Telegraph* 24 July 1878; *Queenslander* 17 July 1880.
243. *Weekly Examiner* 10 March 1877; *Launceston Examiner* 11 February 1880.
244. AMP abolished this in 1877 *South Australian Register* 24 February 1877.
245. *Sydney Morning Herald* 2 March 1878.
246. *Toowoomba Chronicle* 6 September 1873; *Ballarat Courier* 9 November 1880.
247. *Maitland Mercury* 2 August 1877.
248. *Age* 14 October 1872; *Ballarat Courier* 1 November 1873.
249. Geelong railway workers formed a cooperative to purchase food in bulk, *Argus* 11 January 1867.
250. *Leader* 2 March 1872; *Ballarat Star* 19 July 1877.
251. *Age* 21 February 1867.
252. *Age* 23 February 1870.
253. *Age* 7 January 1874, 6 June, 9 August 1877, 2 May 1878.
254. *South Australian Register* 2 February 1872; *South Australian Advertiser* 8 June 1878.
255. *Newcastle Chronicle* 2, 9 February 1871.
256. *Australian Town and Country Journal* 11 October 1873.
257. *Week* 11 November 1876.
258. *Ipswich Observer* 17 March, 24 April 1875.
259. *Geelong Advertiser* 26 March 1877.
260. *Sydney Morning Herald* 27 April 1878; *Age* 23 August 1878.
261. *Argus* 19 March 1879; *Bendigo Advertiser* 4 October 1879.
262. *Age* 4 July 1879.
263. *Age* 20 May 1880.

4 Worker Organisation in Agriculture and Rural Industry

Introduction

Rural worker organisation, dominated by convicts prior to 1840 and over a decade longer in Tasmania, transitioned to free labour but remained largely informal. Western Australian received convicts until 1868, many engaged on public works like road construction, with farmers complaining their 'leisurely' work regimes and short hours caused disaffection amongst free farmworkers required to 'work hard.'[1] Some large landholders sought labour perceived as cheap and subservient. Alexander Berry imported Germans and Chinese indentured for long terms at low wages for his vast Shoalhaven Estate but encountered resistance including go-slows. Aboriginal workers were also employed in rural work (shepherds, mustering cattle) and other tasks like timber-getting, especially in remoter districts and often paid in kind.[2] Farming/pastoral practices largely ignored the climate, causing long-term environmental damage and depleting native food sources. Berry's atypical practice of leasing land to tenant farmers he imported (including one of my ancestors) encouraged intensive land-use, further depleting native food.[3] Overall, the vast majority of pastoral/farm workers were 'European' apart from Queensland.

Rural Activities and the Labour Process

Production and work practices evolved including increasingly large shearing sheds. Shearing was seasonal, occupying a few weeks at each sheep-station and, given continental climatic variations, occurred between August and January at different locations. Sheep-stations relied heavily on itinerant workers—shearers, sheepwashers and shedhands/labourers. Shearing was intense work requiring strength, dexterity and experience. Incompetent or aggrieved shearers could seriously harm sheep, as a *Perth Inquirer* correspondent lamented.[4] Paid by piecework, output restriction was not an issue with competition between 'gun' shearers common. Better located stations or those with good working conditions developed 'regular returns' amongst shearers while remote ones or those with poor conditions or a history of bitter disputes struggled. Reporting regional labour scarcity in 1874 the *Maryborough Chronicle* stated only nine shearers appeared at May Downs Station to shear 20,000 sheep and 'a number of aborigines have been taken on to assist.'[5] Like harvests, wet weather delayed shearing and inhibited travelling between stations while telegraphs enhanced shearers' knowledge of better conditions elsewhere. For landholders, shearing and baling wool before sending to market was the penultimate stage in production, and their most costly single activity. In 1868 the *Pastoral Times* observed:

> At the rate of 18s per 100. . . the 10,000,000 sheep to be shorn this season in Riverina and the pastoral districts of New South Wales will amount to £90,000. . . . The shearers in the Yanko shed (Wilson Brothers) will receive £1,170, as they shear 130,000 sheep.[6]

Shearing sheds resembled factories with sheepwashers, shearers (with their own cook), boys collecting fleece, labourers and others baling wool and loading them on drays. By the 1870s even a modest shed engaged 30–40 workers, bigger sheds over 100 and some considerably more. Despite the work's itinerant nature, these congregations, shearers' practice of travelling in groups, gatherings in towns and labour agents undertaking recruitment facilitated networking and organisation. The *Border Watch* estimated 100 shearers lived in the Mount Gambier District in 1873 with another 100 travelling there to work.[7]

Group-absconding dominated collective action by convicts. This continued amongst free rural labour, apart from shearers and reapers more prone to making unilateral wage demands supported by strikes. For 1851–1880 wages were the dominant issue of strikes and NSCA, followed by hours (mainly recreational absence), working conditions, OHS and management behaviour (Table 4.1). Collective action remained largely workplace-based and informal, though multi-workplace/regional actions, especially amongst shearers, set the ground for unionisation. Shearers' unions were short-lived but their efforts an essential precursor for more successful bodies in the 1880s. The absence of petitioning/deputations reflects limited political engagement.

Informal Workplace Dissent

Court and newspapers record thousands of disputes involving rural workers, hundreds entailing collective action. Master and servant laws administered by 'stacked' benches fell especially hard on rural workers, unscrupulous employers exploiting their draconian provisions. In July 1866 Finlay Campbell charged a shepherd with being drunk after work one evening and not sleeping in his designated hut—agreement

Table 4.1 Worker Organisation in the Rural Industry 1831–1880

Industry	1831–1840	1841–1850	1851–1860	1861–1870	1871–1880	Total 1851–1880
Entire Industry						
Organisations	751	393	168	74	82	323⁺
Raw involvement	2039	1221	541	432	2310	3283
Estimated involvement*	2127	1339	565	577	2531	3673
Strikes						
Won	7	10	5	6	4	15
Drawn	2	4	7	4	4	15
Lost	165	189	75	29	18	122
Unknown	13	10	6	10	8	24
Total	187	213	93	48	34	175
Est. total involvement*	560	614	293	336	390	1019
Number of establishments						
One	182	209	90	42	30	162
Multi	2	3		1	1	2
Regional/town				5	3	8
Non-strike collective action						
Won	11	33	9	10	14	33
Drawn	42	3	4	2	1	7
Lost	323	97	41	10	13	64
Unknown	233	61	22	6	15	43
Total	609	194	76	28	43	147
Est. total involvement*	1578	725	316	328	611	1255
Number of establishments						
One	604	184	66	25	29	120
Multi	5	7	8		3	11
Regional/town		1	2	2	10	14
Colonial						
Issues in collective action (strikes/NSCA)						
Wages	3/	19/3	8/5	28/14	21/29	57/48
Hours	116/	130/	59/	9/	3/12	71/12
Working conditions	81/	78/	28/	17/2	12/13	57/15
Health & safety	23/	28/	12/	7/	3/4	22/4
Management behaviour	31/	19/	6/	6/	3/10	15/10
Jobs/employment	1/	1/	2/	2/4	1/10	5/14
Work methods		2/	1/	3/	1/2	5/2

Industry	1831–1840	1841–1850	1851–1860	1861–1870	1871–1880	Total 1851–1880
Unionism					1/4	1/4
Legislation			/1	/6	1/7	1/14
Pensions					/2	/2
Unknown	1/			1/		1/
Breakdown of organisation and actions of largest subgroup						
Shearers						
Organisation numbers	1	10	5	25	39	69+
Involvement/members*		160	85	300	2480	2865
Strikes		2	3	20	18	41
NSCA	2	6	1	4	13	18
Absconding		2	1	1	4	6
Petitions						
Deputations						
Mass meetings			1		6	7
Marches						
Letters/public notices					15	15
Bans						
Court actions						
Won		1	1	3	3	7
Lost	1	1	2	12	8	22
Drawn		2				

* Adjusted by multiplying number of zero-reporting organisations/years by industry/ occupation median membership in that decade. ⁺For totals, organisation spanning multiple decades only counted once.

cancelled and £2 wage-deduction, causing the *Kyneton Observer* to label the *Master and Servant Act* disgraceful to a civilised country.[8] Records afford only fragmentary insights into collective resistance. Small numbers tried over a single incident reflected the scale of production but also employer attempts to deter dissent through exemplary action. Wider disagreements are evident in sequential cases. On 19 February 1866 two workers were charged with absence/absconding from Page's Lemon Springs' estate, Tunbridge, another two charged with disobedience on the same day.[9] Others may have been involved. As earlier, court cases represented the tip of an iceberg of tacit bargaining and dissent. In Tasmania convict-era expectations hung heavily on rural employers and magistrates, with prosecutions for insolence—daring to talk back. No such offence existed under master and servant law. Verbal reposts were also used as evidence of disobedience or deemed obscene and threatening. In 1855 Robert Townsend prosecuted five hired servants for using 'abusive and threatening language' — 14 days' solitary confinement.[10] In December 1857 two hired servants (one a Ticket-of-Leave holder) charged by their Clarence Plains master for using obscene language received 14 days' imprisonment with hard labour, forfeiting their wages and court costs.[11] This by no means atypical penalty demonstrated the law's centrality in subordinating labour and explains the loathing it generated amongst workers, culminating in political campaigns against them. Tasmania's convict overhang, the goldrushes and better mainland prospects encouraged flight by free and unfree workers. In November 1852 six convicts who had absconded from three neighbouring Falmouth estates were apprehended in Victoria and returned to Hobart, receiving significantly extended sentences and recommendations for close surveillance, suggesting they were serial absconders.[12] Bench-books only record those caught, not successful absconders of which there appear to have been many.

Rural workers organised to improve wages or remedy ration deficiencies including customary extras (like grog) during shearing/harvests like a strike by Tabilk vineyard-hands in 1861.[13] Food quality/quantity caused frequent complaints. When shearers at Alexander Clarke's Mountford Estate went to complain about their meat they were charged with breaching their contract, six Ticket-of-Leave and probationers receiving 90 days' hard labour while eight free men got 30 days' imprisonment and forfeited part of their wages.[14] Evidence attests to tacit/overt bargaining underpinning collective action. In July 1853 probation passholders Thomas Burke and John McCarthy complained about their hut and bedding, telling their Campbell Town District employer, John Murray MacKinnon, they wouldn't stay for the £12 per annum he offered (£3 above the stipulated rate).[15] The frequency and duration of recreational absences were also bargained over. In August 1852 a Longford employer (Hartwell) charged probationer John Sullivan with drunkenness and neglect and three others (John Law, James McDermott and William Smith) with frequently absenting themselves, neglecting their work, threatening their overseer, causing a disturbance at their master's establishment and using obscene and threatening language.[16] Sullivan received 60 days' hard labour while his compatriots got 18 months in chains at Port Arthur. Recourse to courts was less frequent for temporary absence by free labour. Another practice, longstanding amongst seamen, was to renege on agreements for a better option, especially amongst indentured immigrants who unknowingly engaged at below prevailing wages. Severe financial penalties sought to discourage this and compensate aggrieved employers but to limited effect. In December 1864 the Campbell Town Bench four workers failing to enter service at CH Harrison's Mona Vale Estate were fined and ordered to pay Harrison 50 shillings' compensation.[17] Hefty fines were used as a 'backdoor' means of gaoling dissenters.

Queensland employers made widespread use of indentured Europeans and non-European workers. Indenturing entailed significant differences in wages, conditions and behaviour-control, especially for non-Europeans contracted for longer terms, paid less, given poorer rations and more severely ill-treated, sparking periodic protests. In 1852, 37 Chinese servants on Sandeman's Gayndah estate rebelled after discovering their wages were a mere fraction of Europeans.[18] A decade later 18 Indians (one female) at Sandeman's Tenthill estate lodged complaints over unpaid wages and ill-treatment, including being beaten by their overseer Ayrest. The Brisbane Bench found the agreements signed in Calcutta and Port Macquarie too loosely worded to interpret.[19] In August 1870 Maryborough District settler Octave de Libert prosecuted two indentured emigrants, Anthony Leneham and Richard White, for refusing work and 16 months later advertised a £10 reward for anyone identifying the person supplying his Polynesian servants with alcohol.[20]

Ill-treatment of Pacific islanders sparked more numerous collective action, including strikes, absconding and complaints before courts. Protests weren't confined to sugar plantations. In 1869 a dispute involving islander-shepherds at Banchory station included a strike, group-absconding (five ringleaders gaoled) and one islander being shot. The *Peak Downs Telegram* observed they were imported by an insolvent employer unable to pay them and the *Master and Servant Act*'s wage provisions were most unfair to Polynesians.'[21] In 1870 foreclosure of the Strathmore Estate left ten islanders who had completed their three-year agreements cast adrift without passage home while another batch were dispatched to Bowen Gaol, presumably for work-related offences.[22] Despite the overall decline in worker prosecutions in the 1870s Queensland courts continued to routinely impose heavy penalties on islanders. In 1878 Allai, employed by farmer George Forster (Yengarie), forfeited 15s wages and 3s 6d costs for going to town to buy a belt on Saturday afternoon after his half-holiday was confiscated for disobedience.[23]

Courts adjudicating disputes involving European workers occasionally considered customary conditions though it seldom altered outcomes. The 1872 sheepwashers' agreement at Terrible Vale Station proscribed grog, offering 'unlimited coffee' instead. When water levels became high (and cold given the altitude) nine sheepwashers struck when their grog demands were refused. Three then sued for unpaid wages. The Uralla Bench considered agreement terms, what was customary and earlier disputes including an 1869 shearers' strike at another station, but ultimately ruled the men weren't entitled to grog dismissing their claim.[24] Landholders repeatedly complained rural workers breached agreements, demanded higher wages, struck or absconded when it suited them. However, some landholder practices hardly induced trust. A Tarraville District landholder (Hoddinott) hired six shearers, paying their fares. They arrived to find ten shearers already engaged and sheep mostly shorn. They sought work elsewhere but when one sued for the difference between Hoddi-nott's promised pay and what he earned, the Tarraville Police Magis-trate referred him to the County Court, a time-consuming, expensive option designed so by landholder-dominated legislatures to discourage wage claims.[25] It wasn't uncommon for shearers arriving at a station to find they were unwanted. Those engaged by labour agents—who pur-sued their claim—had more success in recouping costs and damages.[26] The sequencing of shearing agreements, and efforts by landholders to manipulate changes to their own advantage, also caused disputes. In November 1868 Cape Wrath station owner McLennan prosecuted seven shearers for refusing to shear 760 sheep at a station not included in the original agreement. They were due to start shearing at another station the following day and complying with his demand would have meant breaching this second contract which the Hamilton Bench ruled was fatal to McLennan's claim.[27] That McLennan was confident enough to prose-cute for actions outside the agreement's terms says something about how pastoralists viewed their powers under the master and servant laws, even if it failed on this occasion.

Shearers possessed bargaining power but many rural workers had to sue simply to obtain their pay. Typical was a claim against an employer (Whiteair [sic]) heard in Melbourne in January 1856. The bench observed the money was six months overdue and rural employers often paid labourers with money-orders subsequently dishonoured.[28] These and other sharp practices had occurred for decades, including offsets for allegedly incompetent work, charges of neglect/absence and charges for goods—the truck-system—occasionally drawing sharp criticism. In 1867 the *Dalby Herald* railed against felonious acts by some landholders, cit-ing one case where men and boys working diligently during lambing were charged for 60 sheep lost due to drought. When challenged the land-owner pretended to be the superintendent—threats to shoot him secured payment. Another station owner paid shearers with orders refused by Dalby shopkeepers. Acknowledging legislative deficiencies, the newspa-per stated these incidents explain 'the arson and murder said to be going on in rural districts.'[29] Wage theft via the truck-system was common, the worst excesses against Aborigines on reserves and sheep-stations where payment by rations was the norm. In 1868 Aboriginal workers at Menin-gie went shearing rather than submit to being paid at the mission-store.[30] Wage evasion continued, mitigated by arbitration in the early 20th cen-tury but reinvigorated when that regime was emasculated under neolib-eralism, facilitating an array of dodgy temporary-visa schemes to import vulnerable workers from the 1990s.

Lopsided laws obliged employers to make restitution plus court costs, only risking gaol if they ignored court orders. Insolvency rendered court victories meaningless.[31] Drysdale District farmer John Carey refused to pay five Chinese engaged 'grubbing-out' in September 1861. A fracas ensued. Carey was ordered to pay wages and fined for assaulting Yung Moon, while Ah Ping, Ah Coong and Ah Chong were fined for threatening language.[32] Heated words and fracas reached courts remarkably rarely given severe hardships non-payment imposed. John Honey refused to pay his reapers, labelling them 'crawlers,' using his whip when they waylaid him and charging one (David Morand) with assault. The Geelong Bench would have none of it, ordering Honey to pay their wages plus costs.[33] Decisions like this were commoner in larger towns with full-time police magistrates even-handedly administering fundamentally stilted laws. A centuries' old, preferred and costly payback option was incendiarism. The same day Peter Newman disputed wages with reapers his wheat-field at Chilcotts Creek caught fire.[34] One reaper (Hall) was charged with incendiarism but convictions were rare. Incendiarism was seldom witnessed—or not by anyone prepared to testify—and summer heat made accidental fires common. Rural newspapers regularly reported incendiarism, those labelled collective but the tip of more widespread subversion. Governments offered substantial rewards to little effect. Mechanical reapers/strippers proved more effective.

While appearing disparate there were clear patterns of and rationales for informal collective action by rural workers, indicating a wider struggle over rewards, acceptable effort levels and customary work practices. These wider contests and customs formed the base for unionisation, especially amongst shearers and rouseabouts. Some employers' pursuit of cheaper labour options and significant wage theft antagonised rural workers. Dalby worker 'Fang Bolt' argued it discouraged them from seeking rural work—an unvirtuous circle of exploitation and prejudice sadly now being repeated.[35]

District-Wide/Regional Organisation and Unions

District-wide demands by reapers stalled given the introduction of reaping machines after 1860.[36] Shearing was immune to this threat—electric-powered shears were introduced late in the century but still required a shearer. Informal district-wide collaboration, apparent since the 1840s whereby minimum rates were specified at the beginning of the shearing season, grew over succeeding decades. Early shearers unions tried to extend and formalise this wage-setting, reinforced by strikes like those at Baringhup and Learmonth (Victoria) in January 1867 and at Walgett (NSW) in 1872 which correspondents conceded changed terms of engagement.[37] District-wide strikes made resort to the courts harder than single-shed actions, although some prosecutions targeted ringleaders as occurred during Jerilderie sheds strike in 1870, with five gaoled while other 'notables' had their agreements cancelled.[38] Individual landholders took action hoping it would have a deterrent effect. When Mossgiel District shearers struck for above sign-on wages in August 1879, Canoble station owner (ALP Cameron) prosecuted 37 shearers for breaching their agreement. Cameron couldn't afford to lose their services, helping to explain why rather than being fined or incarcerated the presiding magistrate (O'Neil) successfully persuaded them to return to work.[39]

Master and servant laws left no scope for re-negotiation after agreements had been signed so one option was refusing to sign an agreement. Shearers arriving at a station and not 'signed-up' could collaborate and make additional demands. In August 1878 Edward Webster, manager of Mossgiel Station, complained that over 80 shearers had arrived, been accommodated and fed on the understanding that 17s 6d per 100 sheep would be paid but subsequently refused to sign for less than 20 shillings per 100.[40] This practice was probably more widespread than reported. However, shearers risked long, expensive and fruitless travel if not signed-on and stations sought to pre-empt it by pre-signing shearers. As district bargaining and strikes became the norm, pastoralists looked for new solutions, including getting solicitors to draft model agreements to be signed by all shearers prior to shearing. As with the charade of Australian Workplace Agreements 120 years later, landholders mimicked each other, devising shed agreements specifying 12-hour days; making shearers financially responsible for daggy sheep, shear-inflicted wounds or other losses to the stock-owner; and dictating work practices like prohibiting dragging of sheep.[41] Rule 7 of one well-publicised agreement prohibited a general 'smoko' break with no more than five shearers being permitted to break at any one time.[42]

Unionisation was a logical response to this. Attempts began in the 1850s, exemplified by the Moreton Bay, Darling Downs and Burnett Shearers and Sheep-washers Committee formed in Drayton in 1854.[43] Union numbers grew after 1870, facilitated by larger numbers congregating at sheds and nearby towns. Shearers' unions formalised district-wide alliances, also communicating with informal associations elsewhere to generalise pay-rates. During the 1874 shearing season unions formed in Toowoomba and Peak Downs together with informal alliances in districts like Rockhampton.[44] This was followed by the first attempted colony-wide body (which would succeed in the 1880s), the Toowoomba Association, renaming itself the Queensland Shearers Union and forming an Ipswich branch in 1875.[45] Similar developments occurred elsewhere with tacit wage expectations evident in shed disputes giving way to informal district-level alliances and then unions. The Adelaide Shearers Union (1872–1873) was followed by shearers unions in Mount Gambier (1873) and Warrakimbo/Port Augusta (1877), complementing informal bodies in districts like Port Lincoln.[46] The Adelaide-based body reflected the more concentrated rural activities of South Australia compared to NSW, Queensland and Victoria. Like others it soon collapsed, was briefly revived in 1877 as a branch of the South Australian Labour League, before another Adelaide-based union with 800 members was established

(1878–1879).[47] In Victoria rounds of district rate-setting in the 1860s were succeeded by union formation at Winchelsea, Inverleigh, Mansfield and Hamilton in 1873—the latter tried forming a Western Districts union. These unions communicated amongst themselves and with the Mount Gambier union.[48] In NSW rounds of informal district rate-setting were reported, including 1870 (Hay and Jerilderie) and 1872 (Bourke, Walgett and Cooma). In 1874 the Tamworth-based Shearers Union and Benefit Association was established to regulate wages and provide friendly benefits, with mobile canvassing agents and claiming coverage from the Hunter Valley to Liverpool Plains.[49] In Tasmania and Western Australia collective action was confined to sheds although informal networks may have existed.

Shearers' unions didn't so much bargain for wage increases as counter employers' shed agreements with unilateral regulation setting minimum wages and piece-rates per 100 sheep shorn, reinforced with strikes or refusing engagements. In March 1873 Gympie shearers demanded 20 shillings per 100 sheep, in September Mount Gambier shearers pledged not to work for less than 15 shillings while the Mansfield Workingmens Association set rates of 14 shillings per hundred (or 17s 6d if not found) and five shillings per eight-hour day for harvest labour (6d per hour overtime).[50] In September 1876 the Peaks Downs Shearers Union sent deputations to sheep-station owners to request a wage increase and repeated this practice, requesting four shillings per score in October 1877.[51] But setting rates unilaterally remained dominant, unionism's spread primarily extending its regional scope. District-wide bargaining required corresponding organisation amongst rural employers and willingness to bargain, then unlikely in an industry marked by intense competition and export volatility. The Peak Downs union fizzled after Wolfang station dismissed unionists.[52] When the Toowoomba District/Queensland Shearers Union protested the truck-system at Jondaryan station forcing shearers to purchase provisions at inflated prices in 1874, it relied on newspapers.[53] Newspapers were little used for communicating amongst shearers so diaries and business records might uncover more extensive organisation than described here. Ultimately, the clash of competing rule-setting between shearers' unions and pastoralists led to the momentous 'freedom of contract' strikes of 1891 when pastoralists sought to exclude shearer union rules.

Conclusion

Collective action by rural workers at workplace and district level had been occurring since the 1790s, mirroring European practices stretching back centuries. Harvests/shearing congregated workers and gave them leverage given the time-sensitive nature of these activities. Reapers and shearers had skills, inhibiting their ready substitution. Experienced reapers could be imported—less so shearers. Mechanical reapers eventually replaced the former. Mechanisation didn't affect shearing and shearers' leverage was enhanced by the primacy of wool exports and larger sheep-stations drawing workers (shearers, rouseabouts/sheepwashers) together in a temporary factory-like setting. Shearers travelled between stations in groups and socialised in towns, enhancing networking. Remuneration was the key mobilising issue, with shearers' unions seeking to formalise and extend wages, work-rules and conditions, setting their own rules against those proffered by employers. There was little bargaining, agreement reached via conflict or silent acquiescence. Regional shearers' unions drew on some structural and organisational power and the logic for enhancing this by extending organisation to colony level and beyond was already clear. Realising the latter, however, took over a decade. Prior to the mid-1880s organisation remained fractured and short-lived with conspicuous regional gaps more readily explained in terms of the strengths/weaknesses of particular networks than economic or other structural factors.

Notes

1. *Inquirer* 13 September 1854.
2. Thorpe, B. (1996) *Colonial Queensland*, University of Queensland Press, St Lucia, 70.
3. Bennett, M. (2003) *For a Labourer Worthy of His Hire: Aboriginal Economic Responses to Colonisation in the Illawarra and Shoalhaven, 1770–1900*, PhD Thesis, University of Canberra, 162–206.
4. *Inquirer* 29 August 1860.
5. *Maryborough Chronicle* 31 October 1874.
6. Cited in *Argus* 1 September 1868.
7. *Border Watch* 12 July 1873.
8. *Kyneton Observer* 21 July 1866.
9. LC390-1-5 Oatlands 19, 26 February 1866.
10. LC83-1-12 Campbell Town 20 September 1855.
11. LC247-1-27 Hobart 4 December 1857.
12. LC247-1-23 Hobart 23 December 1852; LC247-1-22 31 December 1852.
13. *Cornwall Chronicle* 7 August 1861.
14. LC362-1-8 Longford 22 December 1852.
15. LC83-1-12 Campbell Town 18 July 1853.
16. LC362-1-8 Longford 19, 23 August 1852.
17. LC83-1-13 Campbell Town 5 December 1864.
18. *Moreton Bay Courier* 17 April 1852.
19. *Courier* 17 July 1862.
20. *Maryborough Chronicle* 18 August 1870, 14 December 1871.
21. *Maryborough Chronicle* 10 August 1869.
22. *Brisbane Courier* 22 July 1871.
23. *Maryborough Chronicle* 19 January 1878.
24. *Armidale Express* 23 November 1872.
25. *Gippsland Guardian* Friday 31 January 1868.
26. *South Australian Advertiser* 26 October 1865.
27. *Hamilton Spectator* 21 November 1868.

28. *Argus* 6 February 1856.
29. *Dalby Herald* 23 February 1867.
30. *South Australian Register* 7 December 1868.
31. *Argus* 16 November 1859.
32. *Geelong Advertiser* 28 September 1861.
33. *Geelong Advertiser* 19 January 1859.
34. *Maitland Mercury* 9 March 1875.
35. *Queenslander* 3 October 1868.
36. *Argus* 14 January 1867.
37. *Argus* 14 January 1867; *Australian Town and Country Journal* 14 September 1872.
38. *Australian Town and Country Journal* 8 October 1870.
39. *Riverine Grazier* 20 September 1879.
40. *Riverine Grazier* 21 August 1878.
41. For the 1877 Yarrabee Station agreement see McPherson, J. (no date) *The Early History of the Australian Workers Union*, AWU Victoria Riverina Branch, Melbourne, 5–6.
42. *Armidale Express* 27 August 1875.
43. *Morten Bay Courier* 5 August 1854.
44. *Toowoomba Chronicle* 31 October 1874; *Brisbane Courier* 17 November 1874.
45. *Ipswich Observer* 5 June 1875.
46. *South Australian Advertiser* 25 December 1872; *Border Watch* 12 July 1873; *Port Augusta Despatch* 22 September 1877.
47. *South Australian Advertiser* 3 August 1877, 25 July 1878.
48. *Hamilton Spectator* 23 April 1873; *Geelong Advertiser* 7 May 1873; *Bacchus Marsh Express* 12 July 1873; *Alexandra Times* 27 September 1873.
49. *Maitland Mercury* 24 December 1874, 31 August 1876.
50. *Gympie Times* 17 March 1873; *Border Watch* 6 September 1873; *Alexandra Times* 27 September 1873.
51. *Capricornian* 16 September 1876; *Brisbane Courier* 20 October 1877.
52. Spence, W. (1909) *Australia's Awakening*, The Workers Trustees, Melbourne, 14.
53. *Darling Downs Gazette* 25 November 1874.

5   Mining

Introduction

Coal and mineral production predominantly for export assumed considerable importance after 1850. Gold was exceptional in several respects. It was high-priced relative to volume, didn't require extensive smelting and was less price-sensitive given almost insatiable overseas demand reinforced by its status as reserve for then leading world currencies (UK pounds, US dollars or Russian roubles). Alluvial goldmining didn't require much capital so single miners or small groups could engage in it, especially on new fields. As easier won gold petered out, larger underground operations were advantaged. Small-scale production by self-employed goldminers affected worker organisation compared to other mining. Goldmining encompassed small, medium and large capital operations with different interests and capacity to influence governments. While small operators existed, other Australian extractive exports were more the preserve of large capital. Coal, copper, lead and silver were less valuable, mainly recovered through more expensive/challenging underground mining, some like copper and lead required expensive smelting, and all exported long distances—coal mostly to the Americas and copper to Europe. Large capital dominance manifested in influencing governments to provide a steady stream of immigrant labour and removing coal excise duties. In coal, intense competition amongst producers for market share afforded a strong incentive for both multi-mine organisation and one instance of output control by companies. Differences didn't translate to a simple dichotomy between self-employed and waged labour based on operation size. Large metal mines used self-employed workers, like tutwork in copper mining while coalminers were paid on the amount of coal they cut (the hewing rate). Indeed, Hunter Valley coalminers long campaigned to be categorised as self-employed contractors, not employees to escape the pernicious *Master and Servant Act*.

Table 5.1 shows that regional unions of metalliferous and coalminers grew strongly after 1851 with membership doubling in 1861–1870 and tripling in 1871–1880. Compared to other industries, strikes were a more

Table 5.1 Worker Organisation in the Mining Industry 1831–1880

Industry	1831–1840	1841–1850	1851–1860	1861–1870	1871–1880	Total 1851–1880
Entire Industry						
Organisations	109	41	75	79	140	271+
Raw involvement	645	671	6963	12071	47156	66190
Estimated involvement*	673	721	8263	17831	72482	98576
Strikes						
Won	1	3	5	4	17	26
Drawn	2	1		4	2	6
Lost	93	25	6	7	15	28
Unknown		1	9	15	47	71
Total	96	30	20	30	81	131
Est. total involvement*	347	963	212	6065	13478	19755
Number of establishments						
One	96	30	16	20	65	101
Multi			4	7	6	17
Regional/town				2	6	8
Non-strike collective action						
Won			3	5	30	38
Drawn	2	1		2	6	8
Lost	68	16	5	2	13	30
Unknown	11	8	2	14	99	115
Total	81	25	10	23	148	191
Est. total involvement*	276	480	305	2955	21259	24519
Number of establishments						
One	81	25	9	18	114	141
Multi				1	5	6
Regional/town			1	4	26	31
Colonial					3	3
Issues in collective action (strikes/NSCA)						
Wages	1	6	13	26	56	95
Hours	31	2	7	4	12	23
Working conditions	40	24	1	2	15	18
Health & safety	38	5		2	6	8
Management behaviour	12	4		1	9	10
Jobs/employment	1				4	4
Work methods	1		1		7	8

(Continued)

Table 5.1 (Continued)

Industry	1831–1840	1841–1850	1851–1860	1861–1870	1871–1880	Total 1851–1880
Unionism				1	3	12	16
Legislation						1	1
Breakdown of organisation and actions of largest subgroup							
Miners							
Organisation numbers	105	41	68	79	136	269⁺
Involvement/members*	677	721	8309	17786	67509	93604
Strikes	95	30	21	26	76	123
NSCA	77	25	9	22	135	166
Absconding	25	7	2	1		3
Petitions	1	2	12	9	21	42
Deputations		1	1	4	26	31
Mass meetings		3	18	34	52	105
Marches				1	8	9
Letters/public notices		4	3	19	38	60
Bans					2	2
Court actions							
Won	11	3	3	2	1	6
Drawn					2	2
Lost	398	122	8	6	9	23

* Adjusted by multiplying number of zero-reporting organisations/years by industry and occupation median membership for each industry in that decade. ⁺For totals, organisation spanning multiple decades only counted once.

significant form of collective action though still outweighed by NSCA, the latter more likely to involve multiple workplaces. Wages/remuneration was the predominant issue in collective action followed by hours and working conditions. Aside from strikes, miners used petitions/deputations connected to political agitation as well as mass meetings and public notices. Relatively few workers appeared before courts.

Coalminers

Driven by exports, colonial coal production grew substantially. Most colonies produced coal but mining was concentrated in the Hunter Valley, Illawarra and Lithgow Districts, drawing on the vast Sydney-basin coal seam. Coalmining in Ipswich west of Brisbane began to assume importance (producing 230,953 tons in 1861–1870 and 431,079 tons in 1871–1880).[1] Mining involved a range of tasks and specialist roles above and below ground. Those hewing coal were paid piecework based on the number of coal-skips filled. Variations in mining conditions like coal-seam thickness, challenging/deficient conditions including the presence of water, poor quality or small-coal and weight/weighing devices used resulted in complex conventions/rules and numerous disputes. Customs gave lodges/district unions considerable scope to regulate work methods, including allocating workspaces and allowances for harder conditions (water, low-seams and the like). Checkweighmen monitoring mine-owner weighman's assessment of weight, size and quality of coal in skips were elected and paid for by miners as were turnkeepers, responsible for distributing tubs underground.[2] This context should be borne in mind when considering unilateral regulation in mining.

Informal Organisation

Coalmining began in the Hunter Valley in 1791 with considerable collective action by convicts, indentured immigrant and free miners prior to 1851. Collective action was also rife amongst convicts engaged in Tasman peninsular mines where coalmining began in the 1830s. By the 1850s Tasmanian coalmining had moved to the Derwent, New Town and Mersey Valley. The New Town mines experienced collective absconding and temporary absences/strikes by both convict and free workers.[3] In June 1853, 11 Ticket-of-Leave miners striking for increased wages at James Luckman's mine were charged with breaching their agreement. Acquitted on a technicality, seven were re-tried and on evidence of their written demand, sentenced to two months' hard labour for pursuing what the *Colonial Times* labelled a 'communist notion.'[4] In 1855 Mersey Valley coalminers took collective action several times including striking over wage cuts when coal prices fell.[5] In March 1858 New Town colliers again struck for increased wages, this time (like their Mersey Valley counterparts) escaping prosecution.[6] Coalmining remained small scale with limited (reported) collective action prior to 1881. In Queensland informal action began soon after coalmining commenced. In June 1861 Redbank Colliery miners struck for increased wages, the ringleaders tried for criminal conspiracy in the Supreme Court. Following prolonged debates over whether relevant laws applied to the colony, they were acquitted by the jury.[7] Periodic wage strikes occurred at Ipswich mines like the Tivoli in 1872.[8] Informal action also occurred on the Burrum/Maryborough coalfield north of Brisbane, coalminers refusing work until the mineshaft was fully timbered in 1869.[9]

Multi-Workplace and Formal Organisation

In NSW, Queensland and Tasmania there is evidence of multi-mine/regional or formal mine-site organisation (miners' lodges) prior to 1881.

Organisation was strongest in the Hunter Valley where multi-mine organisation occurred in 1851, 1852, 1853, 1854, 1855, 1858, 1860–1862, 1863–1864, 1864–1865, 1868, and continuously from 1870. Colliery lodges operated at Borehole (1857–1864, 1865, 1873–1881), Glebe (1857–1862, 1877–1881), Minmi/Back Creek (1858–1864, 1875–1881), Tomago (1860–1862), Wallsend (1860–1864, 1868–1881), Waratah (1863–1864, 1871–1881), Redhead (1863–1864), Lambton (1864, 1870–1881, loyalist 1879), Cooperative (1871–1881), Anvil Creek (1873–1880), Four Mile Creek (1874), New Lambton (1873–1881), Greta (1873–1874, 1874–1881), New Wallsend (1874–1876), Raspberry Gully/South Waratah (1876–1881), Australasia (1877–1879), Ferndale (1878–1881), Browns New Tunnel/Duckenfield (1878–1881). In the Illawarra District-level organisation existed in 1864, 1873, 1876 and 1879–1881, along with colliery lodges at Mount Pleasant (1873, 1879–1881), Mount Keira (1873–1875), Bulli (1873, 1878–1881) and Coal Cliff (1879–1881). In the western coalfields (Lithgow) there was district organisation in 1870 and 1878–1880 as well as lodges at Eskbank (1878–1879), Lithgow Valley (1878–1881) and Vale of Clywdd (1878–1881). In Queensland District organisation occurred on the Ipswich coalfields in 1872, 1876, 1877 and 1878–1882 and in Tasmania at New Town coalmines in 1858.

Following centuries-old traditions colliers' organisation originated with mine lodges. These formed regional unions in the Hunter Valley, Western Districts and Illawarra in NSW and possibly other colonies where union records haven't survived. After regional unions formed, miners' lodges retained considerable independence. Mirroring robust democracy evident in craft societies, key decisions were vested in regular lodge delegate meetings and critical issues were referred to lodge membership ballots.[10] Like printers, workshop organisation wasn't an adjunct to union organisation, but integral to it. This helps explains more fractured development of district unions in some regions, especially those with only a few isolated mines. From 1851 lodge formation became increasingly common with episodic informal regional organisation to mount wage campaigns until 1857/8 when Hunter Valley coalminers established a district union. It was short-lived as were subsequent attempts in the 1860s. Notwithstanding expanding exports, periodic labour-oversupply undermined unions—one consequence of the 1861 strike was formation of miners' cooperative colliery.[11] In 1870 the Coal Miners Mutual Protection Association of the Hunter Valley (hereafter Hunter Valley Coalminers or the Association) formed which, notwithstanding organisational changes, still exists.

Unionisation on the Southern and Western District coalfields was more belated, notwithstanding support from Hunter Valley Coalminers—in the latter's interests given competition from these fields. In September 1878 Hunter Valley officials assisted in forming the Western District

Coalminers Association.[12] Coalminers' lodges operated at least sporadically in the Illawarra from the 1860s, with attempted district wage-bargaining in 1864. A short-lived district union (1873) was succeeded by a more enduring body in 1879.[13] In Queensland Ipswich coalminers formed a union in May 1876 with objectives (a sliding scale hewing rate/coal-price relationship and arbitration) modelled on the Hunter Valley (see later in the chapter).[14] It was short-lived. In 1877 the West Moreton United Coalminers Committee formed to pressure parliament for coalmine safety legislation, including ventilation and other provisions recently enacted in NSW.[15] February 1878 saw a more enduring body, the Ipswich Coalminers Preservation Association with governing structures similar to NSW, mutual insurance functions (accident, widows and funeral funds) and a strike-fund.[16]

Hunter Valley Coalminers sought to minimise volatility, regulate wages, maximise employment and curtail labour market flooding due to business cycle fluctuations and state-assisted British migration. The union also pursued mutual insurance, and campaigned for improved safety laws, negotiating with employers on ventilation requirements, check-inspectors and checkweighmen incorporated into the 1876 *Coal Fields Regulation Act*.[17] Safety issues caused frequent disputes, often intermeshed with work methods and jobs. In July 1876 Borehole colliery miners complained water was not being removed from man-entry places as per district and lodge rules, rails and props had not been supplied and dirt was not being removed from narrow places in the mine. District delegates noted Messrs Gregson and Turnbull's repeated promises remained unfulfilled.[18] Safety prompted Western District unionisation after two Vale of Clywdd miners were dismissed for telling the Coal Field's Examiner of insufficient timber supports and no-one stationed at the door on the main air course.[19] A Vale lodge was formed, followed by others. The Western Districts union took up safety issues, like faulting and ladders removed from airshafts, with employers and the Minister for Mines.[20] Given mining hazards, accident funds/mutual insurance was critical. Hunter Valley Coalminers centralised lodge funds, creating a more resilient regime where the vagaries of one lodge wouldn't jeopardise accessing benefits.[21] Like metalliferous unions, coalminers organised medical practitioners to treat members, the Lithgow union apportioning funds to retain a doctor.[22] Mutual insurance was extended to periodic relief for unemployed members.

In the Hunter Valley intense competition accompanying the removal of entry restrictions for new mines, together with unionisation, notwithstanding company opposition (destroying the 1862 union only intensifying bitterness), impacted on capital strategies. By 1866 some coal producers sought to remedy 'ruinous' competition proposing the vend system—a scheme for sharing demand for coal originating in 18th-century Britain. Unable to secure agreement or merge all companies, they adopted a degree of price-fixing. However, as production grew, coal prices almost halved to seven shillings a ton in the decade to 1871. In 1872 proprietors adopted the Vend (each company given a quota of total production), aided by the miners' union, which saw both pay and job security advantages. Turner argues this increased and stabilised prices; average prices per ton didn't 'fall below 12 shillings until 1880 making this decade perhaps the most prosperous of the century.'[23] Wages increased without hampering profits, notwithstanding increased production elsewhere especially in the Illawarra. It underpinned the Hunter coal-proprietors association and incentives to settle labour disputes through arbitration—a combination prescient of 20th-century developments.[24]

In late 1873 Hunter Valley Coalminers and owners negotiated a general agreement establishing a sliding scale of wages (hewing rates were adjusted by threepence per ton for every change of one shilling per ton in coal prices) and arbitration councils consisting of two employer and two union nominees with an umpire acceptable to both (with appeal rights to a central board). In 1875 the agreement was extended with additional pay for miners working in locations difficult to produce quality coal. Arbitration of disputes was central and Hunter Valley Coalminers were the first to use it in an ongoing fashion—almost 30 years before Australian governments introduced compulsory arbitration. On occasion the union objected to parties deemed to have 'an interest' in proceedings or delays in decision-making.[25] The agreement provided a platform for resolving complexities thrown up by piecework. A November 1874 delegates' meeting resolved disagreements over work in deficient places (height-wise) would be decided by local boards of arbitration.[26] The Association tried to prevent localised arbitration resulting in deviations from general hewing rates under the 1873 agreement.[27] In February 1875 delegates supported inserting an arbitration clause to resolve disputes between masters and miners in the *Coal Fields Regulation Bill* then before parliament. They also pushed to insert arbitration provisions on safety (rock and roof falls, crossing faults, and water) and related matters (like payment for installing timber supports) into the 1873 agreement.

For the union, arbitration didn't preclude lodge strikes. However, it advocated attempted negotiations or arbitration before threatening to withdraw labour. Keen to avoid practices undermining the agreement, it advised Minmi miners to keep their skips full. In July 1876 it proposed conciliation or arbitration to Alexander Brown in relation to 'low coal and lifting bottoms' (thinning of the coal seam) but telling miners to give 14 days' notice and promising union support if Brown refused—he didn't. The district union used strike funds from lodge levies to aid particular lodges, providing £1 a week to Greta miners in March 1877. Like others, the Association preferred single mine strikes to generalised action which rapidly depleted funds. Despite the agreement on wages there were many disagreements over skip-based piecework including proposals for standardised weights and a Borehole Lodge request all checkweighmen should report on payment for small and round coal.[28]

Lodges joining the Association had to meet minimum wage standards and comply with other rules. In December 1874 Four Mile Creek's application was refused due to 'the prices paid for hewing and other work' although the Association resolved to support them in disputes. It also scrutinised lodge bye-laws and oversaw district-rules on allocating work/ working on Saturday to maximise jobs. Managers had to seek permission for variations. Members breaching rules, like filling coal after five o'clock, were fined or suspended for more aggravated offences. In January 1878 the union warned any member working at Four Mile Creek for 3s 6d a ton (well below the district rate) would not be readmitted to any lodge without payout paying £2. In 1878 the Waratah Lodge was told to refuse admission to two miners cutting coal on wages (prohibited by union rules) for a contractor and Ferndale Lodge miners working on tops for wages were warned to desist or lose all privileges. Fines could be appealed. Job Morgan had a £1 fine rescinded in January 1876 but two Ferndale Lodge members failed two years later.[29]

Lodges referred suspensions and their grounds to Quarterly Delegates meetings, district interventions aiming to ensure consistency. In April 1876 Greta miners were readmitted to the union after a disagreement over hewing rate cuts. In January 1877 the South Waratah Lodge was censured over an agreement on coal prices without district consent (also charged with working on wages Saturday). Amidst deteriorating conditions the South Waratah Lodge was told settle but not for less than six shillings a ton. A year later (1878) agreements at Brown's colliery and Ferndale were censured as inconsistent with district standards. The Cooperative Lodge was censored over its proposed cavil (a balloting method allocating men to a workspace called a bord) of three miners to a bord and urged to follow the Waratah Lodge system.[30] Balloting for cavils was customary to avoid favouritism in workspace allocation, some being easier to work/more remunerative. Similar rules applied in the Western Districts. In December 1878 the Western Districts Secretary was instructed to draw up an agreement covering wet-places and faults and present it to the mine-manager for signature. A month later he was told to instruct the overseer to install a ballot-box for allocating spare workspaces. The Western Districts union resisted management efforts to circumvent rules by getting members to sign 'agreements' instructing members to refuse this and informing managers of this resolution. In April 1879 a resolution reiterated members should abide by rules on bailing of water. Rules were revised to remedy problems. In November 1878 the union resolved no miner should start on Monday after pay-Saturday unless every miner had received all their wages. Union membership was enforced, the Vale of Clywdd Lodge threatening to strike unless three miners reneged on an agreement with the manager not to join the union.

Other rules were negotiated with mine-managers or incorporated into the mine's codes, like requests relating to onsetters hauling up men at pit bottoms and being paid by 10 o'clock on Saturday.[31]

Hunter and Western Districts' union minute-books afford ample evidence of elaborate rules governing work (along with lodge rules and bye-laws issued to all members) and their enforcement amounting to unilateral regulation.[32] Union rules governing work originating in medieval journeymen's associations, its extent and importance are understated in labour historiography. Rules gave miners some control over work/remuneration, effort levels and other matters. It was well-attuned to dealing with fractured capital—even Hunter Valley coal-masters' organisation was incomplete. If anything, district-wide unions and their rules encouraged employer organisation in mining and beyond.

Complaints of unfair dismissal were common. District unions took up cases, resisting termination or seeking reinstatement of men and boys. In April/May 1879 Western Districts deputations demanded Richard Owens and John Williams be reinstated, giving 48 hours' notice of a strike if Williams wasn't employed. Even during the Vend/arbitration era the Hunter union contended with activists being 'blacklisted,' establishing a 1s per week membership levy to support any lodge secretary 'discharged honourably.' Unfair dismissal overlapped with wider issues of job insecurity. Some companies were accused of putting miners off on a regular basis. In January 1880 Vale of Clywdd miners asked to share available work.[33]

From 1877 the Vend was under increasing pressure. To prevent wage-cutting contracts the union supported a year-long strike at Anvil Creek with secret plans for other low-wage lodges to come out. Notwithstanding significant funding, by September 1878 Anvil Creek strikers and their families were suffering severely and in January 1879 were permitted to leave.[34] The Scottish Australian Mining Company never joined the Vend and by 1878 only four companies remained members, five others selling lower-priced coal. The Newcastle Coal Mining Company joined but this was offset by another new producer, Ferndale Colliery. Remaining members announced they would withdraw in October 1878, heralding more intense competition as coal-production capacity far exceeded demand. Appointing a check-agent to monitor ships taking coal from non-associated collieries, the union tried to negotiate Vend continuation with masters. A February 1879 membership ballot strongly endorsed the Vend and non-associated lodges told to warn their managers to join or risk strikes. In March the Vend manager was invited to attend delegate meetings—extended to voting rights in August. Unhappy with its production allocation, Lambton—a founding lodge—bent to management pressure and breached the Vend, ignored warnings and was expelled from the district union in April 1879.[35]

Under pressure the union accepted production increases for Waratah and Glebe (but rejected Greta's request), conceding to coal-owners it couldn't do its part maintaining the Vend. Confronting widespread unemployment, crisis meetings from July 1879 considered wage cuts and cutting production by reducing daily working hours from nine to eight and freezing new hires until men were working nine days a fortnight. The union's position continued to deteriorate. The New Lambton Lodge refused to abide by an instruction to 'lie back' until it matched other lodges, South Waratah miners were locked out for adhering to the Vend, Lambton colliery directors sought UK miners and coal-owners rejected union proposals for a conference.[36] The struggle took a violent turn when David Beveridge and Henry Thomas received two years' gaol after exchanging shots with EN Brown, president of the renegade Lambton Lodge. The union petitioned for clemency. James Jones, John Fletcher and James Steel pleaded guilty to unlawfully conspiring with others molest, threaten, intimidate, obstruct and assault Charles Davis and John Franz at the South Waratah Colliery on 8 October 1879. The Vend's partial output restriction couldn't survive in a competitive export-driven industry with multiple suppliers. As coal prices fell, the union tried to limit wage reductions to the sliding scale and maintain negotiated outcomes. A conference failed, sparking a six-week strike involving 1,400 miners, the union eventually conceding though with some concessions and re-established unity amongst lodges.[37]

Inter-Union Links and Politics

Hunter Valley Coalminers helped unionise Southern and Western Districts and assisted others like the Seamen's Union. Lithgow District miners implemented a strike-levy to aid Bulli miners in early 1879 and September 1880, and sent funds to Hunter Valley miners during their 1880 strike.[38] Collaborative networks of reciprocal financial support were important for worker mobilisation, making unions less liable to collapse even if they lost a major strike. Reciprocity was important although financial flows were imbalanced. Sydney trade societies donated substantial funds to the 1880 miners' strike, as did Illawarra District coalminers (£266), Western District miners (over £20) and Stawell (Victoria) goldminers (£50), totalling over £1,780. Informal groups like the Newcastle railway workshops also donated, indicative of inter-linkages.[39] Wider support, especially in working-class communities, was quickly mustered. Within weeks Western Districts' miners thanked the Lithgow community for contributions to the Hunter Valley strike.[40] Hunter Valley miners sent letters, telegrams and delegates to unions and locations to promote fundraising—a familiar pattern by the 1870s. Collaborative financial networks identified in this book were a critical but neglected aspect of worker mobilisation.

There were also chains of inter-union correspondence. In February 1879 Western Districts' Coalminers sought the Hunter Valley's advice and support after 29 miners were terminated at the Vale of Clywdd mine.[41] Like other colonial unions Hunter Valley Coalminers regularly corresponded with their UK counterparts along with membership clearance procedures. The union occupied an important position within intercolonial networks and union peak bodies, helping the Seamens Union in 1878—the Seamen reciprocated in 1879 as the Vend unravelled. The Sydney TLC asked the union to affiliate in 1874 and requested its involvement in critical meetings, including the 1879 Intercolonial Trade Union Congress (ITUC). The union also joined regional 'labour' deputations to the Colonial Secretary and other government officials.[42]

Notwithstanding close UK links, and many British-born members and officials, the Hunter union was hostile to immigration and exaggerated reports of colonial wages, countering this in British newspaper advertisements.[43] In July 1876 it organised protests against spending an additional £100,000 on state-aided migration proposed by emigration advocate Colonial Secretary Henry Parkes. Expressing alarm at 'the influx of labour into the district,' a deputation told Parkes the existing budget allocation (£50,000) was 'more than adequate.' Their concerns weren't exaggerated. In March 1877, 92 Cooperative Colliery men were balloted out (without union approval), the union urging other colliery managers to use last in/first out (LIFO) in labour-shedding. The union used its general fund to assist 'the distressed in Wallsend and other places' and urged lodges to support the committee appointed to manage relief activities. Coal-masters were approached for a 'friendly conference' on employment.[44] Despite its difficulties, in 1878 the union agreed to strike at any colliery supplying the ASN Company. It organised a monster meeting and petitioned against Chinese emigration, as an indication of solidarity not because there was much prospect of Chinese coalminers being introduced unlike goldmining, seafaring, cabinetmaking and rural work. British migration was a different matter. After the Vend breakup and a lockout loomed in March 1879 delegates debated sending a representative to UK mining districts to discourage emigration and three months later voted on sending £375 to aid striking Durham miners. Another petition opposed allocating additional assisted-migration funds while many miners were working half-time.[45]

Coalminers also mobilised over legislation, placing heavy reliance on legal enactment. From the early 1850s they repeatedly challenged coverage under master and servant laws. Unpaid wages sparked a dispute at the Minmi Colliery in 1864, one mass-meeting speaker labelling the law a tool of 'nefarious capitalists.'[46] Local MLA Atkinson Tighe subsequently made repeated attempts to amend the *Coal Fields Regulation Act* to improve wage recovery but the bills never got past the Legislative Council.[47] The union made further efforts with coalmine regulation bills debated in 1873 and 1875.[48] Other actions included petitioning in support of Angus Cameron's employment of the children bill in November 1876.

The union joined Hunter Valley mayors agitating for improved waterworks which not only improved members' living conditions but built
community bonds, as did annual lodge and district picnics.[49] However,
the pivotal issue was mine safety legislation. The first coalmining law
(NSW 1854) was threadbare and miners agitated for better laws. When
UK coalminers secured worker inspectors (known as check-inspectors)
in the 1872 *Coal Mines Regulation Act*, Hunter Valley Coalminers were
already agitating for similar provisions, sending repeated deputations
to the NSW government which dragged its feet before finally including
them in the 1876 *Coal Fields Regulation Act*. Amidst longstanding mis-
trust of government inspectors, mine-site check-inspectors were rapidly
appointed, carrying out inspections and producing detailed monthly
reports on mine safety. In October 1876 the Hunter union instructed all
lodge secretaries to furnish the General Secretary with a full report from
check-inspectors on the state of their mines 'to be inserted in a book kept
for that purpose.' In March 1877 check-inspectors were asked to report
on the number of men and horses being used in pits.[50] By December 1878
Western District coalminers were also appointing check-inspectors, being
paid for their time out of the union's general funds.[51] Check-inspectors
performed a critical OHS role that grew over time and continues today.
The importance of these measures cannot be overstated. They set a global
precedent for legislatively empowering worker involvement in OHS a
century before other industries, and remain a model for other high-
hazard workplaces.[52]

Metalliferous Miners

Informal Organisation

Numerous informal actions occurred at metalliferous mines, especially
over unpaid wages due to a combination of sharp practices, insolvency
and the industry's volatility.[53] In 1866 the apocryphally named Hit or
Miss Mine Kyneton became insolvent, and sold its machinery, stymying
wage recovery by miners.[54] Aggrieved miners might travel long distances
to court like six miners who prosecuted Enoch Cobcraft's Sunny Point tin
mine, the presiding Inverell magistrate remarking these recurring cases
placed singular hardships on workingmen.[55] Mining was (and remains) a
magnet for speculative ventures, one Bendigo miner railing against lease-
hold systems that rewarded 'capitalist drones' and left those who did
the work unpaid.[56] Anger spilled over on occasion. Reedy Creek miners
assaulted Captain Pearce and took ore to cover their wages. Another
group barricaded the New Raglan Street Quartz Company Ballarat manager and two associates in his office until issued with money-orders.[57]

Dissenting miners sometimes absconded like Northern Territory alluvial goldminers in November 1873 but strikes like one at the Normanby

Copper Mine (Queensland) two months later were more typical.[58] Volatile mineral export demand and prices sparked many strikes. Miners at several north-west Tasmanian tin-mines struck against wage cuts in September 1877. Barely eight months later 160 Mount Bischoff miners struck for increased wages.[59] Informally organised miners also pushed for shorter hours. In 1873 Moonta mine-mechanics demanded a Saturday half-holiday.[60] Mount Bischoff tin miners secured eight-hours in 1876, the directors conceding it was already practiced, highlighting pattern bargaining built on union gains elsewhere.[61] Nonetheless, in mining, hours remained fiercely contested. When Arba (Upper-Ringarooma) tin miners struck for a seven-hour Saturday in 1877 they were replaced.[62] Reported strikes by Chinese miners were rare, one occurring amongst Blue River George's Bay tin miners in 1879.[63]

Multi-Workplace and Formal Organisation

Metalliferous miners lacked customary organisation akin to coalminers' lodges although mine-specific unions were formed. Multi-mine/district unions emerged from the early 1850s with evidence of Victorian organisation in Mount Alexander (1851–1852, 1852), Melbourne (1851–1852), Bendigo (1852–1853, 1855–1856, 1856, 1858–1860, 1859–1860, 1864, 1865–1866, 1867, 1870, 1871, 1872–1901, accident society 1878–1882), Ovens River (1852–1853, 1857–1858), Goulburn River (1853), Ballarat (1854, 1857, 1858, 1866, 1870–1871, 1874, 1880–1898), Forest Creek (1856), Clunes (1857, 1873–1879), Wombat Flat (1857–1858), Stony Creek (1858), Ararat (1859, 1874), White Hills (1859), Inglewood (1860), Pleasant Creek (1860, 1864), Scarsdale (1863, 1870–1871), Eaglehawk (1866, 1871, 1873, 1879–1885), Maryborough (1866, 1873), Huntly (1867, 1872–1874), Walhalla (1867–1868, 1868), Rushworth (1869–1872), Eldorado (1869), Woods Point (1870), Bulldog (1870–1873), Brownsvale (1870), Harrietville (1870), Springdalla (1870), Rosewood (1871), Kangaroo Flat (1872–1874), California Gully (1872–1874), Llanelly (1872), Golden Square (1872, 1874), Stawell (1872–1900), Rokewood (1873), Daylesford (1873), Long Gully (1873), Creswick (1873–1874, 1874–1901), Grassy Gully (1874), St Arnaud (1874), Napoleons' Lead (1874), Cambrian Hill (1874), Haddon (1874), Buninyong (1874), Malmsbury (1874–1875), Blackwood (1874), Maldon (1874), Possum Hill (1876), Springhill (1878–1898), Dunolly (1879–1898) and Goldsborough (1879). In NSW miners organised in Bathurst/Sofala (1851, 1853, 1859), Tambaroora/Hill End (1852–1853, 1857–1858, 1872), Pure Point/Meroo River (1852–1853, 1861), Long Creek (1852–1853), Louisa Creek (1852–1853), Rocky River (1857–1859, 1860–1862, 1869, 1880), Araluen (1858–1859, 1869), Adelong (1859), Moruya (1859), Lambing Flat/Burrangong (1861, 1877–1878), Peel River/Hanging Rock (1861), Lucknow (1864), Grenfell (1868,

1872–1879), Majors Creek/Braidwood (1870), Trunkey (1872), Parkes (1874–1878), Gulgong (1874), Emmaville (1877–1878), Wombat (1878) and Barrington (1880). South Australian miners organised in Kapunda (1862, 1874), Wallaroo (1862, 1864–1865, 1869, 1872, 1874–1878), Moonta (1864–1865, 1867, 1872–1875, 1874–1883), Burra (1873), Humbug Scrub (1873–1874), Callington (1874). Queensland miners organised at Talgai/Warwick (1865), Gympie (1871–1872, 1878), George Town (1872), Mount Perry (1872), Stanthorpe (1872–1873, 1873), Peak Downs (1873, 1875, 1879), Mount Perry (1873), Palmerville (1874), Maytown (1879) and Broughton/Charters Towers (1880). Tasmanian miners organised at Devil's Den (1865), Georges Bay (1877), Brandy Creek (1878), Launceston (1877), Mangana (1878), Lefroy (1880) and West Tasmania (1880). Northern Territory miners organised at Palmerston (1873) and the Margaret River (1880).

Early unions were invariably short-lived but the early 1870s witnessed more successful rounds of unionisation centred on Victorian goldmining centres. A Bendigo union established in 1870 began forming branches in neighbouring localities like Kangaroo Flat and California Gully—some had to be reorganised. Independent unions formed elsewhere like Stawell and Huntly, followed in 1873 by Rokewood Junction, Clunes, Maryborough and Creswick. In 1874 further additions including a renewed Ballarat and Sebastopol union (with branches in neighbouring localities like Cambrian Hill) culminated in the establishment of a colony-wide body, the Amalgamated Miners Association (AMA).

Goldminers, Eureka and Related Dissent

Victorian and NSW government goldfields regulations sparked protests from predominantly self-employed miners. In late 1851 miners at Sofala, Louisa Creek and Mudgee protested regulations and their administration—including favouritism in disputed claims—affecting jobs/remuneration (printing 2,000 copies of their resolutions). The government's dismissive response to petitions aggravated anger.[64] In six months from August 1852, thousands of NSW miners mobilised, forming associations at Tambaroora, Long Creek, Louisa Creek and Bathurst/Sofala.[65] Victorian goldfields miners, too, organised from late 1851 at Mount Alexander, Bendigo, Ovens River, Goulburn River and elsewhere.[66] Pivotal to dissent was the license fee on gold prospectors introduced as a revenue-raising measure in August 1851, especially after the Victorian government announced a £3 per month fee increase from January 1852. Essentially a 'license to hunt' (i.e. search for gold) unconnected to success in finding goal (and thereby earning income) the license was deeply unpopular. Protests intensified in Bendigo, Goulburn River (where miners rioted after an unlicensed miner was arrested) and elsewhere, with threats of armed resistance exacerbated by increasing police searches (twice weekly) for unlicensed miners.[67] Some newspapers warned of insurrection and correspondence received in Geelong (September 1853) referred to miners 'arming themselves in all directions.'[68]

Matters came to head in Ballarat following a series of events, including the murder of a Scottish miner in October 1854 and subsequent acquittal of suspect publican James Bentley. The *Eureka Hotel* was burned and Bentley forced to flee. A meeting of 4,000 miners formed a Diggers Rights Society on 22 October. Angered by further arrests of unlicensed miners 10,000 attended a Bakery Hill meeting nine days later, establishing the Ballarat Reform League with a predominantly Chartist platform—some miners having participated in the UK Chartist movement—including no taxation without political representation. League efforts to negotiate with Gold Commissioner Robert Rede and Governor Charles Hotham failed. While Hotham announced a Royal Commission, Rede increased license enforcement/arrests and more radical opposition took hold. Miners burned their licenses and leaders like Peter Lalor more attuned to direct action took over. A stockade was erected on Bakery Hill with armed miners forming brigades and pledging a Eureka Oath under a flag bearing the Southern Cross like the 1851 Australasian League anti-transportation flag but with no Union Jack. It was a calculated act of defiance—even the first American Revolution flag (Grand Union Flag) included the then British flag in a corner. A significant international contingent included 200 Americans forming the California Independent Rangers under James McGill who went to intercept rumoured troops coming from Melbourne.

At 3 am on Sunday 3 December, 276 soldiers and police stormed the Eureka Stockade. Only a small contingent was present, presuming no attack would be made on the Sabbath. A short battle ensued, killing six attackers and between 22 and 60 defenders, some escaping but later dying of wounds and possibly one woman protecting her husband. Of the known dead, only one Will Quinlan was colonially born (Goulburn, 1832), reflecting miners' ethnic diversity including Irish, English, Canadians and Italians typical of goldrush mining. One hundred and thirty 'rebels' were taken prisoner and 11 (including Peter Lalor and three Americans) were charged with high treason. All were acquitted by a sympathetic jury much to the chagrin of the government. While small, the rebellion must be viewed in the context of more widespread miner protests identified previously. The miners had considerable community support unlike Robert Rede and Governor Charles Hotham whose poor judgement exacerbated matters. Miners' associations opposed any Hotham memorial being erected after his death in Melbourne in December 1855 as an 'affront' (eight Legislative Council members agreed).[69] Eureka also occurred amidst political agitation for greater independence within the colonies (Chapter 11). This helps explain Eureka's ramifications, not simply in replacing the license system with an export levy but challenging the government/judicial apparatus. Fears of another American revolution in such wealth-generating colonies accelerated the shift to democratic self-government within two years.

Participant Monty Porter was celebrated as a 'grand old man' of the labour movement 50 years later and the Southern Cross Eureka flag remains a symbol of radical unionism. Peter Lalor moved to conservative politics (nothing novel there) but the asserted association with worker mobilisation was correct. Most goldminers were self-employed but this didn't place them on the employer side of the capital/labour divide any more than Uber drivers today. Eureka protesters extended well beyond miners and their wives, and many miners were drawn from other occupations to which they later reverted. Young composer Charles Miller printed the Rebel Government's proclamations and ended his days (prematurely) as a companionship member at the *Ballarat Star*.[70]

Politics that sparked organisation remained pivotal as the proportion of wage-earners increased. Like British miners, legislative enactment and demands for direct political representation was central to the Bendigo Miners Protection Association (1855–1856) and unions that followed in Victoria and elsewhere.[71] Goldfields regulation remained a target, especially leasing arrangements favouring larger or speculative ventures which often cost jobs and left miners unpaid.[72] Some protests involved riots, as in Ballarat in 1857, but where miners were formally organised, peaceful protests predominated.[73] Over time the regulatory push extended to wage recoveries, restricting Chinese emigration and safety legislation. Nonetheless, lease covenants requiring they be continuously worked and employ a minimum number of miners remained significant issues. In 1866 Maryborough miners protested a lease locking up land at Majorca (that would employ 60–70) and in 1874 the AMA demanded action on lease breaches and lax administration.[74]

Mutual Insurance and Safety

Like coalmining, metalliferous mining was hazardous. Mutual insurance and mine safety legislation (vehemently opposed by mine-managers) were important mobilising issues.[75] From the 1860s accident funds with appointed doctors became common practices typified by the Northern NSW Goldfields Miners Association (1861–1862) and the Bendigo Miners Mutual Benefit Association—the latter formed following a concert to aid deceased-miner William Foot's family in November 1864.[76] Some bodies confined their activities to accident funds like the United Miners Mutual Benefit Association with branches in Grenfell (1872–1879), Parkes (1874–1878) and Gulgong (1874).[77] However, the Ballarat and Sebastopol Miners Mutual Protection Association (1870–1871) which combined mutual insurance with wages and other issues were more typical. An accident fund was critical to building the AMA—the most important metalliferous mining union—readily acknowledged by founder William Spence.[78] It was important, along with jobs, for miners' associations in other colonies like Tasmania.[79] The mutual insurance/safety nexus was equally important in copper, lead, tin and silver mining. Associations with accident funds were formed by miners at Moonta (with mine-mechanics 1872–1875), Humbug Scrub (1873–1874) and the Moonta and Yorke's Peninsular United Trades and Miners Union (1874–1883).[80] Some mining companies operated accident funds employing their own doctors. However, concerns over company-biased doctors' sparked disputes. In 1869 Wallaroo miners successfully struck for the right to appoint their own surgeons.[81]

Low wages and contract/piecework were seen to compromise safety. In 1868, Ballarat union advocate John Trevena claimed 'three-fourths of the fearful accidents which occur in our mines are attributable to . . . men being compelled to work at such reckless speed in order to earn a crust.'[82] However, removing practices viewed as productive by employers and remunerative by miners accustomed to tribute/tutwork proved difficult. In South Australia the Moonta and Yorke's Peninsular United Trades Miners Association protested use of nitro-glycerine-based dynamite (called lithofracteur) in December 1874 due its well-known toxic health effects.[83] An engineer dismissively refuted their concerns but the union drew on medical support to renew its demands in 1878.[84] The union also protested sanitary conditions in the mines.[85] In 1870 Ballarat and Sebastopol Miners petitioned for legislation to improve mine-ventilation, reduce injuries and establish a School of Mines to increase managers' and mining engineers' competence.[86] It also petitioned for injury compensation through employer liability laws and laws regulating leases and liens to aid wage recoveries, including pieceworkers.[87] Following coalminers' lead, metalliferous miners pushed for legislatively mandated check-inspectors from the early 1880s.

Wages and Hours

Wages and hours of work grew as mobilising issues with the shift to employed labour. In February 1863 Scarsdale (Victoria) miners struck against a wage cut—a catalyst for unionisation later that year.[88] Wage cuts sparked unionisation elsewhere including Daylesford (1865).[89] As with coalmining, piecework impeded shorter/eight-hours notwithstanding union support. Victorian goldminers pushed for eight-hours in 1865, almost 1,000 Bendigo miners later joined by Eaglehawk, celebrating success the following year before spreading to other locations. Gains were piecemeal, some employers demanding wage cuts for even smaller reductions as at Huntly in 1867.[90] In 1873 renewed rounds of unionisation were associated with coordinated and generally successful campaigns for wage increases/uniform rates (the common rule), together with another push for reduced hours in Bendigo, Clunes, Maryborough, Creswick and elsewhere.[91] In January 1874, unions merged to form the Amalgamated Miners Association (AMA), soon boasting 2,000 members and over a dozen Victorian branches—ultimately the basis for a national union.

Wages were the dominant issue for South Australian copper and lead miners followed by jobs, regulation/politics, mutual insurance/safety, working conditions/rules and hours. Wage grievances and management intimidation sparked strikes at the large Wallaroo and Moonta mines. In March 1864 over 350 workers struck, with engine-drivers coming out in sympathy, but notwithstanding offering compromises only won after ten weeks.[92] The union formed had lapsed by June 1865. A decade later, wage cuts sparked another strike involving 2,300 miners, mechanics and labourers in Yorke's Peninsular mines, the miners using ring-meetings to protect leaders and winning after two weeks (three activists were later dismissed).[93] This time the union (Moonta and Yorke's Peninsular United Trades Miners Association) was longer-lived, establishing branches at Wallaroo and Callington. It lost single mine strikes over hours in 1877 and wages/allowances and working conditions in 1878.[94] An eight-hour day was a bridge too far but Saturday half-holiday campaigning in 1874 yielded some success.[95] Like coalminers and goldminers, legal enactment was pursued to facilitate wage recoveries, given frequent insolvencies. In 1874 a bill amending the *Companies Act* was introduced making directors personally liable for servants' wages during their term and a year after they resigned.[96]

Jobs, Anti-Chinese Sentiment and Immigration Restriction

One less remarked aspect of Eureka was increased competition for remunerative work as migrants streamed in, later gold discoveries didn't match the early 1850s and alluvial deposits rapidly depleted. This coincided with an increased Chinese presence, their willingness to accept lower returns feeding racist sentiments. As McGowan demonstrates, distinctive Chinese work methods, notably using large cooperatives, represented an efficient if low-wage means of working alluvial claims.[97] In 1857 Ovens River miners expressly organised to oppose Chinese miners. In 1858 Tambaroora miners rioted and petitioned for Chinese exclusion and anti-Chinese sentiment also sparked organisation by Ararat miners in 1859.[98] Nonetheless, prior to 1860 Chinese miners only garnered mention in a minority of miners' associations, with jobs/regulation (especially leases and the gold export levy), wages and mutual insurance/safety the overwhelmingly dominant issues.[99] In January 1861 several hundred (estimates vary widely) European miners rioted on the Lambing Flat goldfield (now Young) to expel Chinese, burned their huts and cut pig-tails off a number. Over 1,500 miners met, forming the Lambing Flat Goldminers Protection League and petitioning for Chinese exclusion and new leasing arrangements.[100] The disturbance was widely reported but with few details. Overcrowding on a new field was common and the then recession probably exacerbated this, combining with different work methods/remuneration and racism already mentioned. Newspapers mentioned unreported friction/incidents on other fields. The miners received support from Bathurst (who urged peaceful means), Upper Meroo and elsewhere. The Peel River and Hanging Rock goldminers and Rocky River Miners Association petitioned to preclude Chinese from miners' licenses, citing wages/job concerns.[101] The government response deplored the violence, blamed the Upper House for rejecting its Gold Duty repeal bill and established tribunals to resolve leasing disputes. Elsewhere local mining authorities indicated no Chinese would be issued licenses.[102]

The 1861 protests represented a spike largely confined to NSW. Over the next decade goldminers' bodies were preoccupied with legislation/jobs (including arbitrating lease disputes and protecting water access), wages and mutual insurance.[103] In Queensland the short-lived Gympie Miners Protection Association (1871–1872) was notable for its anti-Chinese views.[104] In South Australia, too, anti-Chinese views were conspicuous in one body, the Moonta and Yorke's Peninsular United Trades and Miners Union (1874–1883), albeit the colony's most important metalliferous union. Nonetheless, the union took more concrete measures opposing mine-owner efforts to import British miners especially in 1877. Amidst widespread unemployment with jobless miners deserting the colony, union deputations and petitions/letters pressed the government for alternative work.[105] Similarly, Tasmanian miners' associations were overwhelmingly concerned with wages, regulation/jobs and accident funds.[106]

Victoria experienced a wave of anti-Chinese sentiment amongst goldminers in 1873–1874 during the unionisation push. Like Lambing Flat it related to a specific incident. Amidst generally successful claims for increased wages and (less so) reduced hours, the Lothair Company Black Hills (Clunes) extended Saturday afternoon hours in September 1873 and cut wages to 7s per shift, sparking a prolonged strike by over 100 miners.[107] While unable to obtain replacement European miners, directors rejected the union's offer to work on company's terms for six months until existing liabilities were overcome and then revert to working to union rules.[108] Pre-empting rumours the company was about to engage Chinese strike-breakers, in late October Clunes union officials visited Ballarat and, aided by a government interpreter (Reverend Young), urged the Chinese not to get involved.[109] On 8 December 1873 Chinese strike-breakers in protected wagons and under police escort left Ballarat en-route to the mine. The Victorian government's partisan role in providing police has been largely ignored by researchers although it was savagely criticised by labour-sympathetic political candidates well beyond the mining districts.[110] While anticipating opposition, the company and police underestimated the reaction. Alerted by telegram, around 1,000 miners, their wives and children erected a barricade at the junction of the Clunes/Ballarat road. After considerable jeering and a short, sharp struggle involving pick handles and stones, the police and Chinese strike-breakers were forced to retreat amidst cheering.[111]

Melbourne newspapers *Age* and *Argus* (less so mining-district newspapers) condemned the blocking of a public thoroughfare, assaults on police and impeding the rights of capital. Assaults on the Chinese received minimal coverage, reflecting anti-Chinese community sentiments. A Lothair Mine director told the *Ballarat Star* they only sought Chinese miners because they were unable to obtain Europeans experienced, alleging this was due to intimidating letters sent to European miners.[112] Even if the allegation was true it probably only involved a minority given general support for the strikers. Further, threats and violence against strike-breakers was hardly confined to the Chinese. Nor was the involvement of women unknown especially in mining communities. Illustrating both points in October 1861 Newcastle coalminers' wives attacked nine European seamen loading coal on the barque *Mandarin* during a strike. Miners later intervened to prevent police arresting the 'most violent' ringleader.[113] In both incidents, women, like their husbands, knew the hunger and want for themselves and their children attending a long-running strike. Attempts to break long-running strikes with more subordinate workers was—and remains—a catalyst for disorder, as are wage cuts more generally. In September 1869, 400 miners struck and rioted at several Eldorado mines following a wage cut, with ten police being sent in to restore order.[114] The Chinese miners in Ballarat had been urged by the union to stay out, and being moved to Clunes under armed escort could have had no misapprehension their arrival was likely to be contested.

In the aftermath, the Mayor of Clunes (also president of the Miners Association) was called on to explain his statements to a monster town meeting, including resolutions to resist the 'hazards' of introducing Chinese.[115] Five miners were charged with assaulting police during the affray/riot and fined a total of £80, costs met from a widely supported subscription fund.[116] Miners' unions in Stawell, Maryborough and elsewhere pledged support. The Lothair company stated it would employ 100 European miners at 7s 6d per eight-hour shift.[117] Clunes Union officials again went to Ballarat in January 1874 urging miners not to get involved, their efforts helping inspire formation of a Ballarat miners' union.[118] The company's inability to obtain strike-breakers from any quarter led to a resolution with the mine operating under Miners Association rules and regulations.[119] The Lothair strike intensified anti-Chinese sentiment on the Victorian goldfields and beyond. In March 1874 the Haddon Miners Association offered to pay engine-drivers if they would strike and thereby prevent subletting of the No. 1 shaft to Chinese.[120] Attempted use of Chinese strike-breakers occurred at other goldmines in Queensland, NSW and Victoria.[121] Racism cannot be ignored but nor can the use of Chinese workers as a low-wage option in Australia and elsewhere (like building west-coast end of the Canadian-Pacific railway where they were paid half the going rate of European workers). Capitalism has an enduring strategy of flooding labour markets to reduce labour costs and the Clunes riot should be viewed in this wider structural context even if it makes for uncomfortably complex history. The same drivers continue to undermine labour standards, including wage theft over the past decade associated with the introduction of large numbers of migrants and temporary-visa/undocumented workers in the European Union, North America and Australasia, magnified by high unemployment/labour market exclusion amongst already resident workers, especially the young (see Chapter 12).

Clunes also needs to be viewed within general anti-immigration campaigns by unions, including contemporaneous efforts by coalminers. Like coalminers many metalliferous miners were immigrants but opposed employer efforts to depress wages/conditions. In 1870 Ballarat miners wrote to their British counterparts and for wider UK circulation discouraging emigration, indicating there were numerous jobless miners in the colonies.[122] Overall, anti-Chinese sentiment wasn't a significant mobilising issue. Chinese involvement in mining was largely confined to relatively short-lived alluvial goldmining that was commonly succeeded by underground mining. Unlike China, Britain/Europe had a reservoir of experienced/expert underground miners and mine-owners pursued labour from these quarters. Inexperienced underground workers were unproductive, dangerous and unlikely to be accepted by experienced mineworkers.

Mine-Mechanics, Fitters, Engine-Drivers and Labourers

Labourers and surface workers at large mines occasionally took informal action as at Moonta in 1867.[123] Mine-based tradesmen sometimes joined their trade union while others established mine-specific unions, as did engine-drivers. The Wallaroo/Moonta Miners association of 1864–1865 included engine-drivers but was atypical. In towns like Bendigo, Ballarat and Stawell engine-drivers overwhelmingly engaged in mines formed unions.[124] The Ballarat union advocated only duly-certificated drivers be employed on safety grounds. Safety was also central to its push for eight-hours.[125] The union was labelled defunct in June 1872 but drivers met at *Brophy's Hotel* in November to consider the Ballarat School of Mines examination fees and petition for driver licensing/certification.[126] In Bendigo 'Knocker' complained mine engine-drivers were working 72–84 hours per week and the Bendigo Engineers, Engine-Drivers and Blacksmiths Association (1872–1877) pursued objectives identical to Ballarat.[127] Their legal enactment strategy succeeded, with eight-hours being mandated for engine-drivers in amendments to the 1873 *Factories Act*. In March 1877 the Gurdon Gully mine-manager was fined £2 plus costs for working engine-drivers 11–13 hours following a union complaint.[128] The amendment pioneered limiting male hours on safety grounds. The early

1880s witnessed a renewed round of unionisation amongst mine engine-drivers in Ballarat, Bendigo, Creswick and elsewhere.

Occasionally groups of 'non-miner' mineworkers joined alliances, including both unionised and non-unionised labour. In August 1872 Lambton Colliery engine-drivers, carpenters and underground day-wage labour, like wheelers, combined to demand an eight-hour day. A carpenter (William Wilson) was appointed secretary with delegates representing wheelers and labourers/pit-top men. Not being pieceworkers made it easier for them to pursue eight-hours, although amalgamation with Hunter Valley Coalminers was discussed.[129] In South Australia this divide had already been crossed by the Moonta Miners and Mining Mechanics Association (1872–1875) and Moonta and Yorke's Peninsular United Trades and Miners Union (1874–1883), the latter including surface workers/labourers.

Conclusion

This chapter examined miner mobilisation after 1850 that rapidly became politicised, including a rebellion accelerating the shift to democracy. Key mobilising issues were wages/remuneration, jobs, regulation and OHS followed by working hours. Unionisation in coal and metalliferous mining was marked by large confrontations although in the Hunter Valley there was a multi-year experiment with output restriction/arbitration. Arbitration was supported by metalliferous unions though mainly for disputed leases. Miners' unions saw reduced hours as a way of maximising jobs but were inhibited by piecework. Like British unions they turned to legislation to limit hours, remedy hazards and secure unpaid wages. The 1872 UK Coal Mines Act restricted hours for boys (and indirectly adults) to ten hours and an eight-hour day was legislated in 1908—in Australia this was secured via arbitration.[130] From 1876 NSW coalminers could appoint their own safety inspectors while metalliferous miners too pushed for mine safety laws. Over the next three decades British coalminers and Australian coal and metalliferous miners secured and extended miner-inspector powers, with similar initiatives in Canada, France, Belgium and other countries setting an important precedent for worker involvement in OHS. Mine engine-drivers joined others pushing for certification/licensing on safety grounds, those in Victoria securing an eight-hour provision under the *Factories Act*, another important precedent.

Together with long-established customary organisation (like coalminers' lodges) and community networking, miners' unions drew on structural power associated with the significance of their activities to colonial economies and the skill/experience required for underground mining. Unlike shearers, this was offset by large-scale migration. While predominantly regional, miners' unions had organisational power in the relatively large numbers they could mobilise and by the 1870s were beginning to assert considerable societal powers based on tight-knit communities and the political pressure this could bring to bear. Only the Hunter Valley Coalminers were able to draw on institutional power.

Notes

1. Dunne, E. (1950) *Brief History of the Coal Mining Industry in Queensland*, Paper given to a meeting of The Historical Society of Queensland 23 November 1950.
2. E165-33-1A Western District Coalminers minutes 12 May, 11 July 1879, 12, 26 February, 24 March 1880.
3. LC247-1-23 Hobart 16, 19 September 1851, 20 January, 21 February, 23 September, 8 October 1853.
4. LC247-1-23 Hobart 4 June 1853; *Colonial Times* 11 June 1853.
5. *Launceston Examiner* 24 February, 4 November 1855.
6. *Launceston Examiner* 23 March 1858.
7. *North Australian* 9 August 1861.
8. *Brisbane Courier* 15 November 1872.
9. *Maryborough Chronicle* 9 February 1869.
10. E165-28 Hunter Valley Coalminers minutes 21 January, 18 February 1879.
11. Turner, J.W. (1982) *Coal Mining in Newcastle 1801–1900*, The Council of the City of Newcastle, Newcastle.
12. E165-28 Hunter Valley Coalminers minutes 5 October 1876, 4 January 1877, 4 September 1878; E165-33 Western District Coalminers minutes 7 September 1878.
13. *Empire* 21 July 1864; *Illawarra Mercury* 29 April 1873.
14. *Brisbane Telegraph* 26 May, 8 November 1876.
15. *Brisbane Courier* 9, 19, 20 October 1877.
16. *Brisbane Courier* 21 February, 9, 21, 26 March 1878.
17. E165-28 Hunter Valley Coalminers minutes 11 February 1875.
18. E165-28 Hunter Valley Coalminers minutes 26 July 1876.
19. *Newcastle Morning Herald* 21 February 1879.
20. E165-33-1A Western District Coalminers minutes 22 January, 11 February 1879.
21. E165-28 Hunter Valley Coalminers minutes 4 January, 5 April, 5 July 1877.
22. E165-33-1A Western District Coalminers minutes 20 January 1879.
23. Turner, *Coal Mining in Newcastle 1801–1900*, 75.
24. Turner, *Coal Mining in Newcastle 1801–1900*, 85–86.
25. See E165-28 Hunter Valley Coalminers minutes 20 January 1875, 21 August, 5 October 1876.
26. E165-28 Hunter Valley Coalminers minutes 21 November 1874; *Newcastle Chronicle* 7 November 1874; *Miners' Advocate* 25 November 1874.
27. E165-28 Hunter Valley Coalminers minutes 11 February 1875.
28. E165-28 Hunter Valley Coalminers minutes 20 January 1875, 6, 13, 26 July 1876, 1 March 1877, 4 April 1878.
29. E165-28 Hunter Valley Coalminers Association minutes 1 December 1874, 6, 12 January, 6 July 1876, 3 January, 11 July, 15 October 1878, 2 January, 18 February 1879.
30. E165-28 Hunter Valley Coalminers minutes 6, 12 January, 10 April, 26 July 1876, 4 January, 5 April, 5 July 1877, 11, 16 July 1878.
31. E165-33-1A Western District Coalminers minutes 29 November, 5, 30, 31 December 1878, 22 January, 1 February, 28 April, 17 July 1879.

32. E165-33-1A Western District Coalminers minutes 11 August 1879.
33. E165-28 Hunter Valley Coalminers minutes 1, 30 December 1874, 21 August 1876, 5 October 1876, 15 October 1878; E165-33-1A Western District Coalminers minutes 28, 30 April, 12 May 1879, 7 January 1880.
34. E165-28 Hunter Valley Coalminers minutes 18 September 1877, 9 May, 13 June, 11 July, 4 September 1878, 21 January 1879.
35. Turner, *Coal Mining in Newcastle 1801–1900*, 87–88; E165-28 Hunter Valley Coalminers minutes 3 October 1878, 2 January 1879, 18 February, 7 March, 19 April, 3 May, 7 August 1879; *Newcastle Morning Herald* 21 April 1879.
36. E165-28 Hunter Valley Coalminers minutes 3, 15, 26 July, 7, 14, 19 August, 2, 6, 9 September, 11 November 1879.
37. E165-28 Hunter Valley Coalminers minutes 2 January, 25 March, 19 April, 15, 26 May, 7 June 1880; *Newcastle Morning Herald* 12 January, 10 June 1880; *Maitland Mercury* 6 December 1879.
38. E165-33-1A Western District Coalminers minutes 20 January 1879, 19 May, 27 September 1880; *Evening News* 23 July 1880.
39. *Newcastle Morning Herald* 18 June 1880; *Evening News* 23 July 1880.
40. E165-33-1A Western District Coalminers minutes 27 May 1880.
41. E165-33-1A Western District Coalminers minutes 11, 20 February 1879; *Newcastle Morning Herald* 21 February 1879.
42. *Newcastle Chronicle* 12 February 1874; E165-28 Hunter Valley Coalminers minutes 15 October 1878, 7 August, 9 September 1879, 12 February 1880.
43. *Evening News* 24 January 1873; E165-26 Hunter Valley Coalminers minutes 11 February 1875, 12 January, 20 May 1876.
44. E165-28 Hunter Valley Coalminers minutes 6, 17 July 1876, 22 March 1877, 3, 29 January, 4 April 1878.
45. E165-28 Hunter Valley Coalminers minutes 21 December 1878, 2 January, 20 March, 3 April, 3 May, 3 July 1879; *Evening News* 24 December 1878.
46. *Empire* 13 December 1864.
47. *Newcastle Chronicle* 3 December 1864; *Empire* 29 April 1865, 26 February 1866.
48. *Empire* 1 April 1873; *Sydney Morning Herald* 10 December 1875.
49. E165-28 Hunter Valley Coalminers minutes 23 November 1876, 3 January 1878.
50. E165-28 Hunter Valley Coalminers minutes 5 October 1876, 22 March 1877.
51. E165-33-1A Western District Coalminers minutes 15, 30 December 1878.
52. Walters, D. and Quinlan, M. (2019) Representing Workers on Occupational Safety and Health: Some Lessons from a Largely Ignored History, *Industrial Relations Journal*, 50 (4): 399–414.
53. *Bathurst Free Press* 7 May 1853, 22 December 1855.
54. *Kyneton Observer* 21 July 1866.
55. *Armidale Express* 13 September 1873.
56. *Bendigo Advertiser* 17 February 1875.
57. *South Australian Register* 7 March 1868; *Argus* 20 March 1868.
58. *Northern Territory Times* 6 March 1874; *Queensland Times* 20 November 1873.
59. *Mercury* 7 September 1877; *Cornwall Chronicle* 22 May 1878.
60. *Wallaroo Times* 16 July 1873.
61. *Launceston Examiner* 20 June 1876.
62. *Launceston Examiner* 1 February 1877.
63. *Queenslander* 20 December 1879.
64. *Bathurst Free Press* 10, 24 December 1851.

65. *Bathurst Free Press* 7 August 1852, 15 January 1853; *Sydney Morning Herald* 12 October 1852.
66. *Argus* 27 December 1851; *Geelong Advertiser* 18 October 1852; *Sydney Morning Herald* 10 December 1852; *Freemans Journal* 3 September 1853.
67. *Goulburn Herald* 3 September 1853.
68. *Cornwall Chronicle* 14 October 1854.
69. *Age* 2 February 1856.
70. *Ballarat Star* 22 May 1874.
71. *Bendigo Advertiser* 29 September 1855, 28 July 1858.
72. *Armidale Express* 14 February 1859; *Bendigo Advertiser* 5 March 1859.
73. *Goulburn Herald* 7 March 1857.
74. *Argus* 6 September 1866; *Age* 31 December 1874.
75. *Age* 11 November 1873.
76. *Bendigo Advertiser* 23 November 1864; *Ballarat Star* 5 October 1866.
77. *Evening News* 6 December 1872, 6 January 1874; *Empire* 2 May 1874.
78. Spence, *Australia's Awakening*.
79. *Mercury* 3 November 1877.
80. *Evening Journal* 7 August 1872; *Bunyip* 27 September 1873.
81. *South Australian Chronicle* 28 August 1869; *Wallaroo Times* 19 February 1873.
82. *Ballarat Star* 23 September 1868.
83. *Adelaide Observer* 5 December 1874.
84. *Yorke's Peninsular Advertiser* 19 November 1878.
85. *South Australian Register* 16 April 1875.
86. *Ballarat Star* 12 May 1870.
87. *Bendigo Advertiser* 29 April, 25 May 1870; *Ballarat Star* 6 December 1870.
88. *Argus* 26 February 1863; *Toowoomba Chronicle* 22 October 1863.
89. *Argus* 14 January 1865.
90. *Argus* 12 March 1867. *Bendigo Advertiser* 2, July 1865, 31 July 1866.
91. *Bendigo Advertiser* 13 February 1873.
92. *Adelaide Express* 5, 13 May 1864.
93. *South Australian Advertiser* 8 April 1874; *South Australian Register* 12 September 1874.
94. *Northern Argus* 11 May 1877; *Wallaroo Times* 23 January 1878.
95. *Wallaroo Times* 9 September 1874; *Yorke's Peninsular Advertiser* 30 October 1874.
96. *South Australian Register* 7 November 1874.
97. McGowan, B. (2005) The Economics and Organisation of Chinese Mining in Colonial Australia, *Australian Economic History Review*, 45(2): 119–38.
98. *Ovens and Murray Advertiser* 21 July 1857, 24 February 1858; *Mount Alexander Mail* 20 June 1859.
99. *Mount Alexander Mail* 28 July 1858; *Bendigo Advertiser* 16 February 1858.
100. *Sydney Morning Herald* 19 February 1861; *Maitland Mercury* 7 February 1861; *Goulburn Herald* 16 March 1861.
101. *Maitland Mercury* 5 March 1861; *Newcastle Chronicle* 21 August 1861; *Sydney Morning Herald* 16 September 1861.
102. *Sydney Mail* 9 March 1861; *Armidale Express* 21 October 1861.
103. *Armidale Express* 18 June 1869; *Evening News* 7 July 1870; *Sydney Mail* 19 February 1872.
104. *Gympie Times* 12 July 1871.
105. *Yorke's Peninsular Advertiser* 30 January 1877; *Express and Telegraph* 25 June, 6 December 1877.
106. *Mercury* 3 November 1877; *Weekly Examiner* 18 May 1878.

107. *Ballarat Courier* 24 September 1873.
108. *Leader* 22 November 1873.
109. *Ballarat Courier* 25 October 1873.
110. *Age* 21 March 1874.
111. *Ballarat Star* 10 December 1873; *Australasian Sketcher with Pen and Pencil* 27 December 1873.
112. *Ballarat Star* 17 December 1873.
113. *Sydney Morning Herald* 3 October 1861.
114. *Argus* 9 September, 10 October 1869.
115. *Leader* 3 January 1874.
116. *Age* 24 December 1873; *Advocate* 3 January 1874.
117. *Advocate* 20 December 1873.
118. *Leader* 10 January 1874.
119. *Argus* 6 February 1874.
120. *Kyneton Observer* 17 March 1874.
121. *Townsville Herald* 21 October 1879.
122. *Ballarat Courier* 27 July 1870.
123. *Wallaroo Times* 25 September 1867.
124. *Ballarat Star* 21 January 1874.
125. *Ballarat Courier* 9 January 1872.
126. *Ballarat Courier* 7 June 1872; *Argus* 15 November 1872.
127. *Bendigo Advertiser* 30 October 1871.
128. *Bendigo Advertiser* 21 March 1877.
129. *Newcastle Chronicle* 24 August 1872.
130. McCormick, B. and Williams, J. (1959) The Miners and the Eight-Hour Day, 1863–1910, *The Economic History Review*, 12(2): 222–38.

6 Worker Organisation in Building and Construction

Introduction

The rapid expansion of civil construction, commercial building and housing after 1850 swelled the ranks of building workers. In Sydney, Melbourne and Adelaide unionisation by stonemasons, bricklayers and carpenters built on colonial organisation stretching back decades aided by industrially experienced immigrants. Unionisation amongst other trades (like plasterers) and labourers only consolidated after 1860. The long-term trajectory of unionisation is evident in Table 6.1 in numbers, membership and the shift to multi-establishment, town/regional and several colony-wide collective actions. Strikes were still mostly confined to a single workplace and more likely to be lost than NSCA. Unions avoided costly multi-workplace strikes where possible, deploying other methods like unilateral regulation and using targeted strikes during general campaigns over wages and eight-hours—overwhelmingly the two most important issues—or resisting individual employer counterattacks (Table 6.1). Building unions used demonstrations (marches, mass meetings) to reinforce/cement gains and petitions/deputations to pursue political/regulatory issues like immigration, trade/apprentice regulation, subcontracting, eight-hours and safety (points expanded in Table 6.2).

Another major subcategory was building/construction labourers, large numbers involved in collective action (Table 6.2) demonstrating the importance of considering all workers, not just those forming unions. Amongst railway navvies especially, organisation remained largely informal with strikes (mainly over wages and hours) outnumbering NSCA. Government control of railway construction explains petitions/deputations activity along with labourers working for local government and political activity by labourers' unions. Echoing earlier points, labourers, especially navvies, were more likely to come before courts claiming unpaid wages or being prosecuted for collective action (and lose) than unionised tradesmen.

Table 6.1 Worker Organisation in the Construction Industry 1831–1880

Industry	1831–1840	1841–1850	1851–1860	1861–1870	1871–1880	Total 1851–1880
Entire Industry						
Organisations	32	44	174	192	174	465+
Raw involvement	217	648	10206	8861	16387	35454
Est. involvement*	268	1348	12555	16757	34287	63599
Strikes						
Won	4	6	15	5	12	32
Drawn				3	1	4
Lost	3	6	10	11	16	37
Unknown	7	6	33	24	36	93
Total	14	18	58	43	65	166
Est. total involvement*	42	554	3298	7866	4302	15466
Number of establishments						
One	4	9	32	21	43	98
Multi		3	20	18	13	51
Regional/Town	9	6	6	2	8	16
Colonial				1		1
Non-strike collective action						
Won	2	5	16	16	31	63
Drawn				1	2	3
Lost	2	1	10	10	11	31
Unknown	7	8	51	50	63	164
Total	11	14	77	77	107	261
Est. total involvement*	27	327	2671	3510	4239	10420
Number of establishments						
One	7	5	34	29	36	99
Multi	2	4	10	5	10	25
Regional/town	2	4	31	42	59	132
Colonial				1	1	2
Issues in collective action (strikes/NSCA)						
Wages	11/6	13/8	35/43	26/30	43/51	104/124
Hours	2/	2/1	20/30	14/44	13/55	47/124
Working conditions	3/4	2/3	9/8	6/4	6/7	21/19
Health & safety	2/	2/1	1/2	1/6	5/8	7/16
Management behaviour			/1	1/1	/4	1/6
Jobs/employment			2/6	1/1	2/1	5/8
Work methods		1/1	/1	3/	2/2	5/3

(Continued)

Table 6.1 (Continued)

Industry	1831–1840	1841–1850	1851–1860	1861–1870	1871–1880	Total 1851–1880
Unionism		/1	5/2	2/	5/12	12/14
Subcontracting		/1	7/14	4/13	3/9	14/36
Legislation				/1	1/	1/1
Unknown	/2		/1	/1	2/	2/2
Total strikes/NSCA	18/12	20/14	79/108	58/101	82/144	219/353

* Adjusted by multiplying number of zero-reporting organisations/years by industry median membership in that decade. ⁺For totals, organisation spanning multiple decades only counted once.

Informal Organisation

Informal collective action common prior to 1851 continued. In December 1851 Philip Brady's Hobart painters were charged with failing to work on Monday morning (seven days' solitary confinement). All pleaded guilty, Henry Nicholls stating 'I was not fit to work'—probably due to recreational drinking the previous Sunday.[1]

Collective Action by Navvies and Others Engaged in Railway Construction

While governments controlled, railways construction was undertaken by private contractors/subcontractors using predominantly immigrant navvies. As now, multi-tiered subcontracting was associated with quality and safety problems along with hyper-exploitation of workers. While episodic government budget cuts precipitated crises, problems endemic to commercial/work practices included regular bankruptcy amongst over-extended subcontractors, mismanagement, irregular payment, poor rations and the truck-system. Overwhelmingly, European indentured workers rapidly learned their wages fell well below prevailing colonial rates. Irregular pay and unpaid wages caused numerous disputes. In October 1857 Williamstown magistrates awarded several Geelong Railway Company navvies £1 16s 6d but censured their lawyer for scathing remarks about the company's irregular payment practices.[2] Large railway contractor Cornish and Bruce epitomised sharp practices, long known but unaddressed by law, shifting from weekly to fortnightly and then monthly pay, which together with outright non-payment sparked strikes in 1860. Their behaviour was symptomatic as was the 'endless misery and discord' it generated. The *Ovens and Murray Advertiser* stated contractor behaviour shamed the colony, families in severe distress treated like

Table 6.2 Worker Organisation Subgroup Summary—Construction 1831–1880

Carpenters, Bricklayers and Stonemasons						
Organisation numbers	28	29	121	130	105	292⁺
Est. involvement*	136	852	8587	8163	17719	34469
Strikes	8	12	33	17	22	72
NSCA	9	8	42	38	71	151
Absconding	3	1	1	1		2
Petitions	1	2	6	7	5	18
Deputations			3	8	10	21
Mass meetings		1	24	29	56	109
Marches			7	29	63	99
Letters/public notices	4	5	7	9	10	26
Bans			1	1	3	5
Court Actions						
Won	2	1	1		1	2
Lost	8	1	1		2	3
Drawn					1	1
Building and railway construction labourers						
Organisation numbers	1001	295	50	41	53	140⁺
Est. involvement*	4316	1708	4347	6425	9689	20461
Strikes	138	78	27	22	34	83
NSCA	1028	250	24	17	17	58
Absconding	920	200	10		6	16
Petitions	1	3	4	8	2	14
Deputations			1	9	4	14
Mass meetings			7	22	21	50
Marches		1	9	14	17	40
Letters/public notices			15	5	5	25
Bans	2					
Court Actions						
Won	21	13	5	6	1	12
Lost	730	410	12	8	5	25
Drawn	2	7			1	1

* Adjusted by multiplying number of zero-reporting organisations/years by median occupation membership in that decade. ⁺For totals, organisation spanning multiple decades only counted once.

shuttlecocks shuffling from one office to another pursuing their claims.[3] Occasionally violence ensued. In July 1861 Cornish and Bruce subcontractors' navvies near Kyneton responded to unpaid wages and wage cuts by striking, rioting and damaging unfinished track-work.[4]

Cash-strapped subcontractors doing 'a runner' were symptomatic of chaotic, multi-tiered subcontracting. When a South East Queensland railway subcontractor (McLaren) absconded in January 1865, actions brought against the main contractor (Crowshaw) were dismissed with costs of £2 2s awarded against the first plaintiff, the others abandoning their action.[5] In 1868 James McKenzie western line contractor at Rydal (NSW) left 200 workmen owed five weeks wages. They petitioned parliament their families were starving, one MLA (Cummings) telling parliament some men waiting outside hadn't eaten in days.[6] In South Australia 22 stonemasons and 18 labourers owed £250 by an absconding cash-strapped subcontractor (Rogers) sent a deputation to the Commissioner for Public Works who told them to initiate court action while he investigated.[7] Magistrates seldom considered costs and inconvenience imposed on navvies—men of few means—pursuing legal entitlements. The truck-system (tommy shops selling goods at inflated prices) made it worse. During a protest by Great Southern Railway navvies in January 1864, the non-paying and lying subcontractor (Turvey) was only saved from lynching by considerations for his 'non-offending wife and family.'[8] These problems were endemic to the colonies (and beyond), continuing even after NSW and Victoria passed contractor-liens laws in 1870.[9] Newspapers reported numerous riots/revolts and strikes amongst navvies. Smaller incidents in remote locations often escaped notice, sometimes revealed in passing asides like a Balaklava correspondent who observed 'the Hamley Bridge line of railway is almost in a state of lethargy, many of the hands having left disgusted with the petty autocracy of the "boss." '[10]

Exploitation, wage theft, hazards and regulatory evasion bred by multi-tiered subcontracting weren't confined to railways. In 1856, 40 labourers building foundations for the South Geelong iron-bridge congregated outside the Geelong Police Court in a doomed bid to recover wages.[11] Eighteen months later, 18–20 labourers employed by contractor John Tighe on the Surry Hills (Sydney) reservoir took court action. Five providing drays were rejected as not being servants. The others got their money but not before heated arguments over determining costs, symptomatic of the complexity of recovering wages.[12] In 1858, 57 tradesmen and labourers working on the Collingwood Wesleyan Chapel went unpaid by their contractor, driving some into insolvency.[13] Multi-tiered subcontracting on the Dandenong-Gardiner's Creek Road descended into conflicting claims and, ultimately, Supreme Court proceedings. One subcontractor was gaoled until his men were paid after a claim to Treasury. However, this and unrelated litigation (over partnership in the principle contracting firm Edwards and Co.) left another subcontractor unable to pay his labourers.[14] As an Amherst correspondent noted, governments were at the centre of much contracting and the wage-evasion-related distress it caused.[15] As with navvies, these incidents were symptomatic of hundreds of others.

Labourers pushed for legislative protections. Parliamentary questions mostly yielded answers amounting to ambiguous waffle, blaming small contractors with isolated concessions government funds owed to contractors didn't cover their wages. The small contractor explanation conveniently ignored multi-tiered subletting by larger contractors and under-bidding by subcontractors resulting from this.[16] The NSW and Victorian legislative interventions addressed only some abuses and years too late for many.

Multi-Workplace Organisation and Unions

Informal organisation by navvies sometimes encompassed multiple employers and, less frequently, short-lived unions like the Geelong-Ballarat Railway Labourers Committee (1858), Jackson's Creek Railway Navvies Mutual Protection Society (1858) and Melbourne-Sandhurst Railway Navvies Mutual Protection Society (1858). Some unions attempted mutual insurance but were mainly concerned with coordinating wage disputes. The South and Western Queensland Railway Navvies Committee organised protests including strikes over contractors not paying wages between February and November 1867. As was typical, the government denied responsibility. Shopkeepers' eventually refused credit, imposing considerable distress on navvies' families.[17]

More enduring unions were formed by building tradesmen and later labourers. Carpenters organised in NSW in Sydney (1851, Progressive Carpenters 1853–1910, amalgamated society 1875–1945), Maitland (1860–1861, 1865, 1870), Hill End (1871), Inverell (1873), Newcastle (1873), Bathurst (1874–1875), Orange (1874–1876), Grafton (1876) and Goulburn (1877–1880). Victorian carpenters organised in Melbourne (1850–1853, 1856–1892, 1866, 1880–1900 excluding suburban branches), Warrnambool (1854), Geelong (1855, 1869–1870, 1873–1874)), Bendigo (1858–1859, 1873–1874), Castlemaine (1859–1861), Williamstown (1859, 1879), Maryborough (1859), Back Creek (1859), Ballarat (1861–1873, 1876), Clunes (1869), Hamilton (1870–1871) and Echuca (1874–1875). Victorian bricklayers organised in greater Melbourne (1853–1855, 1856–1869), nearby Prahran (1856–1860, 1874–1879), St Kilda (1857–1860) and Richmond (1858–1862, 1876–1885), and further afield Geelong (1858–1860), Ballarat (1858–1870), Sandhurst/Bendigo (1859–1860, with labourers 1873–1874), Castlemaine (1859–1861) and Back Creek (1877). Elsewhere bricklayers organised in Sydney (1851, 1856–1857, 1861–1943), Adelaide (all with stonemasons 1856–1857, 1865 and 1875–1897), Brisbane (1868, 1875–1877) and Hobart (with stonemasons, 1860).

Victorian stonemasons organised in Melbourne (1850–1853, 1855–1991, breakaway 1860) and its suburbs (Collingwood 1856–1857, 1859–60, east 1860; Richmond 1856–1860; North Melbourne 1856–1857;

Emerald Hill 1857–1861; Prahran 1857–1861; Pentridge 1857–1860, 1861) along with Geelong (1856–1863, 1874), Kyneton (1857–1861) Sandhurst/Bendigo (1857–1873), Castlemaine (1857, 1858–1862), Ballarat (1857–1863), Williamstown (1857–1861, 1865–1868, 1872), Portland (1857–1860), Belfast/Port Fairy (1857–1860), Warrnambool (1857), Wilsons Promontory (1858), Cape Schanck (1858), Beechworth (1858, 1859–1862), Carisbrook (1858), Stony Creek (1858), Sunbury (1858–1861), Batesford/Moorabool (1858–1861), Snapper Point (1859–1860), Maryborough (1859–1863) Riddles Creek (1859–1860), Deep Creek (1859), Kilmore (1859), Malmsbury (1859–1863), Big Hill (1859–1860), Lethbridge (1859–1862), Amherst (1859), Taradale (1859–1863), Stony Rises (1859–1861), Harcourt (1859–1861), Ravenswood (1859–1860, 1860), Black Forest (1860–1862), Woodend (1860–1861), Ararat (1860–1861), Heidelberg (1860), Yackandandah (1860), Wangaratta (1860–1861), Inglewood (1860), Elphinstone (1860), Middle Stump (1860–1862), Bolinda Vale (1860–1861), Heathcote (1860), Two Mile Creek (1860–1861), Warrenheip (1860–1862), Ballan (1860), Campaspe (1861) New Gisborne (1861) and Dollys Creek (1861). In NSW stonemasons organised in Sydney (1853–1991) and its suburbs (Paddington 1858–1860, Waterloo 1868–1872 and Balmain 1880–1888) as well as Menangle Bridge (1861–1863), Singleton (1862–1863, 1865–1866, 1867–1868), Picton (1863, 1864–1865), Lapstone Hill (1863), Emu Plains (1864–1865), Barbers Creek (1864–1865), Muswellbrook (1865–1867), Mount Gibraltar (1865–1866), Berrima (1866), Nattai (1866–1867), Maitland (1866–1867), Clarence Tunnel (1867–1868), Lithgow (1867–1869), Cox's River (1867–1868), Western Railway (1868–1869), Goulburn (1868), Cooma (1869–1871), Mudgee (1869), Newcastle (1869–1871), Sodwalls (1869–1872) and Pipers Flat (1869–1870). In other colonies stonemasons organised in Adelaide (with bricklayers 1856–1857 and 1865, 1876–1880), Brisbane (with other trades 1857–1858, 1860–1991), Ipswich (1868), Gladstone (1868) and in Hobart (with bricklayers 1860, 1875).

Unionisation amongst other trades was largely confined to colonial capitals along with several major towns. Painters organised in Melbourne (1854, with paperhangers and decorators 1856–1895), Ballarat (with paperhangers 1870), Sydney (with plumbers 1857, 1859–1863, 1864–1870, 1870–1872, 1872–1873, 1874–1983), Maitland (1860), Brisbane (1861, 1863, 1865, 1866, 1867–1868, 1872–1873, 1878), Adelaide (1869, with plumbers 1871–1875 and 1875–1878, 1879) and Hobart (with plumbers and paperhangers 1877). Plasterers organised in Sydney (1852–1855, 1856–1857, 1861–1865, 1868–1870, 1872–1974), Melbourne (1853, 1856–1861, 1864–1870, 1871–1880, 1876–1883), Ballarat (1869–1871), Bendigo (1873), Adelaide (1851, 1875–1877, 1878), Port Adelaide (1880) and Brisbane (1868). Plumbers organised in Melbourne (1857, 1858–63, 1859, with other trades 1866, with gasfitters

1873–1901), Ballarat (1880), Sydney (with painters 1857, 1862, with galvanised ironworkers 1870–1872), Brisbane (with galvanised ironworkers 1865, with slaters 1866), Adelaide (all with painters 1869, 1871–1875, 1875–1878, 1879) and Hobart (with painters 1877). Unionisation was more sporadic amongst slaters and shinglers (Melbourne 1856–1859, with plumbers 1866, 1868, 1869, 1873; Sydney 1874–1875; Brisbane with plumbers 1866), gasfitters (Melbourne 1864, with machinists and slaters 1866; Sydney with other trades 1874), paviors (Melbourne 1870–1872). Building and general labourers organised in Sydney (1861–1885, bricklayers' labourers 1866, stonemasons' labourers 1869), Adelaide (with other trades 1854 and 1872–1876, 1873–1880), Kadina (with mechanics 1865), Port Adelaide (with mechanics 1873, 1878), Gawler (with building trades 1875), Moonta (with building trades 1877–1879) and Brisbane (1866, 1875–1876).

Building workers also formed wider alliances mainly to conduct hour campaigns in Sydney (1856–1857), Melbourne (1856–1857, 1874 and with labourers 1876, 1878), Hobart (1855, 1864, 1873, 1880), Brisbane (1857–1858, 1861), Adelaide (1863, 1865, 1874) and Perth and Fremantle (hours and wages 1873) along with jobs/immigration, weekly-wages and subcontracting (Sydney 1866; Melbourne 1872, 1874, 1877). Multi-trade alliances, often including labourers, formed in Warrnambool (1856, 1873), Bendigo (1856–1872, 1873–1874), Castlemaine (1856–1857), Williamstown (1857), Beechworth/Ovens District (1857, 1858–1866), Sale/Gippsland (1864–65, 1866), Ballarat (1869–1870, 1876–1877), Hamilton (1870), Bacchus Marsh (with labourers 1874), Echuca (1876), Launceston (1857, 1864, with iron-trades 1870, 1873–1874), Parramatta (jobs 1856), Newcastle (1867, 1869), Maitland (1869), Grafton (1870), Tamworth (jobs/wages 1871), Hay (1874), Wagga Wagga (1874–1875), Inverell (1878), Armidale (1878), Deniliquin (wages 1879), Goulburn (1880), Port Adelaide (1854, 1863, 1865, 1873), Kadina (1865, 1873), Wallaroo (1865), Mount Gambier (1866, 1873), Moonta (1873, with labourers 1877–1879), Gawler (with iron-trades 1873, 1875), Kapunda (with iron-trades 1873), Port Augusta (1877), Ipswich (1862), Rockhampton (mutual insurance 1863), Toowoomba (wages 1864 and 1865, 1872) and Roma (1875). Aside from odd wages/jobs protests the regional bodies predominantly pursued eight-hours, demonstrating the movement's geographic spread and importance as a mobilising issue.

Unionism spread geographically via both branch/lodge and independent union formation. Most metropolis unions claimed colony-wide coverage or had provision for branches but the Sydney Progressive Carpenters had to revise its rules when Hill End carpenters asked for a branch. Not all wanted branch status. Goulburn carpenters organised for eight-hours in 1877 but only asked Sydney to dissuade workers from taking jobs in the town.[18] Amidst, cycles of collapse/renewal union organisation only slowly consolidated. Even robust unions of carpenters, stonemasons and bricklayers in Sydney and Melbourne experienced tough times during economic downturns like the early 1860s when membership and funds of the Victorian Operative Stonemasons Society and Victorian Operative Bricklayers Society (VOBS) both fell precipitously and many suburban/regional lodges collapsed. The Victorian Stonemasons closed their Central Committee in April 1863 with colony-wide coordination reverting to the Melbourne Lodge.[19]

Jobs, Health Risks and Mutual Insurance

From the late 1820s unemployment, sickness/accident and funeral benefits was a critical function for building trades unions. Along with admitting members, authorising benefit payments constituted the most common activities at union meetings, with stewards visiting sick members.[20] Payments were made for work injuries like bricklayers William Tulk struck in the head by a falling hammer and Robert Wade hit in the eye by an ironstone brick fragment.[21] Sick members found out after hours risked forfeiting pay for that week.[22] Additional payments were made for specific cases. Shortly after establishing a funeral fund (1858) Sydney Stonemasons voted £10 to Robert Hume's widow and two years later subscriptions helped the orphan children of another mason unentitled to benefits.[23] The VOBS paid a former Richmond Lodge member's widow in March 1859 and in January 1873 paid for George Bradley's funeral (member only five months) as he had no friends in the colony.[24] The Sydney Painters took up special collections for widows of deceased members, especially those with families.[25] Some unions also covered loss of tools while Sydney Stonemasons purchased bulk tools in the UK to assist members' costs.[26]

Sickness benefits imposed significant financial burdens. In December 1880 the Stonemasons Collingwood Lodge had 15 members on sick payments, the longest for 580 days.[27] Retaining benefits during economic downturns was difficult. In 1870 the Stonemasons Cooma Lodge proposed a 2s 6d member levy for relieving sick members—lost in lodge balloting although another ballot retained unemployment benefits.[28] In the same year the Sydney Painters' society split over mutual insurance and divisions over temperance.[29] Societies sometimes waived financial arrears for members suffering prolonged illness.[30] Even the long-established Sydney Progressive Carpenters found volatile employment and high subscriptions caused significant numbers to fall into arrears—many forced to resign or lapse their membership. The number of financial members oscillated by 50% or more during boom/bust cycles before declining in the 1880s due to competition from the Amalgamated Society of Carpenters and Joiners (ASCJ), part of a global body better able to ride out these challenges.[31] Labourers' unions providing friendly benefits also struggled, with the Sydney United Labourers having 27 members in arrears in July 1870.[32]

Societies retained medical practitioners to treat members and help (as gatekeepers) administer their accident/sickness benefits.[33] When contractors like Cornish and Bruce made compulsory deductions for medical practitioners this caused friction.[34] Most, like the Sydney United Plasterers and VOBS, were subscribers or regular donors to infirmaries and hospitals (the VOBS had a Life Governor of one hospital) to treat injured or sick members. Orphan asylums and the Melbourne Ladies Benevolent Society also received donations.[35] Notwithstanding challenges mutual insurance met member needs and reinforced industrial solidarity even in remote locations because the opportunity cost of dropping out grew over time.[36] Mutual insurance supported other activities, minimising the number of vulnerable workers who might threaten standards. The 1862 Sydney Plumbers Society's key objectives were to maintain wages and pay unemployment benefits, rules specifying anyone accepting less than 12 shillings per day would be denied friendly benefits for three months.[37]

Unions also took more direct action on workplace hazards, arguing hot weather warranted eight-hours. In 1874 Sydney Stonemasons urged the Contractors Association to erect sheds for stonemasons to work in—not an option for other building workers.[38]

Wages

Increasing wages and setting uniform rates was another critical function. Unions pursued this through unilateral regulation, sanctioning members who broke ranks and boycotting non-compliant firms. Wage cuts by large employers posed a particular threat, resulting in prolonged strikes like that by Melbourne Carpenters working for Turnbull and Dick in 1877, the VOBS supporting them although bricklayers' onsite were non-society men.[39] Piecework threatened the common rule. In 1867 Sydney Stonemasons conferred with employers/contractors on 'day work' and sent delegates to every Sydney site to 'prevent any masons working piecework if possible.' The issue escalated into strikes at several sites. While conceding defeat in May, the union continued the struggle, listing members engaged under piecework. Responding to a complaint at the Sydney Exhibition site in 1870, the Central Committee said it 'had done all in its power to end the evil of piecework and it now remains for the men working there to entirely abolish it.' In October 1875 during proceedings against a member for accepting piecework, a Sydney Lodge member labelling it 'one of the greatest evils we have to contend with.'[40] The accused stated he only accepted piecework because he was injured—ordered to desist immediately without further penalty. Wages provided opportunities for united action but less so than hours. In 1875 Melbourne Stonemasons pushed for weekly (rather than fortnightly) pay.[41] Wage theft and wage losses when firms, especially contractors, went bankrupt also drew unions together. Victorian unions jointly campaigned for wage liens laws and advised on drafting bills like one introduced into parliament in 1876.[42]

Hours

The eight-hour movement was transformative for building unions. Early unions rarely took action over hours but this changed after 1851. In April 1853 Sydney Carpenters resolved to stop work at 4pm Saturday.[43] In August 1855 Sydney Stonemasons issued six-month's notice members would work eight-hour days, strikes gaining an early victory (October) at two church sites.[44] In January a Central Committee was established to coordinate agitation (including mass meetings, conferences with employers and deputations) offering a proportionate reduction in daily wages (from 15s for ten hours to 12s 6d for eight). After several strikes including Tooth's Brewery general agreement was secured by March 1856.[45] Stonemasons working during strikes were expelled and only readmitted after paying fines and apologising.[46] Melbourne Stonemasons rapidly followed suit. Echoing the movement's centrality and wider social dimensions they pronounced the campaign would 'improve our social and moral condition' and it was 'indispensably necessary we be in a perfectly organised condition.'[47] Campaigning entailed deputations, a march on parliament, strikes and advertisements, with membership increasing and new lodges formed during and after victory (21 April 1856). The campaign forged closer intercolonial links, Sydney and Melbourne agreeing to maintain regular correspondence.[48]

In Melbourne the campaign extended to other trades, prompting unionisation amongst carpenters, plasterers and painters. After four earlier attempts since 1839 Melbourne Bricklayers formed a union in April 1856, wrote to their brethren in Prahran and St Kilda and advertised their prescribed working hours on 19 August.[49] Sydney Stonemasons also tried to extend the regime, sending delegates to plasterers and bricklayers (neither organised) and calling a general building trades meeting in June 1856. Only carpenters sent delegates. A three-trade committee (carpenters, stonemasons and plasterers) was formed but soon lapsed. Stonemason deputations also sought support from Sydney notables including the Bishop, *Empire* editor Henry Parkes and merchant Robert Campbell. Only Parkes indicated sympathy and agreed to attend an August public meeting whose resolutions were distributed to different jobs. The society then encouraged all tradesmen to leave their jobs at 4pm, sent deputations to sites where employers threatened to 'pay-off' those leaving, took up a subscription for those dismissed and countered employer efforts to crush the movement. Eight months later matters settled sufficiently for a conference and agreement on starting and finishing times.[50]

Consolidating the eight-hour regime wasn't uncomplicated. Ongoing efforts were required to extend coverage, sanction those working unauthorised overtime and combat employers reinstituting longer hours using a combination of positive reinforcement/community pressure, unilateral regulation and strikes. Public dinners/demonstrations celebrated eight-hour anniversaries from 1857, some unions choosing the date of their own victory (delegates from other unions commonly attended) but eventually coalescing into a single day in each colony. Demonstrations affirmed the importance of the victory, its centrality to unionism and garnered wider community support. Persuasion took several forms including officials/deputations visiting worksites or employers. Sydney Stonemasons sent deputations to the Sydney Corporation in May 1857 and Sir Daniel Cooper regarding his new mansion in November 1858. Cooper stated he only accepted ten hours and piecework so the society banned members from the site.[51] Other employers readily acceded like W Williams in 1861.[52] There was a strong impetus to encompass the entire industry so work would start and finish uniformly. By the 1860s considerable progress had been made though sentiments didn't always match practice. In October 1863 the *Argus* reported amongst 350 painters and paperhangers in greater Melbourne subletting/subcontracting was rife, journeymen experienced intermittent employment and the eight-hour system was recognised 'but not strictly carried out.'[53]

Previously undocumented, from 1856 the eight-hour push began spreading to regions and despite periodic setbacks campaigns gradually encompassed more towns over the next 25 years. In NSW campaigns occurred in Newcastle, Maitland, Bathurst, Grafton, Hay, Wagga, Goulburn, Inverell and Armidale; in Queensland in Ipswich, Maryborough and Roma; in South Australia in Port Adelaide, Gawler, Kapunda, Kadina, Moonta, Mount Gambier and Port Augusta; in Tasmania in Launceston; and in Victoria in Warrnambool, Bendigo, Castlemaine, Williamstown, Beechworth, Sale, Ballarat, Geelong, Hamilton, Bacchus Marsh; Echuca, Back Creek, Clunes and Maryborough.

There was also logic to extending the movement beyond tradesmen. On building sites and in government works it was more practical and defendable for eight-hours to include labourers. Sydney Bricklayers sought eight-hours including labourers at the Sydney Corporation in April 1872. It simultaneously protested a contractor using labourers to do bricklayers tasks at the sewerage works, arguing this denied work to bricklayers and by cutting costs excluded other contractors from competing for the job, including its own members. The latter affords more evidence of the porous border between waged labour and self-employment in building necessitating efforts to proscribe labour-only subcontracting.[54] It also highlights two spheres of labour market control both important to the union, one advantaged by wider alliances the other by craft-based exclusion. Even with craft controls, however, it is important to note that the adverse wages/job-control effects of subcontracting extended beyond the trade.

Sanctions for breaching eight-hours included punishing members and strikes against non-compliant employers. In May 1856 Victorian stonemason Alfred Day was fined £10 for working ten hours in Sydney, a considerable sum Day could only pay by instalments.[55] Fines were typically smaller. In April 1870 the Newcastle Lodge fined Horace Smith £5 while the Sydney Lodge inflicted £2 each on five stonemasons working on the Hunters Hill Public School.[56] Some were merely censured like stonemasons doing overtime on the Stony Creek Bridge in 1858.[57] However, members might be expelled. In 1870 the NSW Stonemasons Central Committee informed Newcastle those working ten hours 'cannot be permitted to remain in the society.' The Sydney Progressive Carpenters expressed similar views announcing that from January 1874 members wouldn't fix joiners' work completed under the ten-hour system.[58] Enforcement included identifying breaches by other trades, the VOBS reporting stonemasons working 8.5 hours at a Hotham site in 1877.[59] Strikes occurred over attempted reversion to longer hours or systemic overtime like one by Lithgow railway-works stonemasons in 1868.[60] Defeat anywhere set a dangerous precedent reinforcing intercolonial and inter-union links. Victorian Stonemasons informed Sydney of strikes on several railway lines in 1858–1859 while the latter took out newspaper advertisements and sent £50 assistance.[61] Extending the eight-hour regime to other industries helped entrench it. Building unions supported eight-hour strikes by Melbourne Coachmakers in 1856 and 1859 and initiated both the Melbourne Trades Hall Committee and Sydney Labour League in 1856 whose successors organised unions in other trades (Chapter 11).[62] Peak bodies were especially important because otherwise supportive societies might be enmeshed in their own struggles as was the case when the Sydney Iron Trades Eight Hours Committee requested Stonemasons' help in 1861.[63]

Disputes also occurred over working through mealtimes and Saturday half-holidays. The half-day Saturday claim could conflict with eight-hours if it involved trade-offs. By 1863 Melbourne Plumbers had opted to work nine-hours on weekdays for a Saturday half-holiday and similar arrangements operated amongst Adelaide building tradesmen a decade later.[64] In March 1870 the Sydney Progressive Carpenters resolved carpenters couldn't work more than 8.5 hours each weekday to secure a half-day on Saturday.[65] In December 1872 Sydney United Plasterers sought cooperation from other building unions for a Saturday 1pm finish but were rebuffed by Bricklayers.[66] In 1874 Melbourne Stonemasons requested other societies' backing on the mealtime and half-holiday issues. Launching a Saturday half-holiday campaign in late 1875 carpenters, bricklayers, plasterers and builders' labourers sent a joint deputation to the Contractors Association. In November 1877 the VOBS initiated its own campaign before joining with others in October 1878.[67] A lockout occurred at the Eastern Markets site after bricklayers tried to emulate stonemasons leaving at midday. The union amended its rule, specifying a 45 hour week (five days at eight-hours and five hours on Saturday) and eventually won its claim. However, the contractor refused to dismiss 25 bricklayers working during the lockout. The committee and pickets determined they be fined from £1 to £10 depending on culpability. The fines and lockout costs imposed on the Prahran Lodge fractured relations with Melbourne eventually also drawing in the Richmond Lodge.[68] This highlighted branch independence and complications that could arise in protracted disputes. Another problem was reconciling claims with some working 8.5 hours during the week for early finishing on Saturday, a practice Sydney Stonemasons viewed incompatible with the eight hour principle.[69]

The eight-hour struggle drew unions into politics. In October 1870 Sydney Bricklayers called a public meeting to petition for a bill introduced by JB Wilson and promoted by the Eight Hour Extension and Short Hours League to extend eight-hours to 'all classes of the community where practicable.' One aim was to prevent non-eight hour based tenders winning out in government contracts.[70]

Craft Control and Unilateral Regulation

Regulating craft knowledge, apprenticeship and apprentice/tradesmen ratios were centuries-old means of controlling labour markets and working conditions. Unlike some manufacturing, technological change had less impact on building. Nonetheless, there were ongoing concerns about employers using unbound apprentices/boy-labour, undermining rules specifying the maximum age for apprentices, and ensuring apprentices were bound by written agreement.[71] Those prosecuted included self-employed members like bricklayer John Locke fined for employing none but apprentices while another member (Westman) was sanctioned for having four boys, three being apprentices. Control efforts included fielding enquiries for country-parents about age, pay and other requirements.[72] To promote local training unions and peak bodies promoted establishing working men's colleges. A few pursued mutual -improvement.[73] The NSW Stonemasons Society maintained a library and paid librarian (sending materials to country lodges) until 1868—its materials lingered on—as did unions in other industries, notably the Melbourne Typographical Society.[74]

Unilateral regulation, relying on compulsory membership and elaborate working rules governing members dominated building union methods, the VOBS notifying employers that from 22 May 1858 members would only work for employers compliant with its rules. The following February, sites with a majority of members were told they could strike against non-society bricklayers.[75] Unions printed rule books with copies issued to every member, a ready guide to work practices/conditions. Rules typically covered accident/sickness and funeral funds, wages, working hours, work methods, apprenticeship/use of improvers, subcontracting, fines and appeal procedures. Rules forbade working with non-society members, and those withdrawing from a workplace in accordance with this were awarded strike pay, the Sydney Bricklayers' minute-books revealing a steady stream of such cases.[76] Rules underwent periodic revision that were extensively debated and decided on by society-wide ballots. Encapsulating union procedures and working conditions, they assisted others forming unions.[77]

Members working below set wages or longer hours, with non-unionists, or allowing labourers to do trade work risked fines, suspension from friendly benefits or expulsion. Societies had a standing or management committee which adjudicated cases along with preparing reports on issues and drafting rule changes.[78] Members reported non-compliant members, the complaint then investigated by calling witnesses and hearing evidence with fines most common for those found guilty.[79] Bricklayer Henry Hills was fined ten shillings for working two days with a non-society member. Refusal to pay risked expulsion or members at the same site withdrawing their labour, as the Sydney Bricklayers did to WD Bull in May 1870.[80] Fines could be reduced for mitigating or personal grounds. In 1860 the Victorian Stonemasons Central Committee urged the Ravenswood Lodge to mitigate Philip Hole's fine because his prompt reporting of subletting avoided 'a rupture' on the job.[81] In exceptional circumstances rules were waived. In March 1867 Williamstown Stonemasons approved overtime for members repairing a dock until the bottom course of stonework was laid as a 'case of necessity.'[82] Sydney Bricklayers exonerated five members laying asphalt blocks in George St from working unauthorised overtime, finding the work was urgent to city business.[83] At the same time, unions assisted members underpaid on a job through no fault of their own, most commonly when they left following a disagreement with their employer.[84]

Sometimes more general action was required. In July 1856 Melbourne Stonemasons established a black book of non-compliant members and Sydney followed suit.[85] In 1871 Sydney Bricklayers sent deputations to three sites using non-society men securing agreements at two.[86] The following year the VOBS sent a deputation to a Brunswick St site breaching eight-hour rules (with mixed results) and responded to another round of complaints in December.[87] Societies wrote to firms violating rules as the Sydney United Plasterers did with Lewis and Steel in July 1877 before ordering members to withdraw.[88] Enforcement became harder during downturns. Matthew Medway took a job at Tooth's Brewery (now back to ten hours) in early 1860, the Stonemasons Society eventually resolving not to expel him.[89] Craft societies maintained strike funds with rules governing their allocation. Funds were sometimes dispatched to branches/lodges when a strike was imminent as the Victorian Stonemasons did for their Sandhurst Lodge in August 1859.[90] Strike levies were also imposed periodically.[91] During downturns societies could only fight a few strategic struggles and only if jobless numbers didn't preclude prospects of success. In 1866 Sydney Stonemasons refused to endorse several strikes but appointed pickets at the St Mary's Cathedral site and Mr Wadsworth's railway job.[92]

Unilateral regulation relied on controlling trade entry and worker movement between locations. The House-of-Call declined, the Sydney Friendly Society of Carpenters and Joiners (later Progressive Carpenters) abandoning it after 1856.[93] Melbourne Carpenters were still operating theirs in 1857, accusing contractor George Cornwell of gulling six members who walked to the St Kilda grammar school site only to find no work.[94] Where possible, craft societies still acted as recruiting points for labour.[95] Echoing another medieval work-distribution device in the 1860s both the Victorian Stonemasons Emerald Hill Lodge and NSW Stonemasons Cox's River Lodge unsuccessfully advocated a tramping allowance.[96] Older/infirm workers willing to take any work threatened unilateral regulation requiring some compromises. Reviewing the case of a 60-year-old member in 1872, the Sydney Bricklayers amended rules so those over 50 years could work with non-society men but not break the eight-hour rule.[97] Another issue for unilateral regulation was the regular movement of workers between employment, self-employment and small employer status. In 1874 the newly formed Sydney Painters rapidly revised rules on members working for themselves when it lost members.[98]

Unilateral regulation encouraged organising nearby locations, forming alliances with 'neighbouring' craft societies and corresponding/swapping rules with intercolonial counterparts.[99] In six years from 1855, stonemasons established over 60 lodges throughout Victoria; not just major centres like Geelong, Ballarat and Sandhurst/Bendigo, but small towns like Belfast/Port Fairy including ones dotted along the spreading railway network[100] Many closed after a year or two as work on bridges/viaducts, commercial or public buildings was completed while others collapsed with some being renewed. Similarly, the VOBS (1856), organised lodges in Prahran, Richmond and St Kilda (now Melbourne suburbs), dispatched a member to Hobart and sent rules and membership cards to the newly formed Adelaide bricklayers and stonemasons society.[101] It collaborated with Sandhurst, Castlemaine and Geelong, negotiating agreements on membership transfers and other matters, and urging Ballarat bricklayers to do the same.[102] In 1858 the VOBS resolved to assist the Melbourne labourers' society where 'practical' and seven years later was asked to give employment preference to their members over non-society men.[103] In May 1873 the Bricklayers and Labourers Societies negotiated joint action to enforce union membership. However, relations soured when the Bricklayers backed out and the Labourers Society introduced a rule specifying the ratio of bricklayers to labourers which was seen to infringe on bricklayers' job opportunities. The VOBS responded by boycotting Labourers

Society members.[104] This incident highlights not only labourers' unions practicing unilateral regulation, but problems posed by conflicting rules.

Widening Alliances, Intercolonial and Global Networks

Exchanging information on trade conditions and discouraging oversupply of emigrants were imperatives. Colonial and British unions began corresponding in the 1830s, becoming regularised after 1850, including swapping trade circulars, reports, publications and rules using enhanced shipping links (vessel numbers and speed), telegraphic communication (enabling rapid messages and funds-shifting) and occasional visits by officials.[105] Within months of formation the VOBS sent letters to other colonial and British unions. Victorian and NSW Stonemasons societies corresponded weekly while regularly communicating with other colonies and their English, Scottish and Irish counterparts.[106] Communication facilitated organisation, Melbourne Stonemasons providing the newly formed Brisbane society with blank minute-books, rules and forms, and looping them into intercolonial correspondence networks.[107] In 1859 Sydney Bricklayers asked the VOBS to assist with eight-hours and help them form a society (following earlier attempts in 1842–1844, 1851 and 1856–1857).[108] Nonetheless it took another two years before a more enduring body was established which began regular correspondence with Melbourne including dealing with a Sydney Exhibition Building-site contractor in 1870. Expressing admiration for the Melbourne Trades Hall, the Sydney Bricklayers Society used VOBS rules to revise its trustee rules.[109] The Sydney Progressive Carpenters also used its Victorian counterpart's rules as a model in 1872 and corresponded with Victoria and Queensland on wages and trade matters.[110] In October 1876 the Sydney United Plasterers Society warned its New Zealand and Melbourne counterparts of a wages strike.[111] Moves to coordinated campaigns also began, Queensland Carpenters indicating they would join any wage demands initiated by Sydney in April 1878.[112]

Specific incidents demonstrate communication's importance. In February 1859 the Stonemasons' Moorabool Lodge wrote to Melbourne complaining Sydney Stonemasons were working on the Batesford Bridge at 1s 6d per hour.[113] In 1860 Sydney Stonemasons sent £21 10s to Victoria to help masons migrate to New Caledonia following the Cornish and Bruce struggles.[114] Funds aided other unions during prolonged strikes. In 1859 the VOBS provided £100 to striking stonemasons (a loan subsequently repaid), £80 to striking coachbuilders and £40 to Castlemaine bricklayers.[115] These were substantial sums and building unions made hundreds of similar payments. Assistance was significant even in 'run of the mill' strikes. Campaigns on wages, union membership, employment, and hours demonstrated the benefits of inter-society coordination, notwithstanding odd disagreements over demarcation, jurisdiction and industrial strategy. Unions competing for members in the same trade were rare and short-lived—typically a 'scab' or breakaway body with one notable exception. From 1875 the UK-based Amalgamated Society of Carpenters and Joiners (ASCJ) established colonial branches, directly competing with existing carpenters' unions. In November 1877 the Sydney ASCJ proposed amalgamation with the Sydney Progressive Carpenters. Amounting to the latter subsuming themselves to the ASCJ it was declined, initiating long-term battle between rival unions, only ending in 1910 although this didn't affect industrial campaigns.[116]

In Melbourne, Sydney and Adelaide building unions led moves to form peak bodies—a conduit for wider information flows and alliances. Securing eight-hours was the impetus for collaboration in building and especially so outside colonial capitals where union of individual trades was fragmentary or entirely absent in many towns. Victorian building unions held a conference in 1872, where proposals for a formal alliance failed but there were subsequent general campaigns by craft and labourers' unions for a Saturday half-holiday and increased wages in 1874–1876. By 1876 an identical log of claims was being pursued in NSW.[117] In 1878 300 Melbourne building workers met at the Old Trades Hall to support bricklayers' striking for a Saturday half-holiday at the Eastern Markets.[118] Other collaborations included pressuring the Commissioner of Public Works over below-rate wages paid by a contractor on the Chief Secretary's building in March 1877. Due to unilateral regulation only 11 carpenters were left on site, WE Murphy and James Stephens arguing against granting the contractor time-extensions on this ground.[119]

Branch/Lodge and Workshop Organisation

As branch/lodge numbers grew, coordinating activities became more challenging. Communication relied on post/telegraph, coaches, steamers and the expanding railway network to dispatch minute and rule books; account sheets; contribution, clearance and membership cards; shop-steward books; and annual reports, and receive in turn branches/lodge remittances/accounts, requests/queries, election/ballot results, proposed rule changes and decisions on collective action. Notwithstanding problems when small lodges struggled/collapsed or there were profound disagreements (rare), the system worked largely due to voluntary efforts by office-holders. Lodge officials were reimbursed for travel and attendance expenses while secretaries received a stipend. Even large metropolitan bodies seldom exceeded 1,000 members, generally far fewer, especially when suburban branches were established. Small size was conducive to democracy, marked by high/compulsory meeting attendance, robust debate over policies/actions and balloting major decisions. Within a month of being formed the Sodwalls Lodge moved to amend resolutions relating to the Stonemasons Society library.[120]

Building unions appointed shop stewards at sites to oversee member-ship, collect and return subscriptions/arrears. Victorian Operative Stone-masons were appointing stewards by August 1856 (issuing specific books for them) and by 1859 the VOBS had stewards on sites like the Bay St hotel Sandridge.[121] In April 1871 Sydney Bricklayers appointed Wil-liam Rudd as steward at the Petersham Anglican Church site to deal with non-society bricklayers—which he seems to have done.[122] In country regions lodges based on railway construction were effectively workplace or contractor-based. Branches/lodges were a springboard for further organisation, the Stony Creek Stonemasons' Lodge appointing shop stewards on the Footscray section of the Melbourne/Murray railway line in 1858.[123]

Subcontracting, Piecework and Other Threats

Subcontracting was (and remains) a threat for building unions given its association with cost-cutting, low wages/piecework, wage-defaults, safety problems and union avoidance.[124] In 1859 the VOBS repeatedly memo-rialised the Institute of Architects to stop subcontracting, investigated ways of abolishing the practice and revised its bye-laws to ban members from accepting it. Contemplating a multi-union campaign, it turned to the Operatives Board of Trade (Chapter 11) but was disappointed with the support received.[125] Twenty years later the union sent anti-piecework deputations to architects and the Commissioner for Public Works.[126] The NSW Bricklayers also campaigned against subcontracting, sending depu-tations to architects and brickmakers in 1870 (with some success) and distributing a printed letter outlining its case.[127]

Railway construction became the focus of intense struggles over sub-contracting and associated practices. Cornish and Bruce, undertaking considerable Victorian government work, built an anti-union reputation. During the 1856 eight-hour struggle William Cornish stood out, eventu-ally securing £1,700 government compensation notwithstanding wage offsets included in the deal. After winning railway construction contracts the firm imported indentured labour from Britain and Germany and other profit-maximising measures, cutting wages, no/slow payment, the truck-system and corner-cutting on work quality.[128] Cornish and Bruce repeatedly sought to break eight-hours and undermine union influence, leading to strikes by stonemasons and others on the Geelong/Ballarat and Melbourne-Sandhurst railway lines in December 1858. By 20 Janu-ary 1859 the Stonemasons Society Central Committee had sent £925 strike pay, lodges contributing another £341 by 17 February and car-penters and bricklayers' societies contributing £200. The Strike Commit-tee telegraphed Sydney and published strike-advertisements in Sydney, Adelaide, Hobart and Launceston. Legal counsel was retained to repre-sent strikers charged with trespassing on their contractor-rented grounds and public meetings organised. A delegation explained their case and asked the Chief Secretary for Cornish and Bruce's contract conditions. The Geelong Lodge persuaded stonemasons from Adelaide and Hobart engaged by Edwards Merry and Co at 14s per ten-hour day to abandon the Geelong/Ballarat railway-works, paying their return fares. Three barristers volunteered their services when the Adelaide men were charged with breaching their contracts. Pickets were sent to Hobson's Bay (Port Melbourne) to dissuade strike-breakers hired by Cornish and Bruce. Delegates and interpreters went to Sunbury to remonstrate with indentured German and other masons continuing to work. These efforts along with public pressure organised by a Citizens Committee of Enquiry secured a 'successful termination.'[129]

The resolution didn't last. Bruce (Cornish had died) continued to import German masons indentured at lower wages and ten-hour days, that together with other practices sparked further strikes on the Geelong-Ballarat line and at his Castlemaine works. The Stonemasons Central Committee appointed a German-fluent agent (Schultz), published a German-language circular, provided £130 strike pay to German masons joining the cause and later utilising a German Committee.[130] Strike action, including carpenters and bricklayers, extended into 1860. In January 1860 the VOBS picketed John Bruce's Melbourne office following warnings from Castlemaine that Bruce was going there to recruit strike-breakers.[131] Stonemasons implemented a strike-levy (black-listing members not contributing) and sent a deputation to Malmsbury after Bruce cut wages there. In July further disputes erupted as Bruce introduced wage cuts affecting navvies, stonemasons and others. Stonemasons at Lethbridge and Moorabool were dismissed and replaced by members of the Free and Independent Stonemasons of Victoria—probably Australia's first scab-union. Negotiations failing, the Central Committee telegraphed Ballarat to withdraw all railway-works labour. Some disputes were resolved but underlying difficulties continued to fester, leading to further flare-ups, like German masons working over eight-hours at Harcourt in October/November 1860. Again, union negotiation efforts failed. As labour market conditions worsened the Central Committee resolved to concede (with conditions) wage cuts to 14s per day on the Geelong/ Ballarat railway-works in January 1861 but was over-ruled and obliged to strike after a lodge-initiated ballot. Attempts to sublet work—another cost-cutting measure—led to further long and costly strikes (the Central Committee releasing £990 strike pay in May–August 1861 alone) on both the Ballarat/Geelong and Sunbury/Mount Alexander railway-works.[132]

These struggles shouldn't be viewed in isolation. As indicated earlier, there were dozens of strikes/disputes on Victorian railway-works involving navvies, most over similar issues to those involving stonemasons, carpenters and bricklayers' unions. Employers imported labour to push down wages. Cornish and Bruce were especially aggressive but symptomatic of practices connected to subcontracting, including privatising public works. Similar struggles played out in other colonies. In June 1868 NSW Western line stonemasons struck when the main contractor refused to take responsibility for wages owed by subcontractors. The Society sent a deputation to the Minister for Works protesting subcontracting on railway lines.[133] Labour-only subcontracting was viewed as akin to piecework, Sydney Bricklayers fining those taking it like two members on a Newtown job in February 1880.[134] Of course, these practices, including the exploitation of foreign workers (now often on temporary visas), are widespread today following renewed waves of privatisation/outsourcing since the 1980s, eroding labour standards and systemic wage theft—an iceberg of exploitation campaigns on modern slavery laws capture only a tiny fragment of.[135]

Contractor/subcontractor insolvencies leaving workers unpaid extended well beyond railway construction. In February 1874 the Sydney Stonemasons Society told architects (Mansfield Brothers) for the Commercial Bank Haymarket building the site would be boycotted until the masons engaged by an insolvent contractor were paid.[136] Non-payment wasn't confined to insolvencies. Sydney Bricklayers proposed rules banning members from taking jobs at sites where another member hadn't received their entitlements. Increasingly looking to legislative solutions, in 1873 the union asked the VOBS for information and copies of the Liens Bill and Eight Hour Bill.[137]

Industry volatility and the finite time-span construction tasks caused organisational stress and membership instability. The post-goldrush construction boom waxed and waned, causing branch/lodge turnover while leaving an iconic heritage of churches, public buildings, dwellings, bridges and viaducts.[138] Work was short term and precarious, especially for older/infirm workers and even periods seen as 'middling' often entailed considerable under-employment. In 1878 Sydney Bricklayers estimated of around 500 bricklayers, 100 had constant employment with another 350 employed casually.[139] Victorian Stonemasons subscribed to industry publications like the *Australian Builder* in an effort to address these challenges.[140] Like others, building unions opposed immigration, especially assisted-immigration, seen to undermine their capacity to protect members' wages and conditions. The Sydney United Plasterers Society supported a February 1878 anti-immigration meeting.[141] In November 1880 the Stonemasons Balmain Lodge expressed alarm 50 English and Scottish masons had been engaged on the Callan Park buildings below 'current wages' after already experiencing difficulties enrolling members at the site. With regard to Europeans, hostility to immigration didn't extend to immigrants themselves or threaten global union networks. At its next meeting Balmain stonemasons accepted a membership application from John Roy based on a clearance from the Dundee Stonemasons Society.[142]

Conclusion

Building trade unionisation began in the late 1820s led by stonemasons and carpenters followed by bricklayers, plumbers, painters and plasterers, slowly consolidating from the mid-1850s based on centuries-old methods of mutual insurance and craft controls/unilateral regulation supported by strikes. Key objectives were friendly benefits, regulating wages and work methods and maximising jobs, but most importantly the eight-hour day which building unions pioneered and then helped generalise through wider alliances pivotal to creating peak bodies like the Melbourne Trades Hall Council. Limited technological change enhanced their structural power along with the rapid construction expansion, albeit still subject to sharp swings. Building unions also led efforts to maximise societal power, union peak bodies being a platform for political agitation and ultimately direct political representation. In contrast, until the 1870s labourers' organisation was predominantly informal. While experiencing considerable membership volatility, labourers' unions attempted mutual insurance and joined eight-hour actions—a mutually reinforcing measure encouraged by craft unions. They also attempted unilateral regulation because notwithstanding their lack of structural power they had little alternative. Labourers engaged in civil construction like railways remained largely un-unionised but engaged in considerable collective action—mainly strikes—relying on numerical strength but often undermined by replacements imported by employers.

Notes

1. LC247-1-21 Hobart 2 December 1851.
2. *Williamstown Chronicle* 10 October 1857.
3. *Ovens and Murray Advertiser* 1 August 1860.
4. *Melbourne Herald* 1 August 1861.
5. *Darling Downs Gazette* 13 September 1865.
6. *Sydney Morning Herald* 9 April 1868.
7. *South Australian Advertiser* 4 March 1869.
8. *Empire* 27 January 1864.
9. *Evening News* 28 April 1876.
10. *Port Augusta Dispatch* 26 October 1878.
11. *Cornwall Chronicle* 19 November 1856.
12. *Sydney Morning Herald* 19 June 1858.
13. *Age* 29 June 1858.
14. *Age* 8 October 1858.
15. *Maryborough and Dunolly Advertiser* 5 November 1858.
16. *Empire* 17 September, 8 December 1863.
17. *Brisbane Courier* 17 July 1867.
18. A2795 Sydney Progressive Carpenters minutes 4 December 1871, 7 January 1872, 26 March 1877.
19. E117-2-2 Victorian Stonemasons Central Committee minutes 5 June 1862, 9, 23 April 1863; E117-60 Victorian Stonemasons Society Williamstown minutes 18 September, 2 October 1865.

20. The earliest surviving craft union rule-book (Sydney shipwrights) included sick steward provisions. DLMQ520 Rules, Orders and Regulations of United Friends Society established 13 December 1829; T46-1-1 NSW Stonemasons Sydney minutes 14 June, 12 July 1858; E235-2 Sydney United Plasterers minutes 8 October 1877.
21. T8-2A-3 VOBS Melbourne minutes 11 May 1874; Z291-17-2 NSW Bricklayers Central Committee minutes 19 September 1879; T46-1-1 NSW Stonemasons Society Sydney minutes 4 August 1862.
22. T8-2A-4 VOBS Melbourne minutes 16 May 1879.
23. T46-1-1 NSW Stonemasons Sydney 1 November 1858, 31 December 1860, 7 January 1861.
24. T8-2A-2 VOBS Melbourne minutes 21 March 1859; T8-2A-3 VOBS, Melbourne minutes 13 January 1873.
25. Z291-17-1 NSW Stonemasons Sydney minutes 22 July 1873; MUA Sydney Painters minutes 22 July, 5 August 1874, 26 June 1875.
26. T46-1-1 NSW Stonemasons Sydney minutes 21 July, 15 September 1862, 14 January 1867, 20 September 1875.
27. E117-39 Victorian Stonemasons Collingwood minutes 29 December 1880.
28. T46-4 NSW Stonemasons Central Committee minutes 9, 23 December 1870.
29. *Sydney Morning Herald* 13 September 1870.
30. E235-1 Sydney United Plasterers minutes 18 September 1876.
31. A2794/1 & 2 Sydney Progressive Carpenters minutes and quarterly accounts 1856-96.
32. ML MSS208 Box 02 Item 7 Sydney United Labourers Protection Society, fine book 4 July 1870.
33. Z291-17-1 NSW Bricklayers Sydney minutes 21 June 1870.
34. T94-17-1 Victorian Stonemasons Stony Creek 25 August 1858.
35. A2794/1 & 2 Sydney Progressive Carpenters minutes 28 March 1864, 20 December 1866; E235-2 Sydney United Plasterers minutes 11 June 1877; T8-2A-2 VOBS Melbourne minutes 2 July 1866; T8-2A-3 VOBS Melbourne minutes 5 May 1873, 14 June 1875.
36. Z291-17-1 NSW Bricklayers Sydney minutes 15 July 1873.
37. ML334/0 Operative Plumbers Trade Society Rules and Practices, Alexander Douglas *Atlas* Office Sydney 1862 Rule 18.
38. T46-1-3 NSW Stonemasons Sydney minutes 3, 11 June 1874.
39. *Argus* 26 February, 10 March 1877; *Age* 7 April, 23 May, 8 June 1877; VOBS Melbourne minutes 6 March 1877.
40. T46-1-3 NSW Stonemasons Sydney minutes 31 December 1866, 11, 25 February, 25 March, 10, 15, 23, 29 April, 6, 30 May 1867, 6 April 1868, 4 October 1870, 20 October 1875.
41. T8-2A-3 VOBS Melbourne minutes 8, 21 March 1875.
42. T8-2A-3 VOBS Melbourne minutes 20 December 1875 and T8-2A-4 VOBS Melbourne minutes 1 May 1876.
43. *Sydney Morning Herald* 20, 23 April 1853.
44. Cahill, R. (2007) The Eight Hour Day and the Holy Spirit, *Recorder*, 253: 1, 5–6.
45. T46-3 NSW Stonemasons Central Committee minutes 8, 24, 30 January, 18, 22, 25 February 1856.
46. T46-1-1 NSW Stonemasons Sydney minutes 9 October 1856.
47. P94-19 Victorian Stonemasons Melbourne minutes 3, 31 March, 14, 28 April, 12, 20 May, 3 June 1856.
48. T46-3 NSW Stonemasons Central Committee minutes 22 April 1856.
49. T8-2A-1 VOBS Melbourne minutes 8 April, 26 May, 30 June 1856; *Age* 19 August 1856.

50. T46-3 NSW Stonemasons Central Committee minutes 27 May, 16 June, 8 July, 13, 18, 21, 22 August 1856, 24 April 1857.
51. T46-1-1 NSW Stonemasons Sydney minutes 17 May 1857, 1, 15 November 1858, 11 May 1859.
52. T46-3 NSW Stonemasons Central Committee minutes 24, 30 April, 7 May 1861.
53. *Argus* 30 October 1863.
54. Z291-17-1 NSW Bricklayers Sydney minutes 9, 23 April, 18 June 1872.
55. Probably the same Alfred Day enmeshed in a dispute when injured five years later. P94-19 Victorian Stonemasons Melbourne minutes 12 May 1856 and E117 Victorian Stonemasons Central Committee minutes 7 November 1861, 7, 31 July, 4 August 1862.
56. T46-4 NSW Stonemasons Central Committee minutes 18 April 1870.
57. P94-17-1 Victorian Stonemasons Stony Creek 4 October 1858.
58. T46-4 NSW Stonemasons Central Committee minutes 4 March 1870; A2795 Sydney Progressive Carpenters Society minutes 6 November 1871, 17 November 1873.
59. T8-2A-4 VOBS Melbourne minutes 16 July 1877; E235-2 Sydney United Plasterers minutes 10 March 1879.
60. T46-8 NSW Stonemasons Lithgow Valley minutes 15, 17 October 1868.
61. T46-1-1 NSW Stonemasons Sydney minutes 29 December 1858, 24 January, 7 February, 21 March, 11 April, 12, 17 December 1859.
62. P94-19 Victorian Stonemasons Melbourne minutes 17 June 1856; T46-1-1 NSW Stonemasons Sydney 20 November 1856; *Sydney Morning Herald* 4 November 1856; E117 Victorian Stonemasons Central Committee minutes 27 October 1859.
63. T46-1-1 NSW Stonemasons Sydney minutes 24 June, 28 October 1861, 6 January 1862; T46-3 NSW Stonemasons Central Committee minutes 25 June, 3 July, 12 August 1861.
64. *Argus* 30 October 1863; *Age* 23 August 1873.
65. A2795 Sydney Progressive Carpenters minutes 14 March 1870.
66. Z291-17-1 NSW Bricklayers Society Sydney minutes 3 December 1872, 30 September 1873.
67. *Age* 19 December 1878; T8-2A-4 VOBS Melbourne minutes 5, 12 November, 3 December 1877.
68. T8-2A-4 VOBS Melbourne minutes 7, 14, 17 October, 4, 11, 18, 22 November, 2, 9, 16 December 1878, 8 September 1879.
69. T46-1-3 NSW Stonemasons Sydney minutes 15, 29 November 1875.
70. Z291-17-2 NSW Bricklayers Standing Committee minutes 13 April 1870.
71. P94-17-1 Victorian Stonemasons Stony Creek 11 October 1858; P94-17-2 Victorian Stonemasons Pentridge minutes 7 November 1858; NSW Bricklayers Sydney minutes 7 June 1870; Z291-17-2 NSW Bricklayers Management Committee minutes 19 June 1876; MUA Sydney Painters Trade Society minutes 8 April 1878.
72. Z291-17-1 NSW Bricklayers Sydney minutes 27 October 1870, 21 May, 19 November 1880.
73. A2795 Sydney Progressive Carpenters minutes 30 October 1876.
74. T46-1-1 NSW Stonemasons Sydney minutes 23 January 1860; T46-4 NSW Stonemasons Central Committee minutes 12 August, 22 September 1865, 4 September 1868; MUA Melbourne Typographical Society minutes 5 September 1868.
75. T8-2A-1 VOBS Melbourne minutes 10 May 1858, 21 February 1859.
76. Z291-17-1 NSW Bricklayers Sydney minutes 21 May 1872.

77. E117-2-1 Victorian Stonemasons Central Committee minutes 14 December 1857.
78. Z291-17-2 NSW Bricklayers Standing Committee minutes 13 April 1870, 24 June 1881.
79. T8-2A-2 VOBS Melbourne minutes 3, 31 October 1864; T8-2A-4 VOBS Melbourne minutes 25 February 1878.
80. Z291-17-1 NSW Bricklayers Sydney minutes 10 May, 24 July 1870.
81. E117-2-2 Victorian Stonemasons Central Committee minutes 16 December 1860.
82. E117-60 Victorian Stonemasons Williamstown minutes 4 March, 2 December 1867.
83. Z291-17-2 NSW Bricklayers Central Committee minutes 22 July 1880.
84. Z291-17-1 NSW Bricklayers Central Committee minutes 9, 16 July 1872.
85. P94-19 Victorian Stonemasons Melbourne minutes 29 July 1856; T46-1-1 NSW Stonemasons Sydney minutes 21 May 1857.
86. Z291-17-1 NSW Bricklayers Sydney minutes 7, 14 November 1871.
87. T8-2A-3 VOBS Melbourne minutes 15, 22, 29 January, 4, 9, 11, 16, 23 December 1872.
88. E235-2 Sydney United Plasterers minutes 9, 30 July 1877.
89. T46-1-1 NSW Stonemasons Sydney minutes 30 April 1860.
90. E117-2-2 Victorian Stonemasons Central Committee minutes 4 August 1859.
91. E117-90 Victorian Stonemasons Lethbridge minutes 8 March 1860.
92. T46-1-2 NSW Stonemasons Sydney minutes 7 May, 5, 19 November, 3, 17 December 1866.
93. A2794/1 Sydney Progressive Carpenters minutes 15 January, 12 February, 22 April 1856.
94. *Argus* 8 April 1857.
95. E235-1 Sydney United Plasterers minutes 25 September 1876, 25 June 1877, 16 September 1878.
96. E117-60 Victorian Stonemasons Woodend minutes 4 April 1861; T46-1-2 NSW Stonemasons Sydney minutes 15 June 1868.
97. Z291-17-1 NSW Bricklayers Sydney minutes 9 April 1872.
98. MUA Sydney Painters Trade Society (later Painters and Decorators) minutes 6 May, 8 July 1874.
99. MUA Sydney Painters minutes 16 December 1874.
100. NSW did the same T46-1-1 NSW Stonemasons Sydney minutes 20 September 1858.
101. T8-2A-1 VOBS, Melbourne minutes 21, 28 July, 29 September 1856, 13, 20 July 1857.
102. T8-2A-2 VOBS Melbourne minutes 19 November 1858, 2 August, 7 November 1859, 2 January 1860.
103. T8-2A-1 VOBS, Melbourne minutes 18 January 1858; T8-2A-2 VOBS, Melbourne minutes 19 June 1865.
104. Z291-17-1 NSW Stonemasons Sydney minutes 23, 30 July, 3, 10, 17 September, 17 December 1872, 14 January, 4, 18 February, 6 May 1873.
105. T8-2A-2 VOBS, Melbourne minutes 28 January 1867; T8-2A-3 VOBS Melbourne minutes 7 August, 2 October 1871, 14 April, 22 September 1873, 16 February 1874.
106. T8-2A-1 VOBS, Melbourne minutes 28 July 1856, 23 February 1857; T8-2A-1 Victorian Stonemasons Melbourne minutes 29 July, 12 August 1856; T46-1-1 NSW Stonemasons Sydney minutes 12 February 1857, 7 February 1858, 20 August 1862.

107. E117-2-2 Victorian Stonemasons Central Committee minutes 22 November 1860, 31 January, 20 June, 10 October 1861, 13 February, 17 July, 28 August 1862.
108. T8-2A-2 VOBS, Melbourne minutes 7 March 1859.
109. *Sydney Morning Herald* 26 November, 11 December 1861; Z291-17-1 NSW Bricklayers Sydney minutes 3, 17 May 1870.
110. A2795 Sydney Progressive Carpenters minutes 16 July 1872, 24 January 1874, 20 May 1878.
111. E235-2 Sydney United Plasterers minutes 30 October 1876.
112. A2795 Sydney Progressive Carpenters minutes 1 April 1878.
113. E117-30 Victorian Stonemasons Moorabool minutes 10 February 1859.
114. T46-1-1 NSW Stonemasons Sydney minutes 9 January 1860.
115. T8-2A-2 VOBS, Melbourne minutes 7 February, 4 April, 10, 17, 31 October, 5 December 1859.
116. A2975 Sydney Progressive Carpenters minutes, 17 November, 5, 17 December 1877.
117. *Argus* 15 April 1876.
118. *Argus* 30 October 1878.
119. *Argus* 16 March 1877.
120. T46-4 NSW Stonemasons Central Committee minutes 6 August 1869.
121. P94-19 Victorian Stonemasons Melbourne minutes 12 August 1856; E117-2-1 Victorian Stonemasons Central Committee minutes 23 December 1856; E117-30 Victorian Stonemasons Moorabool minutes 15 November 1858; E117-60 Victorian Stonemasons Williamstown minutes 18 March 1867; T8-2A-2 VOBS, Melbourne minutes 21, 28 February, 7 March 1859.
122. Z291-17-1 NSW Bricklayers Sydney minutes 11, 18 April 1871.
123. P94-17-1 Victorian Stonemasons Stony Creek minutes 15 September 1858.
124. P94-17-1 Victorian Stonemasons Stony Creek minutes 18 August 1858.
125. T8-2A-2 VOBS Melbourne minutes 17 January, 14 February, 24 May, 29 August, 12 September 1859, 9, 23 January. 20, 27 February 1860.
126. T8-2A-4 VOBS Melbourne minutes 17 February 1879.
127. Z291-17-1 NSW Bricklayers Sydney minutes 17 May, 21, 28 June, 2, 9 August 1870.
128. Maxwell, J. (1969) Cornish, William Crocker (1815–1859), in *Australian Dictionary of Biography*, Vol.3, Melbourne University Press, Melbourne.
129. E117-2-1 Victorian Stonemasons Central Committee minutes 4, 6, 9, 13, 22, 24, 29 December 1858, 5, 16, 20, 22 January, 5, 11, 17 February, 3, 17, 31 March, 9 April 1859.
130. E117-2-2 Victorian Stonemasons Central Committee minutes 15, 17, 22 September, 6, 8, 10, 13 October, 9, 10, 24 November 1859, 26 April 1860.
131. T8-2A-2 VOBS Melbourne minutes 2 January 1860.
132. E117-2-2 Victorian Stonemasons Central Council minutes 1 March, 12 April, 17, 19, 25, 28 July, 1, 8 November 1860, 3, 7, 11, 17 January, 1, 10, 12, 16 April, 23 May, 5 August 1861.
133. T46-1-2 NSW Stonemasons Sydney minutes 29 June 1868; T46-4 NSW Stonemasons Central Committee minutes 1 July 1868.
134. Z291-17-2 NSW Bricklayers Central Committee minutes 9 February 1880.
135. Berg, L. and Farbenblum B. (2018) Remedies for Migrant Worker Exploitation in Australia: Lessons from the 7-Eleven Wage Payment Program, *Melbourne University Law Review*, 41: 1035–1082; Clibborn, S. and Wright, C.F. (2018) Employer Theft of Temporary Migrant Workers' Wages in Australia: Why Has the State Failed to Act? *Economic and Labour Relations Review*, 29(2): 207–27; Knox, A. (2018) Regulatory Avoidance in the

Temporary Work Agency Industry: Evidence from Australia, *Economic and Labour Relations Review*, 29(2): 190–206.

136. T46-1-3 NSW Stonemasons Sydney minutes 25 February 1874.
137. Z291-17-1 NSW Bricklayers Sydney minutes 6 February 1872, 24 June 1873.
138. T46-4 NSW Stonemasons Central Committee minutes 7 July 1865.
139. Z291-17-2 NSW Bricklayers Central Committee minutes 26 April 1878.
140. P94-19 Victorian Stonemasons Melbourne minutes 12 May 1856.
141. E235-2 Sydney United Plasterers minutes 14 February 1878.
142. T46-9 NSW Stonemasons Balmain minutes 15, 29 November, 15 December 1880.

7 Metal/Engineering, Printing and Transport Equipment

Introduction

This is the first of two chapters on manufacturing, the division based on differences in methods and labour market conditions confronting unions recruiting manufacturing workers consistent with the book's focus on mobilisation as well as different circumstances and their consequences. Craft controls and unilateral regulation central to unions described in this chapter were insignificant amongst those examined in Chapter 8. As in building, unionisation of printers, shipwrights, coachmakers, saddler, blacksmiths and wheelwrights began in the late 1820s/early 1830s followed by boilermakers and engineers in the 1840s. Notwithstanding some slowing in the 1860s, overall growth accelerated in 1851–1880. Indeed, the growth of organisations/membership in the metal trades was conspicuous, drawing on expanding manufacturing/engineering, ship-building/repair, mining and railways (Tables 7.1 and 7.2). Overall, NSCA outnumbered strikes by over two to one and known outcomes were more favourable. Apart from 1871–1880, NSCA involved far more workers than strikes, 78.4% of which were confined to one establishment (compared to 67.3% of NSCA). Multi-establishment/regional NSCA outnumbered strikes, including the only colony-wide actions (Table 7.1). Wages and hours were the most prominent issues followed by unionism, work methods and working conditions. Disputes over unionism are higher than other industries, largely associated with repeated but generally unsuccessful challenges to union rules/unilateral regulation by individual employers.

Growing union numbers/membership in metal/engineering outstripped transport equipment and printing/publishing though involving less collective action (strikes, NSCA). Unilateral regulation and mutual insurance were important but unions also made considerable use of mass meetings and marches (less so public notices and the House-of-Call), and engaged politically via petitions/deputations (less so printers, Table 7.2). These workers were unlikely to come before courts. Aside from wage recoveries (rare compared to rural and mining workers), cases were connected to collective action and workers lost most (Table 7.2).

Table 7.1 Worker Organisation in Metal, Transport Equipment and Printing 1831–1880

Industry	1831–1840	1841–1850	1851–1860	1861–1870	1871–1880	Total 1851–1880
Organisations	23	34	60	89	177	266⁺
Raw involvement	126	272	1865	8073	17882	27820
Est. involvement*	168	434	3266	13456	29103	45482
Strikes						
Won	2	2	2	4	22	28
Drawn	1	1			2	2
Lost	6	10	12	3	12	27
Unknown	2	7	14	5	34	53
Total	11	20	28	12	70	110
Est. total involvement*	23	50	324	210	3382	3916
Number of establishments						
One	6	12	20	8	63	91
Multi	3	1	3		6	9
Regional/town	2	1	4	1	11	16
Colonial						
Non-strike collective action						
Won		2	8	16	68	92
Drawn		1	1	4	6	11
Lost	3	3	5	8	11	24
Unknown	4	4	25	32	89	146
Total	7	9	39	60	174	273
Est. total involvement*	20	32	2352	1252	4585	8189
Number of establishments						
One	5	6	25	43	105	173
Multi	1		3	2	11	16
Regional/town	1	2	10	13	41	64
Colonial			1	1	2	4
Issues in collective action (strikes/NSCA)						
Wages	6/2	7/6	12/21	6/33	26/76	44/130
Hours	4/1	8/	13/13	5/17	29/66	47/96
Working conditions	2/7	3/2	5/7	2/6	11/15	18/28
Health & safety			1/1	1/3	1/16	3/20
Management behaviour		/1	/3	1/3	5/5	6/11
Jobs/employment	2/4	/1	/3	1/4	3/22	4/26
Work methods	1/1	/2	1/7	/7	9/32	10/46

Industry	1831–1840	1841–1850	1851–1860	1861–1870	1871–1880	Total 1851–1880
Unionism	1/		1/4	1/6	21/35	23/45
Subcontracting				1/	1/2	2/2
Grievance procedure					/1	/1
Unknown				2/		2/
Total strikes/NSCA						

* Adjusted by multiplying number of zero-reporting organisations/years by median industry membership in that decade. ⁺For totals, organisation spanning multiple decades only counted once.

Informal Workplace Dissent

As in building, informal action continued into the 1850s, especially amongst Tasmanian convicts. In December 1851 several workers at H Davidson's Hobart iron foundry received ten days' solitary confinement for absence.[1] A month later *Tasmanian Herald* editor Jonathon Moore prosecuted convict printers for absence extending from Sunday into Monday (five days' solitary).[2] Informal action also occurred in regional centres, often following union campaigns. Kapunda vehicle and implement-manufacturer Robert Cameron accepted eight-hours but in September 1876 his workers rejected wage cuts and within a fortnight a branch of the United Tradesmens Society was established.[3] This incident highlights synergies between informal and formal organisation.

Multi-Workplace and Union Organisation

Metal trades union numbers grew rapidly after 1851, although cycles of collapse/renewal marked the 1850s and 1860s. Following British models colonial unions formed in specific trades notably engineers, blacksmiths, boilermakers, ironfounders and moulders. Most colonial bodies were independent but a major exception was the Amalgamated Society of Engineers, Machinists, Smiths, Millwrights and Patternmakers (ASE). Established in 1851 and epitomising the Webb's new model union, the ASE formed branches in Canada, the US, Australia, New Zealand and elsewhere. Australian branches were established in Sydney (1852), Melbourne (1859–1920), Adelaide (1864–1920) followed by suburbs/ towns with significant mining, port or railway workshops like Newcastle (1861–1920), Ballarat (1861–1920), Williamstown (1863–1920), Bendigo (1865–1965), Ipswich (1865–1920), Port Adelaide (1874, 1877– 1920) and Balmain (1879). The ASE dominated engineering unionism notwithstanding attempts at independent organisation like the Adelaide

Table 7.2 Worker Organisation Subgroup Summary—Metal et al. 1831–1880

Breakdown of organisation and actions of largest subgroups						
Metal and Engineering						
Organisation numbers	4	8	21	31	67	97+
Est. involvement*		54	972	9009	13381	21362
Strikes	1	6	11	5	24	40
NSCA			7	9	55	71
Absconding						
Petitions				3	4	7
Deputations				3	6	9
Mass meetings			8	26	44	78
Marches			6	29	68	103
Letters/public notices	1			2	11	13
Bans					1	1
House-of-call	1		3		4	7
Court actions						
Won					1	1
Lost		6	6	2	1	9
Transport Equipment						
Organisation numbers	8	14	14	21	53	82+
Est. involvement*	75	62	578	2180	9991	12749
Strikes	5	11	6	4	36	46
NSCA	1	5	10	27	74	111
Absconding						
Petitions	1	1		1	2	3
Deputations				3	12	15
Mass meetings			2	19	35	56
Marches			4	13	36	53
Letters/public notices	5	4		10	13	23
Bans		1			6	6
Court Actions						
Won		1			2	2
Lost	5	5	2		1	3
Printing and Publishing						
Organisation numbers	11	12	25	37	57	87+
Est. involvement*	93	318	1716	2267	5731	9714
Strikes	5	3	11	2	11	24
NSCA	6	8	22	24	45	91
Absconding	2			1		1
Petitions	2	1			1	1

Deputations					4	4
Mass meetings	2	2	21	26	35	82
Marches				1	3	4
Letters/public notices	6	7	11	6	2	19
House-of-call	1		1	1		1
Court actions						
Won	3	1	1	1		2
Lost	9	3	11	3		14

* Adjusted by multiplying number of zero-reporting organisations/years by median industry membership in that decade. ⁺For totals, organisation spanning multiple decades only counted once.

Mechanical Engineers Society (1851) and Hobart Engineers and Ironworkers (1875).[4]

Amongst blacksmiths, farriers and hammermen organisation occurred in Melbourne (1856, 1858, blacksmiths 1859–1874, hammermen 1859–1874, 1879–1880), Sydney (1870, 1872–1875, 1874–1880, 1878–1879), Brisbane (1865, 1866, 1875, 1877), Adelaide (1853, with other iron-trades 1876–1880). Multi-trade bodies were more common in regional towns like Bendigo (1856, 1865, with engine-drivers 1872–1877), Ballarat (1860, 1879), Castlemaine (1872), Heathcote (1872), Stawell (with coachmakers and wheelwrights 1874), Parramatta (1875), Rockhampton (1863, 1868), Ipswich (with wheelwrights 1863), Rockhampton (with wheelwrights 1868), Maryborough (with other iron-trades 1873 and 1877–1878), Warwick (with wheelwrights 1874), Gympie (1877), Gawler (1873), Moonta (1874), Wallaroo (1874), Yorketown (1880) and Mount Gambier (with coachmakers, 1880). Coachmakers, carriage-builders and wheelwrights organised in Melbourne (1852–1860, 1866, 1870, 1873–1890, 1879), Sydney (1854, 1873, 1876–1880), Adelaide (1863, 1871, 1873–1879), Stawell (1874), Horsham (with blacksmiths 1876), Goulburn (1880) and Mount Gambier (with blacksmiths and machinists 1880).

Unionisation amongst boilermakers/ironworkers, ironmoulders and ironfounders was concentrated in Melbourne (1854, ironworkers 1858–1861, ironmoulders 1858–1940, ironworkers 1866–1871, boilermakers 1869–1872 and 1873–1880, 1880–1900), Sydney (1854, 1870, 1871, boilermakers 1873–1972, ironworkers 1874, ironmoulders 1876–1940), Brisbane (with engineers and blacksmiths 1866, ironmoulders 1874–1964, boilermakers 1876), Adelaide (boilermakers 1873, boilermakers, ironmoulders and blacksmiths 1876–1880), Newcastle (boilermakers 1877–1973) and Port Adelaide (boilermakers 1880–1973). Organisation also occurred in Geelong (boilermakers 1858), Ballarat (ironmoulders 1863–1873 and 1874–1880, ironworkers 1869 and boilermakers 1878), Maryborough (with other iron-trades, 1873, 1877–1878) and Gawler (with other trades 1873). The expansion of metal manufacturing facilitated unions amongst tin/zinc plate, galvanised ironworkers, agricultural implement makers, brass-founders and gasfitters in Melbourne (1852–1854, 1857–1864, gasfitters 1864, brass-founders 1865, 1867–1872, agricultural implement makers 1870, 1873 and 1874–1878, 1874–1877, brass-founders 1874–1875), Sydney (1852–1855, 1858, 1870, 1872–1877, 1880) and Adelaide (1872–1874, 1877). Following Britain models there were several attempts at more specialised unions like the NSW Patternmakers Association (1874–1877) and Sydney Engine Fitters and Turners Protective Association (1874–1876).[5] At the other extreme, wider iron-trade alliances were formed to campaign for eight-hours in Sydney (1856, 1861–1862 and 1872–1880), Adelaide (1873), Brisbane (1876), and Launceston (1870) while other alliances were forged over protectionism in Adelaide (1867).

Sydney Shipwrights organised in 1829 (possibly reorganised in 1852/3), with a Newcastle union seeking branch status in 1867. Balmain members also requested a separate branch—and an independent boatbuilders union by 1874.[6] Port Phillip Shipwrights unionised in 1856, with a separate Williamstown union by 1858. Both reorganised in 1866 and 1869 respectively, Williamstown becoming a branch as did an Echuca union established in 1874.[7] After earlier attempts (1847, 1852) Hobart Shipwrights formed a society in 1872.[8] Brisbane Shipwrights formed a short-lived benefit society in Kangaroo Point in 1865 before reorganising in November 1875.[9] Sailmakers organised in Port Adelaide and Sydney by 1873 and by 1874 in Melbourne.[10] Hobart sailmakers secured a nine-hour day (eight on Saturday) in August 1874 but little else is known.[11] Coopers making and repairing barrels, a major storage and transport requirement unionised in Sydney (1869–1873, 1878–1880), Melbourne (1869–1871, 1880–1900) and Adelaide (1875–1876).

Printers' formed unions from 1829 with post-goldrush societies (excluding chapels of which over 30 are known) in Sydney (1851, 1854, 1855–1858, 1867–1871, 1878, 1880–1950), Melbourne (1851–1855, 1856–1865, 1867–1921), Ballarat (1857–1921), Geelong (1866–1881), Sandhurst (1875–1881), Hobart (1852–1855, 1868–1869, 1874, 1875–1876), Launceston (1849–1854), Brisbane (1862, 1865, 1867, 1873–1884), Toowoomba (1867), Maryborough (1875) and Adelaide (1874–1915). Lithographers organised in Melbourne (1858–1860, 1873–1884) and Sydney (1878), and bookbinders in Melbourne (1873, 1878–1899).

Objectives, Functions and Methods

The Labour Process and Struggles Over Craft Control and Work Methods

All manufacturing unions confronted employer attempts to undermine craft controls using cheaper non-craft workers (boys, improvers and semi-skilled men and women) or mechanisation. Members permitting labourers or others to do trade work faced sanctions, typified by the censuring of boilermakers at both Grant's and Bubb's workshops in Sydney in 1878.[12] Resistance to mechanisation was difficult. When Sydney coopers struck against the introduction of machinery by major firms the Sydney TLC refused assistance.[13] Apprenticeship was the basis of craft control. Admission to society membership required completed apprenticeship documents or recognition by an equivalent trade society, colonial or British. 'Improvers' or those whose training was uncertain were subjected to assessment.[14] Prescribing tasks covered by the trade (demarcation) was important to prevent incursions by unskilled workers or those from other trades. In 1872 Sydney Shipwrights revised rules regulating the work undertaken by shipwrights, joiners and boatbuilders (a vessel of up to 12 tons). Three shipwrights were compensated for refusing work at Mr Shea's when a joiner was used to sheath decks.[15] Things became complicated when a separate boatbuilders' society formed (1874) although inter-union communication reduced problems posed by non-society boatbuilders.[16]

Youth labour long caused angst in printers' chapels but disputes became more intense after 1860. In 1867 Melbourne Typographers raised practices at the *Bendigo Advertiser* with its chapel father, who offered only limp support. Rules prescribed boys composing 'matter' receive full rates so there was no wage 'advantage,' the union regularly dealing with breaches or other evasive tactics. In 1872 the society reverted to its 'oldest and best' rule of banning boy-labour and strictly enforcing apprentice/journeymen ratios. Prolonged negotiations with masters over this and wage/work methods didn't prevent further disputes.[17] In 1875 the South Australian union protested two un-indentured apprentices at the *Register* jobbing office while the Victorian union lost a strike over young workers at the *Melbourne Herald*—the latter becoming a non-union shop for some years.[18] In 1879 Victorian typographers warned NSW of another boy-labour dispute at the *Bendigo Advertiser*. The NSW union had its own problems. *Words of Grace* religious-publication proprietors introduced four girls/women to 'work at case.' The reader, however, refused to supervise them after consulting the chapel companionship. The companionship threatened to resign, telling the manager (Johnstone) apprentices could work 'cheaply and expeditiously.' Johnstone replied he was getting cost-estimates for female labour compared to type-setting machines. The chapel referred the matter to the union's Board of Management and following representations the girls were withdrawn.[19]

Resisting encroachments were ongoing in other trades. In March 1874 a Port Phillip Shipwrights' deputation and correspondence with the Commissioner of Public Works restricted labourers' use in docking and slipping activities at the Alfred graving dock, Williamstown. Two years later three Victorian Shipwrights' societies deprecated 'apprentices' moving between establishments, vowing to only recognise those bound to single employer.[20] Sydney Shipwrights devised rules to regulate 'improvers' to combat the erosion of apprenticeship and skill dilution.[21] Sydney Boiler-makers refused to recognise improvers not constantly employed in boiler-shops.[22] These are but illustrations of numerous actions. Unions looked increasingly to legislation. In August 1880 the Victorian Typographical Association urged the Attorney General to legislate to ensure apprentices were properly trained and prohibited from doing health-damaging night work and excessive hours. In October a joint union deputation called for legislation on young workers in printing, workshops and factories.[23]

Controlling Labour Supply

Labour market control was pursued by other means. Echoing the medi-eval tramping system, some unions helped members move to locations with more jobs or to reduce pressures during prolonged strikes. The ASE Sydney Branch sent engineers (some non-members) to Adelaide during the 1874 iron-trades eight-hour strike.[24] The ASE's rules afforded funds to unemployed members emigrating. In 1863 several colonial branches urged a revision with funds being paid on landing.[25] In 1875 Sydney Boilermakers offered to assist distressed members migrate dur-ing their long-running dispute at PN Russell.[26] Members were also cau-tioned against travelling to towns, experiencing a dispute, although local conditions sometimes made this difficult.[27] Australian ASE branches regularly communicated, issuing clearance and travelling cards, admit-ting UK members and provided documentation for those migrating to New Zealand, the US and Canada. They were particularly assiduous in exchanging labour market reports but the practice was widespread. Sydney Boilermakers sent annual reports to the UK along with other material like the 1879 ITUC report.[28] In 1857 the Melbourne Typo-graphical Society initiated an intercolonial typographical circular on the trade conditions. The *Sydney Herald* chapel appointed a correspondent and took out subscriptions for every member.[29] Most inter-union cor-respondence provided conservative views of local conditions but occa-sionally job opportunities were identified. The Newcastle Shipwrights informed Sydney of jobs in November 1877 and seven months later the ASE informed Sydney Boilermakers that Smellie & Co. Brisbane had jobs (there was no Brisbane union).[30] Like pre-1850 unions, notices were published on misleading job advertisements or reports. In 1874 South Australian Typographers refuted reports of printers' shortages in the *Farmer's Weekly*, forwarding it to NSW and Victorian societies.[31] Several societies looked to producer cooperatives during downturns or following industrial defeats. In August 1870 the Sydney Shipwrights voted to use funds to build a new vessel. Regulatory hurdles eventually torpedoed the venture and unemployment grew to 150 by March 1871, rapidly depleting their relief fund.[32]

Mutual Insurance, Health and Safety

Providing friendly benefits for sickness, injury, unemployment and funerals was a key objective. The ASE was an exemplar, advantaged by its ability to administer and transfer funds globally. But mutual insurance was important to almost all. The Victorian Friendly Society of Ironmoulders 1858 rules provided significant benefits for accidents (seven shillings per day), sickness 25 shillings for 13 weeks, 12s 6d for another 13 weeks (and then subject to review), unemployment (advances repaid once re-employed) and funerals (£12 for widows, nominee or nearest relative).[33] Some societies indemnified against loss of tools, as Sydney Shipwrights did for 25 Cuthbert shipyard members when a barge sank in June 1867.[34] Benefits provision occupied considerable time during meetings, reflecting their importance. These measures safeguarded members, provided a sustaining union-function and mitigated the threat posed by old, infirm or injured workers. Like building unions, the Sydney Shipwrights made provisions for members over 60 years, excluding them from making subscriptions. By December 1878 it had 17 aged members with similar numbers two years later.[35] Further, regular contributions were made to hospitals and infirmaries ensuring treatment of members injured at work or who fell ill.[36]

The opportunity cost of falling into arrears was substantial, explaining why the issue occupied considerable time at union meetings. Mutual insurance posed challenges for trades experiencing organisational churning like coachmakers, smaller bodies or workers in remotely located establishments like the Maryborough Union Foundry.[37] In printing, individual chapels like the *Argus* companionship (71 members in 1864) offered sick and funeral benefits with different single and married subscription-rates. Public assistance helped compensate successive deaths in 1856 at Hobart's *Colonial Times* and even larger chapels gratefully accepted wider support.[38] Responding to climatic conditions in October 1872 Sydney Shipwrights altered their rules entitling sunstroke victims to accident pay. In 1876, inconsistencies over accident pay and granting clearances between Sydney and Newcastle Shipwrights prompted negotiations, securing a more formal relationship between the two unions. In circumstances deemed especially deserving, like deaths leaving a widow and young children, societies waived entitlement rules or established a special subscription fund to bolster funeral and other benefits.[39] Unemployment was a pressure point. In 1860 jobless compositors in Melbourne questioned the union-executive's effectiveness and pressed for a benefit fund.[40] Times were still tough in 1867, Geelong Typographers urging small loans to unemployed members. This was rejected by the recently revived Melbourne Society, which preferred to warn British counterparts of the 'deplorable state of trade.' However, by 1875 Melbourne had adopted a voluntary unemployment fund.[41] In 1880 Melbourne Lithographers and Copperplate Printers noted ongoing depression was depleting their unemployment fund.[42] Some, like Sydney Shipwrights, established special funds. Nonetheless, erratic work led to members falling into arrears, being expelled and losing entitlements with Sydney Shipwrights expelling 26 in September 1875 and another 31 between January and May 1877.[43]

Unions occasionally took direct action on OHS, Sydney Shipwrights telling employers to provide safe and efficient staging ropes for working on the sides of vessels in February 1876.[44] Health issues also figured in other struggles. During a 1857 wage-strike, ex-Melbourne *Argus* compositor Joseph Pearce stated 30 to 40 worked between 10 am and 3–4 am six days a week, 'cooped up in a room scarcely 40 x 40—close, sultry, pestilential, amidst the glare of a hundred lights, with straining eyes and dizzy head.'[45] Poor ventilation, gas-lighting and toxic substances (especially chemicals but also metals) accounted for premature cancer/ respiratory disease-related deaths amongst printers.[46] Hazardous exposures were also problems for metal trades and transport equipment workers.

Unilateral Regulation and Strikes

For these unions unilateral regulation was central, rules specifying minimum rates, work methods, apprentice/tradesmen ratios and demarcation. Members were prohibited from hiring/remaining at below-rate jobs although those resigning had to notify the union and give due notice. In June 1867 the Ballarat Typographical Society 'closed' the *Courier* office to members during a dispute over frames, a month later re-opening following an 'amicable' settlement.[47] Members taking action received oppression benefits. Under Victorian Ironmoulders rules (1858) members required executive permission to resign, those refusing acceptable alternative employment could be fined, and those working during a dispute fined or expelled.[48] Union admissions were also vetted. In 1864 the Melbourne ASE chastised Williamstown for admitting young men paid ten shillings per day—below the tradesman's rate.[49] Where permitted, overtime had to be paid rates specified in society rules.[50]

The common rule was extended through unilateral regulation. In November 1867, four shipwrights were dismissed for demanding 12 shillings per day at Pashley's Wharf. The Sydney Shipwrights paid the men six shillings per day and threatened sanctions on shipwrights still working at Pashley's. Wage cuts at Cuthbert and the ASN Co in May 1868 were also opposed, the Cuthbert dispute lasting almost two months. As depressed conditions continued, the union altered rules to specify a lower rate of ten shillings per day for 'new work' on iron vessels, floating docks, punts and patent slips. Work still dried up with more members falling into arrears and ASN Co. shipwrights supporting a management proposed 11 shillings for 'old work.' The society rejected this but by late October ASN shipwrights were only being 'heavily censured' for accepting ten shillings.[51] In early 1869 Cuthbert increased hours at the Fitzroy Dock, this and ongoing disputation at ASN Co carrying through to April, with 20 non-compliant members being fined 6s per day in March. The union continued resisting wage cuts despite losing members to unemployment or expulsion. A December 1870 proposal sanctioning wage cuts and enabling ASN Co. shipwrights to remain members was narrowly defeated 56 votes to 46. Following a prolonged strike over wage cuts and non-unionism at Cuthbert's (March to May 1871) the society reduced specified wages to ten shillings per nine-hour day for all employers (also reducing society official's salaries). Rejoining penalties for those working against society rules were reduced but they were excluded from all but strike benefits for 12 months.[52] These events are indicative of union efforts to maintain working rules even in unfavourable circumstances. It wasn't just intransigence. Fractured capital inhibited general bargaining and any concession risked widespread rule non-compliance, precipitating the union's collapse. There were also good strategic grounds for making wage cuts difficult. In March 1872 shipwrights successfully resisted further wages cut at the ASN Co, two months later reducing hours to eight at the prevailing wage (ten shillings) and in October restoring wages to pre-1871 rates.[53]

Unilateral regulation was a coordination point between independent unions and formal mergers. The Port Phillip Shipwrights Society told the Echuca Shipwrights Society abiding by their working rules, especially wage rates and not admitting Melbourne Shipwrights in arrears, were prerequisites for becoming a branch.[54] Unilateral regulation required tight labour market control, including compulsory union membership. In 1868 Sydney Shipwrights summonsed six members for working with a non-unionist at Waterman's Bay Dock Balmain, expelling those refusing to leave the job. Four years later two non-unionists were permitted to work paying five shillings towards their entrance fees that night and another five shillings on Saturday.[55] In April 1877 Sydney Boilermakers ordered four members in arrears not to work until they satisfied society demands.[56] As in building, employers too were sometimes fined for employing non-society members especially when this required members leaving the job as happened to James Alexander (£5) in September 1879.[57]

While minimising strikes (and legal retribution for them) has been seen to explain unilateral regulation's origins,[58] more compelling was its ability to deal with fractured capital and employer unwillingness to bargain. Unions used funds and levies to support strikes, upholding society principles and rules, as in February 1868 when shipwright Henry Davis was unfairly dismissed from Healy and Harper's floating dock. In 1874 Robert Whiting was fined for failing to join others withdrawing when several Morts Dock shipwrights were working contrary to rules.[59] Similarly, the Sydney Boilermakers fined a member (Slattery) £5 for not joining a strike at Vale and Lacy in January 1874 while a 1s levy assisted those who had walked out. As the strike dragged on, efforts were made to prevent subletting/contracting-out work, members told to refuse 'any work knowingly in connection with Vale and Lacy.' Importantly, the strike had positive effects with 31 new members enrolling in March alone. The society warned other employers non-compliance with its rules would result in labour being withdrawn.[60] Threats were often enough, shop stewards regularly forwarding member-lists to the secretary. However, attempts to get a general agreement with masters failed. The Iron Trades Employers Association refused demands to dismiss all non-society men.[61] Work bans were also used to support industrial action or punish employers defying the society, Sydney Shipwrights banning work on a vessel built by Mr Sheehy at Mort's Dock in January 1875.[62]

Larger establishments could threaten unilateral regulation and the common rule. Responding to wage claims in January 1876 the South Australian Government Printing Office split compositors into three categories with the third class well below the union's prescribed minimum rates. Neither a strike nor petitioning worked so the Typographical Society expelled third-class printers (after 1 May) and published their names in the *Typographical Journal* circulated throughout the colonies.[63] More typical were cases where members were reported for accepting below-rate wages, or members themselves reporting wage cuts. Non-compliant members were fined, placed on probation, expelled or advised to demand the society-rate and, if refused, resign depending on the gravity of the offence, society strength and trade conditions.[64] Unions assisted displaced workers until they found another job and tried to prevent employers obtaining replacement labour. During downturns, requirements to resign were moderated, Adelaide ASE officials telling members to request the ruling rate but not jeopardise their jobs.[65] Unions adopting a tougher line tried alternatives. In early 1870 Sydney Shipwrights made allowances for members in arrears, facilitated re-enrolment of lapsed members and prioritised discharged members when vacancies occurred.[66]

Unilateral regulation extended to work methods. The Port Phillip Shipwrights Society sought generalised agreements with employers on its rules, pressuring holdouts and fining non-complying members, evidenced by its efforts to remove Saturday 'lay days' (days when a vessel could berth without paying demurrage).[67] When individual employers refused to budge there was little option but to withdraw labour. If this failed, after time had elapsed (exacting a cost on the employer) societies authorised members to rehire or readmitted those breaching rules with a substantial fine. By the 1870s unions increasingly turned to negotiated agreements to entrench rules as well as resolve other matters—facilitated by increasing organisation amongst employers. The Melbourne Typographical Society also pushed arbitration to resolve disputes although employers only accepted it occasionally. The rationale was clear. Even small strikes could be costly. A Trades

Hall-approved 13-week strike over boy-labour/wages at the *Melbourne Herald* in 1875 cost the union over £247 in strike pay.[68] Transitioning from unilateral regulation to bargaining and conciliation/arbitration was decades away.

Wages and Piecework

Colonial unions were generally hostile to piecework, arguing it undercut wages, increased work intensity and hazardous work practices, inhibited efforts to secure eight-hours, was difficult to administer and divided workers. ASE branches instructed members to refuse piecework and report any requests as well as sanctioning members accepting piecework except where it was established practice. When in 1877 the Adelaide ASE Secretary told the Adelaide locomotive workshops' chief engineer the union fined members accepting piecework, the engineer expressed shock stating such practices wouldn't last one day in England.[69] While the engineer may have exaggerated, colonial/UK differences were profound. Even where confined to specific tasks like caulking wooden ships, piecework sparked ongoing disputation. Sydney Shipwrights regularly dealt with instances of members charged with breaking the caulking-scale, exemplified by 17 members working on the *Anglo Indian* at Cockatoo Dock in March 1867. Emphasising quality/safety concerns, in 1872 the society approved a caulking rule change appointing leading hands to ensure work was done properly.[70] In January 1874 the Port Phillip Society fined Michael Bolderines £2 for purporting to caulk 90ft of the *Anglican* in less than half the time (eight-hours) specified in rules, thereby endangering 'the safety of the ship and lives of the crew and passengers.' Bolderines failed to pay, was expelled and other shipwrights working for John Laurie then withdrew. Ultimately Bolderines paid £5 to rejoin the society plus 19s 6d compensation to the six members at Laurie's.[71]

In printing and coopering, piecework was too entrenched to oppose, societies and chapels trying to set uniform prices and regulate work methods/task allocation to manage it. In printing, piecework was governed by elaborate rules/customs—some centuries old—including use of composing frames, pay per 1,000 type with different rates for news, repeat-advertisements and headings as well as rates for daily newspapers and jobbing offices. Complexity and employer efforts to cut costs (using non-apprenticed workers and casuals) were both an impetus for unionisation and numerous disputes. Key issues for the Melbourne Society's conference with master-printers in 1870 were uniform piece and day work wages, legally bound apprentices and forming an arbitration committee (with equal representatives) to resolve disputes.[72] In early 1875 the NSW Typographical Association secured an agreement setting piece-rates and minimum wages for a 50-hour week but within six months lost a battle to retain it.[73]

Hours of Work

Metal and transport equipment tradesmen followed building in campaigning for eight-hours and as there it facilitated unionisation. Prior to 1870, gains were limited apart from Melbourne. Once secured eight-hour and overtime limits were incorporated into society rules, as the Victorian Ironmoulders did in 1858—also formalising their opposition to piecework.[74] In 1859 the Melbourne ASE resolved engineers working over eight-hours would only be admitted on the proviso they 'endeavour to get 8 hours established as a general rule.'[75] In May 1872 Sydney Shipwrights told employers they could adjust intermediate hours (meal breaks and Saturday half-holiday) so long as work finished at 4 pm, full-day wages were paid and start/finish times included travelling to vessels moored in the stream.[76] Other tactics included targeting large government worksites. The ASE Melbourne Branch urged the Secretary Board of Land and Work to grant 'the 8 hour privilege to all government workmen.'[77] Campaigns experienced periodic failures and reverses. In September 1865 the ASE's Williamstown Branch acknowledged a Sandridge campaign had failed. In June 1866 the Sandhurst/Bendigo branch reported progress was being stymied by a firm dismissing one member of a deputation, suspending another and vowing to sack anyone asking for eight-hours.[78] Nonetheless, the movement inspired wider alliances and collaboration. In November 1868 Melbourne Carpenters and Joiners asked to meet the Melbourne ASE to determine the best means of adopting and maintaining eight-hours.[79]

In Sydney an iron-trades campaign began in 1861 following a strike at PN Russell engineering where two instigators (William Collins and James Patton) were prosecuted for conspiracy.[80] Melbourne unions sent support, the Melbourne ASE voting a half-day's pay from each member.[81] The struggle still took over a decade, ultimately coordinated by an iron-trades committee—similar bodies formed in other locations. An 1873 Adelaide (and beyond) campaign succeeded. In Sydney a long strike/lockout involving 2,000 ironworkers in early 1874 was ostensibly over abolition of two meal breaks. However, the primacy of eight-hours was evident in the final agreement and willing financial/logistical support of building unions and others.[82] Ex-chief justice Sir Alfred Stephen's efforts to resolve the lockout prompted wider discussion of arbitration.[83] In the transport equipment trades progress was fragmented, Melbourne coachmakers striking twice for eight-hours in the 1850s. From the late 1860s saddlers, harness/collar-makers, carriage-builders and wheelwrights in Sydney, Melbourne and Adelaide took up the cause intermixed with Saturday half-holiday claims. Amongst blacksmiths and wheelwrights the eight-hour push extended to Horsham, Stawell, Rockhampton and Warwick.[84] However, in most regional towns (Ballarat, Geelong, Roma, Parramatta, Goulburn, Grafton, Wollongong, Gawler, Yorketown and

Mount Gambier) the hours push centred on half-holidays, sometimes independently but more often involving retail-workers.[85]

Once secured, unions relied on members or periodic investigations to assess regional compliance.[86] Metal trades unions supported calls for making the eight-hour anniversary a public holiday.[87] Any challenge drew a significant response. Learning Martin and Co. (Gawler) had extended hours in May 1876, the ASE's Adelaide Secretary alerted other colonies and joined the ensuing strike.[88] In 1879 the ASE backed a multi-union strike against another eight-hour busting effort by Martin and Co., the costs precluding support for a levy to aid nine-hour struggles in Britain.[89] Upholding eight-hours meant limiting overtime. Charles Lakie honoured the Port Adelaide Sailmakers overtime ban although as an apprentice he wasn't a member.[90] Non-compliant members were sanctioned unless there were mitigating factors, typically being fined although three Sydney Shipwrights were expelled in 1876. During downturns overtime restrictions were essential to maximise jobs. Pressured for overtime at Mort's Dock, in August 1876 Sydney Shipwrights resolved to allow it 'where necessary' but half the payments would go to the society or all if false statements were made. Risks with such concessions soon manifested, successive investigations finding over half shipwrights working overtime were guilty of rule-breaches.[91] Similarly, in August 1880 the ASE's Balmain Branch banned overtime at Booth's Sawmill.[92]

Workshop Organisation

Printers' chapels originated in medieval times, hence religious terminology like Father of the Chapel. Chapels were central to customs like the annual *Wayse-Goose* dinner/celebration brought to the colonies in 1824.[93] Colonial printers' chapels probably operated from the 1820s (few chapel records survive) and as in Europe chapels helped establish multi-workplace printing unions. The *Sydney Herald* chapel's minute-book (1848–1866) demonstrates it was a base for repeated efforts to establish unions following the collapse of one formed in 1835.[94] In 1867 newspaper and printing chapel delegates re-established the Melbourne Typographical Society. Printing affords more evidence of workplace organisation as a transition point to union organisation. Nonetheless there were tensions. The Victorian Government Printing Office chapel remained aloof, few members joining the union while the *Melbourne Herald* chapel withdrew in October.[95] Chapels acted as unions exercising craft controls, providing friendly benefits and regulating wages and conditions, with activities continuing even after multi-workplace unions were established. They revived unions that collapsed, as repeatedly occurred even in colonial capitals prior to 1870, and in many towns like Newcastle and Maitland chapels remained the only printers' organisation prior to 1881, corresponding with unions in other colonies.

Sydney Herald and *Adelaide Advertiser*'s chapel minute-books detail activities, including administering sickness/distress benefits, pursuing claims/resolving disputes, enforcing unilateral regulation and revising rules on work methods like task allocation.[96] The *Herald* chapel sometimes extended funds to printers or widows at other establishments. In 1852 the *Sydney Herald* chapel requested increased piece-rates, rejecting a £20 bonus for members displaying 'steady behaviour.' It successfully challenged engagement without checking indentures. Almost all printers belonged although an 1859 proposal to make Chapel companionship and Office Benefit Society membership compulsory was lost.[97] As typographical societies became stronger, chapels were instructed to exclude non-unionists.[98] The *Adelaide Advertiser* chapel coordinated claims with other chapels like the *South Australian Register* while the *Sydney Herald* compared pay at other newspapers to bolster its claims. In October 1853 the *Herald* organised a four-chapel meeting setting minimum piece-rates. Agreements were reached with proprietors but piecework and issues like allocating Saturday and Sunday night work caused numerous disputes involving collective action and fining members. In 1859 *Herald* and Government Printing Office chapel delegates conferred on establishing printers' pensions.[99] Chapel minutes detailed debates, resignations and elections, including fining those refusing to undertake chapel posts— enforced democracy.

Other trades instituted representation at least in larger workplaces. Victorian Ironmoulders 1858 rules included check stewards to manage union membership and collect funds.[100] Minute-books confirm workshop organisation, the Sydney Boilermakers appointing delegates to Mort's Dock, ASN Co., the Railway Workshops, Grants, Vale and Lacy, Chapman Brothers and Atlas Ironworks in 1874.[101] Job delegates kept lists of members, collected subscriptions, investigated issues like apprenticeship and demarcation, reported on trade conditions and identified/enrolled non-union members. Their activities were especially critical on remote sites. Officials mentored their activities. In January 1877 the ASN Co. delegate was advised to approach a non-unionist and if rebuffed the 'usual consequences were to follow' (he joined). Similar warnings were issued to unfinancial members.[102] Shop stewards were commonly included on union's Central Committee/Board of Management, like the Melbourne Coopers Society.[103]

Wider Alliances and Collaborative Networking

Intercolonial and global communication began in the 1830s but strengthened over time. The Melbourne Typographical Society (1867) corresponded with unions in Ballarat, Geelong, Sydney, Manchester, London and Edinburgh. It published the intercolonial *Typographical Journal*, reporting conditions, financial members, non-compliant printers and other matters. In addition to discouraging strike-breaking other assistance was afforded. Sydney Shipwrights donated £50 and banned work on vessels sent from Hobart when the Southern Tasmanian Shipwrights Society struck for eight-hours in 1872.[104] Sydney Boilermakers communicated and exchanged rules with Melbourne, Adelaide and New Zealand.[105] Sydney Boilermakers also urged relocating members to establish new unions in Brisbane and Newcastle although in both instances success came several years later. However, Sydney refused an 1878 Ballarat boilermakers' request to establish a branch as beyond its jurisdiction even though the Melbourne union was struggling.[106] Inconsistencies in rules could present difficulties, Port Phillip Shipwrights threatening to sever connections with Echuca when five Melbourne members were fined for breaching Echuca's caulking rules. Tensions over working rules (including a long-running disagreement over caulking rate) also arose with its Williamstown section, though eventually settled.[107] Following a dispute at Macquarie's the Sydney and Newcastle Shipwrights established a joint-committee which took several years to reconcile their rules.[108] Notwithstanding occasional disagreements, shipwrights' societies kept up a stream of correspondence, in August 1878 Sydney informing Melbourne a strike had prevented wage cuts at the ASN Company.[109] Some typographical societies charged printers double entrance fees if they didn't belong to the union in the colony they left or inquired about their standing there. Societies borrowed from each other and the UK when drawing up piecework scales and copied artwork in membership cards and the like.[110] Collaboration set the groundwork for mergers/amalgamation into national bodies from the late 1870s. The South Australian Typographical Association requested copies of ASE rules prior to an international typographical conference (including New Zealand) in Melbourne in 1880, Victorian Typographers having already sent their rules to a re-established Sydney union.[111]

As a global union the ASE had advantages in uniform rules and governing structures, administration costs (like printing and distribution) and dealing with regional volatility or prolonged industrial struggles. The ASE circulated monthly reports on trade conditions in particular towns along with reports to and from the UK. This structure strengthened provision of friendly benefits, including 'equalisation' arrangements transferring funds between branches to accommodate member movements and make contingency payments. In November 1870 the Melbourne ASE received £30 from Adelaide to help address a downturn in trade. There was a downside, the Adelaide branch complaining to the UK General Secretary about heavy drains on reserves assisting the UK Lambeth branch over the past year. In May 1871 Adelaide sent £50 to Melbourne following a further request.[112] These mechanisms alone couldn't deal with labour market mismatches, given substantial colonial government emigration-funding especially for skilled workers like engineers, inevitably drawing craft unions into politics. Colonial ASE branches wanted more independence from the UK to produce an Australia-wide trade report (already done in the US), hold intercolonial delegate meetings, to pursue policies (notably opposition to migration) and operations. Growing Australian and New Zealand membership fueled the independence push led by Sydney which sought support from other branches.

As in building, manufacturing unions collaborated in major campaigns and disputes especially where key principles were at stake. In 1875 Sydney Blacksmiths prohibited members from doing boiler work at PN Russell's during a dispute.[113] Support wasn't confined to related trades. Between September 1873 and January 1874 Sydney Shipwrights contributed to a Sydney TLC fund for Nattai miners and made substantial donations supporting eight-hour strikes by sawmill employees and the iron-trades.[114] Relations between craft and unskilled unions varied, being most favourable where least threatened by changed production methods. In mid-1875 Sydney Boilermakers sent a delegation to the Iron Trades Labourers Association. It resolved to ignore its correspondence but before the year was out had donated £15 to the association (the Typographical Association also donated £10).[115] As in building, friction arose most commonly where labourers encroached on trades-work or where labourers' and craft union rules regulating work conflicted.

Subcontracting and Other Threats

While not so pervasive, subcontracting/contracting problems identified in building occurred in engineering/metal, resulting in court actions and political lobbying by the ASE and other unions.[116] Sydney Shipwrights banned sublet work, in 1873 charging William Monroe with breaching the rule at Vale and Lacy while Henry Watt was fined five shillings per day for contracting to caulk a vessel at Booth's Saw Mill (other members withdrawn). Between January and March 1878 the society was involved in a prolonged dispute over labour-only subcontracting (paid one shilling per hour) at Cockatoo Island. A joint society/TLC deputation urged the Minister for Works to set minimum wages for contract work while those accepting the subcontract were expelled, permitted to rejoin only on payment of a substantial fee.[117]

Government Lobbying and Political Activities

Immigration

Metal trades and transport equipment unions opposed immigration, especially government-assisted and indentured migration. In 1863 the Melbourne ASE instructed the secretary to report on employers' practice of getting 'emigrants at greatly reduced wages from the depot, and forcing them to be accepting of it.' A committee was formed and its report sent to the UK Executive Council requesting dissemination.[118] In 1876 the Adelaide ASE urged the Commissioner of Public Works to discontinue emigration after railway workshop fitters were retrenched.[119] Wider alliances were pursued, Victorian Coachmakers approaching unions in other industries arguing for 'the necessity of taking steps to check State Immigration.'[120] Unions also assisted anti-immigration demonstrations organised by labour councils and from the mid-1870s joined rising anti-Chinese agitation with Sydney Boilermaker TLC delegates supporting Bricklayers on the issue in April 1878.[121]

Promoting Local Industry

Colonial unions' advocacy of local manufacturing evident since the 1830s grew as engineering and other works expanded. Boilermakers, engineers, shipwrights and others pressed labour councils to lobby on government tenders, protested import competition and pressured governments over their industrial undertakings like railway workshops. In 1868 a Melbourne ASE deputation urged government to manufacture locomotives.[122] Coachmakers and carriage-builders also advocated locally built rolling stock aided by import duties, Victorian Coachmakers dispatching three deputations in July/August 1879 alone.[123] Societies collaborated with the Sydney iron-trade, preparing a report on colonially manufactured locomotives.[124] They also lobbied governments to build/expand technical schools so local manufacturing wouldn't depend on emigrant workers—debates still evident today.[125] Typographical societies, too, advocated limits to imported printed work while the Sydney Shipwrights amongst others countered newspaper reports criticising protectionism.[126]

Regulating Apprentices, Labour Standards and OHS

Facing difficulties over non-apprenticed workers, typographical unions turned to legislation. In 1868 Melbourne Typographers told the Eight Hours Association laws should prohibit boys working 'so many hours as to injure their health and to the detriment of journeymen.'[127] From the mid-1870s young female 'improvers' were introduced as an even cheaper alternative. The *Ballarat Star*'s Melbourne correspondent warned, given inroads already made in the UK and US, it would make past problems over 'grass hands' and boy-labour/apprenticeship seem 'mere trifles.'[128] In February 1880 the Melbourne Society's attempt to have ten females apprenticed at Massina and Co. failed. Within months six other printers were engaging un-apprenticed females. In August a deputation sought *Factories Act* amendments mandating indenturing of young workers and restricting their hours. Hopes to garner support from other unions were dashed, bakers and tailors having already resigned themselves to non-trade labour.[129] There was more support for laws having both OHS and public safety dimensions. In 1880 the Boilermakers Society reviewed a Land Boiler Inspection Bill then before NSW parliament, pointing to a recent Lismore boiler explosion and arguing some large boilers were under the charge of 'incompetent men.'[130]

Direct Political Representation

By the 1870s manufacturing unions increasingly supported the push for working-class parliamentary representatives although some like the Sydney Shipwrights criticised candidate selection (Chapter 11).[131]

Conclusion

Printers and shipwrights formed unions from 1829 and over the next decade coachmakers, blacksmiths, wheelwrights, saddlers and engineers followed. Cycles of formation/collapse/renewal continued into the 1860s but unions slowly consolidated in major towns, the UK-based ASE advantaging unionisation of engineers. Union growth in engineering, shipbuilding, coachmaking and printing was facilitated by the post-goldrush expansion of population, urban centres, ports and manufacturing/repair and transport requirements associated with mining, rural/agriculture and infrastructure building. Unskilled labourers/trade-assistant numbers grew, with the first attempts at unionisation after 1870. Key union objectives were friendly benefits, maximising jobs and regulating wages, work methods and hours through craft controls/unilateral regulation, mutual insurance and strikes with some collective agreements but little formalised bargaining. All methods—including mutual insurance—sought to influence labour market conditions. Employers periodically challenged these controls, via non-apprenticed boys and female labour, unskilled or indentured immigrant workers. Unions were mostly able to blunt these threats. Metal/engineering unions became the second major employment sector to secure eight-hours, with coachmakers/carriage-builders, saddlers and wheelwrights following suit. Printers, like miners, were inhibited by piecework. This point, largely overlooked in conventional accounts of the eight-hour movement, helps explain Australian unions' greater hostility to piecework than their UK and US counterparts. It also raises important questions about how labour work/pay regimes in particular countries shaped union strategies and vice versa. As with building, unions primarily drew on structural power while forming wider societal alliances to secure/maintain eight-hours and defend unionism notwithstanding some trade insularity. Colonial unions were drawn into politics through the eight-hour movement, the centrality of colonial governments in economic activity, and maximising jobs via import duties and restricting immigration.

Notes

1. LC247-1-21 Hobart 23 December 1851.
2. LC247-1-21 Hobart 20 January 1852.
3. *Kapunda Herald* 12 September 1876.
4. *South Australian Register* 28 March 1851; *Mercury* 5 May 1875.
5. *Evening News* 10 March 1874; *Sydney Morning Herald* 30 September 1876.
6. ML MLK00049 Sydney Shipwrights Minutes 18 April, 2 May, 25 July 1867; *Sydney Morning Herald* 28 February 1874.
7. *Argus* 26 May 1856, 8 May 1866; *South Australian Register* 27 April 1869; E88-1-1 Port Phillip Shipwrights Minutes 17 April 1874.
8. *Mercury* 2 June 1874.
9. *Brisbane Courier* 28 September 1865, 12 March 1877.
10. *Evening Journal* 1 February 1873; *Sydney Morning Herald* 6 October 1873, 12 July 1875; *Leader* 5 December 1874.
11. *Mercury* 17 August 1874.
12. ML MSS2422 1(7) Sydney Boilermakers Minutes 7 September, 26 November 1878.
13. *Riverine Grazier* 12 March 1879.
14. ML MSS2422 1(7) Sydney Boilermakers Minutes 20 August 1878.
15. ML MLK00049 Sydney Shipwrights Minutes 7 November, 5, 12, 19 December 1872, 18 September 1873.
16. *Sydney Morning Herald* 28 February 1874.
17. MUA Melbourne Typographical Society Minutes 16 July, 17 August 1867, 21 September 1869, 15, 22, 25 June, 2 July, 7 September 1872, 15 February, 28 June 1873.
18. E92-1-1 South Australian Typographical Society Minutes 26 June, 31 July, 14 August 1875.
19. T39-1-1 NSW Typographical Association Minutes 24 June, 6, 16, 20 October 1880.
20. E88-1-1 Port Phillip Shipwrights Minutes 16, 25 March 1874, 19 May 1876.
21. ML MLK00049 Sydney Shipwrights Minutes 21 September 1874.
22. ML MSS2422 1(7) Sydney Boilermakers Minutes 5, 19 September, 3 October 1876.
23. *Bendigo Advertiser* 13 August, 1 October 1880.
24. E162-1-1 ASE Adelaide Branch Minutes 25 July 1874.
25. Z102/10 ASE Newcastle Branch Minutes 14 November 1863.
26. ML MSS7614 1(1) Sydney Boilermakers Minutes 22 October 1875.
27. MUA Melbourne Typographical Society Minutes 28 September, 9 October 1875.
28. ML MSS2422 1(7) Sydney Boilermakers Minutes 19 August, 25 November 1879.
29. *Sydney Herald* Chapel Minutes 13 October 1856, 8 October 1857, 6 July, 2 November, 7 December 1859.
30. ML MLK00049 Sydney Shipwrights Minutes 22 November 1877; ML MSS2422 Sydney Boilermakers Minutes 8 June 1880.
31. E92-1-1 South Australian Typographical Society Minutes 19 December 1874.
32. ML MLK00049 Sydney Shipwrights Minutes 25 August 1870, 15, 29 March 1871.

33. William Dixon Library 331.7616691/1 Friendly Society of the Iron-moulders Society of Victoria Rules and Practices, Melbourne 11 September 1858.

34. Three in arrears were denied. ML MLK00049 Sydney Shipwrights Minutes 27 June 1867.

35. ML MLK00049 Sydney Shipwrights Minutes 14 February 1873, 30 September, 20 December 1877, 31 December 1878, 16 December 1880.

36. ML MLK00049 Sydney Shipwrights Minutes 1 August 1872, 3 July 1873, 6 October 1874.

37. *Maryborough Chronicle* 3 February 1877, 29 June 1878.

38. *Colonial Times* 31 December 1856; *Sydney Morning Herald* 13 January 1864; *Age* 15 December 1874.

39. ML MLK00049 Sydney Shipwrights Minutes 28 October 1872, 21 February, 6 March 1873, 16 September 1875, 17 February, 16 March, 6, 12 April, 11, 25 May, 6 July 1876.

40. *Argus* 7 May 1860.

41. MUA Melbourne Typographical Society Minutes 18 June 1867, 31 July, 28 August 1875.

42. *Melbourne Herald* 27 September 1880.

43. ML MLK00049 Sydney Shipwrights Minutes 30 September 1875, 18 January, 17 May 1877, 2, 7, 21 August 1876, 5, 9, 19 February 1880.

44. ML MLK00049 Sydney Shipwrights Minutes 3 February 1876.

45. *Age* 12 January 1857.

46. *Bendigo Advertiser* 27 February 1865.

47. MUA Melbourne Typographical Society 18 June, 16 July 1867.

48. William Dixon Library 331.7616691/1 Friendly Society of the Ironmoulders Society of Victoria Rules and Practices, Melbourne 11 September 1858 Fines for General Laws 4, 5 and 7.

49. Z102/256 ASE Melbourne Minutes 23 January 1864, 5 December 1868.

50. Z102/256 ASE Melbourne Minutes 16 June 1860.

51. ML MLK00049 Sydney Shipwrights Minutes 9, 14 November, 18 December 1867, 7, 11 May, 26 June, 16 September 1868.

52. ML MLK00049 Sydney Shipwrights Minutes 18 January, 4 February, 4, 17, 29 March, 1 April, 26 October 1869, 14, 21 December 1870, 23, 27 May, 8 June, 6, 27 July, 3 August 1871.

53. *Sydney Morning Herald* 12 October 1872; ML MLK00049 Sydney Shipwrights Minutes 22 March, 9 May, 27 September, 1, 5, 15 October 1872.

54. E88-1-1 Port Phillip Shipwrights Minutes 3 July 1874.

55. ML MLK00049 Sydney Shipwrights Minutes 18, 26 March 1868, 18 January 1872.

56. ML MSS2422 1(7) Sydney Boilermakers Minutes 3 April 1877.

57. ML MLK00049 Sydney Shipwrights Minutes 24 September 1879.

58. Lis, C. and Soly, H. (1994) An Irresistible Phalanx: Journeymen Associations in Western Europe, 1300–1800, *International Review of Social History*, 39(Supplement): 18–19.

59. William Dixon Library 331.7616691/1 Friendly Society of the Ironmoulders Society of Victoria Rules and Practices, Melbourne 11 September 1858; ML MSS Sydney Boilermakers Minutes 20 October 1874; ML MLK00049 Sydney Shipwrights Minutes 28 February 1868, 30 July, 4 August 1874.

60. ML MSS7614 1(1) Sydney Boilermakers Minutes 27 January, 4, 10 March, 7, 21 April 1874.

61. *Evening News* 11 March 1874.

62. ML MLK00049 Sydney Shipwrights Minutes 14 January 1875.

63. E92-1-1 South Australian Typographical Society Minutes 29, 31 January, 4, 12, 24 February, 4, 8, 31 March, 7, 11, 22 April, 12 May 1876; See too *Express and Telegraph* 31 January, 14 February 1876.

64. Z102/10 ASE Newcastle Minutes 6 October, 11 November 1865; E107-1-1 ASE Adelaide Minutes 1 April 1876.

65. Z102/256 ASE Melbourne Minutes 8 May 1869; E107-1-1 Adelaide Minutes 10 May 1878; E162-1-2 Adelaide Minutes 10 April 1879.

66. ML MLK00049 Sydney Shipwrights Minutes 18, 23 November, 16 December 1869.

67. E88-1-1 Port Phillip Shipwrights Minutes 17, 22 June, 3 July 1874.

68. MUA Melbourne Typographical Society Minutes 6 July 1870, 24 November, 17 December 1874, 9 January, 31 July 1875.

69. E107-1-1 ASE Adelaide Minutes 7 August 1877.

70. ML MLK00049 Sydney Shipwrights Minutes 26, 28 March, 16, 25 July 1867, 1, 8 August 1872.

71. E88-1-1 Port Phillip Shipwrights Minutes 18 January, 20 February, 6 March, 17 June, 4 September 1874.

72. MUA Melbourne Typographical Society Minutes 18 December 1869, 8, 22 January, 16 July 1870, 19 August 1871.

73. *Sydney Morning Herald* 18 September 1875.

74. William Dixon Library 331.7616691/1 Friendly Society of the Ironmoulders Society of Victoria Rules and Practices, Melbourne 11 September 1858, Rule 117.

75. Z102/256 ASE Melbourne Minutes 23 April 1859.

76. ML MLK00049 Sydney Shipwrights Minutes 9, 13 May 1872.

77. Z102/256 ASE Melbourne Minutes 25 August 1859.

78. Z102/256 ASE Melbourne Minutes 16 September 1865, 23 June 1866.

79. Z102/256 ASE Melbourne Minutes 21 November 1868.

80. *Sydney Morning Herald* 30 July 1861.

81. Z102/256 ASE Melbourne Minutes 1 June 1861, 9 September 1871.

82. *Sydney Morning Herald* 28 February 1874; T46-1-3 NSW Stonemasons Sydney Minutes 25 February 1874.

83. *Age* 17 February 1874.

84. *Rockhampton Bulletin* 7 April 1868; *Warwick Examiner* 7 November 1874; *Cumberland Mercury* 19 June 1875.

85. *South Australian Register* 16 September 1861, 29 November 1873; *Bunyip* 8 October 1875.

86. Z102/256 ASE Melbourne Minutes 17 September 1864.

87. E162-1-2 ASE Adelaide Minutes 17 January 1879.

88. E107-1-1 ASE Adelaide Minutes 13 May 1876.

89. E162-1-2 ASE Adelaide Minutes 25 April, 10 May, 21 July 1879.

90. *Express and Telegraph* 1 February 1873.

91. ML MLK00049 Sydney Shipwrights Minutes 22 October 1874, 11 May, 10 August, 12 October, 16 November, 17 December 1876.

92. Z102-4-1 ASE Balmain Minutes 2, 11 August 1880.

93. *Courier* 11 October 1858.

94. *Sydney Herald* Chapel Minutes 6 February 1856; T39-1-1 Typographical Association of NSW Minutes 10 April, 8, 29 May, 31 July 1880.

95. MUA Melbourne Typographical Society Minutes 4 May, 1 June, 26 October 1867, 3 September 1870, 15 April 1871.

96. E216 *South Australian Advertiser* Chapel Minutes 1863–1896.

97. *Sydney Herald* Chapel Minutes 31 August, 2, 4 September, 25 October 1852, 5 January 1859.

98. E92-1-1 South Australian Typographical Society Minutes 22 December 1876.
99. *Sydney Herald* Chapel Minutes 3, 23 May, 14 June, 1 July, 20 October 1853, 1 June 1859.
100. William Dixon Library 331.7616691/1 Friendly Society of the Iron-moulders Society of Victoria Rules and Practices, Melbourne 11 September 1858, Rule 28.
101. ML MSS7614 1(1) Sydney Boilermakers Minutes 6 October 1874.
102. ML MSS2422 1(7) Sydney Boilermakers Minutes 6, 20 February, 11 December 1877, 16 April 1878, 24 June 1879, 31 August 1880.
103. T30-1-1 Journeymen Coopers of Melbourne and Suburbs Minutes 18 November 1880.
104. ML MLK00049 Sydney Shipwrights Minutes 10, 21 February 1873.
105. ML MSS2422 1(7) Sydney Boilermakers Minutes 19 May, 1 December 1874, 14, 26 September 1880; E185-3 Port Adelaide Boilermakers and Iron Shipbuilders Minutes 3, 15 September, 29 October, 10 December 1880.
106. ML MSS2422 1(7) Sydney Boilermakers Minutes 19 May, 17 November 1874, 12, 26 November, 12 December 1878, 17 February, 30 March 1880.
107. E88-1-1 Port Phillip Shipwrights Minutes 2, 3 June, 7, 21 July, 7 October, 3 November 1876, 14 November 1877.
108. ML MLK00049 Sydney Shipwrights Minutes 11, 12 May 1875, 6 May, 8 July, 16 September, 2 December 1880.
109. E88-1-1 Port Phillip Shipwrights Minutes 2 August 1878.
110. E92-1-1 South Australian Typographical Society Minutes 7 January 1876, 20 June, 28 July 1877, 5 October 1878.
111. E92-1-1 South Australian Typographical Society Minutes 27 December 1879, 31 January, 7 February 1880; E162-1-2 ASE Adelaide Minutes 14 August 1880; T39-1-1 NSW Typographical Association Minutes 10 April, 29 May, 16 October 1880.
112. E162-1-1 ASE Adelaide Minutes 26 November 1870, 17 May 1871.
113. ML MSS Sydney Boilermakers Minutes 25 September, 5 October 1875.
114. ML MLK00049 Sydney Shipwrights Minutes 18 September, 20 November 1873, 29 January, 5 February 1874.
115. ML MSS Sydney Boilermakers Minutes 29 June, 13 July, 5 November 1875.
116. Z102/156 ASE Melbourne Minutes 25 February 1860.
117. ML MLK00049 Sydney Shipwrights Minutes 14 February, 13, 20 March 1873, 3, 18 January, 7, 21, 23, 28 February, 28 March 1878.
118. Z102/256 ASE Melbourne Minutes 13 December 1863, 23 July, 20 August 1864.
119. E107-1-1 ASE Adelaide Minutes 22 July 1876.
120. T8-2A-3 VOBS Melbourne Minutes 1 June 1874.
121. ML MLK00049 Sydney Shipwrights Minutes 5 July 1877, 8 January 1880; ML MSS2422 1(7) Sydney Boilermakers Minutes 16 April 1878, 20 January 1880.
122. Z102/256 ASE Melbourne Minutes 26 September 1868.
123. *Age* 7, 9 July, 11 August 1879.
124. ML MSS2422 1(7) Sydney Boilermakers Minutes 14 July, 30 September 1879, 20 January, 16 March 1880.
125. Z102/256 ASE Melbourne Minutes 12 September 1868.
126. MUA Melbourne Typographical Society Minutes 15 April, 10 June 1871; ML MLK00049 Sydney Shipwrights Minutes 18 May 1871.
127. MUA Melbourne Typographical Society Minutes 8, 29 February 1868.
128. *Ballarat Star* 10 January 1876.

129. MUA Melbourne Typographical Society Minutes 7, 16 February, 31 July, 28 August, 9 October, 13 November 1880.
130. ML MSS2422 1(1) Sydney Boilermakers Minutes 20 January, 17 February 1880.
131. ML MSS2422 Sydney Boilermakers Minutes 17 October 1876; ML MLK00049 Sydney Shipwrights Minutes 17 September, 9 December 1874, 6 May 1880.

8 Apparel, Footwear, Food/ Beverages and Other Manufacturing

Introduction

In some manufacturing like textiles, clothing and footwear, mechanisation and cheaper mass-produced imports weakening colonial unions by the 1840s accelerated over succeeding decades. In baking and butchering, most worked in small retail/production outlets where long trading hours/ intense competition weakened craft controls. From the mid-1870s refrigeration and large slaughterhouses facilitated meat storage and exports. These factors help explain organisational volatility. While bakers, bootmakers and tailors were amongst the earliest to unionise, growth after 1850 was spasmodic and relatively sluggish until 1871–1880. Weakness/ defensiveness was reflected in the higher ratio of strikes to NSCA although NSCA were larger (Table 8.1). Wages and hours were the dominant issues in collective action followed by working conditions and OHS—the latter largely associated with sweating/long-hours in baking, clothing and bootmaking (Table 8.1).

Far from the Webb's realms of new model unions (Chapter 7) these unions couldn't practice unilateral regulation, made less use of petitioning/ deputations and initially relied more on old methods of hiring—the House-of-Call (Table 8.2). There are subgroups differences. Unlike others, strikes by tailors and bootmakers outnumbered NSCA. Building materials workers used mass meetings and marches in equal measure but other subgroups engaged in few marches principally because only the former seriously pursued eight-hours, joining annual demonstrations. Footwear/clothing and food/beverage unions made more use of newspaper letters/public notices seeking community support on poor wages, long-hours and exploitation (Table 8.2). In clothing subcontracting was widespread and came with a raft of problems, including under-payment/ low wages, irregular employment, intensified work and long-hours.

Informal Workplace Organisation

Informal workplace-based collective action remained common, especially where numbers were insufficient to sustain unions. In August 1851

Table 8.1 Worker Organisation Apparel, Footwear, Food, Other Manufacturing 1831–1880

Industry	1831–1840	1841–1850	1851–1860	1861–1870	1871–1880	Total 1851–1880
Entire Industry						
Organisations	107	103	111	72	161	315+
Raw involvement	564	1151	1002	2299	5432	8733
Est. involvement*	627	1274	1115	4409	20084	25608
Strikes						
Won	2	5	7		9	16
Drawn		3				
Lost	35	30	25	2	9	36
Unknown	8	10	11	6	31	48
Total	45	48	43	8	49	100
Est. total involvement*	334	404	135	56	3418	3609
Number of establishments						
One	37	32	31	5	25	61
Multi	1	3	2	1	8	11
Regional/town	6	10	10	2	17	29
Non-strike collective action						
Won	2	10	14	10	29	53
Drawn	3		1			1
Lost	40	20	12	5	7	24
Unknown	14	14	17	15	40	72
Total	59	44	44	30	76	150
Est. total involvement*	306	145	1278	775	6961	9014
Number of establishments						
One	52	31	22	10	14	36
Multi	2	3	2	1	6	9
Regional/Town	5	9	19	15	53	77
Issues in collective action (strikes/NSCA)						
Wages	13/12	17/18	17/16	6/17	32/24	55/57
Hours	25/2	24/3	23/18	2/14	17/57	42/89
Working conditions	16/37	8/19	9/15	1/17	4/24	14/56
Health & safety	1/6	1/3	1/8	/9	4/35	5/52
Management behaviour	6/3	1/3	3/1		4/	7/1
Jobs/employment	/6	5/4	/2	/1	1/4	1/7
Work methods		3/	3/1	/1	2/1	5/3
Unionism	1/	2/	1/	/2	5/2	6/4

(Continued)

Table 8.1 (Continued)

Industry	1831–1840	1841–1850	1851–1860	1861–1870	1871–1880	Total 1851–1880
Subcontracting	/1	1/1	1/5	/1	4/2	5/8
Legislation	/1					
Unknown		2/1				
Total strikes/NSCA	45/59	48/44	43/44	8/30	49/76	100/150

* Adjusted by multiplying number of zero-reporting organisations/years by median industry membership in that decade. ⁺For totals, organisation spanning multiple decades only counted once.

Bathurst bootmakers thanked their master for increasing wages while hatters working for Bidencope's Hobart struck over reduced wages in 1876.[1] Even unorganised workers had norms about craft-demarcations, butchers at Yengarie (Queensland) refusing to fold hides as beyond their trade in September 1866.[2] Large meatworks/abattoirs using semi-skilled slaughtermen experienced wage strikes like those at the Melbourne Meat Company Maribyrnong (1870) and Lakes Creek near Rockhampton (1880). The Lakes Creek strikers were replaced but the works subsequently became a union hub.[3] Wage grievances also sparked protests in factories, mills and refineries, including the Australian Sugar Company's Canterbury refinery (1852) and Cameron and Co. tobacco manufacturer (1875).[4] In 1867, 300 workers at John Dunn Jnr's Port Adelaide flourmills responded to wage cuts by burning him in effigy, the mill burning down two months later amidst suspicions of sabotage—an inquest blamed Dunn's failure to employ a nightwatchman.[5] Workers also combined over hours. In September 1874 workers at Johnson's jam factory and Franklins Sawmill in Hobart secured a Saturday half-holiday while Maryborough Sawmills workers (Queensland) protested working overtime more than three days per week in 1876.[6] Collective absconding, like that by sawyers and labourers from George Pizey's Pitt St in July 1854, occurred but was rare (or unreported).[7]

Multi-Workplace and Formal Organisation

Bootmaking, Clothing/Apparel and Textiles

Pre-1851 bootmakers and tailors unions were active but mass-imports and later mechanised production progressively undermined craft controls causing considerable organisational volatility. In Sydney, journeymen cordwainers/bootmakers unions are known in 1851–1852, 1860–1864 and 1866, afterward splintering as boot production changed. The NSW

Table 8.2 Worker Organisation Summary—Apparel et al. Subgroups 1831–1880

Footwear, clothing and apparel						
Organisation numbers	36	35	36	21	47	95⁺
Est. involvement*	308	535	196	1200	7057	8453
Strikes	16	24	17	4	24	45
NSCA	22	15	11	9	19	39
Absconding	3	1	1		1	2
Petitions	3	1	1		2	3
Deputations	1			1	4	5
Mass meetings		5	2	5	17	24
Marches		2			4	4
Letters/public notices	6	28	4	3	28	35
Bans	1	1			1	1
House-of-call	1	9	3		9	12
Court actions						
Won		4	4		2	6
Lost	40	21	14	3	2	19
Drawn	1					
Food, beverage and tobacco workers						
Organisation numbers	29	29	35	24	59	108⁺
Est. involvement*	121	254	807	1656	3615	6078
Strikes	11	7	12	2	4	18
NSCA	12	15	18	14	36	68
Absconding	8	3	1			1
Petitions		4	1		4	5
Deputations		1		1		1
Mass meetings		1	7	11	24	42
Marches	1			1	2	3
Letters/public notices		4	15	1	11	27
Bans	1	1	1	1	1	3
House-of-call	3	2	2	10	13	25
Court Actions						
Won	1	5	*	1		1
Lost	29	13	24	1	1	26
Drawn	1		1			1
Building materials and household items						
Organisation numbers	34	32	30	23	35	82⁺
Est. involvement*	182	475	88	1553	8272	9913
Strikes	13	14	10	2	9	21
NSCA	22	12	12	4	16	32

(*Continued*)

Table 8.2 (Continued)

Absconding	10	3	4			4
Petitions	3	3		3	3	6
Deputations		1			4	4
Mass meetings		6	3	8	46	57
Marches			2	7	42	51
Letters/public notices	4	2	4	1	6	11
House-of-call	1	1				
Bans	1		2			2
Court actions						
Won			1		1	2
Lost	19	17	4	1		5
Drawn		1				
Miscellaneous Manufacturing						
Organisation numbers	8	7	10	4	20	30⁺
Est. involvement*	16	10	24		1140	1164
Strikes	5	2	4		5	9
NSCA	3	2	3		5	8
Absconding	1	2	1			1
Petitions					3	3
Deputations					3	3
Mass meetings			1		3	4
Marches			1			1
Letters/public notices					4	4
Court actions						
Won			1		1	2
Lost	7	4	6		2	8
Drawn			1			1

* Adjusted by multiplying number of zero-reporting organisations/years by median industry membership in that decade. ⁺For totals, organisation spanning multiple decades only counted once.

Bootmakers Protective Union (1869–1875 revived 1878–1879) incorporated a separate finishers union (1872–1874). Other short-lived bodies included a cordwainers association (1872–1874 revived in 1879) and operative sewn-bootmakers union (1872–1874). Melbourne followed a similar pattern with craft unions (1859–1860, 1864–1868, 1870–1874) joined by more specialised bodies like bespoke bootmakers (1873) before a more general body, the Victorian Operative Bootmakers Union (1879) formed. In Adelaide unions formed/operated in 1851, 1854, 1860, 1866–1867, 1869, 1873–1874 plus a riveters and finishers union (1870–1871). A successor body (1874–1879 or 1876–1879) became a branch of the United Tradesmen's Society. Unions were even more discontinuous in Hobart and Brisbane, with one Hobart attempt (1854) prior to the Southern Tasmanian Journeymen Bootmakers Society (1874–1882) and four attempts in Brisbane (1860, 1872, 1873–1876, 1879) only one surviving over a year. Unions in Maitland (1856) and Bendigo (1868) rapidly failed.

Clothing-worker unionisation followed a similar pattern although manufacturing growth in Melbourne provided more impetus for organisation including more specialist and semi-skilled workers in factories. There were six unions of tailors in Melbourne (1850–1854, 1856–1861, 1870–1907), two by practical/slops cutters (1876, 1879), and one each by tailoresses (1874–1875), pressers (1874–1875) and foremen tailors (1874–1891), several merging in 1907 to form a more broadly based union. Tailors also unionised in Ballarat (1862–1870, 1877) and Bendigo (1873–1876). In Sydney there were six unions of tailors (1851, 1851, 1861–1864, 1866, 1875–1881) and one by foremen tailors (1880). Adelaide had four unions (1851, 1854, 1866 and 1874–1882) and Brisbane two relatively long-lived bodies (1866–1875, 1878–1892). A Hobart tailors' union (1846–1855) wasn't followed until 1883 with two short-lived Launceston unions (1852, 1875–1877). Other apparel trades began to organise, notably hatters in Melbourne (1873–1878) followed by felt hatters (1883–1896). Given the importance of wool there was also organisation amongst woolsorters/classers in Melbourne (1851, 1865–1908, 1877) and Geelong (1877) and wool-packers in Launceston (1851).

Food, Alcohol and Tobacco Workers

Journeymen bakers unionised from the early 1830s but bodies experienced considerable organisation volatility. Post-1850 unions formed in Sydney (1850–1851, 1852–1853, 1856, 1860–1872, 1869–1881 and a scab body 1871–1877), Melbourne (1850–1851, 1852–1854, 1857, 1859, 1860, bread and biscuit makers 1862–1867, 1863, 1864, 1865–1875, 1869), Adelaide (1853–1854, 1869, 1877, 1878–1880), Hobart (1854, 1856 and 1874), Brisbane (1871, 1876) and Victorian regional towns of Bendigo (1857, 1869–1873, 1873), Ballarat (1860, 1869–1873), Geelong (1869–1873), Castlemaine (1869–1873, with cooks and confectioners, 1873), Kyneton (1873) and Pleasant Creek (1873–1875). Pastry-cooks and confectioners organised in Melbourne (1859–1860, 1874), Ballarat (1872) and Castlemaine (1873). Journeymen butchers unionised in Sydney (1851–1852, 1857–1861, 1874–1880), Melbourne (1857–1861, 1867, 1870, Emerald Hill 1873, 1876–1877, Carlton, Collingwood and Fitzroy 1878), Adelaide (1851, 1871, 1873, 1876 and 1880–1888), Hobart (1865), Brisbane (1869, 1872, 1874 and 1875), Newcastle (1863, 1878–1880), Bendigo (1869, 1873, 1879), Geelong (1869), Ballarat (1873), Toowoomba (1872), Echuca (1878–1880),

Maryborough (1874, 1880–1896), Rockhampton (1879), Mount Gambier (1874) and Port Adelaide (1876). Semi-skilled flour mill workers organised in Melbourne (1872–1873), Bendigo (1874) and Mount Gambier (1874) as did Melbourne brewery workers (1879).[8] Cigar-makers and tobacco workers organised in Melbourne (1875, 1880–1900), Sydney (1875) and Adelaide (1880).[9]

Building Materials, Furniture and Household Items Workers

Prior to 1851 convicts dominated collective action by quarrymen in NSW and Tasmania—exceptions included Sydney Council quarrymen petitioning for wage increases in 1845 and 1847.[10] In Tasmania informal action remained the norm after 1850, Hobart Council quarrymen striking over wages in 1862. Similar workplace actions over wages, subcontracting and the truck-system occurred in South Australia (Adelaide 1876), Queensland (Chinchilla and Dalby in 1878) and quarrymen engaged in Victorian road and rail-construction (including Sandhurst, Broadford and Koroit in 1859; Mount Alexander, Lethbridge and Warrenheip in 1860; Ballarat in 1870 and Kyneton in 1873).[11] Quarrymen's unions were formed in Melbourne and its surrounds. Brickmakers—often self-employed—organised in Sydney (1866–1871, 1879–1880), Greater Melbourne (with labourers at Brunswick, Hawthorn and Prahran 1873–1884), Castlemaine (1856), Ballarat (1860), Echuca (1876), Sandhurst (1877) Brisbane (1866) and Adelaide (1869, 1875, 1877–1879). Pipe/pottery workers attempted organisation in Melbourne (1860) and Parramatta (with brickmakers 1880). Sawyers formed early unions but machine-sawmilling after 1850 facilitated sawmill and timberyard unions in Melbourne (1857, 1869–1880), Castlemaine (1869), Ballarat (1870), Echuca (1873–1878) and Sydney (1872, 1873). Sawyers joined building mechanics and labourers in Fremantle and Perth in a push for increased wages and reduced hours in 1873.[12]

In furniture and household items, cabinetmakers unionised from the 1830s, complicated after 1850 by splintering along UK/US lines into more specialist groups like French-polishers, carvers/picture framemakers and chairmakers as numbers grew in these trades. This splintering was countered by mechanised production and growing competition from Chinese cabinetmakers—more pronounced after 1880. In Melbourne there were unions of cabinetmakers (1855–1860, 1865–1867 with chairmakers, 1870–1884), French-polishers (1864), upholsterers (1866–1892), woodturners (1870), carvers (1874) and furnishing trades employees (1880). In Sydney cabinetmakers organised (1851–1858, 1860 with carvers, 1863, 1872–1877 with chairmakers) along with French-polishers (1878–1879) with an eight-hour cabinetmakers body in Maitland (1870). In South Australia cabinetmakers organised in Adelaide (1856, 1857 with carpenters, 1874–1876, 1878) while those in Moonta joined building trades workers in 1873. Cabinetmakers' unions briefly existed in Brisbane (1864, 1868–1870) and Hobart (1874).

Miscellaneous Manufacturing Workers

This category was dominated by leather trade workers although others sporadically organising included soap/candle makers, jewellers (Melbourne 1869–1874, 1879; Sydney, 1878) and basketmakers (Melbourne 1868–1879 and Adelaide, 1880).[13] Leatherworkers began unionising in the 1830s but only sluggishly and splintering into more specialised groups. Journeymen curriers formed unions in Melbourne (1848–1851, 1853, 1859–1864, 1869–1882) as did saddle, harness and collar-makers (included in transport equipment for this book in 1853–1865, 1866, 1867, 1868–1869, 1872–1890) plus a short-lived Geelong union (1871). After 1870, tanners organised independently in Melbourne (1874–1875, with fellmongers 1879) and Echuca (1873), as did beamsmen (Melbourne, 1876–1878). Other colonies followed a similar pattern. Curriers formed unions in Sydney (1852–1856, 1878–1892) and Adelaide (1851–1852, 1874–1875). Journeymen saddle and collar/harness-makers organised in Sydney (1853, 1873, 1878–1879), Maitland (1872), Adelaide (1873) and Gawler (1875); beamsmen in Sydney (1880) and tanners in Adelaide (1874–1875). Launceston leatherworkers briefly organised in 1876 and Brisbane leatherworkers formed a committee in 1879.

Engine-drivers operating the boilers/steam engines in factories, mills and refineries also unionised in Sydney (1875).[14]

Craft Controls and Jobs

Most trades examined in this chapter had little capacity to use craft-exclusion and unilateral regulation. Even given fragmented records, there were few reported disputes over apprentice ratios, jurisdiction/demarcation or non-apprentice workers—rules Chapter 7 unions had to regularly enforce. The silence suggests weakness, not strength. Leatherworkers attempted craft controls, as did cabinetmakers, tailors and bootmakers, but organisational turnover and unsuccessful wage and hour campaigns were indicative of their weakness. Melbourne cigar-makers were a rare exception, securing agreement to their rules and subsequently defending apprentice ratios and opposing boy-labour.[15] Woolsorters/classers in Melbourne and Geelong, too, asserted control over their vocation, unilaterally setting remuneration, providing friendly benefits and controlling hiring through a House-of-Call.[16] Other societies confronting surplus labour like the Melbourne Operative Bakers maintained a House-of-Call in the 1870s, the practice largely abandoned elsewhere.[17]

Mutual Insurance, Safety and Health

Organisational volatility undermined friendly benefit provision (accident, sickness and death/funeral) even in hazardous trades like baking and leather-making. Curriers in Sydney (1852–1856, 1878–1892), Melbourne (1859–1864, 1869–1882) and Adelaide (1874–1875) pursued mutual insurance as did Melbourne Tailors (1870–1907) and several quarrymen's unions (Melbourne Quarrymens Benefit Society, 1857 and Sydney Quarrymens Protective Society 1873–1881).[18] The Victorian Quarrymens Association (1860) and Sydney Quarrymens Society (1867) focused on wages.[19] However, hours were the pivotal mobilisation issue for quarrymen and the same applied to bakers although friendly benefits were important for several like the Sydney Operative Bakers Friendly Society (1860–1872) and Operative Bakers Society of Victoria (1865–1975).[20] Amongst brickmakers, friendly benefits were as important as wages and eight-hours exemplified by the Victorian Brickmakers and Brickmakers Labourers Society (1873–1884). Sawmill unions, like the Melbourne United Mill Sawyers and Timberyard Employees Society and the Echuca Sawmill and Timberyard Working Mens Eight Hours Association (1873–1878), operated sickness/accident funds, responding to hazards like machine-saws, splinters and wood-dust.[21] Low wages and long-hours (sweating) were major health-related issues for bakers, boot and clothing workers, more closely linked to mobilisation after 1880.

Working Hours

Eight-hours were rallying points for cabinetmakers, upholsters, curriers/tanners, quarrymen, sawmill and flour mill workers. In 1853 Sydney Cabinetmakers joined stonemasons and carpenters' claim for earlier Saturday finishing. Melbourne Cabinetmakers joined the eight-hour push in 1856, with upholsterers (1866) and wood-carvers (1874) following suit as did Maitland cabinetmakers (1870).[22] Migrating to Melbourne from Ireland in 1865, cabinetmaker William Emmett Murphy played a prominent role in the eight-hour movement, becoming secretary of the Victorian Trades Hall Council (THC) in 1877, the movement's first historian and Labour Party activist.[23]

Quarrymen pursued eight-hours in Melbourne (1856, 1858–1861, 1866, 1869–1876, 1878–1880), Sydney (1856–1857, 1869, 1873–1881), Adelaide (1863) and Brisbane (1878), aided by building unions and peak bodies keen to spread the principle. Only Melbourne and Sydney bodies made ground. Melbourne/Brunswick quarrymen joined eight-hour demonstrations from the early 1860s, Richmond quarrymen struck for eight-hours in 1878 while the Sydney Quarrymens Protective Society joined demonstrations by 1875.[24] Hours also predominated amongst sawmill and timberyard workers. In 1857 Melbourne timber trade workers pushed for a Saturday half-holiday and in 1869 the United Sawmill and Timberyard Employees Society (Melbourne and Castlemaine) pushed for eight-hours. Ballarat sawmill workers followed in 1870, as did Sydney Sawmill Delegates in 1872.[25] Nonetheless, apart from Melbourne where the 1869 agreement held for over a decade, gains were short-lived. Echuca sawmill workers won eight-hours in 1873 but two years later had to engage in a bitter strike to retain it, with companies engaging Chinese and other strike-breakers. Some strikebreakers withdrew after discussions with unionists.[26]

Amongst tanners and curriers, eight-hour campaigning was fragmented and slow. Melbourne curriers campaigned in the late 1850s, followed over a decade later by tanners in Echuca (1873), Castlemaine and Melbourne (1874), and Sydney curriers (1880), while Launceston leatherworkers struck for nine-hours in 1876.[27] In most towns saddlers and others found it easier to join the half-holiday movement. Some flourmill workers sought eight-hours but those in Mount Gambier, Port Adelaide and Gawler pursued a weekly half-holiday.[28]

Bakers, Butchers, Clothing Workers Campaigns
Against Long-Hours

Where intense competition/retail practice dictated long-hours (bakers and butchers) or where mechanisation replaced tradesmen with semi-skilled workers (clothing and boot manufacture), eight-hours remained a remote aspiration. Responding to a bootmaker apprentice's conviction for refusing to work 11 hours, Hobart *Mercury* correspondent 'Citizen' pointed to eight-hours in building and argued master and servant laws should prescribe working hours.[29] Bakers and butchers working long-hours, including Sunday's, were keenly aware of eight-hour/half-holiday gains. Most worked in small premises serving as retail outlets although larger baking establishments and abattoirs were evident by the 1870s. Health featured in all hours' campaigns but dominated campaigns against excessive hours. Noting Saturday half-holiday successes amongst clerks and others, in 1854 a journeyman baker spoke for many, calling for ending Sunday work.[30] Bakers' societies campaigned against all-night baking and Sunday work, drawing support from other unions, including stonemasons, but seldom secured even short-lived agreements.[31] In July 1857 the Melbourne *Age* observed that contrasting recent Saturday half-holiday agreements, Master Bakers refused operatives' 'reasonable demands for some release from almost incessant toil, treating them as a new form of serfs.'[32]

Limiting hours and banning Sunday work were core struggles. Melbourne bakers began campaigning in the 1840s, with further claims in 1851. Six years later another body demanded Sunday work be abolished, daily hours reduced from 12 to ten and a 5 am start. Masters accepted the first two claims but it didn't last, with failure repeated in several further efforts.[33] The Operative Bakers Association (1865–1975) struck unsuccessfully for ten hours in 1869, lost another campaign in 1872 and then secured some hour reductions, uniform wage rates and banning Sunday work in 1873.[34] Regional bakers' unions ran parallel claims in 1869 and 1873 in Ballarat, Geelong, Castlemaine and Bendigo with Kyneton and Pleasant Creek joining the 1873 campaign. In 1860 Sydney Bakers sought to a 12-hour-limit and end to nightwork, the only positive outcome being one master increasing wages.[35] In 1864 the union ended Sunday baking but then confined itself to cooperation and friendly benefits.[36] A separate union formed in December 1869 but resistance from several masters stymied hour cuts, a pattern repeated when the union joined the eight-hour push in 1875.[37] In Sydney and Melbourne some journeymen refused to join, even forming scab unions like one in Sydney (1871–1877) which undermined campaigns.[38] The Melbourne Trades Hall and Literary Institute did what it could, promising to prevent non-society men using the Hall in 1871.[39] Efforts were more sporadic elsewhere. In 1854, 20 Hobart master bakers agreed to eliminate nightwork by commencing at 5 am but nothing more occurred until 1874 when the Bakers Short Hour Association requesting eight-hours got all but four employers to agree to ten hours.[40] Of four Adelaide unions only the Journeymen Bakers Association (1869) is known to have pursued a short-lived campaign for ten hours.[41] Overall, gains were modest but foreshadowed more sustained campaigns after 1880 and, ultimately, legislative intervention.

There were strong parallels between butchers' and bakers' hours' campaigns including proscribing Sunday work. In May 1857, 200 Melbourne butchers organised to cut hours and ban Sunday work securing a partial win.[42] Sydney butchers, too, unionised and three years later demonstrated when, at the behest of masters, the government re-opened Glebe abattoirs on Sundays.[43] Newcastle butchers initially unionised in 1863 but Sunday work was still being contested in 1874 and again in 1880.[44] It was the same story in Queensland with repeated attempts to end Sunday work in Brisbane (1869, 1872, 1875), Toowoomba (1872) and Rockhampton (1879).[45] From the early 1870s butchers unions in Melbourne (including Emerald Hill, Carlton, Collingwood and Fitzroy), Ballarat, Echuca and Bendigo pursued early-closing/weekly half-holidays as did butchers in Adelaide (1871, 1873, 1880), Mount Gambier (1874) and Port Adelaide (1876)—the latter campaigning for 60-hour week.[46] In Hobart butchers organised a cricket match with bakers as part of a weekly half-holiday campaign.[47]

In clothing the Melbourne Tailors Trade Protection Society 1872 recruitment drive promoted minimum rates for a ten-hour day.[48] Health concerns were prominent in these campaigns. Female clothing workers often worked longer hours, especially seamstresses working 16-hour days from home for a pittance. Victoria's 1873 *Factory Act*, introduced by

West Ballarat member William Collard Smith, mandated an eight-hour day for women, with inspections by local Board of Health inspectors (the UK model). The Legislative Council nobbled the law by excluding smaller workplaces (less than ten workers) and, in the face of manufacturer influence, inspections were ineffective.[49] Unions, like the Ballarat United Short Hours Association, did what they could, identifying and threatening to expose firms flouting the law.[50]

Wages and Piecework

Securing wage increases/uniform rates proved challenging. In September 1852 Sydney operative bakers' wages claim was rebuffed and subsequent bakers' unions concentrated on reducing hours.[51] Some trades opposed piecework but overall their stance was mixed. In Melbourne hostility to piecework split tanners and curriers, tanners forming a separate union in 1874.[52] In brickmaking, cabinetmaking, tailoring and bootmaking, piecework was entrenched although day wages were sometimes paid. Unions tried to ensure piecework rates incorporated minimum wages and regulated work methods/task allocation to 'manage' this. Setting uniform wages underpinned organisation by Melbourne upholsterers in 1866 and Brisbane cabinetmakers two years later, the latter warning Sydney of misleading job advertisements.[53] Most experienced changes in production methods or import competition affecting wages. Tailors' societies found it increasingly difficult to defend piecework log-rates or prevent the introduction of semi-skilled labour. In 1866–1871 Melbourne tailors' unions prepared 'machine-time' logs but still couldn't prevent wage cuts by individual employers, or general employer attacks on wages and work methods control, the Melbourne Tailors Society collapsing in early 1869.[54] It was rapidly reformed (Melbourne Tailors Trade Protection Society 1870–1907) by activists using the same minute-book which managed to survive, drawn increasingly into the political sphere. In early 1871 a deputation requested Trades Protection League assistance regarding import duties. Writing to the *Tailor and Cutter* the union refuted colonial newspaper wage reports, arguing they encouraged emigrants who experienced 'disappointment' on arrival. When Buckley and Nunn cut wages the union could do little more than protest via correspondence and deputations. Threatened/actual wage cuts continued. Secretary Henry Fowler labelled employer responses to its September/October 1871 log as 'less than flattering.' Declining wages weakened the union's capacity to recruit/maintain members, prompting reduced entrance fee proposals and deputations visiting each shop. By March 1875 efforts to have disputes arbitrated stalled on disagreements over acceptable appointees with employers. Some employers resigned from the Masters Association and broke the log by arguing outwork wasn't covered.[55] The Melbourne union's difficulties grew as subcontracting/outwork became pervasive and employers pressured tailors to train women in factories on 'mysteries of the trade,' leading to disputes and strikes. The changes wrought a general decline of employment conditions.

Competing groups began to organise, notably tailoresses. Melbourne tailoresses briefly unionised in 1846 and no further (known) attempts occurred until July 1874 when the Melbourne Tailoresses Mutual Protection Society was formed at a Temperance Hall meeting, aided by male tailors keen to raise wages from a reputed two shillings a day and reduce their lengthy hours to eight.[56] With about 200 members it lasted about a year. The Melbourne Tailoresses Union formed eight years later with THC and union support as a result of strike over wage cuts eventually joining the amalgamated clothing trades union (1907). Overall, the pattern just described was repeated in other colonies and in bootmaking too. Limitations with voluntary arbitration and employers breaking ranks played out over time in clothing, bootmaking and other industries. Efforts to avoid/rectify these probelms influenced the model of compulsory wages board/arbitration unions advocated/obtained from the 1890s. Union officials/politicians who drove this ensured it was mandatory, roped in all employers no matter how reluctant and regulated work, not just employers.

Workshop Organisation

Some trades had longstanding traditions of workshop organisation. Linebaugh points to 'shop committees' amongst London boot manufacturers in the early 18th century.[57] If similar bodies operated in the colonies prior to 1881, evidence hasn't survived.

Building Alliances and Politics

As prior to 1851, unions publicly condemned misleading job advertisements and corresponded on trade conditions and strikes.[58] In 1867 Melbourne Tailors asked other colonial unions to notify them of any strike to 'prevent any members of this society proceeding there.'[59] Its successor, the Melbourne Tailors Trade Protection Society, arose from a meeting attended by 300 to refute statements by wholesale manufacturers Messrs Morrow and Parry of wages being 50–55 shillings for a 45-hour week. Meeting resolutions argued workers had to take bundles home every night that were completed with the assistance from their wives and children and even then it took 16–18-hour days to earn the specified wages. Further the resolutions argued employers made repeated misleading claims to encourage emigration and more competition for work that further reducing wages.[60] Hostility to UK (and even US) emigration was longstanding and extended to other bodies. In May 1868 the Melbourne Tailors Society entrusted 20 copies of a labour market report to a member returning to England to circulate.[61] From the late 1870s growing numbers of Chinese cabinetmakers in Melbourne and Sydney working for lower wages aroused considerable antagonism, several disturbances and a parliamentary debate over chairs for the 1880 Melbourne Exhibition.[62] Union efforts fueled anti-Chinese agitation in the 1880s.

Trades also sought to curb imports. Sydney cabinetmakers petitioned the Legislative Assembly for duties on manufactured furniture in 1863, complaining they had been rendered destitute.[63] Melbourne curriers told the National Reform and Protection League (1878) and Unemployed Labour Board (1879) there were hundreds of unemployed and widespread distress in the trade.[64] Others petitioning for import protection included Victorian hatters (1875) and cigar-makers/tobacco workers in Melbourne (1865), Sydney (1875) and Adelaide (1880), the latter lamenting they would be thrown out of employment just as the industry was established.[65] Tailors, bootmakers, the Basketmakers Society (1868–1879) and Goldsmiths and Working Jewellers (1869–1874) joined the Victorian Trades Hall Council while their counterparts in Adelaide and Sydney joined union peak bodies in the 1870s.[66]

Conclusion

Bootmakers, bakers, tailors, cabinetmakers and curriers/tanners began unionising in the 1830s but familiar cycles of formation/collapse/renewal only sluggishly gave way to consolidation due to a combination of import competition, mass production and labour-oversupply—many British/Irish tailors and bootmakers migrating to escape the deprivation arising from mechanisation. By the 1870s unions were forming amongst splintered task groups (like cutters) and female semi-skilled factory workers that would eventually merge into more broadly based unions after 1880. Splintering/deskilling also occurred in furniture manufacture. Leather-making experienced import competition, drawing them into political agitation along with bakers and butchers unable to shorten their hours. In general these unions were unable to regulate wages, hours and other conditions more than episodically. Long-hours at low pay (exacerbated by piecework/subcontracting) in bootmaking, clothing manufacture and baking—sweated labour—would eventually be a critical impetus for wage boards/arbitration. Only leather and building materials workers joined the eight-hour push, others pursuing half-holidays. Overall, unions had little structural power and were transitioning—some more rapidly than others—to draw on the organisational power of mobilising large numbers of workers. Boot/shoemakers, clothing workers and the leather trades were drawn to politics, agitating on distress, imports and immigration. However, their very weakness meant this was muted compared to Chapter 7 unions. It also affected their engagement in union peak bodies which became substantial after 1880.

Notes

1. *Bathurst Free Press* 16 August 1851; *Mercury* 4, 5 July 1876.
2. *Maryborough Chronicle* 19, 22 September 1866.
3. *Age* 7 October 1870; *Capricornian* 8 May 1880.
4. *Empire* 4, 5 June 1852; *Newcastle Chronicle* 11 February 1875.
5. *South Australian Advertiser* 11 September 1867; *South Australian Register* 26 November 1867.
6. *Mercury* 15 September 1874; *Maryborough Chronicle* 15, 19 August 1876.
7. *Sydney Morning Herald* 25 July 1854.
8. *Argus* 13 December 1872; *Bendigo Advertiser* 30 March 1874; *Border Watch* 17 October 1874; *Ballarat Courier* 28 April 1878.
9. *Age* 23 July 1875; *Sydney Morning Herald* 17 December 1875; *Hamilton Spectator* 25 December 1880.
10. *Sydney Morning Herald* 18 November 1845, 12 January 1847.
11. *Mercury* 29 September 1862, 17 June 1876; *Dalby Herald* 9 February 1878; *Argus* 17 May, 22 July, 23 September 1859, 21 February, 12 May 1860; *Ballarat Star* 10 September 1870; *Kyneton Guardian* 4 June 1873.
12. *Perth Inquirer* 3, 10 December 1873.
13. ML MSS308 THLI Minutes 24 September 1869; Victorian THC Minutes 17 June 1870; *Age* 19 July 1873, 11 July 1879; *Sydney Morning Herald* 22 October 1878; *South Australian Advertiser* 17 November 1880.
14. *Sydney Mail* 30 January 1875.
15. *Age* 4 December 1884, 11 February, 5 June 1885.
16. *Argus* 19 August 1851; *Australasian* 27 January 1877; *Geelong Advertiser* 19 July 1877.
17. *Age* 6 October 1875.
18. Some large employers like Alderson and Son Redfern tanners provided friendly benefits. *Australian Town and Country Journal* 13 January 1877.
19. *Age* 20 May 1857; *Argus* 12 June 1860; *Sydney Morning Herald* 31 August 1867.
20. *Sydney Morning Herald* 28 March, 24 August 1870.
21. *Age* 6 July 1870.
22. *Peoples Advocate* 7 May 1853; *Age* 22 May 1856; *Argus* 25 May 1866, 6 August 1874; *Maitland Mercury* 10 March 1870.
23. *Table Talk* 26 September 1890; Hagan, J. (1974) William Emmett Murphy, in *Australian Dictionary of Biography*, Melbourne University Press, Melbourne.
24. *Age* 7 December 1878; *Sydney Morning Herald* 25 October 1875.
25. *Argus* 24 November 1857; *Mount Alexander Mail* 9 October 1869; *Ballarat Star* 10 February 1870; T46-1-3 Sydney Stonemasons Minutes 19 November 1873.
26. *Freeman's Journal* 18 December 1875.
27. *Argus* 23 April 1859; *Age* 22 November 1873, 17 September 1874; *Launceston Examiner* 4 March 1876; *Sydney Daily Telegraph* 16 October 1880.
28. *Gawler Times* 21 March, 11 April 1873; *Border Watch* 17 October 1874.
29. *Mercury* 21 May 1877.
30. *Sydney Morning Herald* 31 August 1854.
31. *Sydney Mail* 7 July 1860, 30 April 1864; *Sydney Morning Herald* 10 August 1860; *Empire* 26 November 1860; *Evening News* 25 April 1870; T46-1-1 NSW Stonemasons Sydney Minutes 21 January 1861.
32. *Age* 11 July 1857.
33. *Argus* 30 September 1851; *Age* 11 July 1857.
34. *Age* 25 October 1869, 18 December 1872.

35. *Empire* 16 July, 13 August, 1 October, 26 November 1860.
36. *Sydney Mail* 30 April 1864.
37. *Sydney Morning Herald* 5 March 1870, 6 October 1873, 22 March 1875; *Argus* 3 November 1873.
38. *Evening News* 13 July 1870; *Sydney Morning Herald* 11 July 1871, 30 March 1877.
39. ML MSS THLI Minutes 2 June 1871.
40. *Hobarton Guardian* 8 April 1854; *Tasmanian Tribune* 11 August 1874.
41. *Evening Journal* 14 September 1869.
42. *Argus* 30 May, 18 June 1857.
43. *Sydney Morning Herald* 6 July 1857; *Empire* 1 January 1861.
44. *Newcastle Chronicle* 18 July 1873; *Maitland Mercury* 13 January 1874; *Sydney Morning Herald* 18 May 1880.
45. *Brisbane Courier* 30 April 1869, 23 June 1872, 10 March 1875; *Toowoomba Chronicle* 21 December 1872; *Maryborough Chronicle* 3 April 1879.
46. *South Australian Advertiser* 6 May 1871, 27 September 1880; *Border Watch* 9 August 1873, 4 November 1874; *South Australian Register* 21 September 1876.
47. *Mercury* 5 February 1878.
48. Z308-1 Melbourne Tailors Trade Protection Society Minutes 25 March 1872.
49. Hagan, J. (1964) Employers, Trade Unions and the First Victorian Factory Acts, *Labour History*, (7): 4.
50. *Age* 7 June 1875.
51. *Sydney Morning Herald* 28, 30 September 1852.
52. *Weekly Times* 13 June 1874; VOBS Melbourne Minutes 5 October 1874.
53. *Age* 26 April 1866; *Brisbane Courier* 14 August 1868; *Sydney Morning Herald* 16 September 1868.
54. Z308-1 Melbourne Tailors Society Minutes 5 August 1866, 18 October 1867, 6, 20 January 11 August 1868, 8 February 1869; Z308-1 Melbourne Tailors Trade Protection Society Minutes, 17 August, 11, 18 September, 14, 16 October 1871.
55. Z308-1 Melbourne Tailors Trade Protection Society Minutes 30 January, 20, 27 February, 16 October 1871, 12, 26 February 1872, 3, 5, 22 March, 12, 13, 14 April 1875; *Bendigo Advertiser* 5 May 1875.
56. *Argus* 13 July 1874; *Age* 13 July 1874.
57. Linebaugh, *The London Hanged*, 235.
58. E92-1-1 South Australian Typographical Society Minutes 10 April 1875, 29 January 1876.
59. Z308-1 Melbourne Tailors Society Minutes 18 November 1867.
60. Z308-1 Melbourne Tailors Trade Protection Society Minutes 14, 25 July, 22 August 1870.
61. Z308-1 Melbourne Tailors Society Minutes 11 May 1868.
62. *Launceston Examiner* 31 October 1878; *Bendigo Advertiser* 5 May 1880; *Weekly Times* 14 August 1880.
63. *Sydney Mail* 24 October 1863.
64. *Argus* 10 October 1878, 24 July 1879.
65. *Age* 23 July 1865, 23 July 1875; *Freemans Journal* 18 December 1875; *Hamilton Spectator* 25 December 1880.
66. MUA VTHC Minutes Including Quarterly Accounts 1871–1878.

9 Retailing/Warehouses, Hospitality, Commercial and Personal Services

Introduction

Labour historians have largely ignored pre-1881 organisation amongst service workers like shop-assistants, cooks and waiters. Tables 9.1 and 9.2 demonstrate it involved over 400 organisations and 300 instances of collective action mobilising tens of thousands. The rarity of strikes helps explain this neglect. Early-closing initiated by assistant drapers in 1840 grew into a broadly based mobilisation at least comparable in size to other groups prominent in conventional labour histories. Long-hours and their health effects dominated organisation. The movement relied heavily on community support and moral suasion although growing frustration with short-lived agreements saw a transition to shop-assistants' unions pushing for regulatory intervention first secured in 1885.

Organisation amongst cooks, waiters and domestics remained predominantly informal and the relatively large number of court cases (overwhelmingly lost) reflects this. After 1870 unionisation efforts grew. Hours, working conditions and OHS were the dominant issues (Table 9.2).

Informal Organisation at Workplace Level

Domestic Servants, Retail/Warehouse Workers and Others

In Australia, California and Britain female domestics were widely portrayed as presumptuous, and impertinent, especially by masters/mistresses easily affronted by any questioning of authority. A writer on life in Australia described servant girls as nuisances who demanded £35 a year and two holidays per week.[1] Dissent was extensive enough to acquire a label—servantgalism—a term used repeatedly in colonial, British and US newspapers.[2] In 1861 the *Star* bemoaned servantgalism was at:

> an 'atrocious' pitch in Ballarat. There is no doubt that all mistresses are not absolute perfection . . . but the scandalous airs assumed by too many domestic servants is a grievance . . . hard to be borne.[3]

Table 9.1 Worker Organisation in Retailing/Warehouses and General 1831–1880

Industry	1831–1840	1841–1850	1851–1860	1861–1870	1871–1880	Total 1851–1880
Entire Industry						
Organisations	13	20	60	126	247	402+
Raw involvement	21	421	2191	6632	15875	24698
Est. involvement*	25	1441	4091	14062	31060	49213
Strikes						
Won			1	1		2
Lost	5	2	5			5
Unknown			2		3	5
Total	5	2	8	1	3	12
Est. total involvement*	10	14	19		750	769
Number of establishments						
One	5	2	8		2	10
Multi					1	1
Regional/Town				1		1
Non-strike collective action						
Won	1	14	37	102	167	306
Drawn					3	3
Lost	4	4	3	20	45	68
Unknown	1	1	16	51	111	178
Total	6	19	56	173	326	555
Est. total involvement*	13	1302	2293	16864	28131	47288
Number of establishments						
One	5	2	2	8	25	35
Multi			7	7	27	41
Regional/Town	1	17	48	155	271	474
Colonial				2		2
Issues in collective action (strikes/NSCA)						
Wages	/1	/1	1/2	/2	2/	3/6
Hours	5/1	1/18	7/72	1/200	3/277	11/549
Working conditions	/3	1/1		/1	/1	/3
Health & safety	/1	/12	/43	/147	/312	/502
Management behaviour					/1	/1
Total strikes/NSCA	5/6	2/19	8/56	1/173	3/326	12/555
Breakdown of organisation and actions of largest subgroup						
Shop-assistants						
Organisation numbers	14	21	59	110	228	352+
Est. involvement*	28	1274	3309	7876	15313	26498

(*Continued*)

Table 9.1 (Continued)

Industry	1831–1840	1841–1850	1851–1860	1861–1870	1871–1880	Total 1851–1880
Strikes	5	3	5			5
NSCA	8	19	57	150	250	457
Absconding	3		1			1
Petitions		1	4	3	18	25
Deputations		1		5		5
Mass meetings	2	2	20	67	97	184
Marches				3	5	8
Letters/public notices		3	40	150	220	410
Bans	1	22	7	5	8	20
Court Actions						
Won	1	1	2		1	3
Lost	13	1	5	1	4	10

* Adjusted by multiplying number of zero-reporting organisations/years by industry and occupation median membership in that decade. ⁺For totals, organisation spanning multiple decades only counted once.

There was no recognition female domestics' 'uppity-ness' might reflect societal changes or the unattractiveness of jobs entailing unrelentingly long-hours and low pay. In addition to increasing immigration and establishing servants' homes/bureaus, proposed remedies included importing more subordinate servants from India—mirroring Gulf States importing household servants from poor countries today.[4] Dissent translated into small-scale collective action. In October 1853 probation passholders James Conwell, Mary Heley and Maria Swain received seven days' solitary confinement for a Sunday absence.[5] Marriage didn't negate legal bonds. In February 1854 Hugh Murray Esq (employer and part-time magistrate) prosecuted John Auld for harbouring an absconder after he married Murray's female domestic servant and she left his service before her contract had concluded—Auld fined £10 under the *Masters and Servants Act*.[6] In January 1870 Mary Dwyer and Ellen Corrigan left Mrs Freeman's Retreat Hotel at Brighton, refusing to serve a week's notice and taking court action for wages.[7] For female servants absconding was a rational response to a detested job, some did so collectively and many escaped apprehension. Not so lucky were Sarah Seckington and Mary Ann Flynn caught and prosecuted by their Perth mistress Lady Leake—one day's imprisonment and forfeited wages.[8]

Retail/warehouse workers also engaged in informal dissent. On 1 November 1852 Longford merchant John Pooler prosecuted four probationers for absence (three days' solitary confinement) with the men

Table 9.2 Worker Organisation in Hospitality, Commercial and Personal Services 1831–1880

Industry	1831–1840	1841–1850	1851–1860	1861–1870	1871–1880	Total 1851–1880
Hospitality, Commercial & Personal Services						
Organisations	126	44	63	18	22	102+
Raw involvement	257	1108	386	76	424	886
Est. involvement*	257	1108	388	136	2115	2639
Strikes						
Won		1	5			5
Drawn				1		1
Lost	28	16	19	1		20
Unknown		3			2	2
Total	28	20	24	2	2	28
Est. total involvement*	62	42	50	5	20	75
Number of establishments						
One	28	20	23	2	2	27
Multi		1				1
Non-strike collective action						
Won	4	2	16	8	4	28
Drawn	5	2	1	1		2
Lost	57	18	17	1	2	20
Unknown	33	1	5	3	8	16
Total	99	23	39	13	14	66
Est. total involvement*	212	48	360	63	825	1248
Number of establishments						
One	98	18	26	3	3	32
Multi	1	3			1	1
Regional/town		2	12	10	10	32
Colonial			1			1
Issues in collective action (strikes/NSCA)						
Wages	/3	1/7	/4	1/1	2/2	3/7
Hours	18/6	11/	21/14	/11	/11	21/36
Working conditions	12/95	10/17	4/24	1/2	/1	5/27
Health & safety	1/4		/8	/11	/11	/30
Management behaviour	8/8	4/5	1/1			1/1
Jobs/employment	1/	/3	/3			/3
Total strikes/NSCA	28/99	20/23	24/39	2/13	2/14	28/66

(Continued)

Table 9.2 (Continued)

Industry	1831–1840	1841–1850	1851–1860	1861–1870	1871–1880	Total 1851–1880
Breakdown of organisation and actions of largest subgroup						
Cooks, Waiters and Domestics						
Organisation numbers	131	52	49	5	12	66⁺
Est. involvement*	275	122	201	30	135	366
Strikes	28	24	22	1		23
NSCA	103	28	26	2	3	51
Absconding	78	11	20	1	1	22
Petitions					1	1
House-of-call					1	1
Court actions						
Won	2	5	7			7
Drawn		2	1	2		3
Lost	68	60	38	6	2	46

* Adjusted by multiplying number of zero-reporting organisations/years by median industry and occupation membership in that decade. ⁺For totals, organisation spanning multiple decades only counted once.

getting seven days' solitary for a second absence on 22 November.[9]
Much informal action probably went unreported. In April 1855 workers at Baker's Store in Adelaide secured a half-day to visit the races, only
known through a coronial inquest into a fire at the premises later that
day.[10] Other service workers taking collective action included Indian
snake charmers absconding, Ashton's circus performers striking over
wages (both in 1861) and Melbourne's Princess Theatre cast striking over
unpaid wages in 1879.[11]

Multi-Workplace and Formal Organisation

Cooks and Domestic Servants

Domestic servants' isolation made organisation difficult with only one
known attempted union in Melbourne.[12] Depots lodging emigrants prior
to hiring afforded a hub for informal alliances. In December 1856 the
Melbourne Punch complained 70 women recently arrived on the *Mer-
maid* had made 'most rigid' enquiries of ladies before consenting to
engage.[13] The women had agreed amongst themselves on acceptable
wages and employment conditions. Complaints of excessive demands by
depot emigrants were common and tacit combinations probably more

widespread than newspapers suggest, especially given opportunities to liaise during the voyage. Largely escaping historians' notice, employers combined to boost numbers, including petitioning South Australian parliament to import more domestics in 1872.[14] In a rare satirical repost, female domestics dispatched their own petition urging parliament to 'import eligible employers of domestic servants.'[15] Cooks and waiters, sometimes separately sometimes jointly, formed unions from the 1860s. In Melbourne waiters organised in 1867 and professional cooks and waiters in 1873, with a Waiters Mutual Protection Society (1874–1875) offering friendly benefits. Waiters associations also formed in Sydney (1873–1880?) and Adelaide (1879).[16]

Retail/Warehouse Workers and Hairdressers

Hours of Work

Early-closing/half-holidays dominated organising by retail, warehouse, hairdressers and a widening array of workers including photographic operatives by 1861.[17] Tens of thousands of colonial workers (and far more in the UK) struggled to shorten trading and working hours tied to this. Twelve-hour or longer days, including Saturday and public holidays, were typical. Grounds for reducing hours included recreation and mutual/moral improvement (attractive to religious and middle-class supporters) along with the harmful OHS effects of confined premises with gas-lighting/fumes and extreme summer heat.[18] Long-hours were labelled 'white-slavery' and advocates repeatedly referred to sickness and premature-mortality.[19]

Following UK precedents, campaigns were initiated by assistant drapers, later joined by assistant grocers, chemists, ironmongers, warehouse workers and others. From 1850 organisation shifted to broadly based Early Closing Associations supported by prominent citizens, religious leaders, consumers and the wider community. The ECA model came to dominate but subgroup organisation persevered in metropolises like Sydney. Especially after 1860, organisation spread to smaller towns encompassing virtually all retail-workers, clerks and tradesmen.[20] One group retaining separate organisation were hairdressers with bodies in Ballarat (1859, 1862, 1869), Bendigo (1873), Melbourne (1876, 1878–1883), Echuca (1880) and Sydney (1869 and 1877–1879). Like butchers and bakers, hairdressers worked Sundays and this was the focus of campaigns.[21] Even so, from the 1870s their campaigns ran parallel to other early-closing bodies and some like those in Wollongong joined ECAs.

The substantial geographic reach of the movement warrants acknowledgment. In NSW organisations were first reported in Sydney (1854, 1855, 1856, 1860, 1861, 1863, 1866, 1867, 1869, 1871, 1873, 1874, 1875, 1879, 1880), Bathurst (1856, 1873), Maitland (1854, 1856,

1860, 1866, 1872, 1873, 1877), Parramatta (1861, 1874), Braidwood (1861), Goulburn (1863, 1873, 1877), Newcastle (1863, 1866, 1873, 1877, 1880), Armidale (1864, 1871, 1873), Singleton (1867, 1873, 1874, 1877, 1879), Wollongong (1867, 1870, 1876), Lambton/Waratah (1868), Wagga Wagga (1870, 1872, 1876, 1878), Wallsend (1871, 1878), Orange (1872), Tenterfield (1872, 1874), Hay (1872, 1874, 1877, 1878, 1879), Mudgee (1872, 1878), Grafton (1873), Glen Innes (1873), Morpeth (1873), Yass (1873), Inverell (1873), Muswellbrook (1873), Raymond Terrace (1873, 1880), Murrurundi (1873), Gulgong (1874), Tumut (1874), Albury (1874), Tamworth (1874), Bombala (1874), Adelong (1875), Young (1875), Wombat (1876), Wentworth (1877), Balranald (1877), Brewarrina (1878), Windsor (1878), Deniliquin (1878), Newtown (1879), Camden (1879), Campbelltown (1879), Cooma (1879), Casino (1879), Woodburn (1879), Kiama (1880) and Lithgow (1880). In Queensland bodies formed in Maryborough (1860, 1869, 1870, 1871, 1874, 1879), Brisbane (1862, 1867, 1868, 1872, 1876, 1878, 1879), Rockhampton (1865, 1867, 1870, 1872, 1877), Toowoomba (1867, 1869, 1879), Dalby (1867), Gympie (1868), Ipswich (1870, 1878, 1879), Warwick (1870), Gayndah (1874), Roma (1876), Bowen (1876), Bundaberg (1877), Cooktown (1878) and Townsville (1878). In South Australia bodies formed in Adelaide (1851, 1854, 1856, 1859, 1860, 1864, 1865, 1866, 1867, 1870, 1873, 1876, 1878), Burra (1851, 1872, 1877), Gawler (1859, 1867, 1873, 1874, 1878), Port Adelaide (1859, 1862, 1870, 1873, 1877, 1878), Kooringa (1862, 1872), Wallaroo/Kadina (1862, 1863, 1866, 1867, 1869), Mount Gambier (1863, 1865, 1866, 1867), Kapunda (1865, 1873), North Adelaide (1867, 1873, 1875), Clare (1869), Moonta (1869, 1873, 1875), Strathalbyn (1872), Willunga (1873), Angaston (1874), Narracoorte (1874, 1876, 1877, 1880), Millicent (1874, 1879), Mallala (1875), Truro (1877), Port Caroline (1878), Gladstone (1878), Balaklava (1878), Port Augusta (1878, 1880), Port Pirie (1880) and Yorketown (1880). In Tasmania bodies formed in Launceston (1851, 1853, 1854, 1863, 1871, 1874, 1876, 1878, 1880) and Hobart (1853, 1855, 1856, 1857, 1863, 1869, 1874, 1877, 1880). In Victoria bodies formed in Melbourne (1851, 1853, 1854, 1855, 1857, 1859, 1861, 1864, 1865, 1866, 1872, 1873, 1877, 1878, 1879, 1880), Castlemaine (1857, 1877), Ballarat (1856, 1859, 1861, 1862, 1863, 1864, 1869, 1872, 1873, 1874, 1879), Collingwood/Fitzroy (1857, 1865, 1867, 1869, 1873, 1874, 1878), Geelong (1859, 1867, 1868, 1874), Kyneton (1863, 1873), Avoca (1864, 1865, 1877), Amherst (1864), Golden Square (1864), Sale (1864, 1869), Fitzroy (1865, 1867, 1869, 1874), Prahran and St Kilda (1865, 1878), Creswick (1865), Portland (1866, 1878, 1879), Richmond (1867, 1878), Echuca (1869, 1872, 1877, 1878), Bendigo/Sandhurst (1869), Rosedale (1869), Hamilton (1869, 1873, 1876, 1877), Williamstown (1871, 1877), Kangaroo Flat (1872), Emerald Hill/Sandridge (1873, 1877), Long Gully (1873),

Beechworth (1874), Carlton and Hotham/North Melbourne (1874, 1880), Maryborough (1874), Horsham (1875), Alexandra (1875), Kilmore (1876, 1878), Eaglehawk (1876), Warrnambool (1876), St Arnaud (1876), Clunes (1876), Belfast/Port Fairy (1877), Daylesford (1878), Brighton (1878), Malmsbury (1878), Brunswick (1878), Ararat (1878), Rutherglen (1879) and Mornington (1880). In Western Australia, bodies formed in Fremantle (1867, 1875, 1877), Perth (1876), Guildford (1877), York (1877) and Northam (1880). Evidence isn't exhaustive; an Orange movement operated for years only known from a dispute when a retailer broke ranks in 1873.[22]

There were attempts at colony-wide bodies like the Victorian ECA (1855) and the NSW ECA (1856), modelling themselves on the London and Liverpool ECAs. Nonetheless, ECAs in each town generally remained independent though often running parallel campaigns.[23] Initiatives in one town encouraged efforts elsewhere, radiating to neighbouring towns, assisted by sympathetic newspaper reporting, the *Queanbeyan Age* urging shop-assistants to follow Yass, Wagga and Goulburn.[24] ECAs also corresponded although only fragmentary evidence survives. The Ballarat and Bendigo ECAs corresponded while in 1877 the Melbourne ECA (1866–1882) sent circulars to Newcastle and a copy of its rules to Hay.[25]

Trying to widen the community support including customer boycotts of dissidents, the 1856 NSW ECA appealed for 'Ladies' to attend meetings.[26] Public lectures by eminent speakers (sometimes published) and scientific talks at Mechanics Institutes appealed to self-improvement notions beloved in the Victorian era while simultaneously reassuring recreation wouldn't be misused.[27] Moral and social advancement themes were emphasised in concerts, plays and quadrilles. Emphasising the family dimension, 100 children sat quietly at a Sandhurst ECA meeting in April 1876—the Masonic Hall so packed many adults stood outside.[28] Some ECA extended education beyond their ranks, the Sydney ECA instituting penny-readings for working-class families, drawing admiration from the Goulburn Wesleyan Mutual Improvement Society.[29] Consumer bans/pledges were used even in smaller towns like Kooringa while the Brisbane ECA secured 8,000 customer signatures in March 1880.[30]

Campaigns relied on moral suasion whose limitations included disorganised employers in a competitive industry so few agreements avoided breakaways. Occasionally shop-assistant discipline/solidarity was an issue, with too few committing to the Victorian ECA in 1857 despite officials' best efforts.[31] This helps explain preferences for more narrowly and locally based organisation, switching to easier-to-secure half-holiday goals, and experimenting with different modes of compulsion. In September 1857 Melbourne and Collingwood Draper's Assistants League members pledged not to remain or hire to firms refusing to close early—unilateral regulation—but such actions were rare.[32] Non-compliant firms frustrated retailers, an Adelaide master draper lamenting 'it is impossible to persuade one at least of my fellow-tradesmen to shut so long as there is a bare possibility of another customer venturing in.'[33] Repeated attempts to lock-in retailer solidarity by publishing lists of 'signed-on' and meetings of masters like one chaired by Sir Alfred Stephen (president of the Drapers ECA) in 1874 had only temporary effects.

By 1865 successive short-lived, early-closing agreements had been repeated for decades in Sydney, Hobart and Melbourne. Increasingly, ECAs targeted consumers, especially women, publishing public appeals, issuing circulars and members/pickets distributing handbills outside non-complying firms.[34] Picketing sometimes erupted into confrontations, in February 1867 groom George Birtles was fined for throwing eggs, causing 'injury and annoyance' to ECA 'agents' outside a Sydney draper's shop.[35] Three days later 16-year-old assistant-draper John Daley told the Sydney Central Court that while distributing handbills, George St draper Walter Hancock told him he was doing 'no good' and to go home. At 8 pm when a crowd of 100 had gathered, Hancock punched Daley, causing him to fall to the pavement. Despite supporting evidence from another assistant-draper (Henry Stubbs), Hancock was acquitted. Another ECA member (McNally) charged Hancock's employee (Gorman) with assaulting him, Gorman being fined a derisory shilling without court costs.[36] It is worth contemplating the very different outcome likely had ECA members been the assailants.

By the 1870s, picketing non-compliant retailers was common; 200 Bendigo retail-workers marching on three hold-out premises, who agreed apart from Mrs Stone (her husband being absent), and marked by verbal abuse of both retailers and customers.[37] More violent affrays and sabotage occurred—typically smashing shop windows of non-compliant retailers, as occurred during an 1878 torchlight procession in Richmond. Confrontations occurred even in small towns like Mornington where a dissident's store was daubed with paint.[38] Far from being mindless, sabotage and picketing had a clear socio-economic purpose as well as venting frustration—and occurred in other countries. Nonetheless, sabotage remained relatively rare.[39] Most incidents were confined to noisy picketing like three 'lads' fined for bashing kerosene tins in Parramatta in October 1878, with another fined for remonstrating with half-holiday opponents five days later.[40] Nonetheless, growing frustration with moral suasion led to heated exchanges between pickets, late shoppers and retailers. In 1877 a large group of picketers surrounded a hold-out draper's (Kingston) Newcastle premises, jeering late shoppers and scattering soft-goods on the footpath, notwithstanding police efforts to drive them off.[41] Newspapers expected prosecutions but what they got was a warning from former-draper's apprentice K Richardson:

> Every labouring association in this district is interested in this matter, and they should come forward and help their brethren in their

extremity . . . there are more Mr K's . . . in this district, only waiting their opportunity to oppress the workman and again reduce the
working classes to the level of serfdom.[42]

Condemnation of late shoppers became ever more strident, ladies asked
to choose between freedom and slavery while ECAs also requested help
from working men enjoying eight-hours.[43] Echuca, Wagga and others
enlisted 'ladies' to the cause.[44] By the late 1870s torchlight processions
both celebrated agreements and identified miscreants who risked getting
their windows broken.[45] Agreements lasting years became more common
but most collapsed within months, the *Australian Town and Country
Journal* lamenting customer convenience always trumped 'overworked
assistants.'[46]

While barely mentioned, the growing female workforce benefited,
the Bendigo ECA (1869) claiming to represent 300 men and women.[47]
Sir Alfred Stephen told an 1874 Sydney meeting that 600 persons, over
330 of them women (200 under 20 years old), were 'kept at work in
ill-ventilated rooms for twelve, thirteen, and fourteen hours per day.'[48]
Females joined the agitation but were largely ignored in newspaper
reports. In August 1869 the Brisbane Half-Holiday Association deputed
12 ladies to wait on Mrs Terry to use her influence on dissident retailer
Charles Street.[49] Subsequent reports and letters from female assistants
make it clear female shop-assistants were involved and their contribution lauded.[50] This carried over to the successor Brisbane ECA (1876)
which emphasised the especially harmful effects of long-hours on female
assistants. Large numbers attended meetings and they led a deputation
to a recalcitrant firm.[51] In 1880 'Empo' called on shoppers to do all in
their power to curtail 'the working hours of shopwomen' of Hobart.[52]
The movement had good reason to enrol women lest they be used to
break agreements. In June 1876 a Melbourne ECA member (McCuffery)
reported several retailers were using 'girls' to stay open but such complaints were rare. The same meeting agreed to take no action with
regard to allowing women to sit when not serving customers.[53] In 1877
the Newcastle ECA supported Cameron's *Employment of Females Bill*
restricting hours of female labour in factories and workshops.[54] Unlike
manual workers retail-workers didn't face competition from indentured
immigrants, the schisms in their ranks largely internal. When Melbourne
grocers introduced a half-holiday in 1878 John Collings pointed to Chinese tea-hawkers continuing to operate but argued warehouses sending
out retail orders posed a bigger threat.[55]

Moral suasion's repeated failure prompted other tactics. At a Sydney
ECA meeting in November 1873 one speaker doubted 'they could possibly gain their object by any other means' than striking.[56] The movement drew closer to manual workers. The NSW Eight Hour System and
General Short Hours League cooperated with the Sydney Half-Holiday

and ECA in 1869.[57] In 1877 the Echuca ECA targeted workers pivotal to the town's economy, including eight-hour tradesmen, boatmen and dock labourers. The town's Eight Hours Association pledged support, dispatching a deputation securing a hold-out retailer's acquiescence. Correspondent 'old Bagman' argued Echuca's reputation as an eight-hour hub demanded workingmen should ensure 6 pm closing and the Wednesday half-holiday became as entrenched as it was in Sandhurst, Castlemaine, Belfast, Warrnambool and other Victorian towns. Despite this the ECA collapsed—the Eight Hours Association's helped revive it in 1878.[58] Unions were sent lists of employers paying workers on Saturday and asked to boycott non-compliant retailers.[59] In 1874 Sydney trade societies agreed to support the Drapers ECA although the Stonemason suggested they should affiliate to the Trades and Labour Council.[60] The Sydney TLC co-sponsored (with Sydney Council) a public meeting promoting early-closing. In August 1874 the ECA resolved to affiliate but collapsed soon after.[61] In 1880 the Sydney ECA affiliated to the TLC, changing its name to the United Salesmans Association.[62] While fears of a community backlash may have initially discouraged THC/TLC affiliation, the transition to shop-assistant unions and affiliation occurred in all colonies during the 1880s.

Employee membership of an ECA was increasingly viewed as union membership. In Brisbane pro-early closing employers required employees to join the ECA while holdouts victimised ECA activists, notably ECA Secretary George Russell dismissed by Forsyth and Co. in March 1880.[63] Victimising ECA activists was nothing new: a Melbourne activist (Hayward) was told to resign as ECA vice-president or resign his job in 1866.[64] Other unions increasingly saw the movement as reinforcing their own hour struggles, an early-closing agreement signed in Newcastle in 1880 inspiring calls for a renewed hours campaigning by Hunter Valley Coalminers.[65] In the coalmining Illawarra a half-holiday supporter urged renegade retailers be treated like 'blacklegs'—coalminers' term for strike-breakers.[66]

From the mid-1850s there was a growing movement for a weekly half-holiday, most often on Saturday or Wednesday followed by Friday.[67] In 1856 the Victorian ECA joined clerks and civil servants' Saturday half-holiday campaign, distributing 20,000 handbills and memorialising 169 Melbourne shops. Membership was only 40, demonstrating the importance of seeing mobilisation in terms of all workers involved.[68] In late 1866 a campaign including public meetings in Sydney (over 3,000 attended), Balmain, Newtown and Woollahra, and a pledge signed by 72 leading ladies (including Justice Stephen's wife) secured a Saturday half-holiday agreement covering 4,158 shop-assistants.[69] The HHA undertook considerable follow-up action over the next two years, including monitoring compliance/published advertisements, circulars, soirees/concerts, public lectures, penny-readings, donations for flood-relief and

widows and orphans, and public meetings in working-class suburbs—
one addressed by Henry Parkes.[70] Regular excursions included harbour
voyages requiring multiple vessels accommodating hundreds. Public
notices targeted potential breach-points like country-dwellers attending
Prince Alfred's visit in 1868. The association sought union support and
expressed sympathy for butchers working Sunday. The HHA held its
ground with the odd gain, and a short-lived attempt to extend the holiday to factories/workshops, until 1873.[71]

The Sydney victory was rapidly followed by Newcastle and resonated
in Victoria, Queensland and South Australia. The Melbourne ECA (established October 1866) took several years to secure a Saturday half-holiday
before (like Sydney), extending coverage to more specialist retail/service
outlets including booksellers/printers, watchmakers/jewellers, china and
fancy goods warehouses and musicians/musical-instrument dealers.[72] Progress was slow and efforts to entrench gains ongoing. A May 1871 town
hall meeting (attended by 4,000) called for half-holidays for 'all classes'
and Saturday pay to be abolished.[73] At an April 1873 meeting attended
by 2,000 (including considerable numbers of women) in St Kilda MLA
Robert Murray Smith stated 'guerrilla bands' of dissidents still held-out
in the suburbs—they were still being picked off and breaches staunched
years later.[74]

To varying degrees all HHAs followed Sydney campaign methods, the
1871 Bendigo petition garnered over 4,000 signatures. There were inno-
vations, with calico-placarding and torchlight processions popularised in
the late 1870s.[75] The Grafton HHA used a 'Call Boy' cannon fired at 1
pm closing—stolen in August 1874, the association offered a £50 reward
and considered buying a heavier gun difficult to remove.[76] In Maitland,
church bells were rung. 'Freedom' labelled this coercion, warning half-
holidays induced larrikinism and lamenting farmers unable to shop.
Assistant reposts noted the Melbourne half-holiday hadn't encouraged
larrikinism while 'Greater Freedom' argued long-hours caused consumption (tuberculosis) amongst young women.[77] While overlapping with
early-closing, half-holiday campaigns involved a wider array of workers. Ironmongers' assistants, warehousemen, clerks and others joined the
fray, some hanging on when larger agreements collapsed. In 1866 Sydney
chemists were advised to form an organisation like assistant drapers and
collaborate with the HHA.[78] In 1880 a Saturday half-holiday amongst
Hobart ironmongers led to claims by assistants working for wine and
general merchants, booksellers, drapers and a building firm before transitioning into more generalised agitation.[79]

Half-holidays were easier to secure/retain than shortening daily hours—
a reason for the push, with some Half-Holiday Associations organising
cricket teams to celebrate the break.[80] However, dissidents remained a problem, with business downturns encouraging breaches.[81] Non-compliant
firms increasingly attracted abuse and noisy picketing. In April 1874,

100 assistants surrounded James Gregg's Parramatta drapery, yelling and groaning until Gregg ordered the shop closed. Six months later Gregg resumed his defiance.[82] In towns like Launceston and Maitland critics claimed half-holidays disadvantaged country residents. Others argued assistants were 'not chained to the counter' drawing sharp retorts, a country shop-assistant stating they worked 85 hours in winter and 91 in summer.[83] After an 1876 Launceston push failed, the ECA shifted its claim from Wednesday to Saturday which sporting groups in Launceston and neighbouring towns favoured but not employers.[84] Commenting on cycles of failure, the *Tasmanian Punch* observed:

> It comes on the young men with unfailing regularity every spring, like . . . attacks of love. Then they meet together, call themselves a 'movement' pass resolutions, appoint an indefatigable secretary, and a talented President. Then they die; that is, the movement dies, till the next spring . . . they can't bring themselves to ask enough.[85]

Longstanding half-holiday agreements were secured in Sydney, Melbourne, Bendigo and other towns. By 1875 Kadina had maintained a Wednesday half-holiday since 1867 and Gympie's Thursday half-holiday (begun 1868) was still operating in 1886.[86] The Newcastle Half-Holiday and ECA maintained a Friday half-holiday for nine years, but like others wanted to use this as a stepping-stone for early-closing, lauded in summer as offering respite from oppressive heat.[87]

Selection of days varied, Saturday preferred in colonial capitals because it coincided with bank and public office closure while Wednesday was favoured in country towns.[88] In 1871 Bendigo considered shifting from Thursday to Wednesday to align with neighbouring towns.[89] In Maryborough (Queensland) banks resolved to close at 1 pm on Friday to align with the half-holiday while others like Rockhampton negotiated agreements extending to banks and other businesses.[90] Differences of opinion over the day sometimes splintered the movement, as in Brisbane in 1869.[91] Ballarat operated two half-holidays (Friday and Saturday) in the 1860s, one for clerks and one for retail-workers, reconciling them inhibited by farmer interests.[92] Saturday was the day farmers often travelled to towns and also the day some workers were paid, while religious leaders were concerned late Saturday trading's influenced Sunday church attendances.[93] Half-holiday associations in Brisbane, Hobart and elsewhere tried to remedy pay-day issues, urging bodies like City Councils to pay employees earlier in the week.[94] Melbourne city retailers closed on Saturday but suburbs like Prahran, Collingwood, Richmond and Brunswick followed country practices opting for Thursday.[95] Locking in neighbouring towns could prove pivotal, Gladstone (South Australia) retailers telling assistants they would endorse a Wednesday half-holiday if Georgetown, Laura and Jamestown retailers signed up.[96]

Victories in one location inspired campaigns elsewhere, often radiating out from major centres, but not always.[97] In 1868 Gympie shop-assistants gained a Thursday half-holiday which shifted south to Brisbane then Maryborough while Grafton's 1873 success spread to other northern NSW towns.[98] Campaigning in 1873 the Echuca ECA pointed to agreements in Sandhurst, Ballarat, Castlemaine, Kyneton and other inland towns.[99] HHAs corresponded with each other, swapping information, tactics, copies of rules and agreements.[100] In 1872 the newly formed Rockhampton Drapers ECA asked Brisbane for rules and information.[101] Five years later a succesor body, the Rockhampton HHA, obtained a report from its Ballarat counterpart on how to secure an agreement and win employer support. This included Ballarat employer's subsequent concession that business hadn't been adversely affected by the agreement.[102] The movement was aided by widespread favourable newspaper reporting of British and colonial developments. As with early-closing, while individual employers sometimes helped, assistants were the driving force. Assistants had uniform interests in shortening hours and no competing commercial incentives.[103] In small towns with fewer retailers and stronger community networks an informal request or deputation was often sufficient. A Wednesday half-holiday was secured in Naracoorte in 1880 before assistants had to memorialise retailers, the inauguration celebrated by a large demonstration, sporting events (for children and adults) and concerts, drawing attendees from the surrounding district. Assistants were quick to report breaches (retailer justifications included a blanket for a sick child), a correspondent noting even the Governor couldn't purchase a toothpick on Wednesday afternoon.[104]

Linking the holiday to excursions/recreational events began in the 1850s and became regular and highly organised. In port-towns steamers like the *Commissary-General* in Newcastle, *Transit* in Sydney, *Emu* in Brisbane and *MA Eaton* in Maryborough offered cruises, reinforcing its recreational importance and entrenching the practice.[105] Periodically, HHAs organised excursions with subsidised food/entertainment that still raised funds.[106] Social pressure was leveraged through prominent citizens like mayors, religious leaders, judges and governors. Advertisements urged customers to purchase goods prior to the closing time and patronise compliant firms. Newspaper correspondents publicly shamed non-compliant retailers.[107] In larger towns links were forged with organised labour. Melbourne and Brisbane sought union support for earlier worker payments while the Launceston ECA (1872) met in the town's Working Men's Club.[108] There were synergies between short-hour movements. Shorter hours amongst mechanics and labourers increased time for shopping and made early-closing/half-holidays more viable.[109]

Many retail-worker organisations pursued early-closing and half-holidays, sometimes simultaneously. Unable to secure/maintain either bodies like the Adelaide Ironmongers Assistants Association (1862–1869),

Adelaide Assistant Drapers Association (1859–1895) and Mount Gambier Storekeepers Assistants Association funnelled their energy into maximising public holiday closing notably Easter Monday, Christmas/new year and royal anniversaries. Some employers even broke ranks on 'public holiday' closing, agreements being renegotiated annually.[110] The Wagga Wagga ECA made dual public holiday and early-closing/half-holiday claims. More typically, however, bodies like Newcastle and Grafton HHAs gave either specific or general dispensation for weekly half-holidays when they occurred in a week with a public holiday.[111]

Overall, early-closing and half-holiday movements represented a substantial mobilisation, involving over 300 bodies with a longevity matching manual unions (and paid secretaries in larger towns like Ballarat and Bendigo), tens of thousands of workers and reaching well over 100 towns. Both aimed to shorten hours and multiple organisations ran parallel campaigns with remarkably little friction.[112] They were part of a general push for shorter hours that built and strengthened wider worker alliances. In the small colony of Western Australia early-closing movement constituted almost the only instance of formal organisation prior to 1881. Fremantle shop-assistants secured an agreement in 1868, followed by Perth and Guildford in the 1870s—the latter partly inspired by coachmakers and other mechanics securing a half-holiday in 1876.[113] By 1873 Sydney, Grafton and other HHAs wanted public holidays and half-holidays mandated in legislation, following the UK *Shop Hours Regulation Bill* although this was restricted to 'children, young persons and women' and specified fewer holidays than already prevailing in the colonies.[114]

Mercantile and Other Clerks

Half-Holiday Movement

Mercantile and law clerks helped initiate the colonial half-holiday movement. In December 1853, 16 Adelaide merchants agreed to a Saturday half-holiday and in June 1854 a memorial by 63 Supreme Court clerks also succeeded. Lawyer Joseph Graves involved in the Manchester agreement argued it hadn't inconvenienced employers and clerks used the time for study, leisure and athletic activities.[115] Employee-advocate 'Quill' rejected claims of sectionalism, advocating Saturday half-holidays for workers more generally.[116] His call to follow NSW government officers, legal and bank clerks was heeded, campaigns spreading to public servants and retail-workers.[117] South Australian Banking Company clerks were told approval required support from at least half its customers, a customer-petition reaching this target in August.[118] Few apart from 'a country farmer' complained of being inconvenienced.[119]

Like many retailers, Graves saw personal and social benefits in early-closing. The Saturday half-holiday represented a 'virtuous circle' where spreading gains strengthened the regime, benefiting all. Indeed, inter-dependencies made collaboration essential where businesses dealt with government. In October 1854 mercantile clerks memorialised the South Australian Collector of Customs for the Customs House to close mid-day on Saturday.[120] Seeing logic in closing all government offices, the *Customs Act* was amended and Saturday half-day closing (excluding post-offices) was gazetted for the Province in December.[121] The Saturday half-holiday became general in Adelaide. Ironically, port mercantile and wharf clerks who initiated the campaign lost out due to shipping industry pressure. They seemed to have won in 1865 but only briefly and were still struggling a year later.[122] The Adelaide Warehousemens and Clerks Association (1867–1878) pursued Saturday half-holidays, but had more success securing public holiday closures.

Saturday half-holiday campaigning by clerks followed a similar pattern in other colonies. Sydney agitation began in March 1854. As elsewhere some advocates had participated in earlier UK struggles. 'Live and Let Live' had signed the Dundee half-holiday petition and couldn't understand delays given benefits extended beyond clerks' health and social wellbeing to the whole community.[123] Renewed agitation secured agreement with 60 merchants in August 1854, the committee donating residual funds to Crimean war widows and orphans.[124] Attorneys' clerks weren't included despite a Law Society resolution several years earlier for firms to close Saturday at 1 pm. Auctioneers' clerks too complained of being left out.[125] Melbourne lawyers and merchant's clerks secured a half-holiday in 1854 but the agreement didn't hold.[126] Emphasising the flow-on effects of regulation, it wasn't until 1856 when government leg-islated Saturday noon closure of custom houses that agitation by bank and merchant clerks succeeded (one bank held-out) in Melbourne and Geelong.[127] Ballarat lawyers' clerks (1858) followed along with bank clerks in Castlemaine (1857), Ballarat (1857) and Bendigo (by 1859).[128] Generally lasting longer than retailer agreements, renewal was required on occasion. Ballarat law clerks' Saturday half-holiday was undermined and in 1864 they abandoned it in favour of Friday—a move followed by their Bendigo counterparts.[129] Fragmentary evidence captures broad parameters of campaigning but not every action, the extent of networking or total numbers involved.

Mutual Insurance

Like several pre-1850 bodies, clerks pursued mutual insurance but with little success, a Melbourne provident society failing in 1859 as did further attempts in 1865 and 1868.[130]

Wages

Wages/salaries were not a major mobilisation issue for clerks though sporadic protests occurred. In November 1873, amidst letters complaining about long-hours, National Bank clerks in Melbourne sought increased wages, turning to a petition after proposals to shareholders were rejected.[131]

Conclusion

The early-closing and half-holiday movements amongst clerks, retail and other workers were marked by considerable organisational churning though some agreements proved durable. Both involved thousands of workers but the half-holiday struggle was larger, encompassing a wider array of occupations in numerous towns, 500 attending a March 1876 Bathurst meeting on continuing the agreement.[132] Both involved considerable networking aided by favourable newspaper reporting and activists migrating to the colonies.[133] The early-closing/half-holiday movements relied on moral suasion/ community pressure—public demonstration methods—and later picketing/bans and closer alignment with manual unions. While failing to fully entrench shorter hours, the movement made considerable steps towards creating the weekend (with its profound social implications), mobilising thousands of workers and initiating laws mandating trading/business hours. Other unions used community campaigning in the 19th century warranting more recognition in analyses of worker mobilisation then and now.

Fragmentary records enable few observations about associations' internal workings other than they had office-holders and governance much like other unions. Many retailers were small but bodies like the Sydney Grocers' Assistants Half-Holiday Association (1866) had delegates for major stores represented on their committee of management.[134] Unlike manual unions, prominent citizens and sympathetic employers often held presidential or vice-presidential positions in ECAs/HHAs (employers could be honorary members not unknown amongst craft unions), reflecting their dependence on community support. This practice declined as shop-assistants' unions emerged but earlier bodies were unionate not employers' pawns. Resistance to employer pressure was common, as in 1869 when the Maryborough HHA opposed attempts to suspend the half-holiday because there was a public holiday that week.[135] Agreements were published—rare for other unions. For early-closing in particular by the late 1870s the need for legislation was clear. In September 1878 Melbourne suburban newspaper columnist Figaro stated he saw no relief for shop-assistants 'excepting by an Act of Parliament, and I fancy they are not a sufficient power in the state to command that.'[136] Within seven years they had secured the power, Victoria becoming the first jurisdiction to enact compulsory shop-shutting legislation—an important global precedent.[137]

Of the groups examined in this chapter only shop-assistants could draw on numeric strength to any degree, but all drew on community support/societal campaigning. The early-closing/half-holiday movements weren't just largely overlooked numerically substantial mobilisations, but ones with wider social significance drawing in manual workers and reinforcing worker rights to recreation and health. Stripped of its gendered content, the proverb 'all work and no play makes Jack a dull lad' oft repeated in newspaper editorials is a prescient reminder of the flawed logic lauding dronish long-hours/hard work as key to success, pervasive in some societies but increasingly infecting others.

Notes

1. *Mercury* 5 April 1859.
2. *Age* 13 November 1858; *Empire* 3 November 1859; *Sydney Morning Herald* 27 January 1860; *Argus* 8 February 1861.
3. *Star* 27 April 1861.
4. *Wagga Wagga Advertiser* 29 May 1875.
5. LC362-1-9 Longford 10 October 1853.
6. Victorian Court of Petty Sessions Benchbook 15 February 1854.
7. *Melbourne Herald* 21 January 1870.
8. *Inquirer* 14 May 1879.
9. LC362-1-8 Longford 1, 22 November 1852.
10. *South Australian Register* 25 April 1855.
11. *Geelong Advertiser* 7 March 1861; *Rockhampton Bulletin* 31 August 1861; *Darling Downs Gazette* 17 July 1879.
12. *Hamilton Spectator* 1 July 1871.
13. *Melbourne Punch* 18 December 1856.
14. *South Australian Register* 1 February 1872.
15. *Ballarat Courier* 19 February 1872.
16. *Argus* 27 August 1867; *Age* 27 March 1873, 8 December 1874; *Sydney Morning Herald* 9 October 1873, 31 July 1880; *South Australian Advertiser* 24 July 1879.
17. *Age* 4 December 1861.
18. *Freeman's Journal* 16 November 1867; *Riverine Herald* 14 June 1877.
19. *Kiama Independent* 28 November 1876.
20. *Riverine Herald* 13 June 1878.
21. *Sydney Mail* 30 January 1869.
22. *Australian Town and Country Journal* 8 November 1873.
23. *Empire* 24 May, 6 June 1856.
24. *Queanbeyan Age* 23 October 1873.
25. *Bendigo Advertiser* 22 July 1873; *Newcastle Morning Herald* 14 February 1877; *Riverine Grazier* 2 May 1877.
26. *Sydney Morning Herald* 11 June 1856.
27. *South Australian Register* 31 December 1864; *Illustrated Adelaide Post* 21 May 1869; ML DSM824/E (1869–1870) *Lectures Delivered Before the Early Closing Association*, Samuel Mullen, Melbourne; ML DSM/042/P115 Bromby, Reverend J.E. (1870) *Beyond the Grave: A Lecture*, Delivered at the Melbourne Town Hall 15 November 1870, Samuel Mullen, Melbourne.

28. *Bendigo Advertiser* 6 April 1876.
29. *Goulburn Herald* 24 April 1867.
30. *South Australian Register* 18 October 1872; *Sydney Daily Telegraph* 6 March 1880.
31. *Argus* 8 April 1857.
32. *Argus* 12 September 1857.
33. *Evening Journal* 20 April 1869.
34. *Sydney Morning Herald* 26 May 1871.
35. *Sydney Morning Herald* 11 February 1867.
36. *Sydney Morning Herald* 14 February 1867.
37. *Age* 14 March 1873; *Bendigo Advertiser* 20 March 1873.
38. *Alexandra and Yea Standard* 19 April 1878; *Kapunda Herald* 14 January 1873; *South Bourke and Mornington Journal* 26 May 1880.
39. *Riverine Grazier* 26 November 1873.
40. *Cumberland Mercury* 26 October, 1 November 1878.
41. *Wagga Wagga Advertiser* 14 March 1877.
42. *Newcastle Morning Herald* 13 March 1877.
43. *Sydney Morning Herald* 20 July 1874; *Riverine Herald* 12 June 1877.
44. *Sydney Mail* 30 December 1876.
45. *Riverine Herald* 29 June 1878.
46. *Australian Town and Country Journal* 17 March 1877.
47. *Bendigo Advertiser* 15 June 1869.
48. *Sydney Mail* 2 May 1874; *Empire* 23 July 1874; *Riverine Herald* 14 June 1877.
49. *Brisbane Courier* 11 August 1869.
50. *Queenslander* 4 September 1869.
51. *Brisbane Courier* 24 March, 11 July, 16 September 1876.
52. *Mercury* 13 November 1880.
53. *Argus* 30 June 1876.
54. *Sydney Morning Herald* 26 January 1877; *New South Wales Government Gazette* 6 April 1877, No. 112, page 1376 Petitions.
55. *Argus* 13 August 1878.
56. *Sydney Morning Herald* 29 November 1873.
57. ML MSS2074 Item 45 NSW Eight Hour System and General Short Hours League Minutes 28 October 1869.
58. *Riverine Herald* 12, 19, 21, 28 June, 19, 26 July, 17 December 1878.
59. T8-2A-3 VOBS Melbourne Minutes 25 May 1874.
60. T46-1-3 NSW Stonemasons Sydney Minutes 29 July 1874; ML MSS Sydney Boilermakers Minutes 6 October 1874.
61. *Sydney Morning Herald* 14 April 1874; *Maitland Mercury* 29 August 1874.
62. *Evening News* 25 June 1880; *Sydney Daily Telegraph* 9 July 1880.
63. *Brisbane Courier* 1 March 1880.
64. *Age* 20 December 1866.
65. *Newcastle Morning Herald* 22 July 1880.
66. *Illawarra Mercury* 28 November 1876.
67. *Sydney Mail* 30 October 1875.
68. *Argus* 4 December 1856.
69. ML AS85 913347 Signed resolution adopted 26 November 1866 to abstain from Saturday afternoon shopping.
70. *Sydney Morning Herald* 24 December 1866, 27 July, 8 August 1867, 31 January, 22 February 1868; *Armidale Express* 11 May 1867; *Maitland Mercury* 13 June 1867.
71. *Sydney Morning Herald* 15 February 1868, 28 April, 4 October, 17 December 1869, 25 February 1871, 20 March 1873.

72. *Sydney Morning Herald* 15 February 1868.
73. *Age* 20 November 1869, 13 May, 2 June 1871.
74. *Age* 6, 24 March 1876; *Argus* 8 April 1873, 14 July 1877.
75. *South Australian Advertiser* 18 January 1867; *Bendigo Advertiser* 17 August 1871; *Darling Downs Gazette and General Advertiser* 21 March 1867; *Newcastle Chronicle* 9 March 1875.
76. *Clarence and Richmond Examiner* Tuesday 15 April, 22 July 1873, 23 June, 8 September 1874; *New South Wales Police Gazette* 9 September 1874, No. 36, 249.
77. *Maitland Mercury* 15, 20, 27 November 1873.
78. *Sydney Morning Herald* 25 December 1866.
79. *Launceston Examiner* 18 September, 5 October 1880; *Mercury* 20 September, 5 October 1880.
80. *Maitland Mercury* 19 February 1867; *Newcastle Chronicle* 22 May 1867.
81. *Newcastle Chronicle* 22, 25 April 1868; *Maitland Mercury* 23 April 1868.
82. *Australian Town and Country Journal* 25 April, 7 November 1874.
83. *Launceston Examiner* 15 August 1854, 22, 26, 31 August 1876.
84. *Launceston Examiner* 6 November 1877.
85. *Tasmanian Punch* 17 November 1877.
86. *Wallaroo Times* 15 September 1875; *Queensland Times* 2 January 1869, 4 May 1886; *Gympie Times* 5 February 1879.
87. *Newcastle Chronicle* 28 January 1875.
88. *Brisbane Courier* 24 April 1869.
89. *Bendigo Advertiser* 3 June 1871.
90. *Maryborough Chronicle* 8 October 1874; *Daily Northern Argus* 13 December 1877.
91. *Brisbane Courier* 7 January 1869.
92. *Ballarat Star* 6 November 1865.
93. *Gympie Times* 5 February 1879.
94. *Brisbane Courier* 27 April 1869; *Tasmanian Tribune* 24 November 1874.
95. *South Australian Register* 15 May 1878.
96. *Northern Argus* 8 October 1878.
97. *Weekly Examiner* 19 August 1876.
98. *Clarence and Richmond Examiner* 10 February 1874.
99. *Riverine Herald* 22 November 1873.
100. *Mercury* 9, 11 August 1871.
101. *Brisbane Courier* 3 December 1872.
102. *Daily Northern Argus* 29 November 1877.
103. *Goulburn Herald* 20 November 1867.
104. *Narracoorte Herald* 26 October, 9 November 1880; *Border Watch* 24 November 1880.
105. *Maitland Mercury* 30 July, 20 August 1867; *Sydney Mail* 23 November 1867; *Maryborough Chronicle* 6 February 1869.
106. *Newcastle Chronicle* 29 August 1874; *Cumberland Mercury* 27 November 1875.
107. *Brisbane Courier* 1, 23 February 1869.
108. *Queenslander* 24 April 1869; *Weekly Examiner* 3 February 1872.
109. *Brisbane Courier* 28 April 1869.
110. *South Australian Advertiser* 16 November 1869.
111. *Wagga Wagga Advertiser* 12 March 1873; *Newcastle Chronicle* 22 May 1873; *Clarence and Richmond Examiner* 8 December 1874.
112. *Wagga Wagga Advertiser* 22 November 1873.
113. *Herald* 7 December 1867; *Inquirer* 11 November 1874, 10 February 1875, 2 October 1876, 28 March, 18 April, 26 May 1877.

114. *Clarence and Richmond Examiner* 30 September 1873.
115. *South Australian Register* 21 December 1853; *Adelaide Times* 14, 15 June 1854.
116. *South Australian Register* 26, 27, 28, 30 June 1854; *Adelaide Times* 29 June 1854.
117. *South Australian Register* 3, 13, 15 July 1854.
118. *Adelaide Times* 3, 4 August 1854.
119. *South Australian Register* 20, 22 July 1854.
120. *South Australian Register* 1 November 1854.
121. *Adelaide Times* 2, 17 November, 16, 20 December 1854.
122. *South Australian Weekly Chronicle* 9 July 1859; *Adelaide Express* 5 September 1865; *South Australian Advertiser* 22 November 1866.
123. *Empire* 29 July 1854.
124. *Empire* 2, 10, 26 August 1854.
125. *Sydney Morning Herald* 4 September 1854, 3 July 1855.
126. *Empire* 2 August 1854.
127. *Argus* 18 November, 26 December 1856; *Melbourne Punch* 18 December 1856.
128. *Star* 7 February, 31 July 1857, 21 September 1859; *Bendigo Advertiser* 16 September 1859.
129. *Star* 3 July, 17 August 1861, 17 July 1862, 24 August 1864; *Bendigo Advertiser* 21 September 1864.
130. *Argus* 3 June 1859, 30 June, 1 July 1868; *Australasian* 1 April 1865.
131. *Age* 29 November 1873.
132. *Australian Town and Country Journal* 11 March 1876.
133. *Adelaide Times* 31 October 1854; *South Australian Advertiser* 15 December 1859.
134. *Sydney Morning Herald* 5 December 1866.
135. *Maryborough Chronicle* 16 November, 7 December 1869.
136. *Telegraph, St Kilda, Prahran and South Yarra Guardian* 7 September 1878.
137. Quinlan and Goodwin, *Combating the Tyranny of Flexibility*.

10 Workers in Government and Community Service

Introduction

Prior to 1850 government workers (predominantly convicts) accounted for considerable collective action—all informal apart from several government clerks/officers associations (Table 10.1). After 1851 government remained central to colonial economies, employing many manual and service workers, including teachers. Goldrush inflation sparked protests by government workers whose salaries lagged. Additionally, clerks/officers and teachers began to form associations—a trend strengthening over succeeding decades—followed by railway workers (Chapter 3). Unionisation of teachers and government officers is typically dated to the late 19th/early 20th century but began decades earlier in the colonies, the UK, North America and probably elsewhere. The Table 10.1 combined mobilisation figures for clerks and teachers (almost 20,000) is larger than the estimate for all government workers (15,580) for two reasons. First, clerks included private sector workers—some organisations covering both. Second, median membership of clerks and teachers' associations exceeds other government workers so the figure using a sector-wide median is likely an under-estimate.

Strike action was rare, largely confined to manual workers like labourers and a single establishment while NSCA involved 8.8 times more workers with over half being multi-establishment and 31.7% colony-wide (Table 10.1). The latter far exceeds other sectors but readily explainable because wages/pensions, working conditions of most workers were determined by colonial governments. Wages, working conditions and hours were dominant issues in collective action followed by OHS, jobs and subcontracting (labourers working for local government contractors). Pensions/superannuation was a growing issue. Clerks and teachers readily petitioned government or their agencies (like Education Boards), also using newspaper letters/notices, deputations (more so teachers) and mass meetings. These were directed at employment issues not political claims something forbidden for public servants as were strikes. Court cases were rare.

Table 10.1 Worker Organisation in Government and Community Service 1831–1880

Industry	1831–1840	1841–1850	1851–1860	1861–1870	1871–1880	Total 1851–1880
Entire Industry						
Organisations	1443	511	154	108	120	365+
Raw involvement	6161	2305	1767	1853	5489	9109
Est. involvement*	6227	2428	2044	3397	10139	15580
Strikes						
Won	5	3				
Drawn	1	1	1			1
Lost	175	107	26	6	3	35
Unknown	6	8	14	7	7	28
Total	187	119	41	13	10	64
Est. total involvement*	819	1492	536	357	499	1392
Number of establishments						
One	185	117	40	13	9	62
Multi	2	2				
Regional/Town					1	1
Non-strike collective action						
Won	5	9	28	8	22	58
Drawn	69	19			1	1
Lost	727	254	52	27	20	99
Unknown	654	155	29	33	52	114
Total	1455	437	109	68	95	272
Est. total involvement*	5351	1850	795	1923	8132	10850
Number of establishments						
One	1449	430	66	32	22	120
Multi	1	3	11	5	3	21
Regional/Town	2	2	13	9	24	46
Colony-wide		2	17	22	44	83
Issues in collective action (strikes/NSCA)						
Wages	5/9	9/23	11/48	6/45	8/47	25/140
Hours	86/14	50/23	15/17	2/8	2/31	19/56
Working conditions	91/1421	59/373	16/48	5/23	2/18	23/89
Health & safety	38/23	17/22	4/6	/7	/18	4/31
Management behaviour	24/62	28/67	3/6	1/3	1/6	5/15

Industry	1831–1840	1841–1850	1851–1860	1861–1870	1871–1880	Total 1851–1880
Jobs/employment		2/2	/9	1/10	/6	1/25
Work methods	2/4	1/1	2/		/6	2/6
Unionism					/3	/3
Subcontracting			/3	/11	/5	/19
Legislation		/1		/4	/2	/6
Pensions				/2	6/	/6
Unknown	1/15	2/31				
Total strikes/NSCA	187/1455	119/437	41/109	13/68	10/95	64/272

Breakdown of organisation and actions of largest subgroups

Clerks						
Organisation numbers	2	7	32	30	31	87+
Est. involvement*		168	713	4041	3324	8078
Strikes	1					
NSCA	1	5	29	36	44	109
Absconding						0
Petitions	1	5	20	9	10	39
Deputations		1	1	1	4	6
Mass meetings			8	4	5	17
Marches						0
Letters/Public notices		1	25	16	10	51
Bans					1	1
House-of-call				2		2

Court Actions

Won						
Lost	1					

Teachers						
Organisation numbers		3	22	42	41	92+
Est. involvement*			1867	1495	8412	11774
Strikes						0
NSCA		2	18	14	34	66
Absconding						0
Petitions		4	21	19	16	56
Deputations			3	3	10	16
Mass meetings			5	9	11	25
Marches						0
Letters/public notices			29	11	17	57
Bans						0
House-of-call						0

* Adjusted by multiplying number of zero-reporting organisations/years by median industry and occupation membership in that decade. +For totals, organisation spanning multiple decades only counted once.

Informal Workplace Dissent

As government operations typically involved multiple workplaces and wage/conditions were determined centrally, single workplace organisation was rare. Instances of neglect and recreational absence were common amongst ex-convict constables in Tasmania. Punishments were usually modest (fines) but there were exceptions. In August 1853 two constables were sentenced to nine months' hard labour for deserting their rounds to attend a performance at Hobart's Princess Theatre while two others received prison terms for allowing female prisoners their custody to get drunk.[1] In 1853 several Melbourne police were prosecuted for refusing to collect firewood and water, as were five Geelong mounted police refusing to serve under Lieutenant Taylor.[2] In 1863 Brisbane water police resigned en masse after their accommodation-hulk was condemned and they were afflicted by sand-flies and mosquitos when moved into tents.[3] Workers engaged by government contractors also took collective action. In July 1876 and May 1877 Melbourne night-soil removers working for Mitchell and Newell in Melbourne struck over wages.[4] Government contracting-out wrought frequent wage-defaults and numerous collective protests. Competitive tendering for road construction, local government and other activities was associated with repeated under-bidding, poor business-practices and insolvencies amongst often-small contractors along with outright swindling of workers.[5] In 1864 labourers petitioned the Brisbane municipal council over wages owed by their contractor and in 1866–1870 the South Australian Central Road Board was beset by repeated complaints from contractors' labourers.[6] In 1865 Kiama harbour works labourers refused to work for a new contractor without payment guarantees, having lost wages to his predecessor while Wollongong residents protested harbour works were delayed by 'dishonest contractors.'[7] A contractor's failure to pay wages also sparked a strike by stonemasons and labourers building Adelaide's new reservoir in 1871.[8]

Multi-Workplace and Formal Organisation

Police, Prison Warders, Fire Brigades, Gas Stokers and Nurserymen

Attempted unions were mostly short-lived. Sydney constables formed a benefit society in 1826 but police organisation remained largely informal with post-1850 instances in Melbourne (1851, 1855, 1869 and 1879), Ballarat (1862), Adelaide (1854, 1856, 1860, 1863 and 1878), Port Adelaide (1852), Hobart (1853, 1874), Launceston (1854, 1856) and Sydney (1871). During the goldrushes police pushed for higher wages to offset cost-increases.[9] Wages dominated subsequent actions along with discipline, working conditions and job security.[10] In 1871, 110 Sydney police protested wage cuts and in 1879 married Melbourne police petitioned for increased quarters-allowances.[11] Adelaide police protested retrenchments in 1860 and pushed for reduced hours (1863, 1867 and 1878) as did their Hobart counterparts (1874).[12] In July 1856 firemen formed the Melbourne United Fire Brigades Friendly Society, operating for four years.[13] Gas stokers and firemen predominantly employed by local government formed unions in Melbourne and Collingwood (1873–1881) pursuing eight-hours and improved wages, precedents for wider mobilisation after 1880.[14] Gardeners and nurserymen organised in Melbourne (1873–1874 and 1873–1875) mainly over jobs and friendly benefits while those in Mount Macedon (1879) sought a half-holiday.[15] Melbourne lamplighters established a society but it collapsed after a wage-strike in 1872.[16]

Clerks/Officers and Postal Workers

Wages/Salaries, Conditions and Job Security

Goldrush inflation sparked civil service protests in Melbourne and Sydney in 1852.[17] In 1852 Sydney letter-carriers struck over insufficient pay, petitioning for increased wages two years later as did Adelaide letter-carriers in 1853, 1854 and 1856.[18] Tasmania, where the economy was stagnating, witnessed wide-ranging protests over low salaries and delayed payment in 1853–1855, including middle-ranking officers and clerks, schoolmasters, school inspectors, auditors, letter-carriers, customs boatmen, prison warders and javelin men.[19] Salary cuts and retrenchments sparked protests elsewhere. In late 1854/early 1855 Melbourne civil servants met at *Passmore's Hotel* and the *Bush Inn*, petitioning government to assist retrenched officers.[20] There were similar protests against wage cuts in 1861, non-payment of salaries in 1867 and in October 1880 retrenched officers demanded three months leave of absence on full pay.[21] In 1866 Queensland civil servants protested salary cuts and retrenchments associated with the colony's financial crisis.[22] Similar protests occurred in NSW in February 1871 with efforts to restore salary levels in May 1872.[23] In December 1859/January 1860 South Australian civil servants demanded additional wages for extended working hours.[24] In 1865 Adelaide City Corporation officers and labourers petitioned for wage increases. Only the labourers succeeded, officers failing with a second petition in 1868.[25] Adelaide postal clerks too petitioned for salary increases in 1870.[26] Comparative wage justice mattered, Victorian Crown Lands Department draftsmen and professional officers arguing increases were needed to make their pay comparable with other departments in 1874.[27] By 1870 civil service laws regularised salary payments for permanent appointments and the advantage of annual salary increments to retain competent staff was being acknowledged.[28]

Management Behaviour, Seniority/Promotion and Pensions

Collective action over management decision-making, promotion and superannuation/pensions grew. Some actions targeted specific managers, seven Victorian Mines Department clerks at Trentham charging their manager with victimisation (now labelled bullying) in 1876.[29] More typically issues concerned general civil service employment conditions, especially seniority/promotion and pensions. In 1863 a Queensland public servants' committee influenced provisions in the colony's first *Civil Service Act* but efforts over salary and superannuation failed when the legislation was revised in 1867. The defeat coincided with formation of a civil service consumer cooperative association.[30] Between March 1870 and June 1871 NSW civil servants protested compulsory salary deductions for superannuation under the *Superannuation Bill*.[31] Victorian Mines Department officers sent a protested the *Civil Service Amendment Bill* in March 1879.[32] Municipal officers also organised over these issues. In June 1873 Victorian municipal officers petitioned local councils, including Ballan, Braybrook, Maldon and Indigo requesting (unsuccessfully) a pension scheme.[33] By 1875 activists formed the Victorian Municipal Officers Superannuation Association sending deputations to colonial government ministers requesting a pension for almost 900 officers/clerks in local government.[34]

Hours and the Half-Holiday

In early 1854 the NSW government responded to a civil servants' petition, granting clerks a Saturday half-holiday, closing public offices at 1 pm, followed by similar changes in Melbourne and Perth and sparking agitation in South Australia.[35] 'Scripso' argued opposition from shipping/mercantile interests could be overcome if customs and wharf clerks acted jointly with merchants and solicitors' clerks.[36] Agitation by Port Adelaide mercantile clerks prompted amendments to the *Customs Act* implementing a Saturday half-holiday ultimately extended to all government clerks and resulting in successful claims by other government workers, including Central Roads Board officers.[37] Victoria too legislated to close Melbourne and Geelong Custom Houses noon on Saturday in 1857. A clerk complained the 'mongrel' law didn't apply to the outdoor-department—two-thirds of the workforce—and there were further Geelong complaints about the law.[38] Nonetheless, the law had flow-on effects to the private sector with most bonded stores/port-warehouses agreeing to close at 2 pm Saturday.[39] Legislation didn't always resolve the issue, with Port Adelaide Customs clerks regularly called to deal with late arriving vessels. In late 1860 they failed to get Saturday overtime banned and the struggle remained unresolved six years later.[40] Municipal officers too pursued a half-holiday, a Bendigo request for a Thursday half-holiday to align with commercial clerks being rejected in 1861.[41] Postal workers joined the push, with Melbourne letter-carriers securing a Saturday half-holiday in 1878 quickly extended to postmen in Geelong and other towns, although in Castlemaine and Kyneton it was altered to Wednesday to align with their existing half-holiday.[42] Saturday half-holidays for letter-carriers were adopted in Hobart, Launceston, Sydney and country towns like Goulburn by 1880.[43] The Victorian government refused to extend it to telegraph workers.[44] Despite this rebuff, half-holidays were entrenched for most colonial government workers.

Mutual Insurance

In 1877 Sydney postal workers formed a mutual benefit association but there is no evidence of widespread organisation in this regard.[45]

Government Mechanics, Gardeners and Labourers

Wages and Hours

In February 1871 NSW government manual employees joined civil servants and Newcastle railway workers protesting wage cuts. Although some belonged to craft unions (Francis Dixon attended Newcastle and Sydney meetings) a separate Sydney body (with JW Cox as secretary) was established to coordinate agitation. Fiery speeches deprecated overpaid judges and politicians, lambasted the Attorney General's criticism of trade unions and called for breaking 'the upper crust—or dogfish aristocracy' (by an employer present!).[46] In 1872 Maryborough Council (Queensland) labourers struck for increased wages.[47] In Victoria the National Short Hours League pursued eight-hour claims for customs boatmen and dredge-men (1870) with local leagues doing the same for government labourers in Avoca (1870), Camberwell and Hawthorn (both 1873).[48] Prahran Council mechanics and labourers secured eight-hours in 1874 and in 1878 Council agreed to a Saturday half-holiday setting 48-hours as a condition for all workers engaged by its contractors.[49] Botanic garden and Mount Macedon state forest workers also requested a Saturday half-holiday in 1878.[50] Similar claims occurred in other colonies, like Hobart public slaughterhouse labourers in 1874.[51] In South Australia the half-holiday became political with mayoral/municipal candidates pledging their support at electoral rallies/meetings.[52]

School Teachers

One especially significant area of organisation was school teachers. Initially colonial governments left education to religious groups (apart from South Australia) but began funding denominational schools (Protestant and Roman Catholic).[53] In the 1840s NSW introduced a dual system of denominational schools and secular non-denominational schools (drawing on the Irish National Schools model), both receiving government funding which carried over to Victoria and Queensland when they became separate colonies. Bodies were established to regulate denominational and non-denominational schools but schooling quality and coverage remained problematic.[54] Between 1872 and 1880 five colonies legislated for free compulsory and secular education (Western Australia did so in 1894).[55] Religious schools and small private schools were both affected, especially the latter. The complexities and changes just described shaped teacher organisation, with Protestant, Roman Catholic teachers and state school teachers forming separate bodies, though some covered multiple groups. The dual denominational/non-denominational system raised questions over their respective treatment of teachers amidst often heated debate about the system more generally. From the late 1840s denominational teachers/schoolmasters took informal action over salaries and rent assistance.[56] As elsewhere, inflation in the early 1850s caused salary protests, including denominational schoolmasters in NSW and government schoolmasters in Hobart.[57] Salary cuts also sparked protests, like one by Victorian denominational teachers in 1859.[58] As government intervention increased, it became a focus for agitation. In 1859 school teachers from Sydney and 'elsewhere' petitioned the Legislative Assembly against Local Board control over hiring and firing and compulsory religious instruction in non-denominational schools, also demanding school inspectors have training/practical experience as schoolmasters.[59]

The first association was the South Australian Preceptors Association (established March 1851), the name covering all engaged in education including tutors, assistant teachers and governesses.[60] Explicit recognition of females—who joined—set a precedent.[61] Initially focusing on mutual-improvement, the Preceptors Association was rapidly drawn into government/political realms. The association collapsed after May 1852 but was resuscitated in 1857 (surviving until 1867). It advocated (via memorials to government and correspondence with the Central Board of Education) changes to legislation, competitive exams and ongoing education so teachers, including females, could enhance their skills.[62] The association was concerned about wages, rents and working conditions.[63] In October 1858 it argued certification/qualifications should determine teachers' pay, not enrolments, and this would attract more qualified teachers to the colony.[64] A Northern Preceptors Association was established at Gawler in late 1859, but while initially thriving, was short-lived.[65]

From the mid-1850s teachers organised in NSW, Victoria, South Australia and Tasmania, followed a decade later by Queensland. Early bodies were generally short-lived (five years or less), longevity increasing in succeeding decades. In Victoria associations formed in Geelong (1855, 1875), Melbourne (1856, 1859, 1862, 1864, 1866, 1867, 1873, 1876),

Sandhurst/Bendigo (1857, 1862, 1866, 1870, 1876), Ballarat (1857, 1866, 1877), Mount Alexander/Castlemaine (1858, 1864, 1870), Western Port (1859), Kyneton (1862, 1866), Gippsland (1863), Ovens (1863, 1872), Koroit (1865), Ballan (1867), Grenville (1874), Avoca (1874, 1877, 1878), Bacchus Marsh (1875), Maryborough (1876), Heathcote (1876) and Hamilton (1877). In NSW, associations formed in Sydney (1855, 1856, 1859, 1863, 1866, 1868, 1870, 1872, 1873, 1878), Maitland (1856, 1863, 1873), West Maitland (1866. 1869), Illawarra (1866, 1873, 1880), Newcastle (1866), Goulburn (1867), Shoalhaven (1868), Grafton (1868, 1876), Kiama (1868), West Kempsey (1870), Taree (1871), Braidwood (1872), Dapto (1873) and Dungog (1873). There was less regional spread elsewhere. In South Australia unions formed in Adelaide (1852, 1857, 1871, 1875 and 1876) and Gawler (1858); in Queensland in Brisbane (1868), Toowoomba (1873) and Ipswich (1880), and in Tasmania in Hobart (1859, 1872) and Launceston (1872). In NSW and Victoria some regional bodies became branches but most remained independent. Female teachers were an increasingly important part of the workforce, some belonging to associations in all colonies, newspapers occasionally reporting their involvement. In 1859 women attended a large Sydney meeting on the new Education Bill and an 1863 Hunter Valley teachers' petition included female signatories.[66]

A key mobilisation point was mutual-improvement/professionalisation with regular lectures, library materials and classes, and pressing for government regulation certifying teachers' qualifications—Sydney teachers petitioning for this in 1847.[67] Certification/licensing offered government quality assurance while teachers' benefits included salary, esteem and control of entry into the profession.[68] Legislative reforms in the 1860s included measures for examining, inspecting and certifying teachers directly linked to salaries and promotion.[69] Government funding made it pivotal to efforts to lift teachers' professional standing and employment conditions. Mutual-improvement was consistent with this and gave associations an ongoing function.

Religious interests including Protestant and Roman Catholic teachers associations opposed increased government oversight affecting job prospects, professional standing and wages/working conditions especially when reviews labelled their schools and teachers below standard/inefficient. In 1855–1856 concerns over NSW government inspection/reviews of denominational schools encouraged the formation of a Protestant United Teachers Association (1855–1858, with a Hunter Valley branch 1856) and Australian Catholic Teachers Association (1856–1862). The former collapsed in 1858 but was succeeded by the Church of England Teachers Association (1859–1865).[70] Denominational school criticism of National Schools' sparked counter-protests. In 1857 Fort St School teachers wrote letters to the *Sydney Morning Herald* (converted into pamphlets) rebutting criticism and accelerating the push for

National Schools outside Sydney by reinforcing concerns—oft repeated over the next 20 years—of denominational schools' inferiority, particularly lower qualification/non-merit-based teacher selection.[71] The group also published the *National School Expositor* in 1859.[72] In September–November 1866 Protestant and Catholic Teachers Associations jointly petitioned against the NSW Education Bill especially provisions for 'free education' and abolishing the Denominational School Board.[73] They were opposed by National School teachers and teachers' associations like the Hunter Valley National Teachers Mutual Improvement Society—later the Hunter Valley Teachers Association that included denominational teachers.[74] Both sides mounted deputations.[75] The struggle was complicated. Eighty male and female National School teachers also urged Bill modifications—their petition rejected for lacking a 'prayer.'[76] A deputation representing 95 Sydney National School teachers raised concerns with Colonial Secretary Henry Parkes about linking salaries to student fees (and recovering these fees in poorer districts where some denominational schools didn't charge all students), as well as extending pensions to teachers.[77]

Denominational teachers' associations weren't always hostile to government or at loggerheads with government-school teachers. Even when government funding to denominational schools increased, as in 1860, salaries were lower than government teachers and not always regularly paid. Appointment, promotion and dismissal could be capricious or arbitrary as was provision of adequate and reasonably priced accommodation especially in country districts.[78] Decisions by the Denominational School Board and individual church bodies attracted criticism from teachers and others within denominational system ranks.[79] In August 1859 the NSW Church of England Teachers Association protested hiring and firing decisions by Sydney and Newcastle Bishops.[80] They also asked the Association of National School Teachers to organise a large public meeting of teachers regarding the Education Bill in October 1859 (some Catholic teachers boycotted the meeting).[81] Four years later National and denominational teachers banded together in petitions and deputations to the NSW Legislative Assembly, expressing concern over the Board of Education's oversight/intervention powers.[82] Premier Charles Cowper claimed the new law protected teachers—a claim undermined when National School teacher Robert Philip was charged by Henry Hilley, the school patrons' secretary, with intemperance—charges refuted by parents, church leaders and others in Albury.[83] Some denominational teachers supported legislative reforms in the 1860s and 1870s because they mitigated intrusive local church oversight.[84] However, discrepancies remained. In December 1878 the NSW Council of Education granted equal salary increases to both teacher categories. Denominational teachers were still disadvantaged regarding rent/accommodation assistance, petitioning repeatedly for redress—unsuccessfully as Council deemed it lacked the power to fund their accommodation (although government did partly fund building church schools).[85]

Denominational/non-denominational divisions played out to varying degrees in Victoria and Queensland but not South Australia which didn't adopt the government dual-funding system. A Melbourne Denominational Teachers Association established in 1856 with mutual-improvement objectives became enmeshed in vitriolic press exchanges over rival schooling regimes.[86] Nonetheless, in 1858 the Association merged with the Education Institute of Victoria (1856–1860), formed by government teachers bringing denominational and National School teachers into the same body.[87] There were differences of opinion regarding legislation, especially an 1858 Education Bill, the Institute Secretary asking the Bill's proposer (Ireland) to clarify points in dispute.[88] In addition to mutual-improvement and reviewing legislation, the Institute corresponded with the National Board of Education and the Denominational School Board on employment and professional matters (including inspectors' role and hours/time to attend additional training), one member observing National Board replies were 'invariably of a very indefinite nature, while those of the Denominational Board were of a very different kind.'[89] It also dealt with religious groups administering specific schools, as in August 1858 when three teachers including Mrs Snow were dismissed for refusing to have their salaries 'taxed.' In 1859 the Institute opposed the Bishop of Melbourne's attempt to forestall salary recommendations from the Denominational Board. It also lobbied the University of Melbourne in favour of awarding degrees solely by examination and raised concerns about unfair dismissal of some teachers.[90] By January 1859 teachers' associations in Geelong, Castlemaine and Ballarat affiliated to the Institute (Bendigo soon followed) and the Tasmanian Institute of Education requested rules to help form a similar body.[91] Ballarat advocated the abolition of school fees.[92]

In March 1859 the Institute proposed reorganisation of the Denominational School Board, including electing two teacher representatives. Dr Perry and his clergy's treatment of Sandhurst teachers were condemned.[93] In May 1859 the Institute agreed to correspond and exchange reports with teachers associations in other countries although publishing a journal like NSW was postponed on cost grounds. Just as the body was building momentum it was confronted with fallout from the colony's economic deterioration and budget cuts. The Institute petitioned on behalf of large numbers of male and female teachers retrenched by the National Board of Education.[94] Sandhurst teachers protested Denominational School Board imposed salary cuts, requesting assistance from the Institute and Geelong, Castlemaine and Ballarat.[95] A Sandhurst meeting noted the severe impact on female teachers, their salaries averaging just over £50, insufficient 'for respectable board and residence' and whose contribution was particularly significant in the colony. These points were reiterated in a petition to the Governor supported by the Bendigo community. The signatories were all male but the branch represented a German mistress unpaid for six months, suggesting it had female members.[96] The Denominational School Board's new rules, varying salary cuts for different categories of teachers and criticism of Board inspectors caused a schism amongst denominational teachers. In August a Central Eastern District teachers' meeting generally endorsed the new rules (especially preventing salaries being taxed by local groups); disavowed criticism of the Board and its inspectors but still wanted action on rent allowances.[97] This breakaway formed a short-lived separate association. The Institute told the Denomination Board that the split was caused by Inspector Geary but its complaint was merely 'received.'[98] The Institute collapsed soon after unsuccessfully petitioning the Legislative Assembly for funds (Geelong reverted to independence surviving until 1872).[99] The association was a bold attempt to represent denominational and non-denominational teachers, pursuing actions on salaries and conditions, professionalism/certification, management decision-making and politics that foreshadowed teacher union practices well into the future.

Grievances over 'screwing' down National and denominational teachers' salaries, further retrenchments and belated payment festered well into the 1860s, typified by 'orphan girl' hired at £40 a year as a sewing mistress but complaining after two years she was still owed £18.[100] Delayed salary payments were not confined to Victoria, being the subject of debates in other colonial parliaments.[101] As in NSW, education legislation revisions sparked teacher protests. In 1863 associations protested remuneration and discipline provisions in proposed rules and regulations of the Victorian Board of Education.[102] In 1866 a Geelong Teachers Association submission to the Royal Commission on Education advocated:

1. A national system of secular education, religious instruction to be provided for independently of State legislation.
2. A Minister of Public Instruction.
3. Head teachers to be brought under the Civil Service Act.
4. No gentleman to be appointed an inspector of schools who had not previously taught in a 'well-conducted' elementary school for a period of at least five years.

Geelong collaborated with other districts, though victimisation of activist teachers had a chilling effect as Daniel Kennedy's letter to the *Bendigo Advertiser* made clear.[103] Despite this, teachers associations continued to network. In May 1867, Melbourne and suburban National School teachers petitioned against the Education Bill, calling for appointment of an education minister.[104] In 1876 the Victorian

State Teachers Association protested ministerial decisions regarding enrolment numbers and salary, drawing support from Bendigo which re-established an association.[105] These are but illustrative examples of numerous teacher protests.

While Queensland experienced public debate over the dual denominational/secular school regimes, only the latter organised, forming the Queensland National School Teachers Association (QNSTA) in 1868. Like other colonies it focused on government regulation affecting salaries and conditions. Responding to parliamentary criticism teachers were nothing more than 'political emissaries' a QNSTA member stated their only connection to politics was advancing 'the true interests of education and to obtain for teachers a fairer recognition and remuneration.'[106]

In the 1870s Victoria led colonial government overhauls of education legislation, prescribing minimum tuition standards, free and compulsory education and building numerous government primary schools (and later high-schools) staffed by government teachers. The reform's impact was profound and rapid, state primary schools rapidly filling with students especially from poorer backgrounds. Private operations were so undermined that Ballarat private schoolmasters asked to be incorporated into the state system.[107] Denominational teachers were admitted into the government system but many failed certification exams, were replaced and retrenched, sparking calls for compensation.[108] The Queensland National School Teachers Association complained free education without additional compensation eroded members' salaries (based on pupil numbers with different rates for boys, girls and infants).[109] Others, like the Illawarra Teachers Association, unequivocally endorsed reforms, calling for abolition of public school fees, arguing fee collection was both difficult (some parents refused to pay) and humiliating.[110] Tasmania lagged in these developments. As elsewhere, measures like an Education Board (overseeing teaching standards and programs) threatened the jobs/livelihood of private schoolmasters. In late 1872 and September 1873 Launceston and Hobart private schoolmasters complained about unfair competition from government schools, seeking reduced regulatory requirements. They got little sympathy from politicians concerned with professional standards and extending primary education to the poor.[111] State education had its critics, Captain Onslow telling the NSW Legislative Assembly in 1878 establishing grammar schools in Maitland, Goulburn and Bathurst 'was a species of communism designed to relieve the parents of all responsibility.'[112] The religious school sector felt threatened.[113]

Reflecting the regime shift, public school teachers' unions became dominant in the 1870s, bringing with it a stronger focus on public sector employment issues like pensions. The NSW Public School Teachers Association (established 1873), like several predecessors, published a journal, *The Journal of Primary Education*, promoting its objectives. Henry

Parkes told parliament in March 1874 this publication was different, and the *Bega Gazette* agreed:

> Supposing a teacher had a grievance—for instance, an unjust report on his school by some bull-headed Inspector—was it likely the journal under such management could ventilate the wrong? Now, high officials are thrown overboard, and the journal is a true teachers' organ, fearlessly exposing whatever demands exposure. The teachers are to be congratulated for resolving to free themselves from semi-official espionage . . . the teachers have too long been regarded at a pack of babies, to be patronised as long as they behaved themselves.[114]

The Council of Education (which succeeded the National Board) repeatedly rebuffed association attempts to establish a relationship.[115] This may have affected the tone/content of the journal but tensions were longstanding and predated the union. In February 1872 Sydney District teachers protested a Council circular, making inspectors the sole and final arbiter of teacher performance.[116] In early August 1874 the Council of Education demonstrated it would brook no criticism from the journal, suspending three senior teachers—F Bridges (Fort-street Model School headmaster), A Adams (Wesleyan School headmaster) and W Matthews (Glebe Public School headmaster and union secretary). The suspension of three distinguished teachers angered the community but Council was unmoved, the teachers having to petition for clemency.[117] The intimidation caused the association to collapse.

Overall, 1851–1880 saw the emergence of vigorous teacher organisation with female members. Organisation was drawn to the central role of colonial government in education, affecting professional aspirations, wages, job security, discipline/oversight, pensions, housing and other matters. Teacher associations were also active in the UK, Ireland and the US at this time, suggesting the need for a wider re-examination.

Conclusion

Clerks/officers, police and others working for colonial government had been taking action over workloads and wages since the 1830s and this pattern continued in 1851–1880. While formal organisation remained largely episodic, growing involvement in government regulation of pay, workloads, hours, discipline, promotion, job security and pensions prefigured union growth after 1880. The conspicuous exception was teachers who formed numerous associations from the 1850s and by the late 1870s relatively effective bodies were operating, representing denominational (private) or government school teachers, including women. Not unlike craft unions, these bodies sought to enhance their members' wages and conditions through mutual-improvement and certification/credentialism along with representations to government (and education authorities). However, like civil servants, teachers' connectivity to the state meant their political and industrial activism was circumscribed.

Notes

1. LC247-1-23 Hobart 2, 13 August 1853.
2. *Argus* 9, 10 August 1853.
3. *Brisbane Courier* 6 April 1863.
4. *Age* 11 July 1876, 30 May 1877.
5. *South Australian Register* 26 December 1863.
6. *Brisbane Courier* 11 October 1864; *South Australian Register* 6 September 1866; *Adelaide Observer* 6 April 1867; *South Australian Weekly Chronicle* 21 February 1870; *Bunyip* 11 January 1868.
7. *Kiama Independent* 11 May 1865; *Maitland Mercury* 18 November 1865.
8. *South Australian Register* 18 January 1871.
9. *Geelong Advertiser* 7 October 1851; *South Australian Register* 10 August 1852.
10. *Argus* 21, 24 March 1855, 20 November 1869; *South Australian Advertiser* 19 February 1862.
11. *Mount Alexander Mail* 7 February 1871; *Argus* 9 June 1879.
12. *Adelaide Observer* 2 January 1864, 16 March 1867; *South Australian Advertiser* 8 August 1878; *Mercury* 22 December 1874.
13. *Argus* 5 December 1856.
14. *Age* 17 May 1873.
15. *Age* 28 October 1873, 15 July 1875; *Argus* 12 July 1879.
16. *Age* 11 October 1872.
17. *Argus* 11 April, 20 July 1852; *Sydney Morning Herald* 17 July, 6 September 1852; *Hobart Courier* 11 August 1852.
18. *Empire* 11 September 1852; *Sydney Morning Herald* 26 July 1854; *Adelaide Observer* 21 May 1853; *Adelaide Times* 7 January 1854; *South Australian Register* 28 May 1856.
19. TAHO CSO24/228/8515 Memorials 28 May 1853, 15, 18 February, 2, 3, 21 March 1854; CSO1/72/1829 Memorial 15 November 1855; *Launceston Examiner* 5 April 1853, 9 March 1854; *Hobart Guardian* 18 February 1854; *Tasmanian Daily News* 27 December 1855.
20. *Argus* 22 December 1854, 22 January 1855.
21. *Ballarat Star* 28 February 1861; *Melbourne Herald* 7 April 1867; *Age* 7 October 1880.
22. *Brisbane Courier* 14 September, 13 October, 9 November 1866.
23. *Newcastle Chronicle* 14 February 1871; *Sydney Morning Herald* 20 May 1872.
24. *South Australian Register* 6 December 1859; *South Australian Advertiser* 12 January 1860.
25. *South Australian Advertiser* 15 August 1865; *South Australian Register* 17 January 1868.
26. *South Australian Register* 10 June 1870.
27. *Age* 16 September 1874.
28. *South Australian Register* 17 May 1873.
29. *Kyneton Observer* 16 May 1876.
30. *Brisbane Courier* 18 June, 27 July, 13 August, 18 September 1863, 25 October 1867.

31. *Freeman's Journal* 5 March 1870; *Empire* 8 June 1871.
32. *Age* 20 September 1879.
33. *Bacchus Marsh Express* 21 June 1873; *Ovens and Murray Advertiser* 21 June 1873.
34. *Argus* 21 August 1875; *Ballarat Star* 4 May 1876.
35. *Sydney Morning Herald* 21 February 1854; *South Australian Register* 11 March, 30 June 1854; *Sydney Mail* 8 December 1866.
36. *Adelaide Times* 4 July 1854; *South Australian Register* 25 July 1854.
37. *South Australian Register* 29 December 1854.
38. *Age* 20 January 1857; *Argus* 17 February 1857.
39. *Argus* 6 November 1857.
40. *South Australian Advertiser* 28 December 1860, 31 August 1861; *South Australian Register* 25 January 1861.
41. *Bendigo Advertiser* 23 October 1861.
42. *Age* 15 April 1878; *Geelong Advertiser* 16 May 1878; *Kyneton Guardian* 22 June 1878.
43. *Cornwall Chronicle* 8 May 1878; *Express and Telegraph* 8 August 1878; *Goulburn Herald* 21 February 1880.
44. *Camperdown Chronicle* 27 August 1878.
45. *Telegraph* 10 January 1877.
46. *Evening News* 17 February 1871; *Empire* 21 February 1871.
47. *Maryborough Chronicle* 15 October 1872.
48. *Geelong Advertiser* 15 February 1870; *Avoca Mail* 19 March 1870; *South Bourke Standard* 13 June 1873.
49. *South Bourke Journal* 13, 23 March 1878.
50. *Argus* 12 July 1879.
51. *Mercury* 27 October 1874.
52. *Evening Journal* 20 November 1878; *South Australian Advertiser* 3 December 1878.
53. *South Australian Weekly Chronicle* 13 July 1861.
54. *Argus* 18 August 1859.
55. Shorten, A. (1996) The Legal Context of Australian Education: An Historical Exploration, *Australia New Zealand Journal of Law Education*, 1(1): 2–32.
56. *People's Advocate* 6 January 1849; *Sydney Morning Herald* 22 September 1852.
57. *Sydney Morning Herald* 22 September 1852; *Maitland Mercury* 25 September 1852; *Freeman's Journal* 30; *Hobarton Guardian* 11 March 1854.
58. *Bendigo Advertiser* 16 June 1859.
59. *Empire* 23 September 1859; *Maitland Mercury* 8 October 1859.
60. *South Australian Register* 25 March 1851.
61. *South Australian Advertiser* 11 August, 6 September 1858; *South Australian Register* 21 December 1858, 7 September 1859; *Adelaide Observer* 8 June 1861.
62. *Adelaide Observer* 14 August 1858.
63. *South Australian Advertiser* 6 September 1858.
64. *South Australian Weekly Chronicle* 16 October 1858.
65. *South Australian Register* 29 March 1859.
66. *Freeman's Journal* 5 October 1859; *Argus* 5 September 1859; *Maitland Mercury* 3 January 1863.
67. *Hobarton Guardian* 8 September 1847.
68. *The Bunyip* 9 September 1871.
69. *Sydney Morning Herald* 28 April 1868.

70. *Sydney Morning Herald* 2 August 1855, 24 June 1859; *Maitland Mercury* 22 March, 5 June 1856; *Freeman's Journal* 14 June, 4 October 1856.
71. *Sydney Morning Herald* 13 April, 18 May, 22 June 1857; *Armidale Express* 19 September 1857; *Bathurst Free Press* 14 October 1857; *Illawarra Mercury* 1 April 1858.
72. *Sydney Morning Herald* 7 February 1859; *Freeman's Journal* 26 January 1859, 10 April 1861.
73. The Catholic Teachers Association was revived in 1865 but collapsed again several years later. *Freeman's Journal* 13 October 1866, 9 February 1867.
74. *Newcastle Chronicle* 6 October 1866; *New South Wales Government Gazette* 2 November 1866, No. 212, 2630.
75. *Sydney Morning Herald* 9 November 1866.
76. *Empire* 13 November 1866.
77. *Sydney Morning Herald* 8 November 1866.
78. Delayed payments also occurred in Victoria, *Argus* 18 July 1859; *Freeman's Journal* 7 March 1860, 8, 22 October 1862; *Sydney Morning Herald* 30 November 1865.
79. *Sydney Morning Herald* 4 June 1857, 15 August 1859.
80. *Sydney Morning Herald* 9 August 1859.
81. *Sydney Morning Herald* 3 October 1859.
82. *Sydney Morning Herald* 23 July 1863.
83. *Empire* 15 December 1863.
84. See for example *Maitland Mercury* 27 May 1869.
85. *Sydney Morning Herald* 13 December 1878; *Protestant Standard* 21 December 1878.
86. *Argus* 10, 11, 12, 16 July 1856.
87. *Age* 8 February 1858.
88. *Freeman's Journal* 13 February 1858.
89. *Age* 5 July 1858.
90. *Argus* 23, 24 January 1859.
91. *Argus* 24 January 1859.
92. *Star* 1 December 1858.
93. *Kyneton Observer* 8 March 1859.
94. *Geelong Advertiser* 10 May 1859.
95. *Bendigo Advertiser* 10 May 1859.
96. *Geelong Advertiser* 11 May 1859; *Bendigo Advertiser* 25 May 1859; *Age* 3, 10 June 1859.
97. *Argus* 24 August, 5 September 1859.
98. *Age* 17 October 1859.
99. *Age* 18 January 1860.
100. *Argus* 11 April 1861, 30 April 1864; *Age* 7 February 1862.
101. *Sydney Morning Herald* 8 June 1865.
102. *Hamilton Spectator* 20 March 1863; *Kyneton Observer* 17 December 1863.
103. *Bendigo Advertiser* 2 November 1866.
104. *Bendigo Advertiser* 22 May 1867.
105. *Bendigo Advertiser* 9 October 1876.
106. *Brisbane Courier* 24 August 1869.
107. *Border Watch* 29 January 1873; *Age* 30 January 1873.
108. *Mount Alexander Mail* 30 January 1880.
109. *Brisbane Courier* 12 July 1872; *Warwick Examiner* 20 July 1872.
110. *Wagga Wagga Advertiser* 9 July 1873.
111. *Mercury* 4 November, 20 December 1872, 30 September 1873; *Launceston Examiner* 19 December 1872.

112. *Sydney Morning Herald* 6 March 1878.
113. *Argus* 17 February 1880.
114. *Bega Gazette* 19 March 1874; *Protestant Standard* 14 March 1874.
115. *Protestant Standard* 11 October 1873; *Empire* 27 May 1874.
116. *Protestant Standard* 17 February 1872.
117. *Maitland Mercury* 15 August 1874.

11 Wider Alliances, Peak Union Bodies and Political Organisation

> *Past experience . . . has proved that a better feeling and understanding amongst the various trades is essential to the general interests of the whole, the less we know of our respective positions the easier we become subservient to the designs of capitalists and as we have no other means of ascertaining each other's views but by mingling together, this Board will be found in every respect suitable for the purpose.*
>
> (Preamble to Rules and Regulations of the Operatives Board of Trade, Melbourne 1858)[1]

Introduction

Dealing with wider organisation prior to 1900, Australian labour histories focus on eight-hour leagues, Trades Halls/Trades and Labour Councils and the emergence of the Labor Party. This view represents a retrospective rationalisation because ultimately dominant developments occurred amidst more complex organisational experimentation and alliances. The period 1851–1880 witnessed continuation of informal alliances and mobilisations, mostly unemployed protests, largely overlooked but influencing labourist policy. However, there was also a proliferation of formal political and peak bodies, many intertwined by activist networks. As important were key mobilising issues, some already identified (like hours) while others represented extensions into the political sphere like political representation. This chapter cannot examine the foregoing in depth. Keeping to the book's primary objective it charts different organisational forms, their objectives, methods/functions, interrelationships and pivotal mobilising issues. Diversity is apparent even amongst bodies using the same title. While distinctions have been drawn between union federations, peak councils and purely political organisations, even here blurring is evident.

Mobilising Modes and Structures

Figure 11.1 indicates annual peak union and political body numbers from the early 1830s (post-1880 data is incomplete). The ratio of formal

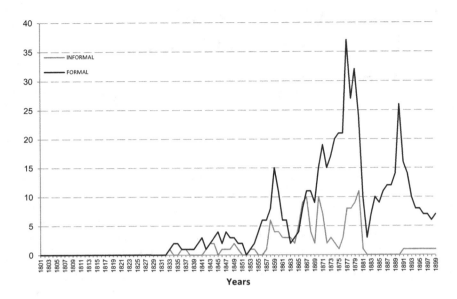

Figure 11.1 Peak Union and Political Bodies: Australia 1801–1900

to informal bodies grew slowly, from 16 of 29 for 1831–1850 to 144 of 237 for 1851–1880. Most informal bodies were short-lived, jobless protests. Figure 11.1 and Table 11.1 indicate peak/political organisation runs parallel to union formation but marked by greater turnover. Notwithstanding the establishment of enduring labour councils, median duration of 1851–1880 formal peak/political bodies was 100 days compared to 145 days for unions. The impact of the 1860s depression/ drought is apparent, with a collapse of formal bodies and falling-off in total involvement from 1851–1860 with most involved in unemployment protests (Table 11.1).

Table 11.1 summarises peak/political organisation numbers, involvement, objectives and actions. Like unions, involvement grew significantly in the 1870s. Key objectives were jobs/employment, legislation, community welfare/poverty, opposing European/assisted-migration, union solidarity and hours. This weighting doesn't match recent labour historiography, particularly the importance of jobs/employment and relative insignificance of anti-Chinese sentiment. Counts are only a guide but reinforced by qualitative evidence in Table 11.1. The most common methods were public demonstrations and political agitation. In terms of usage, mass meetings stand out followed by marches/processions (mostly eight-hours), deputations, petitions and newspaper letters/public notices.

Table 11.1 Number, Size and Activities of Peak Union and Political Organisations 1831–1880

	1831–1840	1841–1850	1851–1860	1861–1870	1871–1880
Formal bodies					
Number	4	14	37	34	87
Involvement	900	1139	22190	5866	43250
Median involvement	900	219.5	450	150	250
Involvement estimate*	2700	2895	29390	11116	63250
Median duration	85.5	40	96	91	77
Informal bodies					
Number	3	10	14	38	42
Involvement		725	5700	11130	12048
Median involvement		41	300	300	135
Involvement estimate*		930	7800	18030	15558
Median duration	1	10.5	7	9	5
All Bodies Objectives					
Jobs/employment	4 (57.1%)	20 (83.3%)	39 (76.5%)	52 (72.2%)	90 (69.8%)
Community welfare		4 (16.7%)	27 (52.9%)	46 (68.9%)	62 (48.1%)
Legislation		6 (25%)	36 (70.2%)	37 (51.4%)	91 (70.5%)
Anti-European immigration	1 (14.3%)	3 (12.5%)	17 (33.3%)	18 (25%)	37 (28.7%)
Non-European/anti-Chinese			1 (2%)	1 (1.4%)	9 (7%)
Union solidarity		1 (4.2%)	11 (21.6%)	17 (23.6%)	33 (25.6%)
Wages	1 (14.3%)	3 (12.5%)	8 (15.7%)	8 (11.1%)	15 (11.6%)
Hours			10 (19.6%)	15 (23.6%)	32 (24.8%)

(Continued)

Table 11.1 (Continued)

	1831–1840	1841–1850	1851–1860	1861–1870	1871–1880
Health	2 (28.6%)	4 (16.7%)	5 (9.8%)	2 (2.8%)	5 (3.9%)
Working conditions			1 (2%)	3 (4.2%)	5 (3.9%)
Friendly benefits	2 (28.6%)	4 (16.7%)	3 (5.9%)	3 (4.2%)	2 (1.6%)
Self-improvement				5 (6.9%)	11 (8.5%)
Subcontracting			3 (5.9%)	2 (2.8%)	3 (2.3%)
Conciliation/arbitration			1 (2%)		2 (1.6%)
Management behaviour				2 (2.8%)	2 (1.6%)
Apprenticeship			1 (2%)		
Unknown	2 (28.6%)	2 (8.3%)			
Total organisations	7	24	51	72	129
All Bodies Methods					
Public demonstration	3 (42.9%)	15 (62.5%)	44 (86.3%)	66 (91.7%)	101 (78.3%)
Political agitation	3 (42.9%)	20 (83.3%)	43 (84.3%)	45 (62.5%)	91 (70.5%)
Petition	3 (42.9%)	15 (62.5%)	19 (37.3%)	22 (30.6%)	24 (18.6%)
Deputation		1 (4.2%)	10 (19.6%)	19 (26.4%)	26 (21.2%)
Inter-union solidarity			9 (17.6%)	15 (20.8%)	31 (24%)
Education			2 (3.9%)	7 (9.7%)	13 (10.1%)
Made demands	2 (28.6%)	1 (4.2%)	14 (27.5%)	5 (6.9%)	7 (5.4%)
Mutual insurance		2 (8.3%)	1 (2%)	1 (1.4%)	2 (1.6%)
House-of-call		1 (4.2%)	1 (2%)		1 (0.8%)
Strike		1 (4.2%)			2 (1.6%)
Strike-fund		1 (4.2%)			2 (1.6%)
Bans		1 (4.2%)			1 (0.8%)
Riot			1 (2%)		1 (0.8%)

Cooperation					1 (0.8%)
Conciliation & arbitration					1 (0.8%)
Collective bargaining					
Conciliation/arbitration					
All Bodies Actual Use of Particular Actions					
Petitions	3 (42.9%)	14 (35%)	27 (19.4%)	30 (14.9%)	37 (8.9%)
Deputations	4 (57.1%)		18 (12.9%)	28 (13.9%)	55 (13.3%)
Mass meetings		20 (50%)	75 (54%)	100 (49.5%)	224 (54.1%)
Marches/processions		1 (2.5%)	8 (5.8%)	24 (11.9%)	69 (16.7%)
Letters/public notices		4 (10%)	9 (6.5%)	15 (7.4%)	27 (6.5%)
Court action			2 (1.4%)	5 (2.5%)	1 (0.2%)
Bans		1 (2.5%)			1 (0.2%)
Total	7	40	139	202	414

* Adding number of zero-reporting organisations by median involvement.

Informal Networks and Mobilisations

Consistent with earlier chapters it is important to consider the informal links, temporary mobilisations and networking which facilitated and complemented formal organisation. In addition to collaboration associated with major incidents like the 1878 seamen's strike there were numerous smaller networks warranting recognition in terms of worker mobilisation. As with union formation, individuals and groups collaborated in successive political and industrial organisation. Launceston operatives John Denney and John Crookes, part of a group leading 1840s working-class anti-transportation campaigns, were prominent in the town's early-closing movement in 1851.[2] Extensive informal networks commonly interlinked formal bodies including single purpose committees like the Labor League's Adelaide General Aid Committee raising over £340 for the 1879 Gawler eight-hour strike.[3] Networking extended beyond the colonies. In 1875 the Adelaide ASE imposed a levy of 1s 6d per member for the Plimsoll and Seamen's Fund campaign to improve maritime safety.[4] Unemployment protests were predominantly informal and episodic but with some carryover of activists (see next). Largely independent of unions, unemployed protests cumulatively involved tens of thousands of workers, rattling the corridors of power and reinforcing calls for protectionism. Campaigns against immigration also rallied tens of thousands of workers but more typically involved unions and like-minded sponsorship as did job protection meetings (less so in regions).

General Unions, Peak Union Bodies and Issue-Based Alliances

Networks of inter-union solidarity manifested in a complex array of bodies. Apart from Trades Hall/Labour Councils, most bodies including Early Closing Associations and the South Australian United Tradesmens Society and its successor United Labor League in South Australia have received limited attention from historians. Like earlier Committees of Trades, United Trades Associations drew on European models (Dublin had a body) involving degrees of multi-occupational unionism (usually in separate branches but with merger aspirations) with peak council functions. Most formed prior to THC/TLCs but independent attempts at amalgamated structures continued, Melbourne United Bakers called a meeting on union amalgamation in 1872—it went nowhere.[5] In 1874 the Melbourne Typographical Society initiated a conference to form an Amalgamated Trades Union for mutual support and arbitration of disputes to which 22 unions (including bakers, ASE and other trades, cabmen, labourers and seamen) with 3,645 members sent delegates.[6] The move closely followed UK Trades Union Congress' Sheffield meeting resolutions. Reorganised as the Trades and Labour Council of Victoria, probably to deal with more reticent unions, it championed arbitration of strikes by agricultural implement makers (successfully) and tanners (unsuccessfully). A November 1874 deputation urged the Attorney General to establish courts of arbitration, with a further deputation to the Governor in May 1875. The Council also promoted negotiation during in disputes, like a *Melbourne Herald* strike over 'boy-labour.'[7]

Eight-Hour/Short-Hour Leagues, Half-Holiday and Early Closing Associations

From the very outset leagues were formed to coordinate eight-hour campaigns, notably the Melbourne Eight Hours Labour League (March/April 1856) and Sydney Short Hours Labour League (November 1856). Based in building, they promoted unions in unorganised trades and widening the campaign. Melbourne quarrymen joined but a merger with the ECA was rejected. The Sydney League helped an iron-trades committee advocating eight-hours (it failed).[8] In October 1859 the Victorian Eight Hours Labour League was initiated in response to attempts by several employers, including a Melbourne coachbuilder (Williams) and contractors Cornish and Bruce to reintroduce ten hours.[9] Leading lights included Charles Don, Benjamin Douglas and John Ivey. It held meetings in working-class centres like Williamstown; established branches in Brunswick, Castlemaine and East Collingwood; and corresponded with eight-hour bodies in towns like Back Creek.[10] The *Argus* labelled Don's activities against Cornish and Bruce's importation of German stonemasons a conspiracy to interfere with the rights of business, lamenting increasingly irreconcilable relations between capital and labour.[11] Failing to amicably resolve the Williams coachworks strike, the League became one of the first colonial bodies to consider arbitration, a practice then being tried in Britain.

From 1857 onwards unions began celebrating their eight-hour victories at annual dinners and picnics/excursions. Beginning in Melbourne, multi-union committees organised more general celebrations on an appointed day. Unions produced elaborate and artistic banners depicting their trade with idealistic propaganda (the ASE's rejecting Mars God of War) to parade in eight-hour marches.[12] Banner designs were commonly modelled on British unions with local modifications like Sydney Bricklayers depicting important city buildings. Paralleling military flags banners were reverent expressions of union solidarity, the rights, values and aspirations of working people. Peak bodies like the Melbourne Trades Hall and Literary Institute (THLI) established banner committees and storerooms. Banners of lapsed unions sometimes passed onto their successors as occurred with Melbourne coachmakers in 1874. Union colours (mauve for the Sydney Plasterers), rosettes and membership certificates, emblems, scarfs, aprons (for stonemasons) and cards performed icono-graphic/symbolic as well as practical functions, as did annual picnics or dinners commemorating the union's establishment. Carrying banners was an honour subject to careful selection. Unions hired bands to lead them at processions, some like the Victorian Bricklayers and Operative Stonemasons having their own bands.[13] Monuments, too, were erected, reinforcing the movement's importance. In 1880 Ballarat erected a monument to eight-hour pioneer James Galloway. Ballarat and Ballarat East declared half-holidays enabling a large procession to the monument with church bells ringing to mark the occasion.[14]

By the 1860s eight-hour celebratory committees were transforming into or operating alongside eight-hour leagues. Like unions, some experienced successive rounds of formation/collapse/renewal. The number of unions involved in demonstrations waxed and waned, some unions collapsing although unorganised workers also marched. There were disagreements, the Adelaide ASE refusing to fund the 1878 eight-hour demonstration due to misappropriations in the previous celebration.[15] However, una-nimity and effective organisation of demonstrations over decades was remarkable. Some eight-hour committees confined themselves to annual celebrations, asking employers to grant a holiday and pressing municipal and colonial governments for a public holiday. In 1872 the Victorian Chief Secretary refused to declare 21 April a public holiday, stating there were already too many holidays but government employees' joining the demonstration wouldn't lose pay.[16] In 1873 and 1874 the Melbourne Eight-Hour Anniversary Demonstration Committee renewed public holi-day requests to employers and government while the Ballarat committee sent deputations to local councils a year later.[17]

Other eight-hour committees campaigned for short-hour arrange-ments, especially in regions with few unions. Some bodies represented a particular industry like building (especially in the 1850s), the iron-trades (as in Sydney in the 1870s) or mining (Bendigo in 1871). Other bodies were principally concerned with securing eight-hour legislation, as in Bris-bane in 1876.[18] But boundaries blurred. The Sydney Iron Trades Eight-Hours Committee supported the 1878 seamen's strike. In February 1879 the Port Adelaide Eight-Hours Pioneers Committee—a body hitherto organising annual demonstrations—formed a funding committee for the Gawler eight-hour strike.[19] Two months later a Bendigo Eight Hours Committee deputation requested public works while urging the Minister for Railways for fare-relief during anniversary celebrations.[20] Some pur-sued more generalised hour campaigns. In 1862 the Ballarat Eight-Hours and General Short Hours League campaigned for a Saturday half-holiday for shop-assistants, dispatching deputations to mining companies urging earlier worker payment.[21] In May 1869 a Melbourne meeting chaired by MLA John Everard inaugurated the National Short Hours League aiming to make the eight-hour system and Saturday half-holiday universal and reduce lengthy hours worked by assistant drapers, bakers and others. Establishing branches (including Geelong, Beechworth and Malmsbury), League objectives included eight-hour clauses in government contracts and legislation mandating eight-hours—making references to the US in this regard.[22] The League sought to extend organisation to other colonies—a Deniliquin branch was considered. It widely distributed its manifesto and reports, and dispatched petitions (with over 8,600 signatures), deputations and memorandums to government. Vice-president Benjamin Douglas spoke at regional meetings urging unionisation.[23] Representing workers from many vocations, the League marked an early attempt at coordinated working-hours organisation. Negotiating eight-hour provisions with colonial and municipal governments, by 1871 it was scrutinising candidates for upcoming elections and had embraced protectionism.[24]

In NSW an Eight Hour Extension and Short Hours League (1869–1871) was formed in Sydney with parallel Maitland (1869–1875) and Newcastle (1862, 1869–1880) bodies and links to the Clarence River building trades.[25] While initially dominated by building unions, these bodies enrolled others (like Newcastle coalminers), assisted organising quarrymen, supported eight-hour claims by stonemasons' labourers and pledged cooperation with the Half-Holiday and Early Closing Association.[26] Like Victorian bodies (Castlemaine and Camberwell), Newcastle and Maitland were not peak councils but conducted campaigns.[27] The NSW League advocated legislation making eight-hours 'the standard day's labour in all occupations' with a petition securing 5,663 signatures by July 1870.[28] Enlisting sympathetic politicians the League found their support dissipated, Henry Parkes and John Bowie Wilson (elected to working-class East Sydney on eight-hour and early-closing pledges) more concerned with other issues.[29] Following a year of unsuccessful agitation, League activists, including stonemason Francis Dixon (1836–1884), promoted a labour council to better represent workers.[30] The Sydney Trades and Labour Council (established May 1871) took up the mantle, deputations urging government to adopt eight hours for its own works, the government responding by enquiring into the Victorian experience.[31] Within three years Dixon led the push for direct labour representation in parliament.[32] Frustration over eight-hour laws wasn't the only driver for the shift from eight-hour leagues to TLCs. The NSW Eight Hours League and others had become enmeshed in other issues, like government-funded migration and social/political developments.[33]

United Tradesmen, Labour Leagues, Trades Halls and Labour Councils

From the 1850s closer alliances of organised labour were being proposed. In some colonies these bodies were precursors to trades and labour/trades hall councils but this wasn't always the case, reflecting organisational experimentation. In Melbourne the eight-hour campaign in early 1856 rapidly led to a Trades Hall Committee (later Trades Hall and Literary Institute, THLI) which began erecting a Trades Hall in 1859—amongst the oldest union buildings in the world—and was the progenitor of the Melbourne Trades Hall Council.[34] Castlemaine (1859–1861) and Ballarat (1862) also sought to build trades halls. In additions to dues and levies, Trades Halls and Labour Councils still depended on borrowing funds from individual unions for erecting buildings and ongoing operations. In 1875 no-interest loans totalling £1,000 to the Melbourne Trades Hall Committee from six societies (stonemasons, carpenters, bricklayers, curriers, plasterers and mill-sawyers) was equal to its assets and over four times its income (from rent etc.) for that quarter.[35]

Congregating unions encouraged collaboration but even in Melbourne the transition to peak council/workers' parliament entailed organisational experimentation. The THLI focused on financing/building/operating a temporary and later permanent trades' hall where affiliated unions could meet (keep their records) along with a library/reading room, storing union banners and supporting eight-hour day demonstrations. The THLI eschewed industrial/political actions with rare exceptions like Garibaldi's struggle against Italian despotism (1860), the Melbourne early-closing agreement (1867–1868) and the Short-Hour Labour League's push for eight-hour provisions in government contracts (1869).[36] Other bodies filled the vacuum. An Operatives Board of Trade was established by building trades (except stonemasons) and labourers' societies in 1858. Representatives included eight-hour pioneers carpenter Charles Vine and plasterer Benjamin Douglas. In March 1859 ironworkers joined during their failed eight-hour strike, the Board calling for eight-hours for all government mechanics and labourers. In July, Board deputations to contractors, builders and the Commissioner of Public Works called for banning government contracting-out work and piecework 'calculated to give every facility to the dishonest contractor and employer to defraud the workman of his rights.'[37] By August 1859 the Board was advocating amalgamation of trades, sending deputations to societies including printers. This seems a last, desperate effort as it struggled getting meeting-quorums and was defunct soon after.[38] The Operatives Board of Trade was followed by the National Short Hours Labour League (1869–1871) and in 1872 the United Trades Association of Victoria which evoked varying degrees of support amongst societies.[39] Meeting at the Trades Hall and surviving until 1877, the latter included leading unionists like David Bennett. The Association supported the struggles of weaker unions like brickmakers, bakers and bootmakers.[40]

The transition to peak councils was more truncated in other colonies. The Sydney Labour League (1856) helped bricklayers and plasterers organise, although its manifesto appealed to working men generally.[41] Subsequently, other peak bodies, mostly eight-hour committees/leagues, came and went, before in May 1871 the Trades and Labour Council was established. The ASE told Sydney Bricklayers reinvigorating the eight-hour movement was central for them but most looked for a wider agenda.[42] The TLC embraced an array of issues including unfavourable labour laws, government-assisted immigration, working-class parliamentary representation, and the iron-trades protectionist push in 1875.[43] It could pursue issues difficult for individual unions and enter into wider alliances, like joining with the Builders and Contractors Association and Engineering Association promoting evening classes on vocational education—precursors to technical colleges/TAFE.[44] Other issues pursued including alienation of harbour foreshores, provision of free libraries and railway services for workmen.[45]

South Australia lacked strong building unions to initiate a Trades Hall/Labour Council. In the early 1870s the United Tradesmens Society was established in Adelaide, forming branches in Gawler, Port Adelaide and Wallaroo while pre-existing societies of printers, coachmakers and stonemasons amalgamated as branches.[46] This loosely federated body (with a Standing Council composed of branch delegates) was a rational counter to organisational 'churn' and extended unionisation to towns where individual trade numbers couldn't sustain separate organisation. Notwithstanding its name, the society included non-skilled workers, reconfiguring as the Labor League of South Australia in 1877 and registering under the *Trades Union Act*. The preface to the League's rules explicated goals of representing all workers and advocating 'the rights of labor—not only on their own account, but for the sake of their children and succeeding generations.' League objectives (rule 2) included just wages, eight-hours, assisting unemployed and affording 'a ready means, by arbitration or otherwise, for the settlement of any dispute that may arise.'[47] The League built a hall (with a library) in Hindley St that became a meeting hub for unions, the Eight Hour Celebration Committee and the Anti-Chinese League. The League acted as a proto-labour council promoting the 1879 Intercolonial Trades Union Congress (ITUC) and sending its own delegate. It provided placards for unemployment protests and financial/logistical support to both members (in the 1879 Gawler eight-hour strike) and other workers like navvies, although the Nairne Railway Navvies Committee rejected its suggestion of arbitration in 1880.[48]

Efforts to formalise union alliances proved difficult in Tasmania, Queensland and Western Australia. In Queensland, bodies organising eight-hour celebrations (initially 1 February) were operating by 1866 and a United Trades Association existed briefly in 1868.[49] A 'Trades Hall' seeming built as a private venture in Burnett Lane in mid-1873 was soon used as a meeting place by the carpenters, blacksmiths, bricklayers, shipwrights and others, the Brisbane Working Mens Association/Union (1875) and a committee advocating eight-hour legislation in 1876.[50]

Key Labour Council Activities

Labour councils were pivotal in coordinating various hour-related campaigns including garnering union support for early-closing and half-holiday campaigns.[51] Councils also provided advice on wage campaigns, organised protests, facilitating fundraising during prolonged strikes/lockouts, mediated remedies and collected information on trade conditions.[52] Multi-union action had occurred since the 1830s but labour councils enhanced coordination, logistical support and long-term strategising. The Sydney TLC coordinated fundraising for the 1876 New Lambton coalminers' strike and helped Hunter Valley Coalminers' secure widespread financial support for distressed families during the prolonged strike against wage cuts in May/June 1880. Much support came from craft unions with deeper pockets, sums given often exceeding donations to other craft unions on strike.[53] Craft unions also imposed bans to support miners, seamen and labourers, with breaches being notified as Newcastle Boilermakers did in 1879.[54] The importance of this in terms of mobilisation and building inter-union solidarity shouldn't be underestimated. Those promoting the aristocracy of labour notion have rarely considered this critical counterpoint, vital to understanding the 1878 seamen's strike and even larger shearers/maritime strikes in 1890–1891.

A growing array of issues became labour council business, including employers withholding wages, problematic even for craft unions with Sydney Shipwrights requesting TLC action in 1875.[55] They brought pressure to bear during prolonged strikes and retrenchments in government workplaces. In 1880 Sydney Boilermakers referred dismissals at Cockatoo Island Dock, arguing action was timely given the upcoming election and government spending on emigration (the effort failed).[56] Labour councils built their affiliate-base but it wasn't plain sailing, with unions disaffiliating after disagreements—almost always temporarily. Sydney Painters did this in 1876 but participated in subsequent eight-hour demonstrations.[57] Virtually from inception, peak bodies engaged in politics, lobbying on legislation like the Navigation Acts (affecting maritime workers) and land boiler inspection.[58] They mounted campaigns for legal enactment on issues like subcontracting/unpaid wages, conducting their own inquiries and collecting evidence.[59] Pushing for elected working-class parliamentarians, the TLC backed Angus Cameron in East Sydney in 1874.[60] Financial support for the campaign varied in part due to union rules. Stonemasons and Shipwrights societies adopted voluntary support rather than a levy while the Progressive Carpenters and Boilermakers made direct donations or paid the requested levy.[61] Even reputedly insular craft societies like the ASE engaged in politics, the Balmain Branch informing the union's General Secretary a member (Garrard) had been elected to the NSW Legislative Assembly in 1880.[62]

In addition to communicating with comparable bodies in the UK and elsewhere, labour councils occasionally took up subscriptions to assist the victims of disasters like a French flood in 1875.[63] This extended union reach into the wider community but it was not new. In 1867 Sydney Shipwrights donated £50 following catastrophic Nepean/Hawkesbury river floods which inundated thousands of homes and killed 13 people.[64]

The 1879 Intercolonial Trades Union Congress

The 1879 Intercolonial Trades Union Congress (ITUC) in Sydney—the first of eight held in different colonial capitals by 1898—initiated efforts to formalise intercolonial links and promote union objectives nationally. While attendance was patchy (including several New Zealand unions and the Sydney United Drapers), ITUC proceedings received detailed coverage in newspapers and a subsequent published report was widely distributed. Issues debated included immigration, tariff-protection, oppressive laws (like master and servant), laws mandating eight-hours, restricting immigration, recognising unions, encouraging local industry, land boiler legislation, reforming marine regulation and work-injury compensation.[65] These were key policy planks for unions, peak councils and workers' political organisations, most reiterated at succeeding Congresses.[66]

Political Leagues and Working Mens Associations

Like peak bodies, political mobilisation entailed informal networks and formal organisation. Thousands of political/industrial activists had been transported and others voluntarily migrated from the 1830s bringing Chartist and other radical ideas to the colonies. Suffolk-born Chartist Robert Booley helped establish the Geelong Peoples Association for political and social advancement within two years of arriving in 1851. The 1854 Ballarat Reform League (Chapter 5) advocated a Chartist platform of free and fair representation, universal manhood suffrage, no property qualification parliamentary members, paid parliamentarians and short duration parliaments. The Bakery Hill mass-meeting some weeks later condemned the Acting Chief Justice for 'stigmatising as riots the persevering and indomitable struggles for freedom of the brave people of England and Ireland for the past 80 years.'[67] Eureka protesters included Californians, adding to republican sentiments found elsewhere, especially amongst the Irish. In 1859 stonemason Charles Don and plasterer Benjamin Douglas formed the Political and Labour Social League.[68] Though short-lived, the League's manifesto encapsulated labourist policies prescient of later bodies—including protectionism, opposing assisted-immigration, laws securing eight-hours and wage recoveries, abolishing government subcontracting and master and servant laws. Protectionism encouraged alliances with other bodies like Labour Tariff Leagues.[69] Don was elected to the Victorian Legislative Assembly for working-class Collingwood later the same year, working by day and attending parliament at night to speak and vote for his class.[70]

Working men's associations (WMA) had existed for decades (a London WMA operated by 1837) although their objectives/functions were by no means uniform. In 1841 the Adelaide Working Mens Association formed to agitate on unemployment and labour standards. Launceston operatives converted a pre-existing body into a WMA in 1849 to boycott those employing convicts.[71] In 1854 another Adelaide WMA was formed to secure shorter hours and intellectual improvements for clerks, shopmen and tradesmen. The anti-transportation Hobart Trades Union (1847–1851) was succeeded by combined Launceston/Hobart campaigning against the pernicious the *Master and Servant Act* in 1855 with the Hobart Standing Committee of the Working classes (aka a WMA) emerging from it. The 1856 arrest of free-emigrant Eliza Maguire on suspicion of being a convict became a lightning rod for protests against legislative/magisterial tyrannies committed on workers (including using the *Vagrancy Act* against itinerant workers) amidst calls for liberty and self-government.[72] Consistent with earlier observations, leadership of these bodies overlapped and the same applied to numerous organisations mentioned a little later in the chapter.

The Melbourne's Working Mens Association used the 1856 extended-franchise elections to support businessman David Moore's candidature (preferring Charles Don in 1857), also raising funds for a new Melbourne Hospital wing.[73] A WMA Central Committee member proposed a Working Womens Association to represent the city's 2,000 'milliners, dressmakers, shopwomen, mantle-makers and domestic servants.' This wasn't actioned although a Working Womens Protective Association was operating in New York by the late 1860s.[74] In August 1857 another body, the Melbourne Working Mens Association of Unemployed (later dropping Unemployed), was established with William Osborne and later Edward Gibbs as its secretary.[75] In September the original WMA sent deputations to government pressing for public works, though tensions remained with Osborne being forced to resign.[76] While the British WMA pressed White Hall for assisted-emigration to Australia, their colonial counterparts mobilising against it, the Melbourne WMA sanctioned a 'Peoples Summary' on the glutted labour market to transmit to 'England.'[77] Joblessness also prompted a Bendigo Working Mens Association.[78] Over the next decade WMAs were established at regional centres primarily concerned with increasing workers' electoral clout, Castlemaine's two preferred candidates topping the 1862 poll though in reverse order.[79]

In NSW a Morpeth Working Mens Political Association was established in 1857 to counter illiberal legislation and promote reform, arguing landholders should contribute to the common good. Access to land was a plank of unemployed protests though never comparable to calls for public works, protectionism and restricting immigration. The Morpeth WMA sought to influence parliamentary elections, forming links with workmen in neighbouring towns like West Maitland.[80] In March 1858 a Sydney WMA was formed amidst unemployed protests but only lasted several months, as did a body formed in February 1859 which tried to establish a registry office entitled the Working Man's Home.[81] In South Australia, too, the unemployed formed a WMA, repeatedly petitioning for public works and cuts to immigration.[82] Gaining little, it collapsed after four months. However, anger simmered. In September efforts were made to establish WMAs in Adelaide and for districts like Gawler to campaign in the upcoming election.[83] At an Adelaide meeting two years later a speaker (Vincent) stated the body was arising from its slumber to deal with 'stump orators' elected on promises to curb immigration who then reneged.[84] In 1866 a South Australian Working Mens Political Association campaigned against immigration and unemployment. Another Adelaide WMA campaigned on these issues and maximising working-men's vote in 1867–1868.[85]

By 1862 a Western Australian Working Mens Association (including women) was operating. The Association's primary functions were social/mutual-improvement and welfare-orientated rather than political although its founding secretary, Leopold Redpath, was a transported-convict and prominent social agitator.[86] Other WMAs with mutual-improvement/social objectives more akin to Mechanics Institutes were formed in Perth (1864), Busselton (1867), Geraldton (1868) and North-ampton (1877) in Western Australia; Longford (1865) and Hobart (1867) in Tasmania; and North Adelaide (1868) and Narracoorte (1871) in South Australia.[87] Perth and Fremantle both attempted mutual insurance. Primarily, social bodies calling themselves working men's clubs also following UK models were formed in Hobart, Launceston and other centres. Sharp distinctions are misleading. A number of 'social/mutual-improvement' bodies were drawn into politics. The Perth Working Mens Association hosted lectures by political candidates seeking working-class support. Its hall was used for industrial/political gatherings of workers, and its officials called for laws abolishing the truck-system.[88]

Associations increasingly acted as working-class political parties. In NSW the Eight Hours Extension League's failure was succeeded both by the Sydney TLC and the NSW Working Mens Union in 1871, Francis Dixon involved in both. Calling for a united non-sectarian working-class voice, WMA Secretary Joseph Pinkston stated politicians were in the habit of saying one thing to get into parliament then doing the opposite once elected.[89] The WMA was succeeded by the Working Mens Defence Association (WMDA, 1877–1880) which rapidly established branches in Sydney's working-class suburbs like Glebe/Pyrmont, Newtown and Millers Point, as well as Newcastle, Parramatta, Bathurst, Braidwood, Casino and Haydonton promoting their own political candidates. In Melbourne a Working Mens Political Association was launched in 1874, speeches asserting workers were the backbone of all progressive countries, with calls for female enfranchisement (not included in key policies), paid parliamentarians along with familiar policies on eight hours, assisted-immigration, protectionism and land-tax.[90] It didn't last. Nor did its successor, the Victorian Labour League (1880), which, like the Victorian Political and Labour League (1859), favoured arbitration of disputes.[91] WMAs were established in Geelong (1871, 1874), Clunes (1871), Copperfield (1873) and other towns, advocating eight hour and protectionist laws, no 'government immigration,' maximum voter registration and other policies 'beneficial to the working man.'[92] In Queensland a Maryborough WMA formed in 1875 to oppose Pacific Island labour, later copying British WMAs by petitioning for emigration to South Australia.[93] Other bodies opposing Pacific Island labour were formed in Mackay (1877) and Rockhampton (1878).[94] Working men's associations also formed in remote NSW towns/regions like the Bogan (1870), Molong (1871) and Quipolly (1875) where jobs, railway-links and free-selector land policies assumed particular significance.[95] Echoing US small farmer/working men's alliances, the Liverpool Plains Free Selectors and Working Mens Association formed in opposition to large landholders/squatters.[96] Some dovetailed agitation with political education via a library and regular lectures. Most proved short-lived though often revived. Others using the WMA title were essentially unions. The Hobart Town Working Mens Progressive Association (1864) and bodies formed in Armidale (1866), Echuca (1873), Bacchus Marsh (1874) pursued eight-hours. Wharf-labourers in Port Adelaide (1872) and Sydney (1872, 1873) and some shearer's unions like Mansfield (1873) also used to called themselves WMAs.[97]

Other bodies calling themselves Labour Leagues, Labour Reform Associations and the like were attempted or formed in Portland, Newcastle and other towns. While advocating an array of policies (including freer access to land), after 1870 almost all opposed assisted-immigration.[98] Their stance echoed numerous informal anti-immigration protests, like one in Port Adelaide in April 1877, often involving unions and their political representatives.[99] The diversity of colonial labour leagues and working men's associations in terms of objective/functions/membership mirrored what was happening in the UK and the US apart from politically conservative and religious WMAs found in Britain.[100] This diversity reflected a period of organisational experimentation, the search for policy cohesion and interest-group alliances, and the drift to more radical political demands. The colonies participated in globally transmitted ideas—in 1874 the Chicago WMA demanding government mandate eight-hours, minimum wages and support the unemployed.[101]

More Radical Bodies

Socialist ideas had been promoted by organisations and individuals in the colonies since the 1840s and the Working Mens International Association in Europe (established 1864) was widely reported.[102] From the 1870s bodies espousing socialist ideas were formed, notably the Democratic Association of Victoria (1872–1873) drawing inspiration from the Paris Communes. It was the first Marxist body corresponding with the London-based International Association of Working Men.[103] Some Victorian unions considered broader political organisation at the time, but this was a step too far for most.

Key Mobilising Issues

Working Hours

The book extensively documented how parallel working hour struggles represented a pivotal mobilisation issue encompassing much of the working population and enjoying widespread community support. Hour claims were trigger points for initiating, sustaining and spreading organisation to different occupations and locations. For most manual workers eight-hours became synonymous with unionism and solidarity. Informal information flows and short-lived organisation helped the spread so it became customary even in workplaces/districts with limited union presence.[104] It was the coalescing issue for wider alliances, leagues and ultimately peak councils which in turn intensified the campaign, resisting employer counter-attacks, galvanising community support and pressing for legal enactment. Eight-hour commemorations were redolent of growing working-class power to affect social change—a civilising of capitalism and cause for wider celebration. Marches included unorganised workers, encouraged with rare exceptions. In 1877–1878 the South Australian Labour League's attempted to exclude them in its push to unionise all workers leading to protests and a threatened separate celebration.[105] In nearby Port Adelaide eight-hour originators called themselves pioneers, contributors to a heroic narrative already being written.[106] Melbourne celebrated its 25th anniversary in 1877 with sympathetic politicians pressing the government to declare the eight-hour anniversary a public holiday—as it eventually became.[107]

Different arms of the shorter hours movement forged closer links over time, mainly the eight-hour movement supporting early-closing/half-holiday campaigns but manual workers also sought weekly half-holidays. The Brisbane Eight Hour Committee supported the Brisbane ECA's half-holiday campaign in 1876.[108] Addressing the fifth eight-hour demonstration in 1878 MLA and future South Australian Premier JC Bray urged mechanics and labourers to break off Saturday evening shopping so retail-workers could have their half-holiday.[109] Eight-hours and early-closing became elemental parts of political discourse not only in cities but smaller communities, with many candidates expressing sympathy for shorter hours lest they anger audiences at public meetings.[110] From the 1860s there were growing efforts to legislate eight-hours, bills repeatedly lapsing. However, Victoria enacted laws specifying eight-hours for specific occupations, notably some women and engine-drivers. Gains in one colony were used as leverage in others as were references to eight-hour leagues in Britain and North America exemplified by the 1876 Queensland movement.[111] The regulatory push wasn't confined to eight-hours or colonial legislatures. Eight-hour bodies urged town councils to declare the anniversary a half-holiday and provide grounds for picnics/entertainment. Half-holiday associations also sought local government support, the Ballarat ECA requesting town council help for its half-holiday campaign in November 1877—rebuffed.[112]

In addition to its impact on leisure, sport and health shorter hours had socio-political implications affording time to contemplate/learn, time to question/discuss, time to demand dignity, and time to engage in politics. Western Districts landholder 'Buster' lamented:

> Every servant man in the colony now joins some debating class or political society, goes in for the half-holiday movement, the eight-hour-a-day system, and will tell you to your tooth that he is educated, has a soul above Day and Martin, and that you can clean your boots yourself.[113]

Wages/Remuneration and Economic Inequality

The book documented extensive wages/remuneration setting by a wide array of workers. There were conspicuous exceptions like shop-assistants although reduced hours without losing pay effectively amounted to a pay increase.[114] The eight-hour movement's contribution to colonial union hostility to piecework represents another interconnection. Leaving these points to one side, several observations can be made. First, the book identified extensive evidence of informal wages/remuneration-related actions. Informal struggles weren't bereft of tactics and had wider impacts on wages and worker mobilisation. Nonetheless, unionisation profoundly widened the geographic and industrial terrain; using leverage-like strikes, bans and craft-barriers strategically to secure larger gains; formalising gains made; and increasing wage stickiness during economic downturns or employer counter-attacks. Second, paralleling this while informal organisation often sought comparable pay unions were far more effective in eliminating pockets of under-payment, and extending its geographic, occupational and intra-industry reach. The push for set salaries tied to qualifications/service with annual increments and pensions by public servants and teachers should also be viewed in this light. The Webb's correctly emphasised the importance of the common rule, foundational for consistency/equity, leveraging up and increasing wage stickiness, and 1851–1880 built its foundations. The common rule didn't just apply within unions. Colonial union leaders understood leveraging wages was easier the more unionised workers there were in their vocation and more generally. Australian craft unions embraced this while their US counterparts pursued a more exclusionist path. Maintaining the common rule entailed ongoing struggles, both subcontracting and piecework offering employers opportunities to undermine it. Third, a largely neglected aspect of wages—now rediscovered—was efforts to counteract wage theft. Non-payment/under-payment affected many jobs and industries but was especially common in rural/farming, domestic service, metalliferous mining and construction. Most recovery actions were informal, suggesting union presence mitigated the problem—a significant but overlooked effect. Importantly, it was union agitation that initiated regulatory remedies through wage/contractor-liens laws.

The combination of these actions in lifting workers' spending power, consumption and living standard—especially in conjunction with complementary influence on labour markets like immigration—has been underestimated. Taken together these campaigns were steps to building a wealthier if not equal society whereas the rise of neoliberalism since the 1970s is delivering the reverse, weakened unions, stagnant wages, heavy personal indebtedness, the re-emergence of multi-generational households and an economic-orthodoxy 'selective' in its recognition of supply/demand forces. Neoliberalism produces a low-wage/low-productivity economy but this connection is side-stepped and wage stagnation is presented as perplexing rather than logical. Capitalism will never deliver high wages if workers simply ask politely; rely on technological innovation; or believe the dominant discourse of financiers, economists and politicians.

Jobs/Unemployment, Protectionism and Immigration

Unemployment and Poverty/Welfare

Largely overlooked by historians, recurring unemployment sparked numerous large protests during economic downturns, encouraging anti-immigration and protectionist sentiments. Mirroring British and earlier colonial protests, they typically entailed calls for public works, with employers responding with claims joblessness arose from unreasonable wage demands and work opportunities abounded 'up-country.'[115] Glowing British newspaper reports of colonial labour conditions and misleading 'gulling' job advertisements galled protesters.[116] Protests followed a similar pattern and it is only possible to provide an abbreviated examination.

In September 1851 widespread placarding facilitated 'numerously attended' meetings of unemployed Adelaide mechanics and labourers protesting distress amongst their families and petitioning for public works. Unsympathetic voices told them to seek work up-country but even the conservative *South Australian Register* recognised that aside from difficulties leaving their families there were few rural jobs during 'the dead season of the year.'[117] Unemployed committee secretary Bryce Ross used subscribed funds to purchase 500 loaves of bread for hungry families, with cooperation from Adelaide's bakers.[118] Gold discoveries and rumours workers were leaving Adelaide caused alarm within employer and government circles. Colonial governments were sensitive unemployed protests might adversely affect UK emigration, explaining their willingness to consider additional public works.[119] In 1854 one recent immigrant complained employers and government authorities combined to flood the labour market/depress wages and he had, like many others, a few weeks' work in six months, exhausting his funds.[120]

In 1854 unemployed protests moved to Melbourne (as had Bryce Ross). Meetings at the Immigrants Home South Yarra (October) and Flagstaff Hill (November) endorsed multi-pronged petitions stating immigrants undertook long and costly voyages under false pretences and calling for affordable-land, a public employment bureau/register, and suitable work matched to skills.[121] Negating criticism, the committee interviewed railway contractors, finding numerous applicants were already being turned away. Of 600 signing one petition, 316 had families including 743 children. The second meeting sharpened the politics, speakers criticising the conquering role of capital over labour in both Britain and Victoria and Melbourne's 'moneyocracy.' They called for a journal to advocate working people's causes including accurate labour market/living-cost data and abolition of miner's licenses.[122] As rebellion brewed on the goldfields (Eureka would erupt a week later), Working Classes Association Secretary Bryce Ross ramped up pressure in a letter to the *Age*. Detailing living-costs (including rent, flour and fuel) for a family of four—shades of the Harvester wage judgement 50 years later—Ross argued land-sale fuelled emigration assistance was flooding the labour market with dire consequences for recent arrivals.[123] The protests resonated months later. During a Legislative Council debate on winding back public works due to the colony's financial straits, Geelong-based pastoralist, shipowner and merchant James Strachan warned more meetings of unemployed labourers could threaten 'the whole social order of the community.'[124]

July 1855 witnessed unemployed protests in Geelong decrying poverty/destitution in Victoria and immigration exacerbating food prices already inflated by rapid population increases. Meetings called for a Glasgow Relief Committee style relief fund—Hobart workers operated a similar scheme during the mid-1840s.[125] Destitution in Geelong was significant because the town served a rich farming/pastoral district and its port was a major disembarkation point for the goldfields. Melbourne also experienced large protests, alarming authorities sufficiently to double the military guard on the city's gold office.[126] Within months conditions improved. Not so in Brisbane where in March 1856 as Sydney and Melbourne stonemasons pushed for eight-hours, a Working Classes Distress Committee petitioned for public works.[127] Economic volatility characterised small and narrowly based colonial economies. This, substantial emigration assistance and push-factors in the UK/Ireland, along with lagged information flows, helps explain periodic mismatches in migration/colonial labour demand. Unemployed meetings were all too common in Britain, with emigration widely portrayed as an escape to poverty and win/win remedy for Britain and its colonies, something colonial newspapers seldom gainsaid.[128] These points apply generally and will not be repeated.

Another round of Melbourne protests occurred in 1857. The first 'monster' meeting was chaired by JW Vine (possibly Thomas W Vine then Melbourne Carpenters Secretary), included previous activists, and was addressed by Scottish-born Chartist Charles Don—soon elected to the Victorian Legislative Assembly.[129] Disillusioned immigrants (many arriving under the Wellington Fund), including other Chartists (like Osborne) were prominent. A Collingwood-meeting speaker labelled the female labour market as a 'slave market.'[130] Initially perplexed by extreme distress in the capital of one of the world's richest countries, the *Age* subsequently conceded serious abuses in the Immigration Depot, including recent arrivals forced to undertake four hours' hard labour prior to breakfast like convicts.[131] Stretching over three months, protests including mass meetings (mostly at the Eastern Markets), deputations and mass marches like one to the President of Land and Works, many carrying 'we will have bread' banners and another a month later by married men carrying swags.[132] They secured soothing words and a few concessions, most notably £5,000 for public works. Newspapers muttered about riots (real and imagined) and dangerous agitators (like Osborne) while authorities (elected and unelected) remained uneasy.[133] Demands for free repatriation to England threatened immigration so central to colonial governments. The *Ovens Constitution* observed that while unemployment wasn't as chronic as Europe, the absence of local manufacturing rendered the colonies' employment-base narrow and volatile.[134] These prescient observations resonated in policy debates over the next half-century and shaped the federation's socio-economic regulatory architecture—something lost to a generation of politicians besotted with neoliberalism.

In 1858 unemployment protests continued in Melbourne (with carryover activists like Osborne and H Linard), also spreading to Sydney, Adelaide and Bendigo—amidst mercantile panic, similar protests were occurring in New York and the UK.[135] Protests followed a familiar pattern, although calls for public works aligned to the popular push to extend railways in Bendigo were picked up elsewhere.[136] Again, political discourse grew more radical. Government offers of four shillings a day to break stone that might be labelled 'red republican' in the UK were derided amidst calls to extend the franchise to every British subject aged 21 years.[137] Movement leaders like Osborne spoke at meetings on electoral reform. In Sydney hundreds marched on parliament demanding import duties for local manufacturing and removing 'mislegislation' to remedy the jobs shortage.[138] The government established an Unemployed Labourers Committee to send workers up-country with a week's rations, protesters labelling this deceptive trickery because there was no work in Bathurst and other designated towns. They urged the Governor to provide public works as his predecessors Bourke (mid-1830s) and Gipps (early 1840s) had done. Arch-patrician and pro-transportation Governor General Sir William Denison refused the petition for its 'threatening and inflammatory language.' The *Empire* urged the unemployed to disown dangerous leaders threatening social order. As in Melbourne the unemployed inserted themselves into electoral reform debates preceding the *Electoral Act* which introduced universal manhood suffrage, secret ballot and more equal electoral districts.[139]

By September protests spread to Adelaide with familiar demands for public works, cutting assisted-immigration and import duties.[140] Influential mercantile, pastoral and mining interests fought to retain immigration outlays. Banker, Burra mines director, and later free-trade MLA Samuel Tomkinson told the Adelaide Chamber of Commerce large sums should be spent even if 'imported labour went to Victoria, for at least they would . . . be fed by South Australia.'[141] A parliamentary motion to suspend emigrant recruitment for six months due to unemployment and an influx of Victorian workers was lost 20 votes to nine. The naysayers were condemned at one of the colony's largest meetings, one speaker stating £40,000 was expended on immigration in the last six months.[142] Protest also occurred in Port Adelaide, Mount Barker and other locations, though intriguingly regional protests were rarely reported in newspapers.[143] The *South Australian Advertiser* conceded the distress was real notwithstanding denials.[144] New gold discoveries could spark a rush of desperate but later disappointed job-seekers. In October 1858 a Rockhampton correspondent reported that amongst arrivals at the Fitzroy Diggings 1,000 had already left cursing while another 1,100 confronted Commissioner O'Connell until reassured he would do all in his power to get them returned home.[145]

Unemployment deepened in 1859, extending into the early 1860s, fuelling protests in Victoria, NSW and South Australia.[146] Economic conditions exacerbated failures amongst government subcontractors, a Maryborough (Victoria) meeting urging direct government involvement in public works.[147] Unemployed labourers in Castlemaine—many married men unable to travel through poverty—petitioned for public work or land to feed their families.[148] Calls for land were made elsewhere but got nowhere. In February 1859 the *Age* bemoaned unemployed meetings were occurring daily in country districts and there 'was unmistakeable evidence of destitution and want among the labouring classes,' hundreds roaming the streets of Melbourne.[149] In Sydney too there was deep distress, a petition of labourers, mechanics, shopkeepers and citizens calling for an end to immigration of 'Chinese or any other class of persons.'[150] An Adelaide Park Lands meeting (April 1859) established a working men's association, pledging to vote against all candidates not supporting cessation of immigration. Amidst references to being treated like serfs, G Vincent recalled the 1851 bread-starvation protests, stating both resulted from immigration benefiting the few while impoverishing labourers and decreasing government funds to employ them. The final speaker (Newton) warned: 'if they persisted in behaving peaceably and orderly,' daily wages would soon be reduced to 3s.[151] The agitation accelerated public works and resonated in subsequent meetings of political candidates.

The same occurred in Victoria and NSW. Widespread distress/unemployment combined with the extended franchise forged alliances between Land Leagues and protectionists, and altered political agendas.[152] The Melbourne *Age* complained protests and gloomy emigrant letters 'home' played into the hands of British employers opposing emigration—for the same reasons colonial employers supported it.[153] Eighteen months earlier the *Goulburn Herald* lamented jobless agitators like Arkins helped populist candidates running against landholding and mercantile interests.[154] In October 1859 Henry Parkes proposed an inquiry into the conditions of the working classes, telling NSW parliament he had witnessed unemployment unwarranted in a new country, demoralising immigrants and sparking numerous protests.[155] Ironically—maybe not—fears of social disorder were most pronounced amongst conservatives like pastoralist MLA Henry Rotton, prone to label the unemployed as lazy and opposing public works measures. Failing to block the inquiry they doggedly opposed implementing its recommendations, sparking further protests.[156] In May 1860 police broke up a torchlight demonstration outside parliament, charging leaders West and Arkins with riotous assembly. Defending himself, Arkins asserted his constitutional rights to demonstrate but got a week's gaol and a 12-month good behaviour bond.[157] Activist William Jennett petitioned for an inquiry into police behaviour.[158] The government quickly followed demonstrations with offers of free passage to railway construction jobs in Maitland.[159]

The Legislative Assembly Select Committee chaired by Parkes in 1859–1860 considered labour market, housing and sanitary conditions, and juvenile vagrancy. Interviewing 15 employers, four labour agents and six workingmen along with government officials (police and health officers), the committee's report depicted socio-economic distress and overcrowded, unsanitary living conditions in working-class districts, and the cascading social impacts of precarious work/unemployment. Carpenter William Robertson told the committee immigration should be stopped while the labour market 'was glutted' and those already 'here are so badly employed.' He argued government should use land-sale funds on railway construction not immigration and sharply criticised employers using courts to mulct the wages of shepherds and others for exorbitantly priced rations or lost sheep in counties like Ipswich. Stonemason Thomas Smith stated he was mainly engaged in jobbing work (subcontracting) and labourers especially were suffering. Labour agents financially benefiting from placing immigrants painted a rosier picture but several employers pointed to declines in manufacturing (like tobacco) and urged higher import duties. Parks was a free-trader but the committee recommended higher duties in its final report.[160] In NSW, Victoria and South Australia agitation secured additional public works and exerted temporary influence on immigration—directly (government funding) and indirectly (discouraging emigration).

Immigration was ratcheted back up in 1862 and unemployed protests soon re-emerged. Isolated protests in 1864 (Geelong and Sydney) became widespread in 1865–1866 (Sydney, Campbelltown, Hobart, Launceston, Melbourne, Adelaide, Brisbane, Maryborough, Toowoomba, Helidon and Ipswich) as severe drought ravaged vast areas, decimating livestock and withering crops while in working-class suburbs like Collingwood soup kitchens fed the starving.[161] In Victorian, South Australian and NSW parliaments protests were ammunition in protectionist debates. The protectionist *Age* criticised its free-trade rival (*Argus*) for being unwilling to recognise 1859–1860 protests as warning signals of tying the country's future to pastoralist interests.[162] Job demands and protectionist sentiment ramped up in protests, including a Hyde Park meeting attended by around 2,500 in October 1866.[163] Adelaide workingmen formed a political association while a Mount Bryan 'old colonist' parodied well-fed, middle-class correspondents advising the jobless to seek work in the drought-ridden bush as about as sensible as Marie Antoinette's (alleged) suggestion the starving breadless eat cake.[164] The Rockhampton *Northern Argus* endorsed calls for severe cuts to salaries of the Governor and other 'extravagant establishment' appendages to help starving Queenslanders.[165] Over 600 Brisbane unemployed protested in August 1866. Railway navvies and other unemployed, many with families, held meetings in Toowoomba and Helidon (300 attendees) calling for public works, land or free passage from the colony. The Helidon meeting threatened to march on Brisbane (122 km away) if the government didn't act, some newspapers reporting they seized a goods train to travel to Ipswich.[166] Further protests including petitioning for passage to America and disturbance in Brisbane, Ipswich and Helidon stretched into October.[167] In September a Brisbane demonstration spilled over into a food riot. William Eaves, Henry Parker (allegedly having shouted 'bread or blood') and John Murray were convicted of riot and unlawful assembly and gaoled for 12, six and three months with hard labour, respectively.[168] Amidst rising anger exacerbated by ration stoppages and poor relief wages, a disorganised government offered concessions (relief work and passage elsewhere in the colony), performed policy backflips (cutting relief wages which provoked strikes) and cancelled immigration.[169]

Colonies lacked UK-style poor/workhouse laws—NSW introduced a law in 1866—with unemployed protesters commonly told to seek assistance from benevolent societies where these existed. This and the colonies' ambitious public works programs reinforced calls for additional public works. The impact of 1859–1861 and 1864–1866 protests wasn't short term, contributing to the protectionist push and matching immigration to labour market conditions (see later in the chapter). Unemployment protests continued into 1867 especially in South Australia (and New Zealand) where thousands, including retrenched mineworkers, attending meetings at Burra, Kapunda, Gawler, Moonta, Port Adelaide, Lyndoch, Nuriootpa and Adelaide calling for railway construction (thereby increasing land values), changes to land legislation and cutting immigration.[170] In Adelaide and Nuriootpa political associations were formed, public works accelerated and some municipalities provided jobs. Protests coincided with Legislative Council elections but its restricted franchise afforded little accountability amongst members—certainly not to the working class.[171] Hundreds abandoned Moonta for another colony, many government-assisted immigrants. Having made considerable sacrifices for prospects of a better life, they took jaundiced views about South Australia with them—not least those experiencing Captain Hancock's employment-practices who compared themselves to African slaves before losing their jobs.[172]

Negative reports filtering back to the UK threatening the colonies' reputation as emigrant destinations encouraged colonial governments to provide temporary public works (sometimes reversing cuts implemented during downturns), papering over evidence of their economic volatility. In November 1867 Hobart unemployed labourers sent a deputation to Colonial Treasurer TD Chapman protesting public works cuts and getting nowhere marched on the Governor's residence a week later.[173] Public works commonly entailed heavy labour—breaking stone/quarry-work, building roads and railways—at minimal wages for which non-labouring workers, like mechanics and clerks, were unaccustomed. Spin-doctoring, internecine factional warfare inside parliaments, delays and backflips meant promised funds didn't always eventuate.[174] Sporadic protests occurred in 1868 when railway-works in Muswellbrook didn't eventuate, goldrush immigration flooded the labour market in Maryborough (Queensland) or work just ran short in Morpeth and Sydney.[175]

August 1869 Adelaide protests and pleas for starving families continued into 1870, spreading to Port Elliot and elsewhere.[176] Mounted police with swords charged one demonstration, epitomising a government more concerned with social control than remedies. Labelling the Mayor as too sympathetic and lumping responsibility for public works onto the City Council, the government mistreated 100 it did employ at the Lunatic Asylum site and dispatched others to drainage work in Mount Gambier, sparking unemployed protests there.[177] By April 1870 protests spread to Sydney followed by Melbourne and Hobart. Protest leader a decade earlier, William Jennett was again conspicuous. Along with general demonstrations, ironworkers, tailors, voluntary rifle corps (the Ballarat Rangers) and roving bushmen/drovers in the remote region of Congolgan (now Concolgon) also protested.[178] Melbourne manufacturing workers demanded greater protection. In October 1870 Hobart unemployed organised mass marches/deputations; Fitzroy meetings called for combined action by the 'labouring classes' across Victoria, while 2,000 unemployed, 'many with large families,' met in Sydney's Hyde Park to petition the Legislative Assembly.[179] As in Melbourne, Sydney unions were involved, coincident with petitions from building trades workers for eight-hour day legislation—a synergistic push to redistribute work echoing Marlow's observations 14 years earlier.[180] Melbourne leaders— including Daniel Henderson a 'man of colour' disparagingly labelled 'Henderson Africanus' by the *Argus* during similar protests nine years later—condemned the conspiracy of rich colonists to suppress wages and prepared a people's manifesto while anti-immigration sentiments played out in electoral campaigns.[181] As earlier, many protesters were recent immigrants demonstrating hostility to immigration doesn't equate to hostility to immigrants—a distinction often escaping contemporary media reporting and some academic literature.

Further protests occurred in Sydney, Melbourne, Geelong and Hobart in 1871 and again in Melbourne and Ballarat in 1873. In Tasmania railway construction mitigated dissent. However, there was also a 'reporting' effect. The *Hamilton Spectator* noted recent Melbourne protests condemning government policies for pauperising the working class were largely ignored by metropolitan newspapers afraid to damage the city's image. It warned the cry for assisted-immigration by 'metropolitans' centralising the colony's resources warranted scepticism and wouldn't resolve up-country issues because—as now—immigrants preferred major cities.[182] In South Australia, workingman 'JB' noted unemployment meetings stopped after immigration was discontinued and those labelling the working-class selfishness never experienced the consequences of a glutted labour market.[183]

Protests revived in the late 1870s. Meetings in Brisbane in April 1877 were followed by calls for public works by Wallaroo, Burra, Moonta and Mount Perry miners retrenched amidst falling mineral export prices— instance boom/bust mining cycles still haunting Australia.[184] Moonta protesters demanded laws prohibiting railway contractors paying unliveable piecework-wages and others skedaddling owing wages.[185] Brisbane meetings raised Polynesian and Chinese labour, rare amongst protests preoccupied with European assisted-immigration. From May 1878 thousands attended protests in Melbourne (including Trades Hall), Emerald Hill, St Kilda, Richmond, Sandhurst (300–400 attendees), Echuca, Stawell, Geelong and Walhalla.[186] The problem was real. City Council debated funding additional public works while suburban councils like Fitzroy dealt with complaints about employing non-residents.[187] On 23 June 1878 a deputation presented the premier with a petition (over 1,000 signatures) and 200 men were subsequently engaged in the Melbourne swamp.[188] Further protests occurred August/September in Melbourne (adequacy of relief wages, concerning to unions, was criticised) and mining districts like Walhalla.[189]

John McLaren who instigated Melbourne protests in January 1879 was discredited by the Seamens Union as having been engaged by the ASN Company to secure labour during the recent strike.[190] Barely a month after inviting colleagues in Echuca, Ballarat, Geelong and Melbourne to attend its eight-hour anniversary the Bendigo building trades was campaigning for work, sending a deputation to the Minister for Public Works.[191] Further demonstrations followed in Victoria (Melbourne, Echuca, Richmond, Geelong and Williamstown), South Australia (Adelaide and Wallaroo), Tasmania (Hobart) and NSW (Sydney). Following earlier colonial precedents, the Victorian Berry government established the Melbourne Unemployed Committee, raising donations to distribute to unemployed workers and their families.[192] In Echuca over 500 unemployed sawmill-hands and bushmen protested the red-gum duty—a year earlier they had challenged license fees.[193] Under the banner 'employ our own labour' Melbourne building trades urged government to build the Swanston St Bridge from brick and stone.[194] Protests rolled into 1880 in Sydney, Melbourne, Brisbane, Echuca, Geelong, Bendigo, Huntly and Horsham. Unemployed protests in regional centres gave the lie to the mantra from employers and others that work was available up-country. Echuca protesters reacting angrily to proposals to send Melbourne unemployed there while other towns like Bendigo felt their pleas impacted less on colonial governments, leaving only meagre municipal resources.[195] The metropolitan unemployed were reluctant to move, one group rejecting an offer of timber-splitting in the Dandenong's.[196]

Some important observations flow from this abbreviated account. There were well over 50 instances of organisation, involving tens of thousands (many recent immigrants), demanding governments provide work, cut state-funded immigration and introduce protective tariffs, as well as becoming enmeshed in the democratic push from the 1850s. These demands threatened policy-settings sacred to influential capital elements though not local manufacturers. Unemployed protests were under-reported at times or were culled from monthly summaries sent to

Europe.[197] Newspapers, like to the pro-immigration/free-trade Melbourne *Argus* and *Tasmanian Times*, reported protests in a demeaning manner, suggesting attendances included many bystanders and were staged to coincide with UK mails.[198] Repeating practices originating in the 1830s, unemployed protesters repeatedly sent 'true' state of colonial labour market reports to the UK. Aggrieved individuals also wrote directly to British newspapers, Sydney-sider JG White telling *Lloyds Weekly London Newspaper* unemployment was significant and the high-wage mantra ignored higher living-costs.[199] While prosperous, colonial economies were volatile, vulnerable to droughts, shifts in export demand and variable capital inflows. Some employers, notably in the iron-trades, occasionally conceded a job shortage. More typically, as today, employers and their political mouthpieces denied unemployment existed, accused workers of being 'loafing mendicants,' too choosy/rejecting lower wages, refusing to move to other locations or claimed labour shortages held back economic development.[200]

From the late 1850s protectionism increasingly figured in unemployment protests, with arguments it would benefit the wider community.[201] By the 1870s, demands relief workers be paid decent wages and not treated in a demeaning fashion by gangers/foremen were common.[202] Union leaders were conspicuous in only a minority of mobilisations like July 1879 and February 1880 when the Sydney TLC organised mass meetings.[203] There were tensions, notably the 1878–1879 Melbourne protests where protectionist-Premier Graham Berry later claimed some protests were engineered by his opponents.[204] Overall, however, protests markedly strengthened protectionism initiated by manufacturing unions. Preoccupied with 1880–1920 as pivotal, labour historians have underplayed how earlier bouts of boom and bust influenced organised labour's views on immigration, protectionism and a range of other issues. It reached beyond manual workers. ECAs/HHAs too were aware economic downturns made it harder to retain agreements they struggled so hard to secure.[205] Finally, it needs to be recognised, as some observers did, that unemployment was the tip of an iceberg of irregular/insecure and underemployment.[206] In construction, maritime, rural industries and elsewhere irregular work was the norm. Though less visible, this experience shaped worker/union attitudes (see earlier chapters).

Jobs and Protectionism

Protectionism was a mobilising issue, especially in Victoria, New South Wales and South Australia. It was central for metal trades, clothing, footwear, textile and other manufacturing-based unions and became dominant within peak councils, political bodies/gatherings and worker-orientated newspapers. Favourable remarks of the effect of US tariffs were made during legislative debates over import/customs duties like NSW in

1864.[207] The NSW Select Committee Report into the Condition of the Working Classes (1859–1860) demonstrated the intertwining of unemployment and protectionism and was reinforced by another NSW Select Committee in 1866. Drawing on evidence of local manufacturers, the 1866 report found 'profitable jobs' created in manufacturing furniture, leather goods and apparel and the flow-on jobs in retailing and so on would far exceed the number of unemployed. Widely publicised in other colonies, it also contradicted allegations protests exaggerated the problem, finding unemployed numbers far exceeded protest participants.[208]

Importantly, protectionism split capital between globalist free-trade rural, mining and mercantile sectors and manufacturing and other businesses benefiting from it—a recurring rift in Australia's political economy. By the 1860s local manufacturers and sympathisers organised bodies like the South Australian Industrial Protection League to produce supportive information and pressure colonial legislatures.[209] Their activities complemented unions and workers' political mobilisations, spawning alliances. In June 1870, 250 attended a Protection to Native Industry and Anti-Immigration League meeting at the *Belvidere Hotel*—a prominent union meeting place. Their anti-immigration petition was presented to the Governor by a deputation led by Irish-nationalist, protectionist and labour-sympathetic Liberal MLA Francis Longmore. Sydney unions recognised the contribution of capitalists like Thomas Mort who built large industrial enterprises. Mort had his share of disputes with unions but at the TLC meeting following his death in 1878 speakers noted the 'great loss to the country.'[210] Equally, protectionist capital saw organised labour as their most influential ally, an 1880 deputation to the NSW TLC making this very point.[211]

Protectionism gained support over time, some 'free traders' changing sides particularly in Victoria. At a meeting in Bacchus Marsh in 1871 the duty on biscuits and lollies was extolled for creating jobs for 800 operatives. Three years later influential protectionist (later premier) Graham Berry told a Geelong meeting tariffs had bolstered the colonial exchequer to finance public works like building railways and eliminated unemployed protests.[212] The latter point was oft repeated at political gatherings. Unemployed protests re-emerged in the late 1870s during Berry's ministry and free traders sought to blame protection. Reposts blamed previous ministries, making conspicuous and telling comparisons with worse distress in 'free-trade' South Australia. Unemployed railway coachmakers pressed the government to expand Williamstown and establish a new manufacturing works.[213] In operating railways, colonial governments expanded local manufacturing both directly and indirectly—synergies unravelled by privatisation and competitive tendering a century later. Liberal political bodies like the National Reform and Protection League portrayed manufacturing as a future plank of the nation, aligning with organised labour (the League sometimes met at Trades Hall).[214] Protectionist sentiment found some voice in most colonies. A Brisbane protection body was established in May 1879 and a South Brisbane meeting endorsed a protectionist candidate in April 1880.[215] These are but few illustrations of how and why protectionism became mainstream labour policy for the next 100 years until sacrificed on the altar of neoliberalism.

Immigration and 'Coolie' Labour

From the early 1830s colonial governments expended growing amounts (partly funded by land-sales), providing assisted-passage for immigrants—few working-class families could meet fare costs. It was one of their largest budget items, supported by influential elements of capital dominating local legislatures but opposed by colonial workers, many of them immigrants. In 1862, barely months after widespread unemployment protests, the colonies competed amongst themselves and with others like Canada to attract British emigrants with bonuses/land-access deals. Victoria alone budgeted £120,000 for the year.[216] Business chambers pressed for immigration, arguing it benefited the economy—it certainly benefited them—even during periods of unemployment—unabated enthusiasm still evident today even as wages stagnate and economies struggle. Calls for cutbacks caused responses paralleling those for unemployment, including labelling unemployed immigrants as 'not adapted to colonial life'—character-traits that magically disappeared when jobs were plentiful.[217] This mixture of assertion and epithets drew hostile reactions from unions and peak councils exemplified by a Melbourne Trades Hall meeting response to a Chamber of Commerce report in 1860.[218]

Government funding of immigration was the touch-point. The Sydney TLC and Melbourne THC repeatedly campaigned against state-assisted migration but more informally organised protests were common like ones in Plattsburg and Balmain in 1877.[219] The Working Men's Defence League also pursued the cause. The Sydney TLC organised large demonstrations against the £76,000 NSW government budget allocation in early 1880 when unemployment was exhausting funds of even wealthy unions.[220] Sydney's Mayor agreed to a meeting on 'the dullness of trade and overstocked labour market' called by worker-sympathetic MLAs and alderman, the Iron Trades Eight Hour Conference Committee, managers of major engineering works like Morts Dock and the Albion Engine Works—and supported by the League for the Encouragement of Colonial Industry.[221]

Hostility tapped into wider sentiments, especially during downturns when community petitions opposing immigration were not uncommon.[222] More commonly than today, newspapers acknowledged migration's capacity to flood labour markets. In 1862 a report stated the 'large influx of immigrants into Brisbane during the past fortnight has choked the labour market . . . the Government are affording facilities to parties to proceed to the northern ports in search of employment.'[223] Immigration's capacity to push down wages and suppress worker combinations and strikes was also widely accepted. In 1872 the *Queenslander* warned the UK 'strike mania' would only come to the colony if opponents of immigration succeeded.[224] *Hamilton Spectator* owner/editor George Mott pointed to the hypocrisy of governments drawing on workingmen's taxes to benefit another class aspiring for wage levels of only 15s per week.[225] In July 1870 the Melbourne Typographical Society authorised its president to join the Protection of Native Industry and Anti-Immigration League and in April 1877 the Sydney Painters considered the wage effects of emigration from the US.[226] The breadth of and rationale for union hostility to immigration has been underrepresented compared to currently fashionable but narrowly conceived 'race' perspectives.

Beyond hostility to 'European' immigration there was deep hostility to the introduction or arrival of non-European workers, especially the Chinese. The distinction between introduction and arrival is important. Aside from the Chinese most non-European workers (including Pacific islanders and those from south-east Asia and the subcontinent) were introduced under private employer-initiated indentured labour schemes. Of these the largest group was Pacific Islanders introduced into Queensland whose hiring differed little from kidnapping in many cases. Some Chinese arrived under similar arrangements but most came to Australia following the goldrushes seemingly funded by community groups/entrepreneurs in China—something warranting more research. Unlike Canada and the US, the Chinese were not used to construct railways—another important difference requiring investigation. Pacific islanders and the Chinese dominated the non-European immigrant population and only the Chinese entered virtually every colony. Labour movement hostility to non-European immigration predated the gold rushes based on racism and their hyper-exploitation by employers. Apart from Pacific Islanders indentured non-European numbers remained small. Much of Australia was climatically unsuited to plantation labour and employer schemes received no official facilitation (unlike today) because unlike other British possessions like Fiji, imperial authorities designated Australia as a site for European settlement and it was feared widespread arrival of non-Europeans would undermine this. The last point was repeatedly made public especially after with the widespread arrival of Chinese. Even prior to the 1878 seamen's strike alleged instances of their depressing effect on wages in North Queensland and elsewhere were being cited not just by worker bodies like the WMDA but community-based anti-Chinese gatherings and newspapers.[227] The seamen's strike strengthened opposition. In January 1879 Melbourne unions (labourers, hatters, seamen, engineers, carpenters, stonemasons, bricklayers and ironmoulders) formed an

Anti-Chinese League (ACL), urging others (hairdressers, wharf-labourers, greengrocers and plasterers) to join.[228] Notwithstanding office-holders like Quennell and Reay from the building trades, it survived less than six months. Its successor (formed June 1880) with wider membership—bookbinders, upholsterers, furniture manufacturing employees, saddlers, shipwrights, felt hatters and coachmakers—corresponded with the NSW TLC Secretary (Roylance) and the Brisbane ACL. It persuaded a sympathetic politician (Dr Quick) to introduce restrictive legislation.[229] But it too proved short-lived.

In addition to labour market concerns the Chinese were seen to threaten an emerging 'democratic' European society. Organised labour drew on this confluence to lever politicians otherwise all too willing to do employer-bidding. Attitudes were shaped by fears the proximity of Asia with a vast population and lower living standards posed a more significant threat of labour market flooding than Europe where immigration relied on substantial passage assistance. Parallel concerns existed in North America where passage costs were less of an issue but experience of Chinese being used to undercut wages was similar. The argument that indentured non-European labour did work Europeans shunned was a convenient middle-class Furphy (an erroneous story claimed to be factual). In Australia railways were overwhelmingly built by European labour and even in North America groups like the Irish played a critical role. Today fruit-picking in many countries is done by foreign workers (including illegal immigrants and Eastern Europeans in the EU) essentially because employers prefer them for their cheapness/exploitability. Hostility to the Chinese was extreme, influenced by their use as strike-breakers and racism but part of wider context antipathy to 'Coolie' migration from anywhere—evident in a Brisbane eight-hour meeting in April 1861. Meeting chair Charles Lilley MLA (later premier) said those pursuing Polynesian legislation sought 'a modified form of slavery' but believed 'coolies' would soon be dissatisfied and demand more.[230] Lilley's predictions proved correct although dissent did little to mitigate the exploitative Pacific Island labour regime.

Organised labour's opposition to immigration should be viewed in a broader context. First, with protectionism and demands for public works it constituted a three-pronged policy to maximise jobs/labour market control. By the 1870s these prongs were integrated into 'labour' policy. Second, opposition (including many immigrants) to immigration occurred in all 'settler' societies. It was common in New Zealand during unemployment protests and other worker gatherings.[231] Intense anti-Chinese sentiment occurred in North America, especially on the west-coast where proximity/travel costs compared to Europe were closer to Australia.[232] Concerns that the European population would be swamped, and references to parallel Anti-Chinese campaigns in California, were used by the Sydney TLC in arguing its case to government ministers.[233] In 1880 a San

Francisco unemployed protester stated once the Chinese were 'cleaned out' they intended to banish capitalists and a proposal to brand convicted Chinese with a capital 'C' received 19 votes in the California Senate.[234] In North America passage assistance wasn't needed and the large influx of Irish was associated with intense exploitation and a degree of antipathy (especially in Canada) not found in Australia. Racism alone doesn't explain organised labour's attitudes to immigration or nuances like San Francisco teamsters mobilising against 'Sydney convicts' in 1850—later used by anti-transportation campaigners in Tasmania.[235] As the foregoing indicates, in 1851–1880 assisted-emigration from the UK dominated immigration protests. This was neither ethnocentric nor hypocritical but a rational worker response to their experience and an attempt to regulate labour markets more to their advantage.

A Better Legislative Apparatus

Workers organised to influence laws well before 1850 and deep hostility to punitive laws like master and servant continued, like agitation in Tasmania in 1855. The period 1851–1880 also witnessed the first concerted efforts to secure laws benefiting workers; their organisations and their communities. Examples included mine and maritime safety, eight-hour limits on engine-drivers and trade union acts already discussed which expanded in succeeding decades. Subcontracting and wage evasion were also targeted. In May 1860 Mount Barker workingmen petitioned for government action on widespread non-payment of wages by contractors building the telegraph, roads and other works.[236] The agitation led to a Truck Bill, one of a number of colonial contractor-liens/truck bills rebuffed by conservative upper-houses prior to successes from 1870. There were also repeated attempts at eight-hour day legislation. In October 1870 Sydney meetings of carpenters and joiners (chaired by William Chapman) and building trades and labourers (chaired by William Gillespie) organised petitions to the NSW Legislative Assembly urging the Eight Hour Bill be passed.[237] These were small but important steps in a regulatory push that gained momentum over time.

Giving the Working Class a Voice

Newspapers

Colonial newspapers like the *Sydney Guardian* sympathetic to workers' interests had operated since 1840, most short-lived but performing a valuable role with links to working-class activists.[238] Some unions took out subscriptions, as the Sydney Progressive Carpenters did with the *Beehive* in 1871.[239] There were repeated efforts to establish/promote pro-worker newspapers. It was amongst the first proposals considered by the Sydney TLC.[240] By the 1870s evening newspapers began that were more easily read after work, the Melbourne *Evening Tribune* proprietors requesting union support.[241] However, evening papers weren't reliable either in the tenor or coverage. The *Sydney Evening News* sparsely reported ASE member Jacob Garrard's candidature for the Working Mens Defence Association in the October 1877 election even though Garrard was a prominent public figure, including playing a leadership role in the 1873–1874 iron-trades eight hour struggle leader. Three years later things hadn't changed with the Sydney Boilermakers complaining bitterly the *Evening News* hadn't reported a single electoral meeting held by Garrard.[242] Despite this, and the TLC preferring another candidate, union support helped secure Garrard's victory in the newly created seat of Balmain. Garrard proved his worth playing a pivotal role in passing a *Trades Union Act* (1881) and *Employers' Liability Act* (1882).

Politics, Voting and Working-Class Representatives

The push for universal suffrage wasn't confined to manual workers. In an 1858 electoral address at the *Star Hotel* Frank Fowler supported his advocacy of secret ballots, stating some drapers warned their employees they would dismiss anyone voting for him because he supported the Early Closing Association.[243] To maximise voting, half-holidays on election days were promoted at both municipal and parliamentary level. In 1862 Eaglehawk Municipal candidate (Dowding) told a meeting a half-holiday for working men was proper because 'every man should have an opportunity of voting.'[244] Dowding's sentiments became more common, reinforced by attempts to manipulate workers' votes.[245] In 1870 conservative Victorian MLA John Thomas Smith sought to influence a Geelong West election by having a half-day's pay deducted from Geelong Waterworks employees who voted—the men threatened legal action.[246] Increasingly, petitions urged local government to proclaim half-holidays, or at least urge employers to grant a half-holiday on election-day. In March 1871 the *Ballarat Courier* noted proclamation of a half-holiday had decisively affected the result.[247] The half-holiday election-day push gained traction. In 1875 NSW Secretary for Public Works John Lackey told parliament Great Northern Railway workers would get a half-holiday to vote and in 1876 their Southern and Western Railway counterparts received the same privilege.[248] Half-holidays were declared for bye-elections with similar calls to aid workingmen vote in remote electorates like Leichhardt (Queensland).[249] In the Victorian 1877 elections local-governments declared half-holidays and all Geelong factories (apart from the Albion Woollen Mills) closed at noon so their employees could vote.[250] In 1878 the government declared a half-holiday for the West Melbourne bye-election 'to admit the wage-earning portion of electors.'[251] The 1880 general election was held on Saturday and a half-holiday declared, resulting in the largest poll turnout in Victorian history and a complete reversal of the 1877 results.[252] Victorian developments were important steps towards holding Australian elections on Saturday, a democratising measure still unachieved in countries like the US and the UK.

Issues of concern in working communities increasingly resonated in their electorates with working-class candidates increasingly holding sway. The Working Mens Defence Association (WMDA) campaigned against £100,000 immigration funding flooding the labour market, increasing living-costs and depressing wages.[253] With a blind president (Martin Guest), the Association's manifesto included encouraging manufacturing, preventing labour market misrepresentation, land and electoral reform, and (later) compulsory and secular education. The Association organised large protest-meetings in working-class suburbs like Balmain, Redfern and Darlinghurst, wrote to unions and coalminer's lodges and organised anti-immigration petitions/deputations in Sydney, the Hunter Valley and elsewhere.[254] The WMDA campaigned against politicians supporting immigration funding (labelled robbery and treason) and elect its own candidates like JM O'Connell and shoemaker/TLC president Thomas White at August 1877 elections.[255] The Melbourne *Leader* stated White's 'extraordinary' polling against Sir John Robertson (only 289 fewer votes) contributed to the collapse of free-trade political dominance. The Victorian Protectionist League too lauded the campaign.[256] In October 1877 the WMDA initiated a conference with delegates from the TLC, Northumberland Reform League and Free Selectors Associations in an unsuccessful attempt to build a wider political alliance.[257]

The October 1877 election was marked by fierce campaigning no more so than in Newcastle where the WMDA was accused of banning retailers failing to support the cause.[258] The WMDA failed to elect candidates but was reconciled by the defeat of Robertson, Parkes and other pro-immigration politicians.[259] At an East Sydney meeting MLA John Davies (ex-ironmonger and blacksmith) pledged support for eight-hours, referring to his success getting City Council workers a half-holiday. Unionist Francis Dixon, another candidate, strongly advocated local manufacturing. Davies was re-elected with the second highest vote.[260] Dixon failed but so did Henry Parkes, also punished for his failure to legislate eight hours. A December move to reorganise as the NSW Political Reform Association (with Davies as president) degenerated into an acrimonious split, one group retaining the title.[261] The WMDA continued advocating trade unionism, extended polling-times to assist working-class voters, abolishing imprisonment for debt, restricting immigration (and banning Chinese), removing obsequious language from petitions, reforming the undemocratic Legislative Council and making common-cause with Victoria on protectionism.[262] Notwithstanding its failure the WMDA was a lightning rod for working-class political mobilisation challenging ruling elite politics—its activities extensively reported throughout Australia. Revelling in its working-class credentials, the WMDA was a labourist-political party promoting policies that within 15 years became core to labour leagues and ultimately the Australian Labor Party. Similar efforts were being made in the US, several adopting the name Labor Party well before Australia. However, these efforts ultimately failed.

Conclusion

Colonial workers mobilised politically from the early 1830s, almost contiguously with unionisation, and these two dimensions grew and interacted over succeeding decades. Colonial unions were drawn to politics by the prominent economic role of government and to counter employers' influence (particularly on immigration). There was a strong impetus to form wider alliances, over 200 peak/political bodies forming in 1851–1880. Over 60% were formal but informal mobilisations, especially by the unemployed, exerted significant political influence— something largely overlooked by historians and reinforcing the need to consider all organisational forms. The most critical issues were jobs/ unemployment, community welfare/poverty, legislation and assisted European immigration along with eight-hours, central to the formation of trades hall/trades and labour councils. While peak union bodies became the conduit for collaborative industrial and political action including the formation of the Australian Labor Party this chapter identified considerable organisational experimentation. Incorporating this complexity affords a more compelling understanding of the interests, activities and conflicts that shaped the organisations and policies of the 20th-century Australian labour movement. It also explains why the 'aristocracy of labour' thesis has little relevance to Australian worker mobilisation.

Notes

1. ML MSS308 Operatives Board of Trade Minutes 23 October 1858.
2. *Launceston Examiner* 24 September 1851.
3. *South Australian Advertiser* 28 March 1879; *Evening Journal* 6 May 1879.
4. E107-1-1 ASE Adelaide Minutes 17 April 1875.
5. *Argus* 1 May 1872.
6. *Melbourne Herald* 15 June 1874.
7. *Argus* 4 September, 25 November 1874, 9 April, 6 June 1875.
8. *Geelong Advertiser* 28 April 1856; *Empire* 8 November, 22 December 1856.
9. *Mount Alexander Mail* 11 November 1859.
10. *Argus* 7, 22 October, 15 November, 2 December 1859, 12 March 1860.
11. *Argus* 18 November 1859.
12. T8-2A-1 VOBS Melbourne Minutes 11 May 1856; T8-2A-3 VOBS Melbourne Minutes 12 May, 18 August 1873; E235-2 Sydney United Plasterers Minutes 26 November 1877.

13. E117-39 Victorian Stonemasons Collingwood Minutes 20 March, 10 April 1860; ML MSS THLI Minutes 4 March 1870; MUA VTHC Minutes 3 April 1874; Z291-17-2 NSW Bricklayer Management Committee Minutes 2 February, 3, 18, 19, 25 April 1877; T8-2A-4 VOBS Melbourne Minutes 18 April 1878.
14. *Ballarat Star* 20 April 1880.
15. E107-1-1 ASE Adelaide Minutes 5 July 1878.
16. MUA Victorian Trades Hall Council Minutes 4 October 1874.
17. ML MSS308 Box 6 Eight Hour Anniversary Committee Minutes 1 May 1873; *Telegraph* 20 June 1874; *Melbourne Herald* 21 December 1874; *Ballarat Star* 12 April 1875.
18. *Brisbane Telegraph* 23 May 1876.
19. *Evening Journal* 18, 22 February 1879.
20. *Bendigo Advertiser* 10 May 1879.
21. *Star* 10 July 1862.
22. *Ballarat Star* 25 November 1869; ML MSS308 THLI Minutes 18 March 1870.
23. *Argus* 8, 19 June 1869; *South Bourke Standard* 11 June 1869; *Mount Alexander Mail* 9 October 1869, 22 March 1870.
24. *Mount Alexander Mail* 4 February 1871; *Geelong Advertiser* 27 February 1871.
25. Z291-17-1 NSW Bricklayers Sydney Minutes 28 June 1870; ML MSS2074 Item 45 NSW Eight Hour Extension and General Short Hours League Minutes 14 April 1870; Noble, R. (1999) The Hunter Valley's Eight-Hour Movement and Its Connection with the First Newcastle Trades and Labour Council, 1869–1886, *Illawarra Unity*, 2(1): 45–55.
26. ML MSS2074 Item 45 NSW Eight Hour System and General Short Hours League Minutes 21, 28 October, 18 November 1869; *Newcastle Chronicle* 3 September 1870.
27. *Newcastle Chronicle* 7 December 1869; *South Bourke Standard* 13 June 1873.
28. ML MSS2074 Item 45 NSW Eight Hour System and General Short Hours League Minutes 24 March 1870.
29. ML MSS2074 Item 45 NSW Eight Hour System and General Short Hours League Minutes 16 December 1869, 16 December 1870, 2 February 1871.
30. A2795 Sydney Progressive Carpenters Minutes 27 March 1871.
31. Z291-17-1 NSW Bricklayers Sydney Minutes 24 June 1873.
32. Nairn, B. (1972) Dixon, Francis Burdett (1836–1884), in *Australian Dictionary of Biography*, Vol. 4, Melbourne University Press, Melbourne.
33. ML MSS2074 Item 45 NSW Eight Hour System and General Short Hours League Minutes 5, 19 May, 9 June 1870.
34. ML 331.88IT Miller, J.J. (1878) Rules of the Trades Hall and Literary Institute Committee, Melbourne.
35. Balance Sheet of Trades' Hall Committee for quarter ended 19 March 1875; T8-2A-3 VOBS Melbourne Minutes 20 December 1875.
36. ML MSS308 THLI Minutes 21 September 1860, 4, 11, 25 October 1867, 3 April 1868, 6, 13 August 1869.
37. ML MSS308 Box 2 Operatives Board of Trade Minutes 17 March, 7 April, 14 July, 4, 5, 18 August 1859.
38. T8-2A-2 VOBS Minutes 1, 15 August 1859; ML MSS308 Box 2 Operatives Board of Trade Minutes 22, 29 September 1859.
39. T8-2A-3 VOBS Melbourne Minutes 19 August, 23 September, 14 October 1872.

40. ML MSS308 THLI Minutes 3 October 1872; T8-2A-3 VOBS Melbourne Minutes 11 May 1874.
41. *Empire* 18 November 1856.
42. Z291-17-1 NSW Bricklayers Sydney Minutes 14 March 1871.
43. *Sydney Morning Herald* 19 July 1876, 30 May, 15 December 1877, 12 February 1878.
44. *Sydney Morning Herald* 5 May, 20 September 1877, 15 January, 19 April 1879; *Evening News* 8 March 1878.
45. *Sydney Daily Telegraph* 24 December 1880.
46. E92-1-1 South Australian Typographical Society Minutes 24 June, 29 July, 12 August, 9, 16, 30 September, 11 October 1876.
47. ML MF IP80 Rules for the government of the Labor League of South Australia, being a revised code of rules by a committee elected for that purpose by the various branches of the United Tradesmens Society and finally adopted by them as a new constitution, 5–6, 7–8.
48. *Evening Journal* 22 September 1879; *Hamilton Spectator* 6 November 1880; *South Australian Register* 4 April, 22 August 1879, 27 November 1880.
49. *Queenslander* 29 February 1868.
50. *Brisbane Telegraph* 23 June 1873, 24 May, 29 June 1875, 23 March, 23 May 1876.
51. ML MLK00049 Sydney Shipwrights Minutes 5 August 1880.
52. MUA Sydney Painters Minutes 2 September 1874, 2 June 1875.
53. ML MSS2422 1(7) Sydney Boilermakers Minutes 14 November 1876, 25 May 1880; ML MLK00049 Sydney Shipwrights Minutes 20 May, 10 June 1880.
54. ML MSS2422 1(7) Sydney Boilermakers Minutes 25 November 1879.
55. ML MLK00049 Sydney Shipwrights Minutes 4 March, 3 June 1875.
56. ML MSS2422 1(7) Sydney Boilermakers Minutes 26 October, 23 November 1880.
57. MUA Sydney Painters Minutes 8 March, 30 July, 14 August 1876, 19 April 1880.
58. A2795 Sydney Progressive Carpenters Minutes 19 January 1880; ML MSS2422 1(7) Sydney Boilermakers Minutes 28 October 1879.
59. *Sydney Morning Herald* 4 October 1878.
60. *Empire* 8 December 1874.
61. T46-1-3 NSW Stonemasons Sydney Minutes 17 June, 1 July, 17, 24 September, 30 November, 28 December 1874, 11 January 1875, 3, 17, 31 May, 14 June, 12 July 1875; ML MLK00049 Sydney Shipwrights Minutes 24 June 1875; A2795 Sydney Progressive Society of Carpenters Minutes 10, 24 August 1874, 26 July 1875; MUA Sydney Painters Minutes 17 June, 9 September 1874; ML MSS7614 1(1) Sydney Boilermakers Minutes 25 January 1875.
62. Z102-4-1 ASE Balmain Minutes 22 November 1880.
63. T46-1-3 NSW Stonemasons Sydney Minutes 23 August 1875.
64. ML MLK00049 Sydney Shipwrights Minutes 3 July 1867.
65. *Newcastle Herald* 8 October 1879.
66. *Evening News* 5 August 1880.
67. McKinlay, B. (1979) *Australian Labour History in Documents*, Vol. 3, Collins Dove, Melbourne, 7, 506.
68. E117-2-2 Victorian Stonemasons Central Committee Minutes 28 April 1859.
69. *Mercury* 28 March 1859; *Portland Guardian* 23 May 1859; *South Australian Advertiser* 11 July 1859.
70. McKinlay, B. (1979) *Australian Labour History in Documents*, Vol. 2, Collins Dove, Melbourne, 7.

71. *Colonial Times* 9 February 1841; *Hobarton Guardian* 14 February 1849.
72. *Hobart Courier* 7 May 1855, 2 July 1856.
73. *Age* 23 September, 15 December 1856; *Williamstown Chronicle* 9 May 1857.
74. *Argus* 10 December 1856; *Armidale Express* 22 May 1869.
75. *Age* 15 September 1857.
76. *Ballarat Star* 12 September 1857; *Age* 31 October 1857.
77. *Age* 19 October 1857.
78. *Bendigo Advertiser* 18, 23 June 1858.
79. *Melbourne Herald* 10 October 1861; *Mount Alexander Mail* 9, 11 July 1862.
80. *Maitland Mercury* 30 April, 2 June 1857, 25 December 1860.
81. *Sydney Morning Herald* 23 April 1858.
82. *South Australian Advertiser* 12 April 1859.
83. *Geelong Advertiser* 2 September 1859.
84. *South Australian Advertiser* 26 November 1861.
85. *Adelaide Express* 30 June 1866; *South Australian Register* 24 August 1867.
86. *Inquirer* 22 October 1862; *West Australian Times* 28 July 1864; *Argus* 1 August 1864.
87. *Perth Gazette* 10 February 1865; *Launceston Examiner* 10 June 1865; *Inquirer* 6 February 1867; *Tasmanian Times* 29 June 1867; *South Australian Register* 3 April 1868; *Fremantle Herald* 2 July 1870; *South Australian Chronicle* 2 December 1871.
88. *Perth Gazette* 14 November 1873, 1 May 1874.
89. *Sydney Mail* 27 May 1871; ML Q320.994/47 Pinkston, J. Address to the Working-Classes of NSW in Connection to the Formation of a League for the Protection of Their Interests Both in the Social and Political Movement of Our Time, 1 June 1871.
90. *Argus* 10 February 1874.
91. *Argus* 8 June 1880.
92. *Leader* 1 April 1871; *Melbourne Herald* 15 April 1871; *Brisbane Courier* 1 January 1874.
93. *Brisbane Telegraph* 29 November 1875, 29 January 1876.
94. *Mackay Mercury* 12 December 1877; *Daily Northern Argus* 27 November 1878.
95. ML Q320.994/47 Address to the Working-Classes in the Colony of NSW, 1 June 1870; *Empire* 12 December 1870, 6 March 1871.
96. *Singleton Argus* 15 September 1875.
97. *Mercury* 31 October 1864; *Armidale Express* 1 September 1866.
98. *Portland Guardian* 8 August 1876; *Argus* 16 June 1877.
99. *Evening Journal* 25 April 1877.
100. The Goulburn Church of England Working Mens Association was a rare exception, *Goulburn Herald* 29 October 1873.
101. *Advocate* 21 March 1874.
102. *South Australian Register* 28 December 1864.
103. McKinlay, *Australian Labour History in Documents*, Vol. 3, 8–9.
104. *Warwick Argus* 24 June 1875.
105. *Express and Telegraph* 30 July 1878.
106. *Express and Telegraph* 7 September 1878.
107. *Ballarat Star* 3 April 1878.
108. *Telegraph* 18 February 1878.
109. *South Australian Register* 3 September 1878.
110. *Bacchus Marsh Express* 11 February 1871.
111. *Mercury* 5 June 1866; *Launceston Examiner* 9 August 1870; *Brisbane Telegraph* 23 May 1876.

112. *Ballarat Courier* 17 November 1877.
113. Day and Martin were a shoe-blacking manufacturer, *Western Independent* reproduced in the *Toowoomba Chronicle and Queensland Advertiser* 18 November 1874.
114. As one shopkeeper lamented *Bendigo Advertiser* 23 May 1873.
115. *Maitland Mercury* 23 December 1848.
116. *South Australian Register* 8 August 1849.
117. *South Australian Register* 29 September 1851.
118. *Adelaide Times* 1 October 1851.
119. *Geelong Advertiser* 20 October 1851.
120. *South Australian Register* 4 October 1854.
121. *Geelong Advertiser* 4 October 1854.
122. *Age* 7, 11 November 1854.
123. *Age* 24 November 1854.
124. *Age* 7 June 1855.
125. *Geelong Advertiser* 10, 11, 17, 20 July 1855.
126. *Argus* 14 August 1855.
127. *Moreton Bay Courier* 8 March 1856.
128. *Hobart Courier* 10 August 1857.
129. *Age* 14 August 1857.
130. *Cornwall Chronicle* 19 August 1857; *Age* 24 October 1857.
131. *Age* 24 August 1857.
132. *Age* 24 September, 20 October 1857.
133. *Portland Guardian* 9 November 1857.
134. Reproduced in *Goulburn Herald* 19 September 1857; *Ovens and Murray Advertiser* 23 March 1858.
135. *Empire* 29 March, 19 April 1858; *Ovens and Murray Advertiser* 3 April 1858.
136. *Bendigo Advertiser* 19 June 1858; *Sydney Morning Herald* 1 March 1859.
137. *Age* 5 April 1858.
138. *Sydney Morning Herald* 23 April, 24 June 1858.
139. *Empire* 27 April 1858.
140. *South Australian Advertiser* 22, 23 September, 9 October 1858.
141. *South Australian Register* 8 May 1858.
142. *South Australian Weekly Chronicle* 2 October 1858.
143. *South Australian Register* 11 October 1858.
144. *South Australian Advertiser* 9 October 1858.
145. *Launceston Examiner* 20 November 1858.
146. *Armidale Express* 19 March 1859; *South Australian Advertiser* 3 September 1860; *South Australian Register* 11 May 1860; *Victorian Farmers Journal* 4 August 1860; *Maitland Mercury* 9 February 1861.
147. *Age* 25 January 1859.
148. *Mount Alexander Mail* 31 January, 4 February 1859.
149. *Age* 14 February 1858.
150. *Maitland Mercury* 8 March 1859.
151. *South Australian Advertiser* 12 April 1859.
152. *Adelaide Observer* 14 May 1859.
153. *Age* 29 October 1860.
154. *Goulburn Herald* 28 May 1859.
155. *Geelong Advertiser* 6 October 1859.
156. *South Australian Advertiser* 28 May 1860.
157. *Empire* 7 June 1860.
158. *Sydney Morning Herald* 24 May 1860.

159. *Empire* 12, 17 May 1860.
160. NSW Legislative Council, NSW Legislative Assembly Select Committee on the Condition of the Working-Classes of the Metropolis Report, *Proceedings: Minutes of Evidence and Appendix*, Government Printer, Sydney, 19 April 1860, 6, 13, 128, 162–63.
161. *Empire* 12 January 1864; *Sydney Morning Herald* 30 September 1865; *Mercury* 9 November 1865; *South Australian Register* 18 July 1866; *Brisbane Courier* 24 July 1866; *Maryborough Chronicle* 25 July 1866; *Portland Guardian* 24 September 1868.
162. *Age* 2 February 1866.
163. *Maitland Mercury* 18 October 1866.
164. *South Australian Register* 31 July 1866.
165. *Northern Argus* 13 August 1866.
166. *Darling Downs Gazette* 21 August 1866.
167. *Queensland Times* 11 October 1866.
168. Wilson, P. (1971) The Brisbane Riot of September 1866, *Queensland Heritage*, 2(4): 14–20.
169. *Queenslander* 1 September 1866; *Brisbane Courier* 19 October 1866.
170. *Kapunda Herald* 14 June 1867; *South Australian Register* 15 August 1867.
171. *Wallaroo Times* 31 July 1867; *South Australian Register* 5 August 1867.
172. *South Australian Register* 21 August 1867.
173. *Mercury* 7, 15 November 1867.
174. *Kapunda Herald* 17 January 1868.
175. *Maitland Mercury* 9 June 1868; *Maryborough Chronicle* 21 April 1868; *Star* 25 August 1868.
176. *Cornwall Chronicle* 14 August 1869; *Evening Journal* 18 November 1869; *South Australian Advertiser* 10 January 1870.
177. *Adelaide Observer* 19 March 1870.
178. Probably the same William Jennett later involved in the Working Mens Defence Association. *Evening News* 12 April 1870; *Empire* 29 June 1870; *Geelong Advertiser* 18 July 1870; *Tasmanian Times* 1 October 1870.
179. *Mercury* 4 October 1870; *Melbourne Herald* 10 October 1870.
180. *Empire* 21 October 1870.
181. *Melbourne Herald* 25 October 1870; *Age* 8 November 1870; *Argus* 31 July 1879.
182. *Hamilton Spectator* 7 June 1873.
183. *Adelaide Observer* 5 April 1873.
184. *Queenslander* 7 April 1877; *Wallaroo Times* 7 December 1877; *Maryborough Chronicle* 24 July 1877; *South Australian Advertiser* 13 October 1877.
185. *Yorke's Peninsular Advertiser* 26 April 1878.
186. *Melbourne Herald* 20 May, 12 June 1878; *Bendigo Advertiser* 8 June 1878; *Hamilton Spectator* 8 June 1878; *Gippsland Times* 6 September 1878.
187. *Argus* 21 May 1878; *Bendigo Advertiser* 15 June 1878; *Mercury and Weekly Courier* 13 July 1878.
188. *Argus* 9 July 1879.
189. *Melbourne Herald* 16 September 1878.
190. *Age* 27 January 1879.
191. *Bendigo Advertiser* 5 April, 10 May, 11 June, 24 July 1879.
192. *Age* 18 July 1879.
193. *Riverine Herald* 15 January 1878, 28 June 1879.
194. *Argus* 25 August 1879.
195. *Riverine Herald* 18 April 1880; *Bendigo Advertiser* 7 May 1880.
196. *Border Watch* 28 August 1880.
197. *Adelaide Observer* 23 July 1859.

198. *Tasmanian Times* 4 October 1870.
199. *Lloyds Weekly London Newspaper* 27 June 1858; *South Australian Advertiser* 21 June 1859.
200. *Geelong Advertiser* 23 July 1855; *Adelaide Observer* 18 August 1855; *Argus* 26 July 1860, 15 June 1870, 31 October 1871; *North Australian* 7 February 1865; *Bendigo Advertiser* 16 August 1872.
201. *Age* 24 July 1860.
202. *Wallaroo Times* 14 June 1879.
203. *Sydney Daily Telegraph* 28 July 1879; *Sydney Morning Herald* 2 February 1880.
204. *Geelong Advertiser* 10 February 1880.
205. *Telegraph, St Kilda, Prahran and South Yarra Guardian* 6 July 1878.
206. *Melbourne Herald* 21 May 1878; Quinlan, M. (2012) The 'Pre-Invention' of Precarious Employment: The Changing World of Work in Context, *The Economic and Labour Relations Review*, 23(4): 3–24.
207. *Sydney Morning Herald* 3 February 1864.
208. *Empire* 5 December 1866; *Age* 10 December 1866.
209. *Kapunda Herald* 28 June 1867.
210. *Australian Town and Country Journal* 25 May 1878.
211. *Sydney Daily Telegraph* 9 January 1880; *Maitland Mercury* 2 March 1880.
212. *Bacchus Marsh Express* 11 February 1871; *Age* 21 March 1874.
213. See *Melbourne Herald* 20 May 1878; *Argus* 15 September 1878; *Bendigo Advertiser* 24 June 1879.
214. *Age* 10 June, 2 August 1879; *Argus* 11 June 1879.
215. *Brisbane Telegraph* 24 May 1879, 5 April 1880.
216. *Argus* 25 January 1862; *Empire* 30 July 1862; *Launceston Examiner* 25 September 1862.
217. *South Australian Register* 28 October 1858; *Geelong Advertiser* 6 October 1859.
218. *Argus* 7 May 1860.
219. *Maitland Mercury* 9 June 1877.
220. ML MLK00049 Sydney Shipwrights Minutes 8 January, 5, 9, 19 February 1880.
221. *Sydney Morning Herald* 7 June 1880.
222. *Adelaide Observer* 22 November 1873.
223. *Maryborough Chronicle* 27 November 1862.
224. *Queenslander* 5 October 1872.
225. *Hamilton Spectator* 18 April 1874.
226. MUA Melbourne Typographical Society Minutes 2 July 1870.
227. *Australian Town and Country Journal* 24 August 1878.
228. ML MSS308 Box 8 Anti-Chinese League Minutes 10 January, 28 February 1879.
229. ML MSS308 Box 8 Victorian Anti-Chinese League Minutes 10, 17 June, 19 August, 16 December 1880.
230. *Moreton Bay Courier* 13 April 1861.
231. *Sydney Mail* 26 June 1880.
232. Price, C. (1974) *The Great White Walls Are Built: Restrictive Immigration to North America and Australasia 1836–1888*, Australian National University Press, Canberra.
233. *Australian Town and Country Journal* 31 August 1878.
234. *Australasian* 26 June 1880.
235. *Colonial Times* 11 October 1850.
236. *South Australian Register* 11 May 1860.
237. *Australian Town and Country Journal* 22 October 1870.

238. Irving, T. (2006) *The Southern Tree of Liberty: The Democratic Movement in New South Wales Before 1856*, Federation Press, Sydney.
239. A2795 Sydney Progressive Carpenters Minutes 14 August 1871.
240. ML MLK Sydney Shipwrights Minutes 3 August 1871; Z291-17-1 NSW Bricklayers Sydney Minutes 27 June 1871, 8 July 1880; T46-4 NSW Stonemasons Central Committee Minutes 7 July, 4 August 1871.
241. T8-2A-3 VOBS Melbourne Minutes 13 April 1874.
242. ML MSS2422 1(7) Sydney Boilermakers Minutes 23 November 1880.
243. *Freeman's Journal* 9 January 1858.
244. *Bendigo Advertiser* 2 September 1862.
245. *Star* 2 November 1864; *Bendigo Advertiser* 12 August 1865.
246. *Bendigo Advertiser* 23 March 1870.
247. *Ballarat Star* 16 March 1871.
248. *Maitland Mercury* 31 July 1875, 6 June 1876.
249. *Western Star* 9 February 1878; *Daily Northern Argus* 17 October 1878.
250. *Geelong Advertiser* 12 May 1877.
251. *Bendigo Advertiser* 9 April 1878.
252. *Camperdown Chronicle* 2 March 1880.
253. *Evening News* 14 June 1877.
254. *New South Wales Government Gazette* 10 August 1877.
255. *Evening News* 17, 18 August 1877.
256. *Leader* 8 September 1877.
257. *Sydney Morning Herald* 16, 17 October 1877.
258. *Mercury* 15 November 1877.
259. *Newcastle Herald* 7 November 1877.
260. *Australian Town and Country Journal* 27 October 1877, 5 January 1878.
261. *Sydney Morning Herald* 18, 19 January 1878.
262. *Maitland Mercury* 4 April 1878; *Sydney Daily Telegraph* 29 July, 4 November 1879, 11 May 1880.

12 Concluding Observations

Research on worker mobilisation consists of disparate strands, earlier studies focusing on formal organisation giving way to studies of informal networks/alliances, wider social movements and more recently research into organising methods and mobilisation amongst precarious workers, notably immigrants. Attempts to reconcile these disparate strands into an overarching analysis are rare.[1] Identifying worker organisation may grow through increased membership of existing unions; or the formation of new organisations has value but must be placed in historical context, including relationships with informal organisation and issues pivotal to that shift not just recruitment techniques. In 1851–1880 worker mobilisation primarily occurred through new bodies but this shift didn't occur in a void. Informal organisation, the major venue of collective action by workers in 1788–1840, slowly gave way to unions led by tradesmen and followed by labourers, miners, seamen, transport workers, retail-workers, dockworkers and shearers. The shift wasn't uniform, with thousands of workers were still combining informally in 1870s.

Worker mobilisation can also be understood in terms of layers of resistance/organisation. *The Origins of Worker Mobilisation* identified four layers of worker resistance, namely individual resistance often drawing on informal norms; informal workplace-based collective action; informal multi-workplace/regional alliances; and formal organisation predominantly occupation-based. To this must be added a fifth layer (present before 1851), namely wider alliances pursuing peak union and political roles, the latter splitting into a sixth layer of worker political parties. These layers were transitional in the development of worker mobilisation and class consciousness although far more complex than a simple linear progression. Each stage up allowed workers to pursue a wider array of issues and deploy different methods and strategies. This is not a transition from resistance to organisation. Resistance remains integral to worker organisation, including tensions/pressures for renewal/reshaping organisational forms and strategies from below. One illustration of this was the rise of syndicalism and workshop organisation/rank and file revolts against bureaucratic union leaderships in Europe, North America and Australasia during the early 20th century. Today similar tensions play out as rank and file workers and even unions revolt against political parties they formed over a century earlier, now dominated by a careerist/pseudo-globalist middle-class leadership abetting the emiseration of working communities by pursuing the impossibility of neoliberalism 'light.'[2]

Patterns of worker mobilisation in Australia 1851–1880 share parallels with developments elsewhere requiring serious re-examination. Even colonial newspapers copiously reported similar developments in Europe and North America. Migration was a transmission belt for ideas and organisational experiences amongst workers—some recent, some centuries old—and the same applied to capital, as the colonies were integral to the global economy. The period also witnessed changes to transport (steamships, railways) and communication (telegraph) that accelerated information flows and networking.

As elsewhere, patterns of organisation (and differences between then) were influenced by particularities of colonial political economies (like political structures, role of the state/laws, industry-mix), labour markets (Australia's historical reliance on convicts can be contrasted with the US's greater reliance on slavery) and imperialism. Nonetheless, workers were active agents shaping organisation and its objectives. The eight-hour day idea originated in the UK but Australian and New Zealand workers pioneered its implementation. Colonial unions were more hostile to piecework than their UK counterparts. Higher colonial wage levels made piecework less seductive but more critically undermined efforts to reduce working hours. Having said this, the distinctiveness of national patterns of worker mobilisation requires more critical and systematic examination. The Knights of Labor were not so much evidence of American Exceptionalism (organisation spread to Britain/Ireland and Australia) as an example of wider forms of organisation being tried by workers.[3] This book identified other similarly broad bodies in Australia and they are likely to be found elsewhere. At the same time craft-exclusionism was stronger in the US. Whether this was simply a strategic choice or linked to the more violent resistance of capital or the violence generally found in ex-slave societies (see Brazil) is a moot point.

This book contributes to understanding worker mobilisation by examining a wide array of organisations and their interactions. The period witnessed a proliferation of organisations and organisational forms. Preoccupied with manual workers the Webb's identified two predominant union types—new model craft unions and new unionism—composed of employees. The largely unchallenged result was that organisation amongst groups like clerks, teachers and government workers was traced from the late 19th/early 20th century—with them slowly taking more unionate form. This book demonstrates these depictions were misleading and mobilisation entailed a wide group of workers from an early period.

This included associations predominantly composed of self-employed workers in road transport (cabdrivers and carters) and mining. At a broader level there were peak bodies like the United Tradesmen's Society, Labor Leagues, Eight Hour Day Leagues, Short Hours Leagues, Operative Boards of Trade as well as Trades Hals/Labour Councils that eventually emerged as the dominant peak-body type.

The proliferation of organisations and organisational forms in 1851–1880 represented an arguably critical phase in worker mobilisation, entailing both complexity and volatility. Comparisons between social and natural history are fraught given the immense time-scale difference that, unlike Darwinian natural selection, human organisation entails Lamarckian evolution (learned traits passed on) and biological evolution divergences whereas social evolution often involves convergence and exchange/borrowing. Gould noted homo-sapiens are a minor twig in a much bigger bush and we should not acquaint our arrival as indicating any culmination or directional logic in evolution. Nonetheless, Gould argued there are parallels worth considering, notably that both biological evolution and social evolution/human technologies do not dictate optimality for survival (the QWERTY keyboard layout is but one example).[4] Models presuming optimisation as a natural state, like utility maximisation and market stability notions beloved by neoliberal economists, represent a deeply flawed understanding of human society. The notion of punctuated biological evolution or long periods of stasis interrupted by relatively rapid bouts of evolution pioneered by Gould may have more value when considered in an organisational context. In 1851–1880 and arguably longer, worker organisation was diverse and volatile— few surviving over a decade. Viewed from the long-term perspective of worker mobilisation stretching back over 700 years this period might be characterised as one of experimentation and relatively rapid evolution. Consistent with natural history methods, Thompson argued we need to examine the totality of worker organisation, ideas and agency—including perceived failures if we are to understand worker mobilisation and class formation. Viewing worker organisation only in terms of organisational types that were seen to survive or dominate is partial, ahistorical as Thompson suggests, and misleading because it presumes an overarching shift to optimal forms—note the re-emergence of informal or wider social alliances in the wake of neoliberalism.

The book examined many 'failed' organisations that weren't entirely unsuccessful nor were their objectives and methods inappropriate. The Eight Hour Leagues for example were especially influential, carrying over into the 20th century, if progressively a shadow of what they had been. Some organisations responded to a particular phase of the capitalism/labour process like those representing self-employed workers (but note its return!), or reflected the needs/ambitions of workers in particular occupations (like mutual-improvement/professionalisation amongst teachers). In organisational ecology small and newly formed bodies are vulnerable to any significant challenge but, as the previous sentence indicates, the evolution of worker organisation is more complicated than this. Some self-employed miners' organisations (not all) encountered internal schisms in terms of their objectives reflecting contradictions in their relationship to capitalism. Organisational turnover facilitated refashioning bodies to address schisms like this although some bodies evolved internally. Judging organisation from the perspective of those surviving well into the 20th century provides a stilted understanding.

Relating the foregoing to notions of union power, several points can be made. Summarising much pre-existing literature on the subject, Lehndorff et al. identified four sources of union power: structural power, organisational power, institutional power and societal power.[5] This book identified all four sources. Structural power was most evident in craft unions although strategically located unions in maritime and mining also used it along with organisational power. Institutional power was limited though fitfully growing. Finally, societal power was central for many, especially in hour-related campaigns. Public demonstrations were pivotal alongside growing political mobilisation, reinforced on occasion by informal action.

Mobilisation Points and Issues

The foregoing discussion connects to other insights about worker mobilisation. Declining union membership globally over the past 40 years sparked renewed interest in how unions organise and ways to mobilise vulnerable groups through community alliances. This literature is largely ahistorical and de-contextualised, ignoring past parallels and lessons to be drawn from this. The starting point needs to be a historically informed understanding of capitalism and the labour process. Capitalism remains essentially a three-trick pony endlessly recycling these strategies to extract a surplus from labour, namely:

- Work intensification—working harder within a given time-span via performance pay etc.
- Work extensification via longer hours, pseudo self-employment (subcontracting, franchising and home-based labour)
- Expanding labour that can be drawn upon to increase competition (like the young, the old, immigrants and temporary workers).

These strategies are not mutually exclusive and are used in different combinations across the economy and within particular industries. Technology is a tool, facilitating shifts toward one strategy like closely supervised factory production (with Taylorism and Fordism) in the late 19th and early 20th and more recently greater use of outsourcing/ subcontracting taking advantage of digital surveillance/control technologies and enhanced transport coordinating elaborate supply chains. Once this is recognised, the use of digital technologies to intensify work, reversal of the decline in working hours, renewed growth of informal and precarious work, unprecedented global migration (including temporary workers), global supply chains (essentially subcontracting on steroids) and gig-work (largely entailing app-enabled subcontracting) becomes more comprehensible. So what is the role of the state in this? The state performs a central role allocating social power and resources. Historically, the state-facilitated rise of capitalism by subordinating labour from 14th century onwards through laws/courts and shifting labour globally through slavery, indenturing and convict transportation. Workers pushed back, their influence peaking with the post Second World War Keynesian Accord. However, from the mid-1970s governments have facilitated the rise of neoliberalism, undermining more than a century of slowly built protective infrastructure, renewing highly exploitative labour practices (like subcontracting), eroding collectivist industrial relations and the welfare state, resulting inevitably in heightened levels of inequality. Reversing these socially harmful policies is not only possible but essential for sustainable society.

This book examined an important historical point when organised labour began to seriously challenge capital's modes of work and labour markets. In the century after 1850 organised labour wrought substantial changes, including regulating hours, wages and working conditions, building the welfare state in advanced industrial countries and making them richer in the process by spreading income sufficient to significantly lift consumption. Neoliberalism, a return to more unfettered capitalism favouring the rich and powerful and weakening labour, has been marked by growing precarious work/job insecurity and stagnating wages, producing rising income/wealth inequality not only in the 'old' industrial countries, but elsewhere including Asia, notwithstanding its economic growth.[6] These consequences were entirely predictable. Indeed, surviving 'New Deal'-era economists did so.[7] We witness a rise of authoritarian states and corrosion of democracies (corrupted by corporate interests and the selling-out by social-democrat/Labor parties), unions undermined, and protective legislation has been cutback (as 'red tape'), bypassed or simply evaded, leading to growing calls to refashion labour law.[8] However much Davos attendees sniff into their teas and the OECD tries to put a positive spin on things, rising inequality is the norm for capitalism. As such, it is not only inherently unstable, but incompatible with building a sustainable global society that addresses over-population, resource depletion, environmental degradation and climate change. These problems aren't a coincidental 'perfect storm' but closely interlinked and so are the remedies.

Issue-Based Mobilisation

Mobilisation is not simply about organisational forms, strategies or tactics, but something intimately connected to issues and their 'selection' may result in different trajectories of mobilisation. What made short-hour movements so critical is that they not only redistributed work to maximise jobs/increased wages but provided a basis for campaigning/organising encompassing all workers and where the entire community could benefit. Large eight-hour and early-closing demonstrations become more comprehensible in this light—affirming community support orchestrated by organised labour. Shorter hours didn't entail some workers gaining at others' expense (as with craft restrictions), especially if problems of payment/shopping times could be reconciled—as they ultimately were. The alliance and mutual support between various streams of the short-hour movement was a major but largely forgotten achievement securing leisure time, not least the beginning of the weekend. In 1885 Victoria initiated the mandating of trading hours, providing a critical legislative control, but one built on campaigns stretching back decades. The eight-hour movement has rightly received considerable attention from Australian labour historians although they haven't charted the interaction of informal and formal organisations (as this book did), the web of organisations involved or the concerted push for legislation. Further, ignoring other short-hour streams has resulted in a partial account of struggles that mobilised so many workers. Australian unions weren't the first to see the mobilising potential of working hours—the early 1830s ten-hour campaign in UK being a prime example. The parallel hour campaigns in Australia, Europe and North America after 1850 warrant systematic investigation, exploring both similarities and why some outcomes differed.

A mobilising issue with wider community benefits largely lost to history was health, now being rediscovered in campaigns for minimum staffing levels in hospitals and nursing homes and establishing minimum pay for contractors/supply chain regulation. The hours and health interconnections so well understood in the past are also being rediscovered. Shortening 'full-time' working hours would make a more tangible contribution to work/life balance (so much publicly extolled so little seriously pursued), improve health/wellbeing and the capacity for more community engagement. Restructuring work to minimise adverse OHS effects remains as relevant today as 150 years ago.

Another mobilisation point requires comment. Like hours, struggles to restrict immigration, including indentured labour, could draw working communities together, and many other elements of colonial society too when it came to the Chinese, epitomised by the 1878 seamen's strike. Organised labour's concerns about immigration weren't unfounded. Capital secured active state financial support to boost European immigration to increase labour supply and their control, while some sought what they viewed as more readily subordinated labour from Asia and the Pacific Islands. Though now unfashionable with historians, campaigns to restrict immigration aided worker mobilisation, forming one of the three planks of the federation accord (immigration restriction, arbitration and protectionism) while the US labour movement began to make further progress when it managed to restrict immigration in the 1920s.[9]

A century later a wave of global migration (1946–1975), including large numbers moving within Europe and from Europe to North America and Australia, didn't undermine wages and working conditions, promoting notions of 'multiculturalism' and universal benefits from migration. However, there were historically contingent reasons for these outcomes, which coincided with the long post-war boom dominated by Keynesian full-employment and wealth/income redistributive policies (including progressive taxation and the welfare state), unions at their most influential, a robust manufacturing sector and pronounced growth in labour's share of national income. That much of Europe had a long union history probably also shaped immigrant behaviour and expectations. In Australia these factors were underpinned by a clear compact engineered by organised labour's political and industrial wings about the parameters of migration, including tweaking intakes during economic downturns; ambitious government policies of public works (like the Snowy Mountains Hydro/irrigation scheme) and boosting manufacturing; a pervasive regime of legally enforceable labour standards under compulsory arbitration; and recognition using migration to break down labour conditions would jeopardise the program.[10] None of these safeguards were present in Australia between 1851 and 1880, or for any period outside 1946–1975.

During the subsequent unprecedented wave of global migration from the late 1980s, these safeguards were either absent or rapidly corroding like collectivist regulation of work. In the 'old' industrialised countries Keynesian policies were abandoned for neoliberalism and – with rare exceptions like Germany – manufacturing went in decline, driven by global supply chains and outsourcing/offshoring. Repeated rounds of privatisation, outsourcing, restructuring/downsizing and plant-closures hollowed out whole communities. Full employment became meaningless (the official OECD measure of one hour's work in the survey period is a parody of 1960s definitions), while precarious/insecure, informal and insecure work, under-employment and hidden unemployment grew substantially; and union density fell precipitously. Many of the new wave of immigrants held temporary visas or were undocumented, increasing their vulnerability to exploitation.[11] Migration created jobs but unlike the post-war boom this didn't match population growth and was associated with deteriorating conditions in already low pay sectors like hospitality, harvest work and retailing as well as a rising tide of wage theft.

Hollowed-out communities include migrants and their children (like the US 'rust belt' and south-west Sydney, once manufacturing hubs). With notable exceptions like Bernie Sanders, avowed 'progressives' studiously avoid an informed policy-debate on migration (let alone population), shouting down critics as racist (some are). They aid neoliberal elites advocating the 'free' movement of labour. It is hardly surprising we see a channelling of the 1930s as community concerns ignored by the major established political parties translate into a rising level of anti-immigrant sentiment which ultra-right-wing political parties and proto-fascist movements tap into. Global inequality needs to be addressed at source. The current migration wave doesn't do this, arguably acting as a transmission belt for driving down labour standards and not just in rich countries.

The Money-Side of Mobilisation

Issue-based mobilisation required building wider communities of interest to maximise the organisational and societal power worker organisation could muster. While examination of craft unions has generally focused on their exclusionist methods, this book demonstrated they regularly made significant donations to non-craft unions and wider community groups, practices extended by predominantly craft union led peak and political bodies. In 1889, led by unions, the colonies sent £30,000 (almost two-thirds of the total strike-fund) to aid the London Dockers strike.[12] As much as evidence of burgeoning international solidarity, it was an effort to pre-empt widespread emigration. While the scale was noteworthy, the practice of deploying funds to purse wider industrial causes, aiding other unions, preventing significant industrial defeats and building wider alliances, had been growing since at least the late-1850s.

Mobilisation and Inequality: The Effects

The term inequality is now used to describe all manner of perceived injustice, diluting its original focus on socio-economic deprivation. Nonetheless, the concept remains central to any examination/understanding of worker mobilisation. In 1997 Acemoglu and Robinson argued ruling elites' fear of revolution helped explain the association between the Gini coefficient (in Britain it peaked at 0.627 in 1871 when 10% of the population received 62.9% of the country's income) and extension of the franchise with flow-on redistributive effects in the first decades of the 20th century.[13] It wasn't simply growing worker organisation but violent upheavals (events like Eureka) that precipitated concessions—something yet to trouble today's global elite with its ongoing efforts to wind back worker organisation. Acemoglu and Robinson found the US was an outlier and the same shift wasn't evident in Asian countries like Korea and Taiwan. While democratic movements are evident in these two countries, in China, Thailand and other parts of Asia authoritarianism is on the rise and worker movements show little sign of gaining traction. This is consistent with research finding no clear association between democracy and economic growth—the effects on overall wealth from redistributive measures that increase overall consumption is another matter but one largely lost in a welter of pronouncements on the illusory trickle-down effect.[14] Could it be that historically contingent socio-economic, religious and political developments in Western Europe that flowed onto their 'white settler' outposts in North America and Australasia were instrumental in the more forceful rise of labour? Rising inequality provides preconditions for mobilisation but human agency and the force of ideas, customs and earlier histories of dissent shape worker responses. If it is simply a question of lagged effects—how long?

Leaving the last question to one side, re-examining the past has much to offer in terms of informing future struggles, not least that worker organisation continues to matter and holds the key to again reshaping and civilising the world of work. In focusing on the how and why of worker organisation, the book identified substantial areas where work arrangements were reshaped, or at least modified in the face of attacks by capital. The most apparent gain was with regard to working hours (eight hours, early-closing, half-holidays especially) which spread far and wide across the colonies, affecting the social relations of production and leisure activities not only in major towns but numerous small communities. Notwithstanding setbacks and exceptions, a large part of the workforce were required to work fewer hours in 1880 than 1851—a considerable achievement. Time meant recreation, weekend sport, a healthier lifestyle and more access to education and socio-political engagement. Effectively it also meant higher pay for hours worked—a strategy for raising living standards that unions, especially those in Australia, were to exploit over the next century. There is also evidence organised labour's opposition to immigration enhanced real wages in Australia when compared to Canada.[15]

Unions also affected wages directly. The precise effect overall or in particular trades is difficult to measure with precision but it was substantial not only helping unskilled labourers like wharf-labourers, but also making wages 'sticky' during downturns. Then as now, simply asking employers politely yielded few pay rises, even during the goldrush cost-inflation. Higher wages directly contributed to improved living standards. More careful research on comparative wage levels/earnings is likely to prove illuminating regarding economic inequality. In refuting the 'prosperity' element of American Exceptionalism Archer notes that between 1870 and 1890 GDP per capita was actually considerably higher in Australia, fell behind in 1900 (the 1890s depression impacted more on Australia) but reached parity (actually a bit higher) in 1910. Further, by the early 1890s, if not before, real wages in Australia for skilled and unskilled workers at least equalled the US and was higher than the UK—and wage disparities were more compressed.[16] Consistent with this and union's contribution to a less inequitable society, Panza and Williamson's study found that by 1870 Australia was a far more equitable society than the US, the UK (where inequality actually peaked in 1871) and Continental Europe. After this time Australia matched global trends—income inequality declining significantly from World War One until the 1970s and reversing significantly thereafter—but retaining a lower level of inequality.[17]

Union presence affected work relations in other ways, including curbing management discretion, bolstering apprenticeship and moderating workloads, although these proved harder 'asks'—the latter still does. Unions had other less heralded effects including providing avenues for friendly benefits and mutual-improvement. Organisation also reshaped the wider policy frameworks in ways that advantaged labour. This included pressure for unemployment relief, curbing immigration, protectionism, the provision of technical and other education and initiating laws affording some protection regarding wages, health and safety. More substantial gains along the same trajectory followed in the next 30 years. Employment-enhancing tariff/protectionism was unlikely to have been secured without organised labour's support given hostility from powerful mining and rural interests—a schism in Australia that continues.[18] Joining bodies representing engineers and architects pushing for technical education unions helped ensure there were both job opportunities for the young but also educational infrastructure essential to industry and the expanding economy more generally. Those relying on market forces or government 'leadership' to propel such outcomes would do well to consider the emasculation/privatisation of the TAFE sector by successive governments over the past two decades to what is now conceded as a crisis (without attributing its politically manufactured causation). The book also charted how worker mobilisation was essential to building democracy. This included the campaign for universal adult franchise (for males at least), that elections should be held on public holidays, adopting the secret ballot and – not least – establishing bodies to promote working-class interests and elect working-class representatives into local government and parliament.

A Final Word

Neoliberalism is delivering escalating inequality and social fracturing globally. Reducing socio-economic inequality and improving community wellbeing requires suitably regulated labour markets, business organisation and welfare regimes, associated with economic policies directed to secure full-employment and redistribute income and wealth in ways benefiting the entire community. This book traced the beginnings of organised labour's push to do this, including initiating civilising collectivist industrial relations mechanisms and demanding democracy to ensure some political say and protection for the community. The conscious degradation of these protections under neoliberalism is all too evident and calls to reverse direction and build more equal and sustainable societies are growing.[19]

Notes

1. Van der Linden, M. (2008) *Workers of the World: Essays Toward a Global Labor History*, Brill, Leiden.
2. Friedman, G. (2008) *Reigniting the Labor Movement: Restoring Means to Ends in a Democratic Labor Movement*, Routledge, London.
3. Parfitt, *Knights Across the Atlantic*.
4. Gould, S.J. (1991) *Bully for Brontosaurus*, Penguin, London, 66.
5. Lehndorff, Dribbusch and Schulten, *Rough Waters*, 10–11.
6. Huang, B., Morgan, P.J. and Yoshino, N. (eds.) (2019) *Demystifying Rising Inequality in Asia*, Asian Development Bank Institute, Tokyo.
7. Kaufman, B. (2018) How Capitalism Endogenously Creates Rising Income Inequality and Economic Crisis: The Macro Political Economy Model of Early Industrial Relations, *Industrial Relations*, 57(1): 131–72.
8. Wolff, E. (2017) *A Century of Wealth in America*, Harvard University Press, Cambridge; Johnstone, R., McCrystal, S., Nossar, I., Quinlan, M., Rawling, M. and Riley, J. (2012) *Beyond Employment: The Legal Regulation of Work Relationships*, Federation Press, Sydney; Isaac, J. (2018) Why Are Australian Wages Lagging and What Can Be Done About It? *The Australian Economic Review*, 51(2): 175–90.
9. Archer, *Why Is There No Labor Party in the United States?*
10. Lever-Tracy, C. and Quinlan, M. (1988) *A Divided Working-Class? Ethnic Segmentation and Industrial Conflict in Australia*, Routledge, London; Quinlan, M. and Levertracy, C. (1988) Immigrant Workers, Trade Unions and Industrial Struggle: An Overview of the Australian Experience, 1945–1985, *Economic and Industrial Democracy*, 9(1): 7–41; Quinlan, M. and Levertracy, C. (1990) From Labour Market Exclusion to Industrial Solidarity Australian Trade Union Responses to Asian Workers, 1830–1988, *Cambridge Journal of Economics*, 14(2): 159–81.
11. Toh, S. and Quinlan, M. (2009) Safeguarding the Global Contingent Workforce? Guestworkers in Australia, *International Journal of Manpower*, 30(5): 453–71.
12. Donovan, P. (1972) Australia and the Great London Dock Strike: 1889, *Labour History*, 23: 17–26.
13. Acemoglu, D. and Robinson, J. (1997) Why Did the West Extend the Franchise? Democracy, Inequality and Growth in Historical Perspective, *Department of Economics Working Paper*, MIT, Cambridge.
14. Przeworski, A. and Limongi, F. (1993) Political Regimes and Economic Growth, *Journal of Economic Perspectives*, 7(3): 51–69.
15. Greasley, D., Madsden, J. and Oxley, L. (2000) Real Wages in Australia and Canada, 1870–1913, *Australian Economic History Review*, 40(2): 178–98.
16. Archer, *Why Is There No Labor Party in the United States?* 23–27.
17. Panza, L. and Williamson, J. (2019) Always Egalitarian? Australian Earnings Inequality c1870, *Centre for Economic History Australian National University Discussion Paper*, No. 2019-01.

18. Wilson, J. and Shanahan, M. (2012) Did Good Institutions Produce Good Tariffs? Evidence from Tariff Protection in Victoria, *Australian Economic History Review*, 52(2): 128–47.
19. Vaughan-Whitehead, D. (ed.) (2018) *Reducing Inequalities in Europe: How Industrial Relations and Labour Policies Can Close the Gap*, Edward Elgar/ ILO, Geneva.

Index

Printed in the United States
by Baker & Taylor Publisher Services